Fichtner · English and German Syntax

Edward G. Fichtner

# English and German Syntax

A Contrastive Analysis on Generative-Tagmemic
Principles

1979

Wilhelm Fink Verlag München

ISBN 3-7705-1563-3
© 1979 Wilhelm Fink Verlag, München
Gesamtherstellung: Hain-Druck KG, Meisenheim/Glan

# TABLE OF CONTENTS

# PREFACE

This book contains a word-placement calculus for English and German, i. e., a system of rules or instructions for putting together simple and moderately complicated sentences in the respective languages. The need for a syntactic description of German with this potential became apparent to me as early as 1963, in the course of my first semesters as a teacher of German at St. Joseph's College in Philadelphia. Many of my colleagues have since observed that the description of that language as presented in the majority of our textbooks is adequate for the production of only the most primitive sentences. Once the student passes beyond a point which lies roughly between the middle of the second semester and the middle of the third, any knowledge of the structure of the foreign language which he may acquire is likely to come, not from the rules and statements of our textbooks and grammars, but through his own linguistic intuition. To be sure, some students advance to the point where they can study the language formally, but they are few. The concept of German structure and, by contrast, that of English in this volume should extend the predictive potential of our apparatus of formal statements about those languages, and help to bridge the gap between the rudiments of syntax and the point at which the student has had enough exposure to the language to begin to rely on his own "Sprachgefühl."

Initially, it was my intention of offer this conception of the language in the form of a textbook. In 1965, Professor Henry H. H. Remak of Indiana University, at that time consulting editor of the Blaisdell Publishing Company, suggested to me that the time was ripe for a new introductory German text which would incorporate the discoveries of modern linguistics. I began work on the project, but as time went on, it became more and more obvious that the picture of English and German structure drawn by linguists working in those fields had not yet clarified to the degree necessary to serve as the basis for such an undertaking.

The ideas on German structures presented in these pages began to take shape at that time. A preliminary version was presented in 1968 and 1969 in tutorials at Queens College. These efforts culminated in an article published in 1970 which contains the concepts which are fundamental to this approach: the slot-and-filler infrastructure, which is characteristic of tagmemics; the generative principle of the transformationalists; and the polar functions of topic and comment, which constitute an American adaptation of basic ideas of the Prague School. Also very influential during this period was Lohnes and Strothmann's basic German textbook (1968); indeed, the concept of the clause nucleus, which is so important in defining the infrastructure of German, is a redefinition and extension of their "irreducible verbal pattern." A course on "Sprachwissenschaft und Sprachpraxis" taken during the summer of 1970 at the University of Freiburg acquainted me with the strengths and weaknesses of *Dependenzgrammatik*.

Several studies on specific problems then followed. In addition to the article referred to above, there were a number of oral presentations. The theory of the tense and aspect system of German (Chapter 8) was given as a paper at a meeting of the Northeast Modern Language Association in 1971 in Philadelphia. An early version of the treatment of the English infinitive (Chapter 14) was read to the Queens College Linguistics Club in 1972; I am obligated to my former colleague, Dr. Hans-Bernhard Drubig, now of Tübingen, for going over that paper with me and for making a number of valuable suggestions. The description of the basic finite clause patterns of English (Chapter 10) was presented in lecture form at the Pädagogisches Institut der Stadt Wien in March of 1974. The book was substantially complete in that year, but at the urging of the publisher, a revision was undertaken. Through this abridgement, sections dealing with the role of accent in syntax, with the passive voice, and with negation, were removed. I hope to publish these separately at a later time.

Most of the research for this book was done at the New York Public Library and at the Österreichische Nationalbibliothek in Vienna; a debt of thanks is due to those institutions and their staffs for their help. Queens College of the City University of New York generously granted me a sabbatical leave for the academic year 1973-74, during which work on the book advanced significantly. Lastly, I am grateful to my wife, Dr. Paula Sutter Fichtner, for serving as a linguistic informant in several languages and dialects, and for her patient encouragement during the period of fourteen years that this book has been in the making.                                                     E. G. F.

Queens College and Graduate School, City University of New York
December 1976

# CHAPTER 1

## WHAT IS SYNTAX?

Many years ago, in a well-known monograph entitled *Was ist Syntax?*, John Ries distinguished the two dominant schools of thought on the subject in his time by the answer which their representatives would give to the question posed in the title of his work. In the one group, he said, are those who take meaning as their point of departure, and for whom syntax stands in close relation to semantics. In the other are those who assume the priority of word form and sentence structure, and who hence regard considerations of meaning as remote from the concerns of syntax. There was, in addition, a third group, one which attempted to bridge the gap between meaning and form, but which earned for its efforts only the unflattering label of *Mischsyntax* (Ries 1927:9).

Ries's book appeared for the first time in 1898, and at that time he was confident that his own view, namely, that syntax should be concerned with word forms and sentence patterns, would carry the day. And indeed, it has been the case until very recently that any considerations of meaning were regarded as out of place in establishing or determining the fundamental structural elements of a language. Bloomfield, for example, felt that linguistics was, and ought to be, a science of observable beharvior, and that the meaning of a word belonged in the same class of non-observable psychic events as "feelings" and "volitions" (Bloomfield 1935:139). This suspicion of meaning as being a transitory psychic state which could not be observed and which therefore could not be relied on to distinguish the various forms of a given language persisted until well into the last decade. The change which has come about is associated with the name of Noam Chomsky. His rupture with the earlier school also revolves around this question of mental states: he argues that the complexity of linguistic utterances, and hence of language structures, requires the participation of some kind of process or mechanism in the brain (Chomsky 1959:575). In this way, "mental acts" again have become the proper object of linguistic investigation, and among these mental acts are what Bloomfield called "meanings."

In subsequent writings, Chomsky has developed his conception of language into a widely accepted model, one often referred to as the "*Aspects* Model" because it was presented for the first time in his work, *Aspects of the Theory of Syntax* (1965). In this model, there are three major components: a syntactic, a phonological, and a semantic component. The syntactic component consists, not of words, but of underlying abstract elements which can be interpreted in two ways: phonologically, as sound; and semantically, as meaning. Since the actual utterance is regarded as surface structure, and the meaning of the utterance as deep structure, the syntactic component, in effect, mediates between deep and surface structure. This view, or a variant of it, is subscribed to today by a majority of those linguists who are concerned with syntax (cf. Di Pietro 1971:35).

Research inspired by these concepts has thrown much light on the nature of many processes which operate within the various natural languages. Nevertheless, there is still a need for descriptions of English and of German which can help teachers and learners of those languages to construct sentences which are not only grammatically correct, but which also sound idiomatic and natural. Unfortunately, the teacher of English or German still finds himself confronted with a picture of the target language which is likely to be inadequate in this important matter of word order. The work of linguists of the thirties and forties has resulted in a substantial number of solid and extensive studies which treat the sound structure of the two languages in a way which is useful to the classroom teacher, e. g., Moulton's study, *The Sounds of English and German* (1962). The morphology of the language had been treated adequately, if not always elegantly, by the older grammarians, e. g., Curme (1952). But in the area of syntax, we appear to have made very little progress toward a conception either of English or of German sentence structure which would have the features and qualities which would make it a useful adjunct to foreign language pedagogy.

The present work is an attempt to remedy this deficiency. In it, a description of English and German syntax is presented which is intended less as a theoretical contribution to the field than as the descriptive and contrastive components of what has been called a "pedagogical grammar" (Noblitt 1972:317). It attempts to supply what the teacher needs in respect of syntax, namely, a set of simple and consistent statements covering the most important, if not all cases of word arrangement in the sentence – in other words, a word-placement calculus for composing authentic, well-formed

English and German sentences. In the treatment of each major construction, a comparison of the structural features of English and German will constitute a third step after the description of the pertinent patterns of the two languages.

In consequence of this aim, the reader will encounter certain departures from current practice in the literature on syntax. Perhaps most noteworthy is that, after certain preliminary considerations, it has been found possible to ignore questions of meaning to a significant extent – in effect returning to Ries's position. Furthermore, instructions have been abbreviated or omitted entirely when these would apply to areas of the foreign language where the student's or teacher's intuition might reasonably be relied on as a guide. It is unnecessary, for example, to define the word or the prepositional phrase, as these are likely to be familiar to him from his native language, or from his study of the target language. On the other hand, where the patterns of formation are unclear, as in the boundary of the infinitive when embedded in its matrix clause, or where the structures of the respective languages differ markedly from one another, as in the distribution of nominals and adverbials within the clause infrastructure, detailed formulations are obviously called for. It is hoped that this approach will throw light on the fundamental structures and processes involved in clause formation and sentence building in English and German, and facilitate the presentation of these structures by teachers, as well as their comprehension and use by students of the two languages.

CHAPTER 2

HOW SENTENCES ARE GENERATED

In order to compare and contrast the two languages, a theory of syntactic structure is required which is applicable to both English and German — a theory which will permit the distinctive and characteristic features of each language to emerge clearly, and which at the same time contains enough common elements to make meaningful comparisons possible (Schwarze 1972:16). If we can construct such a theory, we can then compare them, feature by feature, remarking points of similarity, and noting points at which the patterns of the two languages conflict.

The generative-tagmemic approach which follows seems to meet these conditions. To begin with, the completed structure or sentence is produced by the application of different kinds of rules through a series of stages. These stages are represented in the following diagram:

$$\begin{array}{c}\text{lexical}\\\text{items}\end{array} \rightarrow \text{IS} \rightarrow \text{VM} \rightarrow \text{CF} \rightarrow \text{MS} \rightarrow \text{SOP} \rightarrow \begin{array}{c}\text{finished}\\\text{sentence}\end{array}$$

As the phrase indicates, the lexical items with which we intend to express our thoughts are distributed in a specific sequence in the frame called the "infrastructure" (IS). The infrastructure of English contains seven slots or tagmemes, that of German has six. In each language, there are specific limitations on the kinds of elements which may occupy these segments. Once these syntactic elements have been assigned to their respective tagmemes, the resulting infrastructure is subject to several further operations. The next in order is the "modification of the verb" (VM). In both languages, there are three common verb modifications — all optional — so called because they may be applied to all five clause types. The latter are generated at the stage of "clause formation" (CF), in which the infrastructure may be further transformed into a finite clause, either dependent or independent, or a number of nonfinite clause types — infinitive, participles, or gerundive. The infrastructure is then subject to further alteration by one of a series of "morphosyntactic rules"

(MS), by which one or more of the elements of the clause may be changed in various ways. If the infrastructure is an independent finite clause, it only needs a last transformation according to the patterns of "standard orthography and punctuation" (SOP) of the respective language in order to emerge as a finished sentence. If the infrastructure is a dependent clause — either finite or nonfinite — it is reincorporated into the infrastructure of its matrix clause, and accompanies that clause through its own transformations until it, too, emerges as a finished sentence.

In the later chapters of this book, each of these transformations will be thoroughly examined. In preparation for those sections, let us review the sequence of procedures described above in somewhat greater detail. As the diagram indicated, the lexical items chosen to comprise the utterance are first arranged in the infrastructure (IS). This consists of the following seven tagmemes in English:

SUBJ + ITVAV + VERB + NOMNL + VPART + VCOMP + TRMAV

| | |
|---|---|
| SUBJ 'subject' | NOMNL 'nominal' |
| ITVAV 'intraverbal adverb' | VPART 'verb particle' |
| | VCOMP 'verb complement' |
| VERB 'verb' | TRMAV 'terminal adverb' |

Note that these categories are not the same as form-classes: we find nouns and pronouns in both the SUBJ and NOMNL tagmemes, and adverbs in the ITVAV, VPART, VCOMP, and TRMAV segments.

The infrastructure of German contains only six tagmemes:

UPPRN + MDLAV + AVNOM + CLNAV + NCOMP + VERB

| | |
|---|---|
| UPPRN 'unaccented personal pronoun' | CLNAV 'clause nucleus adverb' |
| | NCOMP 'nucleus complement' |
| MDLAV 'modal adverb' | VERB 'verb' |
| AVNOM 'adverbo-nominal' | NCOMP + VERB 'clause nucleus' |

Again, there are two kinds of adverbs: those in MDLAV, and those in the CLNAV tagmeme. On the other hand, there are two slots which may contain either nouns or adverbs: AVNOM and NCOMP. Unlike English, there is no specific tagmeme occupied by the grammatical subject. And while the tagmeme VERB appears in both languages, in English it is in the middle of the infrastructure, but in German it stands in final position. These features will receive more detailed scrutiny in Chapters 4, 5, and 6.

Similar contrasts mark the stage of verb modification (VM). In

English, the possibilities are three in number: PASV 'passive voice'; LMDR 'limited duration', sometimes referred to as the 'progressive forms'; and CRLV 'current relevance', also called the 'present perfect tense'. In German, we find these three: PASV 'passive voice'; TRMV 'terminative aspect', also called the 'present perfect tense'; and MODL 'modal auxiliary'. Whereas both languages share a passive voice modification (PASV), the traditional "present perfect" differs enough to receive the designation CRLV in English and TRMV in German. The remaining pair, the English modification LMDR and the German MODL, have nothing in common. In Chapters 7, 8, and 9, we will study these modifications at greater length.

If the infrastructures and the verb modifications manifest numerous points of contrast, the patterns of clause formation in the two languages are more alike. In English as well as in German, there are the following five:

FNTZ 'finitization', by which dependent and independent finite clauses are produced (cf. Chapters 10, 11, and 12);

INFZ 'infinitivization', which generates infinitives (cf. Chapters 14, 15 and 16);

PRTZ (AV) 'adverbial participialization', which produces adverbial participial clauses (cf. Chapters 17, 18 and 19);

PRTZ (AJ) 'adjectival participialization', by which adjectival participial constructions are generated (cf. Chapters 17, 18 and 19);

GNDZ 'gerundivization', by which the verbal nouns called gerundives are produced (cf. Chapters 20, 21 and 22).

Naturally there are numerous differences in detail, e. g., between English and German participial constructions, but these and other peculiarities will be treated in the chapters indicated. In anticipation of several examples to follow, it may be noted here that the modification FNTZ 'finitization' includes several changes which affect the last verb form present after the common verb modifications, if any, have been applied. In English, there may be as many as four, of which only the last, PSNM 'person and number', is obligatory: MODL 'modal auxiliary'; PAST 'past tense'; SJNC 'subjunctive mood'; and PSNM 'person and number'. In German, there are only three: PAST 'past tense'; SJNC 'subjunctive mood'; and PSNM 'person and number'. Again, of these three, only the last is obligatory. It should be noted that the modification MODL 'modal auxiliary' is a common verb modification in German, but a finite verb modification in English. Of these clause types, only the finite clause has the potential to become an independent syntactic structure, i. e., a sentence. Both infinitives and gerundives are complex nouns, and participles are either adverbial or adjectival in character. Even dependent finite clauses assume the character of simple syntactic elements: relative clauses are essentially adjectival; subordinate clauses introduced by Eng. *that* or *whether* and Grm. *daß* or *ob* are nominal in character; others have an adverbial function.

Once the clause has been formed, it may yet be subjected to the operation of one of the morphosyntactic rules (MS). By means of these, certain elements are modified in form in conjunction with certain changes in the disposition of elements in the infrastructure. These rules are six in number:

RLTVZ 'relativization', by which a given noun, adjective, or adverb becomes a relative pronoun or adverb;

ITRGZ 'interrogativization', by which a noun, adjective, or adverb is transformed into the appropriate interrogative form;

PRNMZ 'pronominalization', by which a noun is transformed into a pronoun;

CJNLZ 'conjunctionalization', by which an adverb or pronoun in a matrix clause produces a corresponding conjunction which introduces an embedded clause;

SJCTZ 'subjectivization', by which an element from a dependent clause which has been removed from that clause is transformed into the "pseudosubject" of the matrix clause; and

AVBLZ 'adverbialization', a transformation through which a series of elements is reduced to a single adverb.

These will be explained at appropriate points in coming chapters.

Of the four groups of rules described above, the first assigns the various syntactic elements to their position in the infrastructure (IS). The remaining three – verb modification (VM), clause formation (CF), and morphosyntactic (MS) rules – effect a change in the form of one or another of the elements in the infrastructure. Once the infrastructure has been formed, further changes in the position of elements are brought about by the operation of one or more of five "EDICT-rules." Each of the letters of the word "EDICT" stands for one operation which may be applied either to an element in an infrastructure, or to the infrastructure itself. Their meaning is as follows:

E 'embedding', the placing of one clause in or behind a matrix clause or clause element;

D 'deletion', the removal of an element from an infrastructure;

I 'insertion', the placing of a new element into an infrastructure;

C 'commentization', the shift of an element or an infrastructure to the end of the infrastructure in which it stands;

T 'topicalization', the shift of an element to the beginning of the infrastructure in which it stands.

Since the element to which these operations are to be applied is not specified in the definition of the rule, it is necessary to do so when the operation appears in the course of generating a given construction. In such cases, the letter designating the operation is followed by a virgule (" / ") which precedes the element to which the operation is to be applied. For example, in sentences containing a dependent clause, this latter must at some point be embedded. This operation is expressed by the symbols "E / IS2" or more simply "E / 2," which means "embed infrastructure number 2 (into infrastructure number 1)." In the infinitivization transformation of German, INFZ, it is necessary to delete the grammatical subject and to insert the element *zu* before the last verb form present; these operations are abbreviated as "D / SJ" and "I / zu(&LVF)," respectively. Commentization and topicalization frequently occur in the course of generating a sentence; formulas like "C / 2" and "T / FV" mean "commentize infrastructure number 2" and "topicalize the finite verb," respectively.

Throughout this work, we have used, and will use the word "structure" in the sense of the "syntactic structure" of the languages in question, taking the term "syntax" as meaning "word order." Within the limits of these definitions, then, it is possible to say that the "structure of English" and the "structure of German" are constituted by the various sequences in which the rules and operations described above may be applied. The analyses and descriptions in the chapters which follow will consist for the most part in the tracing of these sequences, and in determining the conditions under which one or the other of the various operations may be applied. Before going on to these matters, however, it might be useful to generate a few simple sentences here, in order to see how the different kinds of rules are supposed to be applied, and how they operate in concert to generate authentic sentences in English and German.

Let us assume that it is our purpose to generate the German

equivalent of the sentence: "Why had he stayed home last week?" The German equivalents of the syntactic elements in this sentence would be: *er, bleiben, zu Hause, letzte Woche,* and the element which is the answer to the question word *why?*, which could be, e. g., *wegen Krankheit*. These elements must first be assigned to the proper tagmeme of the infrastructure: *er* is an unaccented personal pronoun (UPPRN); *bleiben* is the verb (VERB); for reasons which will be presented later, we must classify *zu Hause* as a nucleus complement (NCOMP); and *letzte Woche* and *wegen Krankheit* are both adverbonominals (AVNOM), and within this tagmeme, adverbs of time normally precede adverbs of manner, cause, and place; there is no word or phrase in English which would have to be translated by a modal adverb (MDLAV) in German, but the attitude of the speaker — in this instance, one of interest and curiosity — may be expressed by the word *denn*. The distribution of these elements in the infrastructure is thus as follows:

| UPPRN | MDLAV | AVNOM | CLNAV | NCOMP | VERB |
|-------|-------|-------|-------|-------|------|
| er | denn | letzte | ... | zu | bleiben |
| | | Woche | | Hause | |
| | | wegen | | | |
| | | Krankheit | | | |

This structure will be represented in most cases as follows:

IS: er denn letzte Woche wegen Krankheit zu Hause bleiben

Once the lexical items have been combined in syntactic elements, and these arrayed in the infrastructure, the various VM, CF, and MS rules may be applied. The first of these has to do with verb modification (VM). The use of the socalled pluperfect tense in German requires the common verb modification TRMV 'terminative aspect', by which the last verb form present (LVF) is changed into its corresponding participial form (PRT); it is then followed by the appropriate auxiliary, *haben* or *sein*; the formula is: TRMV: (LVF + $PRT_T$) + H / S.

TRMV: er denn letzte Woche wegen Krankheit zu Hause geblieben SEIN

(As a matter of convenience, elements which arise or are changed in some way as the result of the operation of one or another of the rules applied to them will be spelled in capital letters.)

The next set of rules are the clause formation (CF) rules. Since the sentence to be generated is a finite clause, we must apply the modifications subsumed under the symbol FNTZ 'finitization'. These are the optional modifications of the last verb form: PAST 'past tense'; SJNC 'subjunctive mood'; and the obligatory modification PSNM 'person and number'. In the sentence being generated, the first and third of these are called for:

PAST: er denn letzte Woche wegen Krankheit zu Hause geblieben
WAR-
PSNM: er denn letzte Woche wegen Krankheit zu Hause geblieben
war

As the clause is an independent finite clause, it would normally be subject to the modifications T / FV 'topicalization of the finite verb' and T / X 'topicalization of any element (except the modal adverb and certain other elements)'. However, these changes are superseded by the operation of certain MS rules. The morphosyntactic rule which we wish to apply here is ITRGZ 'interrogativization', by which one element in the infrastructure is transformed into the appropriate question word. Our English question inquires into the reason for the subject's staying at home, and therefore the element *wegen Krankheit* is interrogativized:

ITRGZ: er denn letzte Woche WARUM zu Hause geblieben war

Because this is a direct question, the finite verb is topicalized, an operation which is omitted in indirect questions:

T / FV: war er denn letzte Woche WARUM zu Hause geblieben

As the next step, the interrogative element itself is topicalized:

T / ITRG: WARUM war er denn letzte Woche zu Haus geblieben

At the last stage in the generation of our sentence, it is rewritten with the standard orthography and punctuation (SOP) required by the authoritative bodies in the countries where the respective language is used:

SOP: "Warum war er denn letzte Woche zu Hause geblieben? "

By means of the steps above, we have generated the German equivalent of the English question: "Why had he stayed home last week? " It might now be instructive to apply the same procedures to the English sentence. As the initial step, we must assign the various syntactic elements to the appropriate tagmemes in order to form the infrastructure: the word *he* is the subject (SUBJ); the verb (VERB) is *stay; home* is a verb particle (VPART); *last week* is a terminal adverb (TRMAV); as in the case of the German sentence, we assume that the interrogative word replaces an element originally in the infrastructure, e. g., *because of illness*, which would be a verb complement phrase (VCOMP). The elements comprising the infrastructure, then, must be arranged as follows:

SUBJ ITVAV VERB NOMNL VPART VCOMP TRMAV
he  ...  stay  ...  home  because last
                            of ill-  week
                            ness

In English as well as in German, this array of elements is customarily represented as follows:

IS: he stay home because of illness last week

There is a common verb modification (VM) which applies here, that of CRLV 'current relevance':

CRLV: he HAVE stayed home because of illness last week

The clause is to become a finite clause; hence, the modifications associated with the symbol FNTZ 'finitization' apply. Of the four possible finite verb modifications, only PAST 'past tense' and PSNM 'person and number' apply here:

PAST: he HAD stayed home because of illness last week
PSNM: he had stayed home because of illness last week

This would constitute an acceptable sentence as it stands. However, the morphosyntactic (MS) rule of ITRGZ 'interrogativization' must be applied to the element which, in effect, answers the question, i. e., the phrase *because of illness*:

ITRGZ: he had stayed home WHY last week

It is now necessary to topicalize a verb form, as in German; instead of the finite verb (FV), however, the first auxiliary (AUX1) is moved to the head of the clause:

T / AUX1: had he stayed home WHY last week

Again as in German, the interrogativized element is now topicalized:

T / ITRG: WHY had he stayed home last week

As the next and final step, this is rewritten to conform to the standard orthography and punctuation (SOP) of English:

SOP: "Why had he stayed home last week? "

Thus, by assigning suitable operations to each of the four stages in the generation of the sentence – formation of the infrastructure (IS), the common verb modification of the verb (VM), formation of the appropriate clause type (CF), and the application of the morpho-syntactic rule (MS) called for by the meaning which we wish to convey – we have been able to generate correct, indeed, idiomatic utterances in each of the languages, despite the superficial differences in word order. Moreover, because each sentence has been generated by a fundamentally similar – if not completely identical – set of procedures, it is possible to compare and contrast the languages at each stage in the production of the output sentences. Some differences between English and German are to be found in the infrastructures of the languages:

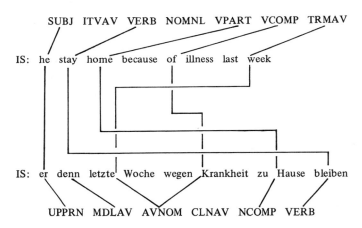

Others become conspicuous at the stage of verb modification, particularly the fact that German verbs "generate to the right," whereas their English counterparts "generate to the left":

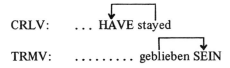

The topicalization of a verb form is characteristic of finitization in both languages, but in German it is the finite verb (FV) which is topicalized, whereas it is the first auxiliary (AUX1) in English. While the full implications of this difference do not emerge in the present instance because there is an auxiliary already present in our examples to which both rules can apply, one only needs to change the tense of the verb so that there is only one verb form present prior to topicalization in order to see why the distinction is important, e. g.:

> IS: he stay home because of illness last week
> VM: none
> CF: FNTZ
> PAST, PSNM: he stayed home because of illness last week
> MS:
>
> ITRGZ: he stayed home WHY last week
> T / AUX1: DID he stay home WHY last week

The verb form *stayed* has no expressed first auxiliary; hence, the appropriate form of the dummy auxiliary *DO* must be topicalized.

> T / ITRG: WHY DID he stay home last week
> SOP: "Why did he stay home last week? "

A derivation of the German counterpart of this sentence reveals a difference of some magnitude:

> IS: er letzte Woche wegen Krankheit zu Hause bleiben
> VM: none
> CF: FNTZ
> PAST, PSNM: er letzte Woche wegen Krankheit zu Hause blieb
> MS:
> ITRGZ: er letzte Woche WARUM zu Hause blieb
> T / FV: blieb er letzte Woche WARUM zu Hause

In German, the finite form of the verb (FV) is the one which is topicalized, whether it is an auxiliary or an inflected form of the lexical verb (i. e., a verb which has a lexical or dictionary meaning). The remaining steps in the derivation are:

> T / ITRG: WARUM blieb er letzte Woche zu Hause
> SOP: "Warum blieb er letzte Woche zu Hause? "

By means of the generative-tagmemic approach described and exemplified above, it has been possible to establish a battery of rules which generate only acceptable utterances in English and German. The same set of rules can be used to explain the vast majority of sentence patterns which a native speaker of one language is likely to encounter in the other. Moreover, because of the nature of the approach, it has been possible, too, to make a point-by-point comparison of English and German at every level, and to identify areas where the structures of the two languages come into conflict. The remainder of this book comprises just such an analysis and a comparison of the numerous structures of English and German. Before proceeding to this task, however, it is necessary to consider certain fundamental characteristics of language which play a great role in the distribution of elements in the utterance.

# CHAPTER 3

## SOME PROBLEMS OF SYNTAX

Before undertaking a detailed examination and comparison of the various structures of English and German, we must describe certain general features of language, and indicate their position in, or relation to, the generative-tagmemic word-placement calculus which is presented in this work. Of all the questions in the field of linguistics today, one of the most challenging is the relationship between meaning and structure, i. e., between semantics and syntax. A link between these two facets of language may be found in the area of *valence theory*. Another problem has to do with structurally unmotivated variations in word order. The fundamental concepts of *topic and comment* go far to illuminate the phenomenon, familiar to the teacher and often disturbing to the student, of "different ways of saying the same thing," i. e., different patterns of word order containing the same vocabulary items.

The influence of the context on the sentence may be observed in connection with patterns of topicalization and commentization. It also makes itself felt in the various patterns of deletion of syntactic elements — patterns which are subsumed under the general term of *ellipsis*. Syntactically independent sentences in a continuous text may be linked together by the insertion of *intersentence adverbs*, elements which are not present in the infrastructures of those sentences. In the sections of this chapter which follow, we shall examine these concepts to see what role they play in determining the order of elements in the sentence.

## *Valence*

It is obvious that language exists in order to transmit certain items of information from one person to another. Because the generative-tagmemic approach concentrates on the disposition of elements in the sentence — that is, it purports to assign words and phrases to their positions in the utterance largely, if not completely, without reference to their meaning — it is necessary to specify how, on this theory, the essential function of communication takes place. The link between the neurophysiological events which we call the "meaning" and the production of the lexical items which are to be distributed in the infrastructure is established by the concept of "valence."

Taken from the science of chemistry, the concept of valence was applied by Tesnière (1965) to the characteristic patterns of association between the verb and various nouns. Tesnière's idea has been redefined and expanded (summary in Helbig 1971b), and has been applied in a number of suggestive ways. As used here, the term has two meanings: "lexical" valence, and "grammatical" valence. The former refers to the semantic compatibility of words, as determined by the circumstances of our experience. The term "grammatical" valence reflects the potential which a verb has to attract certain nouns and adverbs as co-valent elements or *Mitspieler*. The well-known example *Colorless green ideas sleep furiously* is a sentence in which the lexical valence of every noun and adverb is in conflict: *ideas* are neither *green* nor *colorless*, nor could they be both at the same time; neither do they *sleep*, a condition which in any case rarely occurs *furiously*. If we change these items to others which are compatible with one another lexically, without changing the grammatical structure, the sentence is completely unobjectionable: *Healthy young children sleep peacefully*. If we now change the adjectives in this sentence to nouns, and the adverb and the noun to adjectives, the relationships inherent in the grammatical valence of these words are disrupted: *Health youth childlike sleep peaceful*.

In terms of generative-tagmemic theory, then, the relationship between meaning and word order is defined in terms of lexical and grammatical valence. Whether lexical valence may be further analyzed into binary features is a matter which can not be explored here. What is relevant to the problem of word order is the conclusion implicit in the foregoing analysis, namely, that lexical and grammatical valence affect the position of syntactic elements only indirectly. Both kinds of valence have their own properties and characteristics, and influence one another reciprocally at the interface between their respective areas of operation. Moreover, valence affects word order in some ways. Nevertheless, it is possible — indeed, pedagogically desirable to treat the distribution of words and phrases independently and apart from those considerations of meaning and form which are implied by the terms "lexical" and "grammatical" valence.

By defining and delimiting these concepts of valence, we have seen that it is at least theoretically possible to select compatible lexical items and to modify them in conformity with their potential for combining with the verb. But when we assign them to their positions in the infrastructure, problems of a different sort arise. What we called valence were complex systems of semantic selection and morphological covariation which were nontemporal (or nonspatial) in character. It lies in the nature of language that the lexical items which comprise the utterance must be arranged in a sequence. The very fact of this sequential distribution gives rise to certain properties which reflect, in Bolinger's (1952:279) telling phrase, the "geometry" of language. Language is one-dimensional, in that an utterance has length, but no width or breadth; it is one-directional, because it always moves ahead in time, and can never reverse its direction. These characteristics of the linguistic utterance are the origin of certain properties which attach to specific elements in the sequence by virtue of their position. Let us consider the following elements, which have been stripped of all their lexical and grammatical peculiarities, i. e., which are merely abstract syntactic elements in a series:

$$X_1 + X_2 + X_3 + X_4 + X_5 + X_6$$

Despite the fact that these six syntactic elements have no distinguishing characteristics, they are not identical: the first, $X_1$, is preceded by no other element, but is followed by the remaining five; the last, $X_6$, on the other hand, is preceded by all the other elements; all the rest are both preceded and followed by at least one other element.

These observations acquire great significance when we consider their implications for the effect of word position on the listener: the first word, $X_1$, ist not preceded by any other word, and consequently its impact is undiluted by any conflicting stimuli; conversely, the effect of the last word in the utterance, $X_6$, is not diminished by the appearance of a following element. What this means, then, is that the first and last elements in any sequence have, for opposite reasons, a kind of prominence not shared by those elements in the interior of the sequence.

Natural languages like English and German incorporate these

features of language as such into their structures in order to establish certain communicative priorities. If an element is not preceded by any other, i. e., is in initial position, the speaker has a virtually unlimited choice in selecting the word or phrase which he wishes to occupy that position. If an element is not followed by any other, i. e., is in final position, it becomes the focus of the utterance, because it is not followed by any other modifying or delimiting element. As to this latter, it is apparent that a final element, unmodified by any other element, is the one which would attract to itself lexical items of superordinate semantic value within the economy of the utterance. Elements in this position will be referred to as the „comment" or the „comment elements." The initial element has two characteristics which make it, too, suitable for special purposes in the area of syntax: first, as that element is unmodified by any prior element, the speaker, having a wide choice in selecting the word or phrase which he wishes to place there, can use that feature to tie the sentence to different areas of the discourse; second, by virtue of the fact that this first element casts its semantic shadow over the remainder of the utterance, it naturally sets the "topic" of the sentence about which the "comment" then supplies further new information. This means that we must revise our abstract sentence to include these new factors:

$$\text{TOPIC}_1 + X_2 + X_3 + X_4 + X_5 + \text{COMMENT}_6$$

To a greater extent than English, German has incorporated the special prominence of the topic into its structure, by permitting a wide variety of elements to stand in utterance-initial position. Consider the possibilities which arise in connection with an example used previously:

IS: er letzte Woche wegen Krankheit zu Hause bleiben
TRMV: . . . geblieben SEIN
PSNM: er letzte Woche wegen Krankheit zu Hause geblieben ist
T / FV: ist er letzte Woche wegen Krankheit zu Hause geblieben

At this point in the derivation, as many as four different elements may be topicalized:

T / X:
er ist letzte Woche wegen Krankheit zu Hause geblieben
letzte Woche ist er wegen Krankheit zu Hause geblieben

28

wegen Krankheit ist er letzte Woche zu Hause geblieben
zu Hause geblieben ist er letzte Woche wegen Krankheit

To be sure, not all of these would be acceptable in any context; on the other hand, each would be acceptable in a suitable textual environment. The structure of German is such that the speaker may select from a large number of elements that word or phrase which he wishes to place in the topic position.

Topic and comment as structural features of language arise out of the interaction of the "geometry" of language and the "psychology" of the message-sender and receiver in the communicative situation. Though they have been incorporated into the structure of German, and to a lesser extent into that of English, they are not so much features of the syntax of those languages as features of language as such. They reflect not only these fundamental characteristics of language, but also the circumstances in which a given utterance is being formed, where their effect is felt through the optional application of the EDICT-rules of topicalization and commentization during the generation of the utterance. For this reason, we will refer to them again and again as motivating factors for numerous syntactic operations.

*Ellipsis*

The influence of the context extends not only from the discourse as a whole to the individual sentences which comprise it, but also from some elements of a given sentence to others in that same sentence. This influence results in the selective deletion of some elements in the sentence, a phenomenon which we will call "ellipsis." Because the grammar which is to be presented in the following chapters is conceived not only as a set of instructions for making up sentences, but also as an instrument for analyzing them, it is necessary for the latter process to take this phenomenon into account. There is a certain amount of redundancy in speech, but too much is evidently repugnant to users of language, as they find it an easy matter to throw overboard any verbiage which seems useless to them. In order to analyze the structure of the elliptical sentence, we must first restore those elements which have been omitted.

To be sure, some deletions are virtually a matter of taste. The sentence *Der Aufstieg war schön, aber schwierig* is clearly a simplified form of:

1) der Aufstieg war schön
    aber
2) der Aufstieg war schwierig

This illustrates the main principle of ellipsis, namely, that elements which merely repeat other elements already expressed, e. g., *der Aufstieg* in Clause 2, may be deleted. Most cases of ellipsis are of a somewhat different kind, neither completely optional nor always obligatory. They represent a consensus among speakers of a language as to how much explicit structure is necessary in a given context. The following sentence is typical:

"Ich werde natürlich nicht hemdärmlig dastehen wie jetzt, sondern in feierlichem Schwarz mit Zylinder, neben mir die Gattin, vor mir meine zwei Enkelkinder ganz in Weiß mit Rosen" (Friedrich Dürrenmatt, *Der Besuch der alten Dame*, 7th ed. [Zürich, 1963], p. 14).

If this sentence is in fact the product of a system of generative rules, then it must be possible to show that it has been formed by a rigorous and consistent application of the rules which constitute that system. This is possible only if we restore the elements which have been deleted. Applying this procedure to the present example reveals the following patterns of deletion (deleted elements are enclosed in parentheses):

1) ich werde natürlich nicht hemdärmlig dastehen
2) wie (ich) jetzt (dastehe)
    sondern
3) (ich werde) in feierlichem Schwarz mit Zylinder (dastehen)
4) neben mir (wird) die Gattin (dastehen)
5) vor mir (werden) meine zwei Enkelkinder ganz in Weiß mit Rosen (dastehen)

Reconstituted in this way, the sentence can be seen to consist of four independent finite clauses with verb-second word order − Clauses 1, 3, 4, and 5 − and one subordinate clause − Clause 2 − with verb-last word order. The motivation behind these deletions is again the principle that an element, once uttered, need not be repeated in a parallel structure. The first clause is the only one which is present in its entirety. The writer has used it as the foundation of the sentence, so to speak, and consequently any elements present in the clause may be omitted in subsequent clauses. The pronoun *ich*, for example, present in Clause 1, is deleted in Clauses 2 and 3. Similarly, the lexical verb *dastehen*, once expressed in Clause 1, is deleted in all four of the remaining clauses. And last, the auxiliary verb *werden* is represented only in the first clause. Once these restorations have been made, the parallel structures become obvious, and the analysis of the sentence, clause by clause, may proceed.

Another example shows that not all patterns of deletion are as simple:

"Das wuchs, wuchs über beide, den jungen Maler und den alten Papst, hinaus und erst recht über die Höflinge, die die Bücher gewälzt hatten, um immer noch mehr zu finden, eine noch gelehrtere Anspielung, eine noch schmeichelhaftere Allegorie" (Marie Luise Kaschnitz, "Goldene Bienen," *Engelsbrücke: Römische Betrachtungen,* Fischer-Bücherei 820 [Frankfurt, 1967], p. 146).

The presence of repeated elements — *wuchs, wuchs* and *über beide, . . . über die Höflinge* — suggests that here, too, we have a case of parallel structures with substantial deletions. Restoring the sentence on this assumption yields the following:

1) das wuchs . . . . . . . . . . . . . .          (hinaus)
2) (das) wuchs über beide . . . . . . . .          (hinaus)
3) (das wuchs über) den jungen Maler . . . . .          (hinaus)
    und
4) (das wuchs über) den alten Papst . . . . .          hinaus
    und
5) (das wuchs) erst recht über die Höflinge . . .          (hinaus)
6) die die Bücher gewälzt hatten
7) um immer noch mehr . . . . . . . . .          zu finden
8) (um) eine noch gelehrtere Anspielung . . . .          (zu finden)
9) (um) eine noch schmeichelhaftere Allegorie . .          (zu finden)

The phenomenon observed in the previous sentence, i. e., that repeated elements in parallel structures may be deleted, is apparent here in Clauses 8 and 9, where the phrase *um . . . zu finden* must be supplied on the pattern of Clause 7. In Clauses 1 through 5, the author has elected to delete the word *hinaus* in the first three clauses, which, coupled with the repetition of the verb *wuchs*, leads the reader rapidly into the heart of the sentence to its most important word, *Höflinge*. We are prepared for this by the three repetitions of the phrase, *über beide, (über) den jungen Maler,* and *(über) den alten Papst,* in Clauses 2, 3, and 4, respectively. It may be that we have here the reason why the author chose to place the prefix *hinaus* at the end of Clause 4 instead of at the end of Clause 5: the words *Höflinge, die* are at the exact arithmetical midpoint of the sentence, the 19th and 20th, respectively, of 38 words; to insert the word *hinaus* between them, e. g., *über die Höflinge hinaus, die,* would be to interrupt the movement of thought precisely at the peak of the utterance. This observation serves to underscore the point that, in this matter of ellipsis and deletion, we are very much on the borderline between syntax and style.

If we ignore this phenomenon of ellipsis, we can easily be misled into weak or erroneous interpretations of syntactical structures. One of the main problems of German syntax is the order of adverbial elements. At a lecture some years ago, a speaker tried to explain the difference in meaning between the sentences below solely by reference to the order in which the elements *nicht* and *nur daran* happened to appear, the hypothesis being that one could ultimately set up a kind of chart which would show all the possible sequences in which these and other adverbs might stand, and read the meaning from it. The examples in question were:

1) (er hat an alles gedacht,) nicht nur daran
2) (er hat an alles gedacht,) nur daran nicht

Actually, these sentences reflect different processes of topicalization and deletion. To begin with, the segments in question have contrary meanings. Sentence 1 means '(he thought of everything,) not only of that', whereas Sentence 2 means '(he thought of everything) except that'. An adequate analysis should show how these two phrases are derived from underlying structures where there is a close relation between meaning and meaning-bearing elements, and how these meanings are then signaled by the sequences which appear to the reader or hearer.

In both of the infrastructures underlying the phrases in question the verb is *denken;* preceding both is the prepositional compound *daran*, a nucleus complement (NCOMP), which is modified in both cases by the adverb *nur*. Crucial to the interpretation of these sentences is the role of *nicht*: in Sentence 1 it modifies the adverb *nur* — an example of clause-element negation — so that *nicht nur daran* is a single clause element, and *nicht nur daran denken* the clause nucleus; in Sentence 2 it is a separate syntactic element, a clause nucleus adverb (CLNAV), in which function it stands before the clause nucleus *nur daran denken* — an example of clause-negation. It is this difference in the role of *nicht* in these infrastructures which gives these phrases different meanings. Note that in the following derivations the patterns of topicalization and deletion are the same. Separating the syntactic elements in these infrastructures by virgules for the sake of clarity, we may derive the first of these phrases as follows:

IS1: er / nicht nur daran / denken
FNTZ (= TRMV, PSNM): . . . gedacht hat
T / FV: hat / er / nicht nur daran / gedacht
T / X: nicht nur daran / hat / er / gedacht
D / Y: nicht nur daran / (hat / er / gedacht)
SOP: "Nicht nur daran . . ."

("Y") here is an ad hoc abbreviation for the lexical and auxiliary verbs and the pronoun subject.) The second of these phrases may be generated as follows:

IS2: er / nicht / nur daran / denken
FNTZ (= TRMV, PSNM): gedacht hat
T / FV: hat / er / nicht / nur daran / gedacht
T / X: nur daran / hat / er / nicht / gedacht
D / Y: nur daran / (hat / er) / nicht / (gedacht)
SOP: "Nur daran . . . nicht . . . "

Thus we see that the difference between these phrases is more than simply the question of the "sequence of adverbs." As in the case just presented, a correct analysis is possible only after the deleted elements have been restored.

The last case to be considered here is one of the most complex problems in German syntax: the role of the conjunction *als*. One would not think a four-word sentence could contain many difficulties, and yet this sentence can only be analyzed after the restoration of elements, the deletion of which in idiomatic German is obligatory:

er gilt als Querulant 'he is considered a chronic litigant'

The key here is the noun *Querulant*: it must be in the nominative singular, because all other cases, singular and plural, would have the form *Querulanten*. This means that it can only be the subject of a verb or a predicate noun. Analyses of similar constructions lead us to the conclusion that this sentence must be interpreted as having three clauses with much of their word material deleted:

1) er gilt
2) als (jemand gilt)
3) (der) Querulant (ist)

Constructions of this kind show how necessary it is to reconstitute the sentence before undertaking an analysis of its grammatical structure, and illustrate, too, the effect of ellipsis on the surface structure of language.

## Intersentence Adverbs

The influence of the context can be observed in a text in yet another way. In both English and German, there is a small group of words which serve to indicate the logical or rhetorical relationship between the sentences in which they stand and the context, e. g., *furthermore, moreover, however, nevertheless, otherwise, hence, therefore,* and the like. Unfortunately, there is no agreement on what to call this class of expressions. Traditionally, they have been called "conjunctive adverbs" (Long 1961:275), but they have also been labeled "sentence connectors" (Krohn 1971:288), "transitional adverbs" (Whitehall 1956:70), "sequence signals" (Fries 1952:250), or "sequence words" (Hathaway 1967:148). Though objections have been raised by the last-named to the applicability of the word "adverb" to this class of words, we will use the term "intersentence adverbs" for them in this discussion.

In any case, what is important to the subject at hand is that these words are asyntactic elements, in that they are not present in the infrastructure, but rather are inserted into the generated sentence at various points after it has been set into its place in the discourse. The potentiality of these words for occupying different positions is one of their most conspicuous characteristics. In the sentence *John couldn't have done it alone*, the word *however* can be inserted at no fewer than four points:

> (however) John (however) couldn't (however) have done it alone (however)

Similarly, in the sentence *Tomorrow he will bring the document back to the embassy,* there are four possibilities:

> (however) tomorrow (however) he will (however) bring the document back to the embassy (however)

We can briefly summarize the positions represented in these

34

examples in a few short statements. Intersentence adverbs in English may appear:

1) pre-initially or post-finally, i. e., immediately before or after the sentence;
2) following a topicalized element or an accented subject in initial position;
3) following the first auxiliary.

German also has a small group of word which function much as these intersentence adverbs in English, a group which includes *aber, also, doch, hingegen, jedoch, indessen,* and a number of less frequently used words. Again we are confronted by the problem of labels for the category: Lederer (1969:411 ff.) discusses them individually, but does not assign them to a specific grammatical category; Brinkmann (1971:762 ff.) also recognizes their distinctive syntactic function, but does not place them in a specific form-class, either. They have also been called "modal sentence adverbs" (Fichtner 1970:24).

To be sure, this class of words is less clearly defined in German than in English, a fact which may explain the vagueness with which they are often treated. Whereas they can be identified without difficulty when they stand within the clause, in initial position they have a tendency to assume the patterns of distribution of either adverbs or conjunctions, as the following examples show:

ich möchte mit dir gehen,
1) *jedoch* ich habe keine Zeit
2) *jedoch* habe ich keine Zeit
3) ich habe *jedoch* keine Zeit (Lederer 1969:347)
ich habe ihm Geld angeboten,
1) *doch* er wollte es nicht
2) *doch* wollte er es nicht
3) er wollte es *doch* nicht (after Lederer 1969:411)

In the first clause in both groups of examples, the word precedes a nonverb element which itself precedes the finite verb; thus *doch* and *jedoch* in these instances appear to be conjunctions. In the second example in each group, it immediately precedes the finite verb, thus functioning as a topicalized adverb, one which was shifted to initial position from within the clause. The third sentence also suggests that these adverbs do in fact have their origin in the interior of the clause, as they stand within as syntactic elements with as yet unspecified functions.

This form-class of intersentence adverbs also tends to overlap the category of conjunctions, to judge by the case of the conjunction *aber*:

> Karl geht in die Schule,
> 1) *aber* Hans bleibt zu Hause
> 2) Hans *aber* bleibt zu Hause
> 3) Hans bleibt *aber* zu Hause (Lederer 1969:411)

In the first sentence, *aber* functions as the coordinating conjunction it is usually considered to be; in the second and third, it is more like the other intersentence adverbs already described.

We may summarize the range of possibilities for the position of this form-class as was done for English:

> 1) in initial position, these intersentence adverbs may stand before a topicalized nonverb element, as though they were conjunctions, or before the finite verb, like topicalized adverbs;
> 2) these adverbs do not appear in post-final position at all — a point of contrast with English, e. g.:

> ! Karl is going to the movies, however
> ? ? ? Karl geht ins Kino jedoch

> 3) in clause-medial position, they may stand between an accented topicalized element and the finite verb, immediately after any untopicalized personal pronoun, and immediately preceding the clause nucleus adverb (CLNAV), e. g.:

> in dem Fall (aber) soll ihm (aber) der Botschafter das Protokoll (aber) nicht ins Ministerium schicken lassen

As was noted, both languages have evolved, to differing degrees, a class of asyntactic elements which we have called intersentence adverbs. These serve to relate the various sentences of the discourse to one another, as the communicative intention of the speaker or writer may require. Because they do not in most cases appear in the infrastructure, they will simply be deleted from those sentences which will be analyzed in subsequent chapters.

# CHAPTER 4

## THE INFRASTRUCTURE OF ENGLISH

At this point, we turn to the composition of the infrastructure of the English clause. In a previous chapter, we stated that the infrastructure was the basic sequence of elements from which every kind of clause, and hence every sentence, was constructed. It is a peculiarity of English, however, that there are no shifts of major elements, such as that of the verb in German, so that at the beginning we can describe the infrastructure of English by describing the structure of independent finite clauses.

### Organization of the English Infrastructure

For purposes of description, it is useful to group the seven tagmemes of the English infrastructure into four zones or fields, i. e., the preverbal field, the verb, and the first and second postverbal fields:

$$\boxed{\text{SUBJ} + \text{ITVAV}} + \quad \text{VERB} \quad + \boxed{\text{NOMNL} + \text{VPART}} + \boxed{\text{VCOMP} + \text{TRMAV}}$$

| PREVERBAL | | POSTVERBAL I | POSTVERBAL II |
|---|---|---|---|

This chapter will be taken up with the description and classification of words and phrases by reference to their form and function, and their assignment to these segments (cf. Cook 1967, 1969, Fries 1952).

The first step will be to define the four tagmemes of the two postverbal fields: in the first, the nominal (NOMNL) and the verb particle (VPART); and in the second, the verb complement (VCOMP) and the terminal adverb (TRMAV). We will defer a discussion of the verb (VERB) to the chapter on the morphology of that word-class, except where the analysis of one or the other of the various segments makes it necessary to take it up. Finally, we will examine the preverbal field — the subject (SUBJ) and the intraverbal adverb (ITVAV) — and establish the kinds of words and phrases which may be found there. We now turn to the first postverbal field, and to the first of the tagmemes to follow the verb, i. e., the nominal (NOMNL).

## The First Postverbal Field: The Nominal (NOMNL)

In this tagmeme we find the element traditionally called the object noun(s) or the direct and indirect objects. Whether there is one noun or two will depend on the valence of the verb: some, like the verbs *see, forget, receive, answer, contain,* etc. are followed by one object only; others, like *give, send, write, find, get, make,* etc. may take two objects. We will refer to these objects as the first and second noun objects, with the understanding that the second, when present, precedes the first. The tagmeme NOMNL may hence be rewritten:

NOMNL: (2NnOj) & 1NnOj

This formula satisfactorily describes sequences like *John received the letter,* where *the letter* is the first noun object. As speakers of English know, however, it is possible to transform this noun into a pronoun, and for this purpose, it is necessary to construct a morpho-syntactic rule which will apply here to the first postverbal field of the English infrastructure: pronominalization (PRNMZ). This means that the sentence above may be modified by the operation of this rule as follows:

IS, FNTZ: John received the letter
PRNMZ / 1NnOj: John received it

More complex situations occur when both a first and a second noun object are present, e. g., in sentences like *He gave his friend the book.* Speakers of American English can vary this phrase in five ways, and speakers of British English in six, by pronominalizing one or the other element, and by changing the second noun object into a prepositional phrase with *to* or *for*:

   he gave his friend the book
1) he gave him the book
2) he gave the book to his friend
3) he gave the book to him
4) he gave it to his friend
5) he gave it to him
6) he gave it him (British English only)

The last sentence, though acceptable in British English, is no longer idiomatic in American English, and hence will be excluded from further consideration. An example with *for*:

   he found his nephew a job
1) he found him a job
2) he found a job for his nephew
3) he found a job for him
4) he found it for his nephew
5) he found it for him

The question arises as to how these variants can be described within the framework of a system of generative rules. One rule, pronominalization (PRNMZ), has already been devised, although there are quite evident limits as to its applicability; one cannot apply it to both objects, nor to the first noun object alone, e. g.:

   IS, FNTZ: he gave his friend the book
   PRNMZ / 1NnOj: ? ? ? he gave his friend it
   PRNMZ / 2NnOj: ! he gave him the book (ex. 1 above)
   PRNMZ / 1,2NnOj: ? ? ? he gave him it

(One or more question marks preceding an utterance indicates that it is unidiomatic, unacceptable in most cases, or completely wrong; an exclamation point or points indicates that it is acceptable or preferable.) It is apparent that additional modifications are necessary if we are to account for all of the acceptable sequences which English admits of: specifically, we must formulate rules to insert a preposition — *to* or *for*, depending on the valence of the verb — and to move the phrase so produced to the end of the field. In addition to the morphosyntactic rule of pronominalization (PRNMZ), then, we must compose instructions using the EDICT-rules for insertion (I) and commentization (C), restricting these to the confines of the first postverbal field. Thus, to formulate the utterance *He gave the book to his friend*, we must first insert the preposition before the second noun object, and then commentize the entire object phrase. These operations may be represented as follows:

   IS, FNTZ: he gave his friend the book
   I / Prp (&2NnOj): he gave to his friend the book
   C / OjPhr: he gave the book to his friend
   SOP: ! "He gave the book to his friend." (cf. ex. 2)

This sequence of operations may be augmented by the pronominalization rule to generate another acceptable sequence:

IS, FNTZ: he gave his friend the book
PRNMZ / 2NnOj: he gave him the book
I / Prp (&PrnOj): he gave to him the book
C / OjPhr: he gave the book to him
SOP: ! "He gave the book to him." (cf. ex. 3)

As the symbols indicate, when the second noun object is pronominalized – PRNMZ / 2NnOj – a pronoun object (PrnOj) is created,
before which a preposition is placed – I / Prp(&PrnOj); the resulting
object phrase is then commentized – C / OjPhr.

This series of transformations may be varied by the application of
the pronominalization rule to the first noun object:

IS, FNTZ: he gave his friend the book
I / Prp (&2NnOj): he gave to his friend the book
C / OjPhr: he gave the book to his friend
PRNMZ / 1NnOj: he gave it to his friend
SOP: ! "He gave it to his friend." (cf. ex. 4)

Obviously it would be possible to apply the pronominalization rule
twice, to each object, but following the sequences indicated above:

IS, FNTZ: he gave his friend the book
PRNMZ / 2NnOj: he gave him the book
I / Prp (&PrnOj): he gave to him the book
C / OjPhr: he gave the book to him
PRNMZ / 1NnOj: he gave it to him
SOP: ! "He gave it to him." (cf. ex. 5)

As we conclude the task of formulating rules for the generation
of the various noun and pronoun sequences within the tagmeme
NOMNL, we must ask if these cannot be reduced to a single formula,
the application of which would generate all of the acceptable patterns, but no unacceptable sequences. Such a formula must specify
which of the operations described above might be optional (oC . . .),
which might be obligatory (+C . . .), and which might be prohibited
(xC . . .). We began with the formula:

NOMNL: (2NnOj) & 1NnOj

This means that a single noun in the nominal tagmeme is to be
construed as a first noun object; a second noun object may precede
it. The various transformations presented individually above may be
condensed into the following formula:

oPRNMZ / 2NnOj → o[ +I / Prp (&2NnOj;PrnOj) → +C / OjPhr →
oPRNMZ / 1NnOj ].

These symbols mean that the second noun object may be optionally
pronominalized: oPRNMZ / 2NnOj. This operation may be followed
optionally by the series of transformations within the square
brackets: o[ . . . ]; If one elects to make these changes, one must
insert a preposition before the second noun object, or, if that has
been pronominalized, before the resulting pronoun object: +I / Prp
(&2NnOj;PrnOj). One must then commentize the resulting object
phrase: +C / OjPhr. After completing these operations, the pronominalization of the first noun object is optional: oPRNMZ / 1NnOj.

In the following section, this formula will be modified somewhat
to include a transformation which arises in connection with the
presence of the verb particle (VPART) in the first postverbal field.
Before turning to that feature of the English infrastructure, there are
several aspects of the NOMNL tagmeme which may require some
elucidation. For one thing, one might inquire as to the rationale for
a series of alternative sequences for two noun objects and their
pronoun surrogates. Here, as at several other points in the structure
of English, a series of alternative positions has evolved — which we
will call transpositions — which permit the rearrangement of word
material in a given segment in such a way as to reflect the topic-comment organization of the sentence. As we noted in an earlier chapter,
this structure makes itself felt through the position of the topic and
comment elements at the beginning and end of the utterance, as well
as by their accents, whereby the first accented element is usually the
topic, and the last one the comment. The flexibility in the order of
noun objects permitted by these transpositions allows either the first
or the second noun object to serve as comment. This becomes clear
when we superimpose the topic-comment organization on the sentences similar to these used as examples above, and add the appropriate accents, so that the following are produced (in which topic
and comment are marked by the subscript "T" and "C," respectively):

$BILL_T$ gave TOM the $BOOK_C$
$BILL_T$ gave the BOOK to $TOM_C$
$BILL_T$ gave him the $BOOK_C$
$BILL_T$ gave it to $TOM_C$
$BILL_T$ $GAVE_C$ it to him

41

We have replaced the pronoun *he* with the noun *Bill*, since in most cases a pronoun is not important enough to serve as topic. The last sentence also reflects this principle: when both nouns, i. e., the first and second objects, have been reduced to pronouns, the role of comment devolves upon the last major syntactic element in the sentence, in this case, the verb. This is the exception which "proves" the rule, namely, that transpositions in word order serve to a great extent to adapt the sequence of clause elements inherent in the syntactic structure of the language to the order required by the topic-comment organization of the utterance, which reflects the communicative priorities of the individual situation.

Another matter of concern is the ever-present problem of syntactic ambiguity. This arises with the use of the prepositions *to* and *for* in the object phrase (OjPhr). These prepositions have a number of functions in English, of which this is only one. The question which will arise again and again in this investigation is how we can identify and distinguish between different syntactical functions of morphologically identical structures. In every case, we must try to find some kind of test which will enable us to differentiate, objectively and unambiguously, the various syntactical functions of structures which from the point of view of form are identical. Returning to the present case, we might pose the question thus: is there any way in which we can distinguish between an object phrase, and other kinds of prepositional phrases introduced by *to* and *for*. Let us consider the following sentences:

1) he tore the book to shreds
2) he sent the book to his friend
3) he carried the book to his desk
4) he made a whistle for his son
5) he kept the book for days
6) he left the room for no reason

From the point of view of a grammar based on formal classifications, the phrases *to shreds, to his friend, to his desk,* and *for his son, for days, for no reason,* would all be considered identical. Yet, if a simple test be applied, one based on the transposition of elements which we have just observed in connection with the NOMNL tagmeme, all but two of these sequences can be excluded from the category of object phrase which we are concerned with here. That test is to re-transform the prepositional phrases back into second noun objects. If an acceptable sentence results, then the phrase in question is a genuine object phrase; if not, then the phrase with *to* or *for* has some other function, as yet undefined. Let us now apply this test, to see which sentences, so changed, would be regarded as acceptable to a native speaker of English:

! he tore the book to shreds → ? ? ? he tore shreds the book
! he sent the book to his friend → ! he sent his friend the book
! he carried the book to his desk → ? ? ? he carried his desk the book
! he made a whistle for his son → ! he made his son a whistle
! he kept the book for days → ? ? ? he kept days the book
! he left the room for no reason → ? ? ? he left no reason the room

Of the six sentences which have been subjected to this test, only the second and fourth can be changed according to the pattern specified, and still remain acceptable. This means that only the phrases *to his friend* and *for his son* may be regarded as true object phrases arising by means of the transformation of a second noun object.

There is yet another problem which occurs in connection with the NOMNL tagmeme — one arising from the varying valence of the verb. It was noted that some verbs may be followed by one object, others by two. Our formula for the composition of the tagmeme states that any single noun following a verb is to be regarded as a first noun object, and since our generative rules specify in every case which element the various transformations apply to, there is no possibility of confusion: the only transformation which may apply to a first noun object standing alone, according to the formula devised above, is pronominalization (PRNMZ).

However, there are two kinds of verbs which may take two noun objects. Those which have appeared in our examples so far are verbs which could take what in traditional grammar are referred to as "indirect objects." such as appear with verbs of donation (*give, send, hand, pass,* etc.) or of narration (*tell, write,* etc.). There is another class of verbs, however, which may also be followed by two noun objects: these are verbs of designation like *designate, call, name, elect, appoint, make,* etc., as in these sentences:

the club designated Jim its representative
they named Tom chairman
the chairman made Fred his parliamentarian

Not only do these verbs manifest different transformational patterns in the passive voice, the only transformation which can be applied to them in the formula presented above is the pronominalization of the second noun object (PRNMZ / 2NnOj), e. g.:

IS, FNTZ: they elected Henry president
PRNMZ / 2NnOj: they elected him president
SOP: ! "They elected him president."

But it is not possible to apply the remaining rules:

I / to(&PrnOj): they elected to him president
C / OjPhr: they elected president to him
SOP: ? ? ? "They elected president to him."
PRNMZ / 1NnOj: they elected it to him
SOP: ? ? ? "They elected it to him."

As we will discover in a later chapter, this inconsistency occurs because these constructions actually contain embedded infinitives, and hence the nouns following them are not necessarily objects of those verbs.

*The First Postverbal Field: The Verb Particle (VPART)*

It is a feature of the valence of many verbs in English that they are often associated, either optionally or obligatorily, with a kind of adverb which we will call a "verb particle" (VPART). There are not many of these particles; not a few also function as prepositions; and they are very common. A fairly complete list would include: *on, off, in, out, up, by, down, over, under, through, back, forth, about, around, away, home, along, together,* and a few more. When combined with verbs, especially verbs of motion, they form a great number of expressions which find extensive use in every kind of discourse. A single example should suffice to show the effect of these particles on the meaning of a lexical verb:

he turned the corner (i. e., without a particle)
but:

he turned *around*
he turned *away*
he turned *back*
he turned *up* in Rome

as well as:

he turned the radio *on*
he turned the light *off*
he turned the box *over*
he turned the offer *down,* etc. etc.

This combination of lexical verb plus verb particle may be used without an element in the NOMNL tagmene, i. e., with an intransitive verb, as in the first four examples in the list above. When used without an object, the verb particle simply follows the lexical verb:

| (. . . VERB) | NOMNL | VPART |
|---|---|---|
| he sat | . . . | down |
| she went | . . . | home |
| they drove | . . . | away |

When used with object nouns or pronouns in the nominal segment, however, a number of variations in word order are admissible:

she put the cat *out*
she put *out* the cat
she put him *out*
they put their pencils *down*
they put *down* their pencils
they put them *down*
he turned the radio *off*
he turned *off* the radio
he turned it *off*

It is apparent from these sentences that there is a certain variation possible in the relative position of the first noun object and the verb particle: either the object may precede the particle, or it may follow it. Adapting the principle developed in connection with the elements in the nominal tagmeme, we may describe these patterns of word order by means of a generative rule which modifies a basic sequence. Inasmuch as the elements of the NOMNL tagmeme immediately follow the verb, we may place the verb particle (VPART) after that segment. The reversal of word order noted in the examples may be represented by the additional rule "C / 1NnOj." which means that the first noun object may be optionally commentized, i. e., moved to the end of the first postverbal field. This implies the following change in the order of elements:

NOMNL & VPART: (2NnOj) & 1NnOj & VPart
oC / 1NnOj: (2NnOj) & VPART & 1NnOj

or, in an actual derivation:

IS, FNTZ: they put their pencils down
oC / 1NnOj: they put . . . down their pencils

This change is another of the transpositions which are incorporated into the structure of English in order to adapt the sequence of syntactic elements to the communicative priorities of the speech situation through the medium of the topic-comment principle. With these factors indicated by subscript "T" and "C," respectively, the sentences above could be rewritten as follows:

they PUT$_T$ their PENCILS DOWN$_C$
they PUT$_T$ DOWN their PENCILS$_C$

As was noted earlier, the valence of many verbs allows a second noun object. If we combine the rule presented above with those developed for the distribution of first and second noun objects, we can use one formula to generate all of the possibilities for the position of elements which are admitted by the patterns of modern English. That formula would provisionally contain the following five terms:

1) oC / 1NnOj →
2) oPRMNZ / 2NnOj →
3a) o [ +I / Prp(&2NnOj, PrnOj) →
3b) +C / OjPhr →
3c) oPRNMZ / 1NnOj ]

The following examples demonstrate the application of these rules:

IS, FNTZ: the teacher gave the student the test back

oC / 1NnOj: . . . the student back the test
SOP: ! "The teacher gave the student back the test."

oPRMNZ / 2NnOj: . . . him the test back
SOP: ! "The teacher gave him the test back."

oC / 1NnOj: . . . the student back the test
oPRNMZ / 2NnOj: . . . him back the test
SOP: ! "The teacher gave him back the test."

+I / Prp(&2NnOj, PrnOj): to the student the test back
+C / OjPhr: the test back to the student
SOP: ! "The teacher gave the test back to the student."

+I / Prp(&2NnOj): to the student the test back
+C / OjPhr: the test back to the student
oPRNMZ / 1NnOj: it back to the student
SOP:! "The teacher gave it back to the student."

If all of the foregoing combinations of rules yield acceptable utterances, the following does not:

oC / 1NnOj: the student back the test
I / Prp(&2NnOj, PrnOj): to the student back the test
+C / OjPhr: back the test to the student
oPRNMZ / 1NnOj: back it to the student."
SOP: ? ? ? "The teacher gave back it to the student."

Since the rules generate an unacceptable utterance, they must be modified to exclude the operation of both the rule C / 1NnOj, for the commentization of the first noun object, and PRNMZ / 1NnOj, for the pronominalization of that element. This compels us to rewrite our formula as follows:

1)   oC(xPRNMZ) / 1NnOj →
2)   oPRNMZ / 2NnOj →
3a)  o [ +I / Prp(&2NnOj, PrnOj) →
3b)  +C / OjPhr →
3c)  oPRNMZ(xC) / 1NnOj ]

The symbols "C(xPRNMZ) / 1NnOj" and "PRNMZ(xC) / 1NnOj" mean that the operations of commentization and pronominalization may not both be applied to the first noun object in the same derivation. It is not difficult to see why this should be so: commentization throws the noun object into a position of greater prominence; a pronoun, on the other hand, is a noun deprived of its individual semantic value in the utterance, and consequently, the importance of a noun is diminished by pronominalization. These two processes thus lead in opposite directions.

With one exception, the rules set forth above are sufficient to account for all of the acceptable sequences of elements in the first postverbal field. The one reservation has to do with certain characteristics of valence which affect the range of variation which is allowed when certain verb particles are present. For example, it is acceptable (if not elegant) to say *The teacher handed the student the test back*, but the sentence *? ? The student handed the teacher the test in* is not idiomatic English. In the preceding section, we established a generative formula with five terms, the application of which would generate all, and only, the acceptable sequences in the NOMNL tagmeme. We found that it was possible to retain this formula to account for the various patterns which arise when a verb particle is present. The modification which is required by the examples above may be formulated as the statement that the operation of Rule 3 is, in many cases, not optional, but obligatory. Whereas the utterance *The teacher handed the student the test back* is acceptable as it emerges from the stage of verb modification, the other sequence must be modified by the obligatory operations of Rule 3:

IS, FNTZ: the student handed the teacher the test in
+I / Prp(&2NnOj, PrnOj): ... to the teacher ...
+C / OjPhr: the student handed the test in to the teacher
SOP: ! "The student handed the test in to the teacher."

The other rules remain optional, as before. As a practical matter, it may simplify this construction for the learner to regard Rules 3a and 3b as obligatory until his *Sprachgefühl* is sufficiently developed to enable him to recognize those combinations of lexical verb plus verb particle which admit of the optional pattern. On that assumption, we may summarize the rules which apply to the transpositions within the first postverbal field as follows:

NOMNL & VPART: (2NnOj) & 1NnOj & VPart
Rule 1) oC(xPRNMZ) / 1NnOj →
Rule 2) oPRNMZ / 2NnOj →
Rule 3a) +, o [ +I / Prp(&2NnOj, PrnOj) →
Rule 3b) +C / OjPhr →
Rule 3c) oPRNMZ(xC) / 1NnOj ]

There is one further question which arises here, one which will come up in the next section of this chapter as well. In our discussion of nominal elements, we found it necessary to distinguish between prepositional objects and other prepositional phrases introduced by the preposition *to*. In the present case, too, we can observe that most of the words listed as verb particles may be used as prepositions. Some kind of test, therefore, must be found by which the word *off*, for example, when used as a verb particle, may be distinguished from the same word *off* when used as a preposition. In concrete terms, we must find some way to differentiate between the prepositions and verb particles in pairs of sentences such as these:

he turned off the light
he turned off the highway

he looked up the street on a map
he looked up the street for a taxi

We can do this by means of a test much like that employed in earlier sections in this chapter. We need only to shift the position of the noun, so that it stands before the particle in question, as though it were a first noun object. If the sentence substantially retains its original meaning, aside from the shift of comment element, and is still acceptable, then we may regard the word in question as a verb particle. If it does not, then the word is a preposition. Applying this test to the sentences above yields the following results:

he turned off the light → ! he turned the light off
he turned off the highway → ? ? ? he turned the highway off

he looked up the street on a map → ! he looked the street up on a map
he looked up the street for a taxi → ? ? ? he looked the street up for a taxi

On the basis of this test, we have established that the words *off* and *up* in the first and third sentences are verb particles. Their function in the second and fourth sentences will be discussed later in this chapter.

This difference of syntactical function, i. e., the difference between preposition and verb particle, is reflected in the accentual condition of the word in these uses (cf. Taha 1960). The verb particle, as a major syntactic element, bears a more conspicuous accent or intonation contour than the preposition. This accounts for the distribution of accentual prominence in these examples (accented words are capitalized):

he TURNED OFF the LIGHT
he TURNED off the HIGHWAY

he LOOKED UP the STREET on a MAP
he LOOKED up the STREET for a TAXI

The verb complement can be either a one-word adverb, i. e., a verb complement adverb (VCAdv), or a prepositional phrase, i. e., a verb complement phrase (VCPhr). As their labels suggest, both of these elements modify the verb. As to their position, they ordinarily follow NOMNL and VPART. The limits on their movement within the clause can be made clear by a few examples. We can say, for example:

he placed the vase on the table carefully

a sentence in which *carefully* is a verb complement adverb, and *on the table* a verb complement phrase. We cannot shift either of these to a position preceding *the vase*, which is the first noun object. This would produce the following sentences, all of which are unacceptable:

? ? ? he placed carefully the vase on the table
? ? ? he placed on the table the vase carefully
? ? ? he placed carefully on the table the vase

Similar restrictions on the relative position of verb complements and verb particles are exemplified in the following sentences, in which *up* is a verb particle, *quickly* a verb complement adverb, and *from the couch* a verb complement phrase:

! he got up from the couch quickly
! he got up quickly from the couch
? ? ? he got from the couch up quickly
? ? ? he got quickly up from the couch
? ? ? he got from the couch quickly up

Within the VCOMP tagmeme, however, there is a certain flexibility in the positions of verb complement adverb and phrase as to which may stand in first or second position. Thus, all of these sentences are correct:

he got up from the couch quickly
he got up quickly from the couch

they sat at the table quietly
they sat quietly at the table

he walked across the room slowly
he walked slowly across the room

As in the case of the various noun and pronoun objects and the verb particle, this limited variability of position is of use in connection with the topic-comment organization of the sentence, e. g.:

he WALKED$_T$ across the ROOM SLOWLY$_C$

he WALKED$_T$ SLOWLY across the ROOM$_C$

Since many prepositions can also function as verb particles, we must again distinguish between these two uses of the same lexical item. In other words, we must be able to distinguish between the two functions of *on* in these sentences:

! he put on his hat
! he sat on his hat

In our discussion of the verb particle, we tested for the function of that element by shifting the first noun object to a position following the verb particle. Reversing this test would yield the following results:

he put on his hat → ! he put his hat on
he sat on his hat → ? ? ? he sat his hat on

It is thus clear that the word *on* in the second sentence is a preposition, and not a verb particle.

An equally useful test is to pronominalize the noun in question, a procedure which makes use of the fact that pronoun objects must precede verb particles, whereas they follow prepositions of which they are objects. As a result, we can find sentences which clearly contrast these functions, e. g.:

he put on his hat → ? ? ? he put on it
    *but*: ! he put it on
he sat on his hat → ! he sat on it
    *but*: ? ? ? he sat it on

In such cases, we can immediately determine whether a given member of the form-class of prepositions is functioning as a verb particle, or as part of a prepositional phrase which is in turn functioning as a verb complement phrase.

In the preceding section, we noted certain differences in accentuation deriving from the fact that most prepositions are minor syntactic elements. Consequently, the sentences we have been scrutinizing would be accented somewhat differently:

he PUT ON his HAT
he SAT on his HAT

Similarly, one can hear the difference between:

he TURNED OFF the RADIO
he TURNED off the HIGHWAY

In these cases, the verb particles can be recognized by their greater accentual prominence.

Another problem arising out of the form of the verb complement phrase is the possibility of different relationships to other elements in the context. What, for example, is the relationship of the phrase *in the park* to the other elements in these sentences:

1) he ate his sandwich in the park
2) he fed the pigeons in the park
3) he admired the gardens in the park

There are two possibilities in each case: either the phrase is connected in some way with the preceding noun, or it is connected in some way with the verb. The former possibility can often be interpreted as an elliptical relative clause, e. g., the third sentence could be expanded to read:

3) he admired the gardens (which were) in the park

This kind of relationship we will call "adnominal." In the other case, the phrase in question can be said to be used "adverbially." The first sentence could be recast to read:

1) he ate his sandwich (and he ate it) in the park

This sentence, too, is elliptical, except that here it is a repetition of the verb which has been left out.

It should be noted that the identification of these differing relationships derives, not from our recognition of distinctive patterns of word order, but from our general knowledge of the relationship of parks to sandwiches and gardens. Under these circumstances, it is not unlikely that cases should arise which are ambiguous in this regard, e. g., the second sentence above, *He fed the pigeons in the park*. This sentence is syntactically ambiguous, because it is susceptible of two interpretations, either that he fed the pigeons which at that time happened to be in the park, or that he fed the pigeons and this feeding happened to take place in the park. The proper interpretation must be inferred from the context. It is here that considerations of meaning and interpretations of syntactic structures intersect.

One might ask if there were any test by means of which these two uses of a prepositional phrase might be distinguished. Often pronominalization will suffice. If the noun to which a given phrase might be adnominal can be transposed into a pronoun without substantial distortion of meaning, then the phrase in question is adverbial in function, as in these examples:

he ate his sandwich in the park → ! he ate it in the park
he fed the pigeons in the park → ! he fed them in the park
he admired the gardens in the park → ? he admired them in the park

Another useful test is to transform the sentence in question into the passive voice, to see where the prepositional phrase in question makes the most sense. If two alternatives seem to be possible, it is likely that one is dealing with an ambiguous case. Applying this to our examples, we find:

he ate his sandwich in the park →
 ! his sandwich was eaten by him in the park
 ? ? his sandwich in the park was eaten by him
he fed the pigeons in the park →
 ! the pigeons were fed by him in the park
 ! the pigeons in the park were fed by him
He admired the gardens in the park →
 ? ? the gardens were admired by him in the park
 ! the gardens in the park were admired by him

In the first example, the phrase in question, *in the park*, clearly modifies the verb, active or passive. In the third, on the other hand, it remains with the noun *gardens* when it becomes the subject. As we noted, the second sentence is ambiguous in this regard. It is by tests of these kinds that one can distinguish between adnominal prepositional phrases and true verb complement phrases.

We have found the third tagmeme, VCOMP, then, to consist of two elements: the verb complement phrase (VCPhr) and the verb complement adverb (VCAdv). We can represent the two different possibilities in the sequence of these elements by means of a generative rule. For reasons which will become clear in the following section, we take the sequence of phrase plus adverb as the underlying pattern, which is then modified by topicalization. The rules for transposition in this tagmeme are thus as follows:

VCOMP: VCPhr & VCAdv
oT / VCAdv: VCAdv & VCPhr

This is only one of the transpositions which may take place within the second postverbal field, however. The other involves the terminal adverb tagmeme, to which we now turn.

## The Second Postverbal Field: The Terminal Adverb (TRMAV)

As we have analyzed it thus far, the syntactic structure of the English clause contains a number of adverbial elements: the verb particle, the verb complement phrase, and the verb complement adverb. Each of these has a specific function within the economy of the clause, each is found in certain positions, and each has a certain potentiality for movement to other positions within its segment. Terminal adverbs (TRMAV) constitute yet another class of adverbial expressions, one which can be distinguished from other adverbial clause elements in certain specific ways: by their content – they may be adverbs of place or circumstance, but for the most part are adverbs of time; and by their position – they occupy the final position in the structure of the clause, following the verb complement (VCOMP). They differ from the other adverbs whose positions we have charted, however, in one additional and significant respect: a terminal adverb is normally unaccented, and connotes contrast when it assumes an accent. These conditions are exemplified in the following pairs of sentences (accented elements are in capital letters):

JOHN ARRIVED in MUNICH last night
JOHN arrived in Munich LAST NIGHT, and FRANK is to arrive TOMORROW

he WORKS at the OFFICE all day
he WORKS at the OFFICE ALL DAY, and WATCHES TELE-VISION ALL NIGHT

RUTH will be LEAVING for BERLIN next week
RUTH will be leaving for Berlin NEXT WEEK, and HELEN in TEN DAYS

As in other cases of contrast, all accents are deleted except for those

54

on elements which are being contrasted. Because terminal adverbs are normally unaccented, the presence of an accent in itself connotes contrast.

In an earlier chapter, we noted the special potential for prominence inherent in the final position of an utterance. This being so, it is understandable that a speaker might want to move a terminal adverb from its normal position at the end of the sentence, if its presence would tend to divert attention from a more important element which precedes it. In other segments, a transposition often presents a way out of a stylistically awkward situation. In the case of the terminal adverb, too, it is possible to shift it from the end of the sentence to another position, one in which it immediately precedes the verb complement, but follows any nominal element and the verb particle. In other words, it is topicalized to the beginning of the second postverbal field.

Let us consider some examples. The following sentence shows an unaccented terminal adverb in nonfinal position (in italics):

> "Gesticulating wildly, a North Carolina lawyer wound up a case *several years ago* with a massive sweep of his arm, lost his balance, and tumbled head first into the jury box" (*Time*, July 6, 1970, p. 57).

Without distorting the essential syntactic relationships, this sentence may be simplified to read as follows:

> a lawyer wound up a case several years ago with a massive sweep of his arm

The verb is *wound*, and is followed by the verb particle *up*; the first noun object is *a case*; in the second postverbal field, the phrase *with a massive sweep of his arm* ist a verb complement phrase; and the expression *several years ago* ist the terminal adverb. Normally, these elements would be distributed in their respective tagmemes as follows:

| ... VERB | NOMNL | VPART | VCOMP | TRMAV |
|---|---|---|---|---|
| wound | a case | up | with ... | several |
| | | | sweep ... | years |
| | | | arm | ago |

We note, first of all, that the first noun object, *a case*, has been shifted to the end of the first postverbal field:

IS: . . . a case up . . .
C / 1NnOj: . . . up a case . . .

Moreover, the terminal adverb has been moved to the beginning of the second postverbal field, a shift which we represent by the use of the EDICT-rule "T" for topicalization:

IS: . . . with a massive sweep of his arm several years ago
T / TrmAv: several years ago with a massive sweep of his arm

As a result of the two transpositions in the first and second post-verbal fields, the infrastructure now stands as follows:

IS: a lawyer wind up a case several years ago with a massive sweep of his arm

Hence, the communicatively more important elements *a case* and *with a massive sweep of his arm* now stand at the end of their respective fields.

Summarizing those transpositions which may take place within the second postverbal field, we noted in the foregoing section that it was possible to topicalize the verb complement adverb (VCAdv), and that the terminal adverb (TrmAv) may also be so treated. Because of the way in which the basic structures have been ordered and the rules formulated, it is possible to generate all of the possible combinations of elements in this field which are acceptable by the application of these two rules, both optional, in the following order:

oT / TrmAv → oT / VCAdv

Let us take as an example the following sentence:

IS, FNTZ: the speaker pointed to the party's accomplishments proudly last night

Here, the expression *to the party's accomplishments* is a verb complement phrase (VCPhr), the word *proudly* a verb complement adverb (VCAdv), and *last night* a terminal adverb (TrmAv). This sequence itself, without further modification, constitutes one acceptable pattern:

SOP: ! "The speaker pointed to the party's accomplishments proudly last night."

The application of either rule also generates an acceptable pattern:

T / VCAdv: . . . pointed proudly to the party's accomplishments last night

SOP: ! "The speaker pointed proudly to the party's accomplishments last night."

T / TrmAv: . . . pointed last night to the party's accomplishments
proudly

SOP: ! "The speaker pointed last night to the party's accomplishments proudly."

It is also possible to apply both rules to the same finitized infrastructure, to be sure in the proper order:

T / VCAdv: . . . pointed proudly to the party's accomplishments
last night

T / TrmAv: . . . pointed last night proudly to the party's accomplishments

SOP: ? ? "The speaker pointed last night proudly to the party's
accomplishments."

T / TrmAv: . . . pointed last night to the party's accomplishments
proudly

T / VCAdv: . . . pointed proudly last night to the party's accomplishments

SOP: ! "The speaker pointed proudly last night to the party's
accomplishments."

By means of the following generative rules, then, any three elements
may be arranged in as many as four different sequences:

oT / TrmAv →
oT / VCAdv

In this way, we can generate all of the sequences acceptable in
English, but none of the others:

    the speaker pointed
!  to the party's accomplishments proudly last night
!  last night to the party's accomplishments proudly
!  proudly to the party's accomplishments last night
!  proudly last night to the party's accomplishments
?? last night proudly to the party's accomplishments
?? to the party's accomplishments last night proudly

While not uninfluenced by sentence rhythm and lexical compatibility, these shifts of position serve largely to allow a variety of syntactic elements to come to stand in the communicatively important
comment position.

The transpositions which obtain in the first and second postverbal fields mitigate, to a considerable extent, the rigidity of the English infrastructure. There are additional shifts of word position — intraposition and extraposition — which also have this effect. These movements will be considered in connection with the transformations of the finite clause.


*The Preverbal Field: The Subject (SUBJ)*

In the conception of English structure which is at the foundation of this work, the lexical verb is considered to be the axis about which the preverbal and postverbal fields are arranged. There is only one preverbal field, however, which contains the two tagmemes ITVAV "intraverbal adverb." which immediately precedes the lexical verb, and SUBJ "subject," which stands before that adverb when it is present.

The central position of the verb is more than just a spatial metaphor, because all the elements of the clause may be regarded as connected directly or indirectly to the verb. Adverbs may modify the verb directly, or indirectly by modifying other elements which in turn modify the verb; nouns, too, may stand in various functional relationships to the verb.

The relationship of the noun to the verb is complex, in that the relationship may, in a given case, have a number of aspects (for the following, cf. Brockhaus 1969). Most obviously, there is the "functional" relationship, in which the noun serves as subject or object, the difference being the role played by the noun in the action represented by the verb. A familiar example shows this clearly:

the dog$_{\text{subject}}$ bites the man$_{\text{object}}$

the man$_{\text{subject}}$ bites the dog$_{\text{object}}$

In these two sentences, both nouns appear in each function, as subject and as object, and the difference between the sentences depends on who is sinking whose teeth into whose leg.

In addition to this aspect of function, there may be a difference of case. In English, we have only a few remnants of this phenomenon in the pronoun declension; in German, it is an important feature of the morphology of the noun as well. To a marked extent, the case of the noun in German is correlated with its function: the subject function is almost always signaled by the nominative case (the exception being the "dative subjects" of certain verbs in the passive voice); objects are usually in the accusative, occasionally in the dative case; only a few verbs in German in common use today, e. g., *bedürfen*, have objects in the genitive, a case which is more and more being confined to marking the relationship of one noun to another (Waterman 1957).

All of these cases reflect various kinds of relationships of the nouns involved with the verb. Yet the subject, in the nominative case, is distinguished from other nouns such as objects by an additional peculiarity: subject and verb are linked in a pattern of morphological co-variation which depends on the person and number of the subject. This phenomenon, called "agreement" or "Kongruenz," is familiar to us from both languages:

you play ball = you $+\emptyset$ play $+\emptyset$ ball
Johnny plays ball = Johnny$+\emptyset$ play$+$s ball
the boys play ball = the boy$+$s play$+\emptyset$ ball
the boy plays ball = the boy$+\emptyset$ play$+$s ball
du spielst Ball = du$+\emptyset$ spiel$+$st Ball
Hans spielt Ball = Hans$+\emptyset$ spiel$+$t Ball

In addition to the functional relationship between subject and verb, then, these sentences also illustrate a reciprocal morphological or "grammatical" relationship between them.

The foregoing observations have applied with equal force to both English and German. We now come to a further characteristic of English structure, one which is not shared by German: in English, the subject is not only a functional and grammatical element, but it has a specifically "syntactic" role as well. In the next chapter, we will examine this important difference between the two languages from the point of view of German. The subject has a syntactical role in English, because it is always found in the same position in the clause: with some rare exceptions, the subject in English always precedes the lexical verb; moreover, except when affected by subsequent transformations, it is the first element in the clause. For these reasons, we regard the subject as having the same character as the syntactic elements in the postverbal field: it has a predictable form, and is found in a predictable position, relative to the other members of the clause.

The subject, then, is the first of our preverbal elements. As to its position, it may be described by this formula:

SUBJ + . . . + VERB

Following the practice established earlier, we can describe the element occupying the tagmeme as follows:

SUBJ: NnSj; PrnSj

This means that the subject may be either a noun or a pronoun; it is unnecessary to formulate a rule for the transformation of a noun into a pronoun, because no changes in word position are involved. We turn now to the second element in the preverbal field, the last clause element which we have to introduce.

*The Preverbal Field: The Intraverbal Adverb (ITVAV)*

In addition to the three classes of adverbial expressions which were identified in the postverbal field — verb particles (VPART), verb complements (VCOMP), and terminal adverbs (TRMAV) — there is another kind, one which is found in that segment of the clause lying between the subject (SUBJ) and the lexical verb. We call these "intraverbal adverbs" (ITVAV), because they may be found distributed among the various auxiliaries which may precede the lexical verb in English. They are few in number, but very common. Some of those most frequently met with are: *almost, already, also, always, barely, even, just, often, soon, still*, etc., which are nonrestrictive; and *hardly, never, rarely, scarcely, seldom*, etc., which are restrictive intraverbal adverbs. The terms "restrictive" and "nonrestrictive" have to do with the movement of these adverbs to other parts of the clause; this will be explained in the chapter dealing with finite clauses.

As to the label "intraverbal," the segment VERB consists of a lexical verb (LexVb), one bearing the specific meaning of the verb, and as many as four auxiliary verbs (Aux1, Aux2, etc.). These may be represented as to relative position as follows:

Aux1 + Aux2 + Aux3 + Aux4 + LexVb

For our purposes, it is of no importance which of the four possible auxiliary verbs, if any, is present. Whatever the combination may be, the first auxiliary always follows the subject:

he will$_1$ come$_{LexVb}$
he has$_1$ been$_2$ working$_{LexVb}$

he might$_1$ have$_2$ been$_3$ killed$_{LexVb}$
he could$_1$ have$_2$ been$_3$ being$_4$ watched$_{LexVb}$

By adopting this convention in regard to the various auxiliaries of the lexical verb, we are now in a position to describe the position of the intraverbal adverb quite succinctly: it follows the first auxiliary, though it may be transposed to precede it. These possibilities are illustrated in the following sentences, all of which have at least two auxiliaries:

he was *still* being interviewed when . . . .
   he *still* was being interviewed when . . . .
he would *never* have been caught if . . . .
   he *never* would have been caught if . . . .
it will *soon* be decided . . . .
   it *soon* will be decided . . . .

The difference between the two sequences in each case again rests on the principle of topic and comment: the closer one gets to the beginning or end of the sentence, the more vivid the impression conveyed by the word which happens to stand there. Indeed, in the transposed position, both verb and adverb are frequently accented, e. g.:

he NEVER WOULD have been caught, if it HAD'T been for the BANK inspectors

We may express this transposition in the following formula:

ITVAV: (Aux1) & ItvAv & (Aux2 . . . ) & LexVb
oT / ItvAv: ItvAv & (Aux1) & (Aux2 . . . ) & LexVb

This means that the normal position of the intraverbal adverb (ItvAv) is behind the first auxiliary (Aux1) when that form is present; the adverb may be topicalized optionally to a position immediately preceding the auxiliary.

The distinction between the two patterns of intraverbal adverb placement is dependent on one condition: the presence of a least one auxiliary. As we know, the morphology of the English verb does not require an auxiliary verb in every case, and constructions without auxiliaries, e. g., the present tense and the simple past tense, are among those most frequently used. When no auxiliary is present, the possibility of transposing the intraverbal adverb simply disappears, as in these examples:

he has *never* read it
he *never* has read it
he *never* read it

we have *always* traveled by train
we *always* have traveled by train
we *always* traveled by train

Cases of this kind are interesting for the light that they throw on the nature and operation of language. We have here an example of a phenomenon encountered in both English and German from time to time — a case where one subsystem of the language, the system of auxiliary verbs, partially nullifies the effective functioning of another, the transposition of intraverbal adverbs. Cases of this kind support the view that languages are best regarded, not as homogeneous entities, but as complexes of interacting subsystems, jointly serving the purpose of expression and communication.

There is another important distinction between superficially similar elements which becomes crucial in connection with the placement of intraverbal adverbs. Here, as well as elsewhere in this book, we must recognize that the verb *be* in English sometimes behaves in a fashion different from that of other verbs. For this reason, we regard this verb as a separate category, i. e., there are two kinds of verbs in English, LEXVB and BE. In the present case, we observe that one-word forms of the verb BE, unlike those of lexical verbs, function as if they were Aux 1 or first auxiliaries.

Some examples may make this clearer. It has been shown that the intraverbal adverb normally follows Aux 1, but may be topicalized so as to precede it, e. g.:

he would *often* work late at the library
he *often* would work late at the library

It was also pointed out that there is no possibility of contrasting positions when there is no Aux 1 present, e. g.:

he *often* worked late at the library

The verb BE follows these patterns only in part. When an auxiliary is present, it is in no way different from *work* or any other lexical verb:

he had *often* been in the library
he *often* had been in the library

But when the form of BE is not preceded by an auxiliary, it differs from other verbs in that the intraverbal adverb normally follows it, but may be transposed before it, just as if the one-word form of BE were an Aux1:

he is *often* in the library
he *often* is in the library

In this case, as well as in some others we will examine, the verb BE is something of an anomaly.

## *The English Infrastructure*

As the basic structure of German and English, we have postulated a fundamental pattern in which all of the constituent elements of the clause were distributed. This pattern, which we called the infrastructure (IS), was in turn to constitute the basis for the formation of all other syntactic configurations in those languages. Once having distributed the elements of the clause according to the patterns defined by the infrastructure, changes would be made by means of certain kinds of rules, through which the clauses would ultimately be modified and combined into sentences. Since the infrastructure has this quality of being the basic syntactic building block of English, it might be useful at this time to draw together our findings concerning the fields of the infrastructure, the segments in them, and the transpositions which we have found to apply to these segments.

In regard to the crucial relationship of form-class and syntactic function, we notice only one segment which contains a form-class not appearing in any other element, i. e. VERB. This segment contains only lexical and auxiliary verbs, and these appear nowhere else in the infrastructure. Nouns, on the other hand, appear as such in the segments SUBJ and NOMNL, and of course in some of the other segments as objects of prepositions. It is clearly the adverbs which show the greatest variation in syntactical function. Indeed, of the seven segments of the English infrastructure, no fewer than four contain adverbs: the intraverbal adverb (ITVAV), the verb particle (VPART), the verb complement (VCOMP), and the terminal adverb (TRMAV). These categories are defined in part by form: the verb particles consist of only one word, as do the verb complement adverbs and intraverbal adverbs. Verb complement phrases are, by definition, prepositional phrases. Terminal adverbs may be either.

There is a semantic criterion, too, which helps us assign these adverbs to the proper tagmeme. The terminal adverbs indicate details of circumstance, usually of time, whereas the intraverbal adverbs seem to limit the intensity of the action of the verb. Verb complement adverbs and phrases tend to specify or describe the details of the action of the verb. A sentence which illustrates the distribution and function of all three adverbial tagmemes is the following:

> John could scarcely$_\text{ItvAv}$ have taken the money
> secretly$_\text{VcAdv}$ from the vault$_\text{VcPhr}$ last night$_\text{TrmAv}$

All of these adverbial segments allow for restricted adjustments of word order in the form of transpositions, as does the nominal segment, too. Indeed, only the subject and the verb admit of no such shifts of their component elements. These two elements share another distinction, in that they are the only two elements which must be occupied in every infrastructure. Though the subject may be deleted in various ways by subsequent transformations, no infrastructure in English is complete unless it contains a subject and a verb. The other segments may or may not be occupied, depending on the lexical and grammatical valence of the verb.

As we have seen, the infrastructure of English consists of seven tagmemes, which have described and defined above. We may represent this configuration in the following way:

> SUBJ + ITVAV + VERB + NOMNL + VPART + VCOMP + TRMAV

We also noted certain adjustments in the position of the syntactic elements in each of the three fields, adjustments which were called "transpositions." These are summarized here:

> Preverbal Field: SUBJ & ITVAV
> ITVAV: (Aux1) & ItvAv & (Aux2 . . . ) & LexVb . . .
> Rule) oT / ItvAv: ItvAv & (Aux1 . . . ) & LexVb . . .
> First Postverbal Field: NOMNL & VPART
> NOMNL & VPART: (2NnOj) & 1NnOj & VPart
> Rule 1) oC(xPRNMZ) / 1NnOj →
> Rule 2) oPRNMZ / 2NnOj →
> Rule 3a) +,o [ +I / Prp(&2NnOj, PrnOj) →
> Rule 3b) +C / OjPhr →
> Rule 3c) oPRNMZ(xC) / 1NnOj ]
> Second Postverbal Field: VCOMP & TRMAV

Rule 1) oT / TrmAv →
Rule 2) oT / VCAdv

These transpositions operate as part of the process of forming the infrastructure, and serve to adjust the position of the constituent elements of the various tagmemes to the communicative requirements of the context.

These possibilities are represented graphically in the chart on this page. Each tagmeme occupies a separate row; transpositions are indicated by arrows. From such a diagram, the three fields of the English infrastructure become clearly visible. It is this structure which lies behind every clause in English, and which serves as the point of departure for the transformations to be described in the chapters to follow.

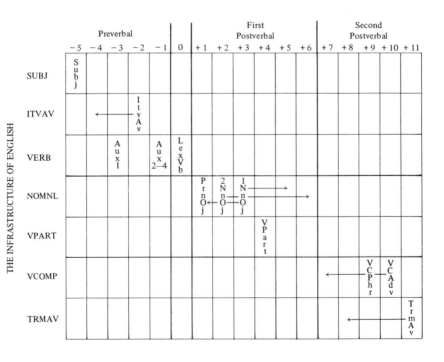

CHAPTER 5

THE INFRASTRUCTURE OF GERMAN


*The Clause Nucleus: The Verb (VERB)*

In our exploration of the infrastructure of English, we were able to take the verb as our point of departure, and to work forwards and backwards from that element to the beginning and end of that structure. Indeed, we found it possible to divide the English clause into three segments, arrayed about the verb as a kind of central axis:

|  |  | FIRST | SECOND |
|---|---|---|---|
| PREVERBAL + | VERB + | POSTVERBAL + | POSTVERBAL |
| FIELD | | FIELD | FIELD |

When the lexical verb was accompanied by auxiliary verbs, these were found before it, separated from the lexical verb only by other auxiliaries or by an adverb. And although it will be shown in the chapter on finite clauses that the first auxiliary in English is susceptible of certain shifts of position, it is still not inaccurate to say that the position of the various verb forms in English is relatively stable, and that it reflects closely the sequence of elements in the infrastructure of the language.

In German, on the other hand, it is not immediately clear what the "normal" position of the verb is: under appropriate circumstances, the verb may appear at the beginning, end, or even in the middle of the clause, as in these examples:

Er blieb gestern zu Hause. (verb-second word order)
Blieb er gestern zu Hause? (verb-first word order)
(Ich weiß, daß) er gestern zu Hause blieb. (verb-last word order)

Given the importance of the verb in the structures of both English and German, it is imperative to determine its basic position before proceeding to a description of the German infrastructure.

Let us approach the problem by considering the sentences above. We note that it is mathematically possible to arrange the four syntactic elements of those sentences — *er, blieb, gestern,* and *zu Hause* — in no fewer than 24 different patterns ($4! = 1 \cdot 2 \cdot 3 \cdot 4$):

| | |
|---|---|
| ER BLIEB GESTERN ZU HAUSE | GESTERN BLIEB ER ZU HAUSE |
| er blieb zu Hause gestern | gestern blieb zu Hause er |
| ER GESTERN ZU HAUSE BLIEB | gestern er blieb zu Hause |
| er gestern blieb zu Hause | gestern er zu Hause blieb |
| er zu Hause gestern blieb | gestern zu Hause blieb er |
| er zu Hause blieb gestern | gestern zu Hause er blieb |
| BLIEB ER GESTERN ZU HAUSE | zu Hause er blieb gestern |
| blieb er zu Hause gestern | zu Hause er gestern blieb |
| blieb gestern er zu Hause | ZU HAUSE BLIEB ER GESTERN |
| blieb gestern zu Hause er | zu Hause blieb gestern er |
| blieb zu Hause er gestern | zu Hause gestern blieb er |
| blieb zu Hause gestern er | zu Hause gestern er blieb |

Of these 24 possibilities, only five would be regarded as completely acceptable specimens of modern Standard German — those printed in capital letters in the list. Our aim is to set up a series of generative rules which, when applied, will produce all of these five acceptable sentence patterns, and only these, in a simple and consistent manner. Because generative rules of the sort used here require a base structure to which the various transformations apply, we will assume that the base structure which requires the fewest and simplest modifications to produce all of the acceptable sentence patterns which occur is the one which reflects the fundamental structure of the language. By this device, we hope to establish the position of the verb in the infrastructure of German.

Traditional grammars, insofar as they approach the problem of word order from this perspective at all, usually take the pattern having verb-second word order as "normal," and derive the other patterns by various changes carried out on that basic sequence. For the sake of the example, let us adopt this view for a moment, and see if we can produce the simplest set of rules possible under this assumption. On this hypothesis, the pattern *Er blieb gestern zu Hause* contains the same sequence of elements as the infrastructure, and hence is not generated. The remaining four patterns must be produced by varying this pattern in some way. The usual practice is to derive verb-first and verb-last word order by moving the finite verb to the beginning and end of the clause, respectively. These operations produce the sequences:

blieb er . . . gestern zu Hause

er . . . gestern zu Hause blieb

Though this accounts for three of the five possibilities, it still leaves those sequences beginning with *gestern* and *zu Hause* yet to be generated. These are usually explained by a statement to the effect that the subject follows the verb when an element other than the subject comes to stand before the verb. Implicit in this formulation is a kind of double transformation:

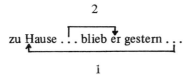

The second of the two patterns in question is explained in like fashion:

$$2$$

zu Hause . . . blieb er gestern . . .

$$i$$

Now let us try to formulate a series of transformational rules which will account for these five patterns on the assumption that verb-second word order most closely approximates the sequence of elements in the infrastructure. We regard the following sequence as tantamount to the infrastructure:

IS, FNTZ (= finitized infrastructure): er blieb gestern zu Hause (= verb-second word order)

Rule X (= move verb to beginning of clause): blieb er gestern zu Hause (= verb-first word order)

Rule Y (= move verb to end of clause): er gestern zu Hause blieb (= verb-last word order)

To generate the two remaining patterns, *gestern blieb er zu Hause* and *zu Hause blieb er gestern*, we can establish a rule by which either adverb is shifted to the beginning of the clause (Rule Z). However, this can only take place in conjunction with another operation which moves the subject *er* to a position immediately following the verb, because otherwise we would generate sequences like:

IS, FNTZ: er blieb gestern zu Hause
Rule Z (= shift adverb to beginning):

1) ? ? ? gestern er blieb zu Hause
2) ? ? ? zu Hause er blieb gestern

Hence, Rule Z must include two operations: the movement of the adverbs to initial position, and the shift of the subject to a position immediately following the verb. The two sentence patterns in question, then, are produced as follows:

IS, FNTZ: er blieb gestern zu Hause
Rule Z1 (= move adverb to initial position):
   1) gestern er blieb zu Hause
   2) zu Hause er blieb gestern
Rule Z2 (= move subject behind verb):
   1) ! gestern blieb er zu Hause
   2) ! zu Hause blieb er gestern

In this way, we can generate the five sentences in our corpus, taking verb-second word order with the subject in initial position as the basic pattern: Rule X generates verb-first word order, Rule Y verb-last word order, and Rule Z those cases of verb-second word order with adverbs in initial position.

However, in view of the fact that as yet we have only managed to produce five acceptable utterances with three rules, we should perhaps consider some alternatives which might possibly reduce the number of rules needed. If we look at the five sentences which constitute the corpus of our grammar, we notice that three of the five contain the sequence *blieb er*. This suggests to us that we might be able to reduce the number of rules if we would take verb-first word order as our point of departure. On this hypothesis, moving the verb to the end of the clause would produce verb-last word order; verb-second word order, on the other hand, would be generated by shifting a nonverbal element to the beginning. These changes are expressed in the following rules:

IS, FNTZ: blieb er gestern zu Hause (= verb-first word order)
Rule M (= move the verb to the end of the clause): er gestern zu Hause blieb (= verb-last word order)
Rule N (= move any nonverbal element to the beginning of the clause):
   1) er blieb gestern zu Hause
   2) gestern blieb er zu Hause
   3) zu Hause blieb er gestern
     (= verb-second word order)

Obviously this is some improvement, since we have reduced the number of our rules by one. Moreover, each rule generates its own kind of word order, which is an additional simplification, compared with our first attempt.

One might not think it possible to achieve any further reduction in the number or nature of these rules. For the sake of the example, however, let us consider the third possibility. On this assumption, we begin with verb-last word order as the fundamental pattern. We can then generate verb-first word order by moving the verb to the beginning of the clause, and, as in the foregoing example, verb-second word order by moving any other element to the beginning, too. These transformations are represented in the following rules:

IS, FNTZ: er gestern zu Hause blieb (= verb-last word order)
Rule A (= move the verb to the beginning of the clause): blieb er gestern zu Hause (= verb-first word order)
Rule B (= move any nonverbal element to the beginning of the clause; condition = this rule may operate only after Rule A has been applied):
1) er blieb gestern zu Hause
2) gestern blieb er zu Hause
3) zu Hause blieb er gestern (= verb-second word order)

As in the previous example, it has been possible to generate all five sentences in our corpus with only three rules (counting the infrastructure as a rule for the purposes of this demonstration). It might therefore seem that both of the last sets of rules are equally effective and suitable as descriptions of procedures for the production of the different patterns of word order in German. And indeed, it is true that it makes little difference with which word-order pattern one starts, if one is considering only two possible sequences, that is, the rules:

IS, FNTZ: blieb er gestern zu Hause
Rule M: er gestern zu Hause blieb

or the sequence:

IS, FNTZ: er gestern zu Hause blieb
Rule A: blieb er gestern zu Hause

In the former case, verb-first word order is modified in order to produce verb-last word order; in the latter, verb-last is modified in order to generate verb-first word order. Yet there are reasons why the latter set must be regarded as superior to the former.

The first reason has to do with consistency. As we saw, in the former example, which had verb-first word order as its starting point, the verb was moved to the end of the clause by Rule M, and nonverbal elements to the beginning by Rule N. In the last example, which began with verb-last word order, the verb was moved to the beginning by Rule A, and nonverbal elements to the beginning by Rule B. This means that a further simplification can be achieved if we acknowledge that the difference between Rules A and B does not lie in what they do, but in what elements they operate on. In other words, the shifting of the verb and of nonverbal elements to the beginning of the clause is actually the same procedure applied to different components of the clause. This means that, for all practical purposes, we can regard our last set of rules as having only one transformation, one which is applied more than once, and to different elements in a specific sequence: first to the verb, and then to one of the nonverbal elements of the clause. The shift of an element to the beginning of the segment in which it stands is in fact identical to the EDICT-rule of topicalization (T). Hence, the five sentence patterns which constitute the corpus we have tried to describe may all be generated by the application of this single rule to specified elements in a certain order: first, to the finite verb (FV), and then to any nonverbal element (X). The generation of the sentences in our corpus thus takes place as follows:

IS, FNTZ: er gestern zu Hause blieb (= verb-last word order)
T / FV (= topicalize the finite verb): blieb er gestern zu Hause (= verb-first word order)
T / X (= topicalize any nonverbal element):
1) er blieb gestern zu Hause
2) gestern blieb er zu Hause
3) zu Hause blieb er gestern (= verb-second word order)

Though we will discover that there are certain restrictions and constraints which apply to these procedures, they are the basic steps by which the three word-order types in finite clauses in German may be produced.

The foregoing analysis leads us to the conclusion that the basic position of the verb in German is at the end of the infrastructure. Our analysis is confirmed when the generative rules above are applied to sentences containing an auxiliary verb, e. g., *Er ist gestern zu Hause geblieben.* On the hypothesis that verb-last word order is "normal" word order in German, we would take the following as the starting point:

IS, FNTZ: er gestern zu Hause geblieben ist (= FV-L, i. e., finite-verb-last word order)

Since there are two verb forms, the lexical verb *geblieben* and the auxiliary *ist*, it is necessary to specify which of the two is to be topicalized. Our knowledge of German indicates that it is the finite verb, whether a lexical verb or an auxiliary, which is shifted to clause-initial position:

T / FV: ist er gestern zu Hause geblieben (= FV-1, i. e., finite-verb-first word order)

As in our earlier example, it is now possible to topicalize any of the nonverbal elements to generate several examples of verb-second word order:

T / X, e. g.:
1) er ist gestern zu Hause geblieben
2) gestern ist er zu Hause geblieben (= FV-2, i. e., finite-verb-second word order)

This demonstration leads to two conclusions. First, the patterns of topicalization by which FV-1 and FV-2 word order are generated apply both to utterances where the finite verb is a lexical verb (*er blieb gestern zu Hause*) and to those where the finite verb is an auxiliary (*er ist gestern zu Hause geblieben*). We will see this confirmed, with some qualifications, in a later chapter. Second, it supports our conclusion that the normal position of the lexical verb in German is not in the interior of the infrastructure, but its end. This does not imply that the other patterns are in some way "abnormal"; it means that verb-last word order is operationally prior to verb-first and verb-second word order in the system of rules by which the various patterns of word order in German can be generated. It is significant here, too, that the lexical verb, when it is not the finite verb, remains in final position in the clause.

There is an additional reason for regarding the end of the clause as the fundamental position for the verb. Many German verbs are composed of two elements, the lexical verb properly speaking, and a "separable prefix." This gives rise to a great number of variants based on simple verbs, e. g., *bleiben* yields *aufbleiben, ausbleiben, wegbleiben, zurückbleiben*, etc., and *gehen* produces *ausgehen, eingehen, nachgehen, untergehen,* etc. The sequence of prefix and lexical verb which we find in these verbs is retained when the verb in a finite clause is in final position; but when the verb shifts to the beginning of the clause, the separable prefix remains in its original place at the end of the clause. Taking the sentence *Er blieb gestern abend bis zehn Uhr auf* 'he stayed up until ten o'clock yesterday evening' as a test case, we can apply to it the rules which we applied to the other infrastructures above:

IS, FNTZ: er gestern abend bis zehn Uhr *aufblieb*
T / FV: *blieb* er gestern abend bis zehn Uhr *auf*
T / X, e. g.: er *blieb* gestern abend bis zehn Uhr *auf*

As this derivation shows, the prefix *auf* retains its position at the end of the clause through both transformations. This again points to the end of the clause as the place where the verb "belongs."

Like the separable prefixes, there are a number of other elements closely related to the verb which also stand at or near the end of the clause. In our first example, the phrase *zu Hause* stands in that position; the utterance *Er blieb zu Hause gestern*, though barely acceptable in colloquial speech with a specific intonation pattern, is not acceptable standard German. The verb is closely bound to elements like *zu Hause,* and combinations of prepositional phrase plus verb are familiar stylistic devices in modern German (cf. Daniels 1963). The tightness of the bond between *zu Hause* and *bleiben* is illustrated by a transformation omitted in one of the examples above. It was noted that after topicalizing the finite verb, any nonverbal element might be topicalized. However, this statement must by qualified to include even the lexical verb in the following case:

IS, FNTZ: er gestern zu Hause geblieben ist
T / FV: ist er gestern zu Hause geblieben
T / X: zu Hause geblieben ist er gestern

So close is the link between *zu Hause* and the lexical verb that the two elements are topicalized as a single unit. Given its connection with the verb, the position of *zu Hause* near the end of the clause is additional support for the view that the lexical verb stands at the end of the infrastructure. It also calls attention to a further structural feature of German, i. e., the "clause nucleus," the combination of the lexical verb and a preceding nonverbal element, e. g., *zu Hause bleiben.*

In consequence of these observations, we take here as our point of departure the principle that, in German, "normal" word order is verb-last word order (cf. Bach 1962; Fichtner 1970). Furthermore, we once again regard the lexical verb as the point of departure for our analysis of German clause structure, just as we took the English verb as the key to the structure of the clause of that language. If we assume the verb to be the last element in the clause, we may represent the infrastructure symbolically thus:

. . . + VERB.

*The Clause Nucleus: The Nucleus Complement (NCOMP)*

In the foregoing section, it was determined that the verb occupies the final position in the German infrastructure. It was also noted that the verb frequently (though not always) enters into a close union with a nonverbal element which was called the "nucleus complement" (NCOMP). One of the most common kinds of nucleus complements is the prepositional phrase, e. g., *zu Hause* in the clause nucleus *zu Hause bleiben*. Combinations of this kind are among the most familiar features of the language, and examples could be cited from any text, e. g., *aus der Fassung bringen, nach Hause gehen, zur Aufführung gelangen, auf einen Einfall kommen, in Anspruch nehmen, in Ordnung sein, zur Verfügung stehen, unter Beweis stellen, in Kraft treten, zur Verantwortung ziehen,* and countless more. Their firm bond with the verb is manifested by their position immediately before the verb, and by the fact that no other syntactic element may intrude between them and the verb.

Unfortunately, the kind of nucleus complement represented by the examples above has the form of a prepositional phrase, and just as in the case of English, it is imperative to be able to distinguish the prepositional phrase used as a nucleus complement from others having other functions. Our discussion has already suggested one criterion, that of position: only a prepositional phrase which immediately precedes the verb may be regarded as a nucleus complement. However, since this sequence of elements occurs frequently in German, some further means of determining the syntactical function of such a phrase must be devised. Let us consider the following sentences (adapted from Helbig 1969) in light of this problem:

er möchte

A

in der Stadt wohnen

das Buch auf den Tisch legen

B

auf seinen Freund warten

in die Straßenbahn einsteigen

C

uns am Vormittag besuchen

sein Brot in der Schule essen

All of these sentences are alike in that the verb is immediately preceded by a prepositional phrase. Yet, as the letters A, B, and C suggest, they fall into three groups. Our task is to establish some procedure or procedures whereby we may determine the syntactic function of each kind of prepositional phrase: whether it is a nucleus complement, or some other kind of adverbial yet to be defined.

One such test is the omission test. If the nucleus is closely related to the verb, one would naturally expect that its absence would result in a distortion of the sentence. Applying this test to our three groups yields the following results:

er möchte

A

? ? ? wohnen

? ? ? das Buch legen

B

! warten

! einsteigen

C

! uns besuchen

! sein Brot essen

We note that of the three groups, only the sentences in Group A are doubtful. Evidently the phrases *in der Stadt* and *auf den Tisch* are essential to the verbs *wohnen* and *legen*, respectively – more so, at least, than the other phrases left out of the sentences in the other groups in this test.

A true adverbial expression, on the other hand, is one which applies not merely to the verb, but to the entire utterance. The fact that a prepositional phrase is not essential to the verb does not necessarily mean that it applies to the entire sentence. One way to see if a phrase applies in this way is to place it in an indefinite relative clause containing a compatible form of a neutral verb like *geschehen* 'happen'. If the phrase applies generally to the entire utterance, the sentence and the relative clause will be acceptable. If the phrase applies to a specific element, the clause will seem to be distorted in meaning. Applying this test to these three groups of sentences leads to the following results:

er möchte

A
??? wohnen, was in der Stadt geschehen soll
??? das Buch legen, was auf den Tisch geschehen soll
B
??? warten, was auf seinen Freund geschehen soll
??? einsteigen, was in die Straßenbahn geschehen soll
C
! uns besuchen, was am Vormittag geschehen soll
! sein Brot essen, was in der Schule geschehen soll

This test shows that the phrases in Group C apply in a general way to the entire clause, while those in A and B stand in a different relationship to their utterances.

The reason for the close relationship between the prepositional phrases and verbs in Group A is not hard to understand. The expression *auf den Tisch* is indispensable to the meaning of the verb *legen* for the reason that, neither in German nor in English, can one simply "put" something; it has to be "put somewhere." This conceptual bond links the phrase *auf den Tisch* closely to *legen*, so that they constitute, syntactically as well as semantically, a single unit. Similar considerations apply to *in der Stadt* and *wohnen*: the expression *??? er wohnt* is not idiomatic German. One cannot say simply "he dwells" in English, either; one must "dwell somewhere," a fact which explains the close relationship between these elements, too.

What all such phrases have in common is that they serve to specify or delimit the action of the verbs which they accompany. If the action of the verb is such that it has an inherent limit, like *legen* or *fahren*, the prepositional phrase which functions as nucleus complement usually specifies the goal or aim of the action, e. g., *auf den Tisch* is the goal of *legen*, just as *nach Hause* is of *fahren*. If the verb, on the other hand, represents an action which may continue more or less indefinitely, like *wohnen* or *bleiben*, then the nucleus complement phrase frequently describes the place where this action takes place, e. g., *wohnen* may take place *in der Stadt*, just as *zu Hause* may be the place where the action of *bleiben* occurs (Helbig 1970).

Exactly the opposite line of reasoning applies in the case of the phrases and verbs in Group C. One can eat one's bread *in der Schule* or in many other places. It is not even necessary to specify where the eating of it takes place, as the omission test makes clear. Consequently, there is no close link between the phrase *in der Schule* and the concept represented by *essen*; rather, the expression applies in a general way to the thought of the entire clause, as the indefinite relativization test shows. The notion of *besuchen* is similarly not restricted to any point in time; hence the phrase *am Vormittag* stands in a relatively loose relationship to that verb.

In light of these considerations, Groups A and C present no insuperable difficulties as to the relationship of the prepositional phrases of those sentences to their verbs: the phrases *in der Stadt* and *auf den Tisch*, then, may be designated "prepositional phrase nucleus complements." The phrases in the sentences in Group C, on the other hand, have a general adverbial function; their syntactical characteristics will receive definition later in this chapter.

If, in this way, we have distinguished between the sentences in Groups A and C, we have not mentioned the pair in Group B at all, which contained the sentences:

er möchte
auf seinen Freund warten
in die Straßenbahn einsteigen

These sentences constitute an anomaly, because they pass only one of the tests we have constructed for distinguishing nucleus complements from other adverbial prepositional phrases. As we noted, when the phrases in question are omitted, we have the acceptable sentences:

! er möchte warten
! er möchte einsteigen

This suggests that these phrases are not nucleus complements, but exemplify another use of the prepositional phrase. If they are merely adverbs like those in Group C, then we should be able to place them in an indefinite relative clause. However, as we saw, this operation yields:

? ? ? er möchte warten, was auf seinen Freund geschehen soll
? ? ? er möchte einsteigen, was in die Straßenbahn geschehen soll

It is apparent that, by the tests we have used, we cannot unambiguously determine whether these prepositional phrases are nucleus complements or merely some other kind of adverb. To solve this riddle, we must enter into the complex area of negation.

To gain a better perspective on this problem, it might be useful to recall why we are interested in defining the nucleus complement in the first place. As in the case of English, we will find that the basic structure of the German clause consists of a series of segments or fields to which the various words and phrases are at least initially assigned. As far as German is concerned, we must anticipate our findings here to the extent that we note that the syntactical category which precedes the nucleus complement is that of the clause nucleus adverb, the most prominent member of which is the adverb *nicht*. We can make use of this feature of the language in our attempt to establish whether the phrases in Group B function as nucleus complements or not.

The question of negation is too involved to receive adequate treatment at this point. For the present purpose, it is sufficient to acknowledge the existence of two (though not the only two) kinds of negation in German: "clause nucleus negation" and "contradiction." In the former, the word *nicht* stands before the clause nucleus, and both *nicht* and the nucleus complement are accented. In contradiction, which is the denial of a previous affirmative statement, the negative adverb stands before the clause nucleus, and is the only accented element in the sentence. Contradiction may be regarded as an emphatic form of clause nucleus negation. As we will see presently, the clause nucleus negation test and the contradiction test will show that the phrases in Group B can function either as nucleus complements, or as another kind of adverb. Let us now apply these tests to our groups of sentences to see what they can tell us.

If a native speaker were asked simply to negate the sentences of Groups A and C without any specific emphasis or context, he would in all probability produce the following utterances (accented words are in capital letters):

er MÖCHTE

A
NICHT in der STADT wohnen
das BUCH NICHT auf den TISCH legen
C
uns am VORMITTAG NICHT BESUCHEN
sein BROT in der SCHULE NICHT ESSEN

For Group B, he could produce two possibilities for each sentence, depending on the accentual condition of the original affirmative statement:

er MÖCHTE
auf seinen FREUND warten → NICHT auf seinen FREUND warten
auf seinen FREUND WARTEN → auf seinen FREUND NICHT WARTEN
in die STRASSENBAHN einsteigen → NICHT in die STRASSENBAHN einsteigen
in die STRASSENBAHN EINSTEIGEN → in die STRASSENBAHN NICHT EINSTEIGEN

As we see, the position of *nicht* in clause nucleus negation shows plainly the double nature of the prepositional phrases in Group B: when only the noun in the phrase is accented, i. e., when the accent on the verb is deleted, it functions as the nucleus complement; when the verb is accented as well, the prepositional phrase functions syntactically as an adverb much like those of Group C.

The fundamental relationship between these phrases and their verbs is betrayed only when these sentences are negated by contradiction. Here the sole accented word *nicht* stands before the nucleus complement:

NEIN, das ist FALSCH — er möchte:
A
NICHT in der Stadt wohnen
das Buch NICHT auf den Tisch legen
B
NICHT auf seinen Freund warten
NICHT in die Straßenbahn einsteigen
C
uns am Vormittag NICHT besuchen
sein Brot in der Schule NICHT essen

The clause nucleus negation test applied earlier suggested that Group B might be a syntactic mixture, in that the negative adverb *nicht* could stand either before the prepositional phrase, as in Group A, or before the verb, as in Group C. The test of contradiction above clearly shows the basic, if partial affinity of the phrases in Group B to the verb.

In conclusion, it may be helpful to summarize the results of the four tests which we have applied to these three groups of sentences. By the omission test, we ascertained that some prepositional phrases were essential to the meaning of the verbs they accompany (those in Group A), and that some were not (Groups B and C). Of the latter two, the phrases in Group C applied in a general way to the entire utterance in which they stood, whereas those in Group B had no such general reference – conclusions based on the indefinite relativization test.. These tests also indicated that, while Groups A and C could be fairly clearly identified as nucleus complements and general adverbs, respectively, Group B seemed to partake of the nature of both.

The hybrid character of the phrases in Group B became even more evident when the sentences in that group were changed by clause nucleus negation and by contradiction. The test of contradiction showed that these phrases are fundamentally nucleus complements. Yet the prepositional phrase and the verb are not so completely fused semantically that the negative adverb cannot intrude between complement and verb, when the latter is accented. As the clause nucleus negation test made clear, the phrases of Group B resembled those of C in this respect. It is apparent that the determination whether a prepositional phrase is functioning as a nucleus complement in a given case is not altogether a simple matter. Yet is is an essential operation for a description of German syntax, because of the great importance of the clause nucleus within the economy of the infrastructure.

On the basic of our conclusions concerning the prepositional phrase nucleus complements, we have tentatively established that the negative adverb *nicht* serves as a boundary marker between the clause nucleus and the remaining elements of the infrastructure, i. e.:

... nicht + NCOMP + VERB

While this criterion serves well enough when the element in question has the form of a prepositional phrase, matters become complicated when the verb is immediately preceded by a noun. Let us approach this problem by examining the sentences below (for the following, cf. Fichtner 1970, also Stickel 1970:75 ff.):

er wollte einen Wagen kaufen
er wollte den Wagen kaufen

At first glance, these sentences seem to be completely identical, except, of course, for the articles. In most systems of grammar, the two nouns *einen Wagen* and *den Wagen* would be construed as having the same function within the sentence: they are both direct objects of the verb *wollte ... kaufen*. Yet any speaker of Geman, asked to contradict these sentences, would produce the following utterances:

er wollte KEINEN Wagen kaufen
er wollte den Wagen NICHT kaufen

The word *keinen* in the first sentence is historically a contraction of the negative adverb with *ein-*. Hence, the negative adverb may be regarded as standing before *einen Wagen*. In the second sentence, the word *nicht* stands unambiguously before the verb.

In regard to these examples, we find that we are now in a position to make certain inferences. First, we can say that *den Wagen* and *einen Wagen* are syntactically two different kinds of noun phrases, despite their formal similarity. Second, if we accept the premise that the clause nucleus consists of a verb immediately preceded by a complement, then *einen Wagen* would be part of such a clause nucleus, whereas *den Wagen* would not be. Third, this being so, then *den Wagen* must be a further, as yet undefined syntactical element which stands before *nicht*. As a result of these considerations, we may now represent the structure of these two sentences as follows:

er wollte:
. . . . . $NEG_3$ einen $Wagen_2$ $kaufen_1$
den $Wagen_4$ $NEG_3$ . . . . . $kaufen_1$

As to the first sentence, when accented NEG precedes *ein-*, it assumes the contracted form *kein-*. For purposes of syntactic analysis, however, it is helpful to resolve the contraction. In both cases, *kaufen* is the verb, which stands in first position in the sequence of elements in the clause, reading from right to left. The role of nucleus complement is filled by *einen Wagen* in second position. The second sentence has no nucleus complement. Both sentences have the element NEG in third position, which is the clause nucleus adverb tagmeme (CLNAV). The expression *den Wagen* is in fourth place; it belongs to a syntactic class which we have yet to define. These sentences suggest that nouns preceded by *ein-*, e. g., *einen Wagen*, may serve as nucleus complements, while phrases like *den Wagen* sometimes do not. Moreover, the criterion by which a noun in this function may be identified is again the relative position of the negative element in contradiction. Thus, the clause nucleus in the first of these two sentences is *einen Wagen kaufen,* but in the latter sentence, merely *kaufen.*

German contains many examples of nouns as nucleus complements: *Klavier spielen, Deutsch sprechen, Blumen schenken, Einfluß üben, Folgen haben, ein Gespräch führen, eine Reise machen, einen Korb bekommen*, etc. In all of these examples, a noun in the singular or plural is preceded either by the pointer word *ein-*, or by no pointer word at all. Nouns which meet either of these conditions, as well as another to be discussed below, will be called "nonspecific" nouns. This designation is useful because we can now say that nonspecific nouns may serve as nucleus complements, and that, when the sentence is negated, the accented element NEG is placed before the clause nucleus. Where the noun in question is preceded by a form of *ein*, then NEG and the pointer word combine in the familiar pattern as *kein-*. As an example of this secondary morphological change, compare the following sentences, affirmative and in contradiction:

er kann ein Auto kaufen → (contradiction) er kann NEG + EIN Auto kaufen → er kann KEIN Auto kaufen

er kann Auto fahren → (contradiction) er kann NEG Auto fahren → er kann NICHT Auto fahren

The expression *den Wagen*, on the other hand, is an example of a "specific" noun. These nouns, which may be preceded by all of the remaining pointer words, usually do not serve as nucleus complements.

Up to this point, we have tacitly regarded the difference between specific and nonspecific nouns as lying in the the kind of pointer word which precedes them. The essential difference, however, is only secondarily a matter of the kind of word which stands before those nouns. Rather, it is primarily a logical difference. If a noun refers either to a class of entities, or to an unspecified member of a class of entities, it is a nonspecific noun. If it refers, on the other hand, to a certain member of a class of entities, it is a specific noun. In our original example, the phrases *einen Wagen* did not refer to any specific automobile but rather to any member of the class of objects called 'automobiles'; hence, it can be deemed a nonspecific noun. The expression *den Wagen*, on the other hand, referred unmistakably to a specific automobile, and hence was a specific noun.

It is a useful rule of thumb to say that nonspecific nouns may be preceded by a form of *ein-*, or by ∅ ("zero"), whereas specific nouns may be preceded by possessive adjectives, definite articles, or by any other pointer word. Nevertheless, the logical or semantic basis for the distinction must be kept in mind, because there are exceptions. There is one case, for example, where *ein-* precedes a specific noun, and a number of instances where *der, die, das* or another pointer word precede nonspecific nouns. The first "exception" is an exception only to the rule of thumb, not to the fundamental principle that nonspecific nouns refer to any member of a class. The pointer word *ein* refers to a specific member of a class when it means 'one', as in this example:

er GLAUBTE ALLE FEHLER GEFUNDEN zu haben, aber TROTZ seiner MÜHE hat er EINEN Fehler NICHT gefunden

Because the word *ein-* here refers to a specific mistake, the word *Fehler* functions as a specific noun, and hence cannot be part of the clause nucleus. Since *nicht* must precede the clause nucleus in contradiction, it stands before the lexical verb *gefunden*. (I am indebted to Prof. Dwight Bolinger for drawing my attention to this case.)

The other exceptions are also exceptions only to the rule of thumb, i. e., that nonspecific nouns are preceded by ∅ or *ein-*, whereas specific nouns may be preceded by any other pointer word. There is a fairly large number of cases in German where nouns which are nonspecific in function are preceded by the definite article. These nouns have such an abstract meaning that they are no longer felt as referring to specific entities. Often they serve, with their accompanying verbs, as circumlocutions for simple verbs (cf. Daniels 1963:92 ff.). Some examples, along with lexically compatible verbs, are: *die Fähigkeit haben* (= *können*), *die Möglichkeit bieten* (= *erlauben*), *das Versprechen geben* (= *versprechen*), *den Anschein erwecken* (= *scheinen*), *den Wunsch hegen* (= *wünschen*), *den Spieß umdrehen* (= *entgegnen*), etc. Since these nouns do not refer to specific entities, despite the "definite" article, they function as nonspecific nouns, and hence can form part of a clause nucleus as the nucleus complement. Hence, when contradicted, sentences containing these expressions have the adverb *nicht* in the position before the noun, as in these examples (clause nuclei with *nicht* are italicized):

er hat *nicht die Fähigkeit gehabt,* in seinem Beruf weiter zu avancieren

das Schicksal hat ihm *nicht die Möglichkeit geboten,* auf die Universität zu gehen

der Student hat *nicht den Anschein erweckt,* das Gedicht gelesen zu haben

Despite the presence of *der, die das,* cases like the foregoing must be regarded as containing nonspecific nouns.

It lies in the structure of the German language that a few nouns can be construed either as specific or nonspecific, depending on the context. Such cases are of especial interest here, because they are the exceptions which "prove" the rule. The noun *Vorzug,* for example, can mean either 'special train which departs during the rush hour in advance of the regularly scheduled train'. or else, as an abstract noun, 'advantage'. When sentences containing this noun in these two meanings are contradicted, the position of *nicht* helps us to distinguish between the specific and nonspecific functions of the noun. In these examples, the clause nuclei and *nicht* are italicized:

obgleich er sich sehr beeilte, konnte er den Vorzug *nicht erreichen* (specific)

er wollte absolut fair sein und seinem Schwager *nicht den Vorzug geben* (nonspecific)

Another example is the humble noun *Zeitung.* When used in reference to a certain newspaper, it functions as a specific noun. But it can also be used to refer to any member of the class of newspapers, in which case it serves, by our definition, as a nonspecific noun. These uses may be observed in the following contexts:

"Nein, vielen Dank, Herr Ober, aber ich muß unbedingt sofort zurück ins Amt. Ich kann im Moment die Zeitung *nicht lesen.*" (specific)

" ... und früher hat mein Mann jeden Tag die Zeitung gelesen, und das hat ihn maßlos geärgert. Wegen seines hohen Blutdrucks hat es ihm der Arzt verboten. Von nun an also darf er *nicht die Zeitung lesen.*" (nonspecific)

In the latter example, the word *Zeitung* no longer refers to any specific entity; rather, in conjunction with the verb *lesen,* an activity is described. Indeed, the word has lost its concrete character in this passage to such an extent that, in the second sentence, it would not at all be felt as incorrect, especially in northern Germany, to say:

er darf nicht Zeitung lesen

It is very likely that the disappearance of the article in this expression has been encouraged by the feeling that the noun here is properly a nonspecific one. While nouns like *Vorzug* and *Zeitung* are not numerous, they vividly illustrate the contrast between the specific and nonspecific functions of the word class, and help to make clear the principle by which nouns may become part of, or be excluded from the clause nucleus.

There are a few common exceptions to this rule, i. e., that only nonspecific nouns may function as nucleus complements; these arise, first of all, in connection with the verbs *heißen* and *bleiben*. The following instances of specific nouns (marked "+SP") which function as nucleus complements with these verbs will not strike the reader as unfamiliar:

er kann (NICHT) *Max (+SP) heißen*
er wird nächstes Jahr (NICHT) *Vorsitzender (+SP) bleiben*

In the foregoing pages, we have established that two kinds of syntactic elements may occupy the NCOMP tagmeme: prepositional phrases which meet certain criteria, and nonspecific nouns, with a few exceptions. However, there is another kind of word which may function in this capacity: one-word adverbs. Some examples may serve to recall a kind of use which is well known to speakers of German. In these cases, the position of *nicht* in contradiction serves to identify the boundary between the clause nucleus and the rest of the infrastructure (clause nuclei are italicized):

das Kind wollte in der Nacht (NICHT) *allein bleiben*
der Mensch will (NICHT) *alt werden*
er hat sein Benehmen (NICHT) *falsch verstanden*
gottseidank hast du dich diesmal (NICHT) *flegelhaft benommen*
der Stromausfall hat die Fabrik (NICHT) *lahm gelegt*
der Kellner hat den Wein (NICHT) *kalt gestellt*

It remains only to note certain peculiarities which arise in connection with the verb *sein*. For one thing, it may not stand without a nucleus complement; when simple existence is asserted, another idiom is used:

??? ein Gott ist . . .

! es gibt einen Gott

For another, any kind of specific or nonspecific noun, adjective, adverb, or adverb phrase may serve as its complement:

Hans wird morgen (NICHT) *in der Stadt sein* (adverbial preposinational phrase as clause nucleus)

Fritz soll heute (NICHT) *hier sein* (one-word adverb)

Inge und Barbara können (NICHT) *gleichen Alters sein* (adverbial noun phrase)

er wird wohl (NICHT) *müde sein* ("predicate" adjective)

das kann (NICHT) *Erich sein* (specific proper noun)

das dürfte (NICHT) *sein Buch sein* (specific common noun)

Meier kann (NICHT) *Arzt sein* (nonspecific noun)

It is thus possible that an expression which forms a clause nucleus with *sein* may serve merely as an ordinary adverb with other verbs. The phrase *auf dem Lande* in the following sentences illustrates these possibilities:

er soll jetzt (NICHT) *auf dem Lande sein* (with *sein* as nucleus complement)

er will sich auf dem Lande (NEG + *ein* = KEIN) *ein Haus bauen* lassen (as adverbial expression with other clause nucleus)

The phrase *auf dem Lande* in the second sentence has a function which we will explore more fully later in this chapter. These examples underscore the fact that a nucleus complement in German is primarily a syntactic function, and only secondarily a matter of the form-class to which a given expression belongs.

At this point, we have defined the clause nucleus as consisting of the verb preceded by the nucleus complement. This sequence may be represented thus:

. . . NCOMP + VERB

We now turn to those elements which may precede the clause nucleus.

## The Clause Nucleus Adverb (CLNAV)

In the previous section we found it helpful to use the word *nicht* as a convenient way of defining the initial boundary of the clause nucleus. We accepted this as a fact, without inquiring further as to why *nicht* could be used in this way. The reason is that *nicht*, as well as several other common adverbs, may function as "clause nucleus adverbs" (CLNAV), and in that use stand immediately before the clause nucleus. Adverbs which often appear in this function include: *auch, doch, immer, (ein-)mal, nicht, nie, selbst.*

It must not be overlooked that many of these adverbs have other functions as well — functions which account for their occasionally appearing elsewhere. The words *auch* and *nicht*, for example, may also precede nominal elements, becoming part of those structures, e. g.:

auch FRITZ ist hier
nicht FRITZ ist hier, sondern HANS

Similarly, the word *immer* may modify a comparative adjective or adverb, e. g.:

er fuhr immer schneller

These uses must be distinguished from the function of these words as clause nucleus adverbs. When they serve in the latter capacity, they are placed immediately before the clause nucleus.

In this function, these words are almost always accented. The subsystems of negation and accent intersect at this point: we have already noted that clause nucleus negation and contradiction may be distinguished by their accent patterns:

er HAT mir den BRIEF ins FACH gelegt (declarative affirmative sentence)
er HAT mir den BRIEF NICHT ins FACH gelegt (clause nucleus, i. e., "normal" negation)
er hat mir den Brief NICHT ins Fach gelegt! (contradiction)

The last sentence above may in turn be contradicted by the use of accented *doch* in place of *nicht*, with all other accents deleted:

er hat mir den Brief DOCH ins Fach gelegt! (contradiction of a contradiction)

The clause nucleus adverb *auch* has its own subsystem of accentually signaled reference. The accents in the sentence *Erich will heute auch ins Theater gehen* may be distributed in two different patterns, depending on the sentence which each presupposes as context:

(ERICH will HEUTE ins MUSEUM gehen)
Erich will heute AUCH ins THEATER gehen
(HANS will HEUTE ins THEATER gehen)
ERICH will heute AUCH ins Theater gehen

In both cases, however, *auch* functions as a clause nucleus adverb, and as such stands before the clause nucleus *ins Theater gehen*. In this way, we have increased the number of tagmemes which have been identified in the German infrastructure to three:

... CLNAV + NCOMP + VERB

We again turn to those which precede these segments.

*The Adverbo-Nominal Tagmeme (AVNOM)*

As we have seen, the elements which may stand in the first three fields of the clause in German are limited in number, and carefully defined as to form-class and function. There are fewer restrictions on those which may appear in the fourth segment of the clause, the "adverbo-nominal tagmeme" (AVNOM). Indeed, it is not entirely wrong to say that what cannot be placed in any other field can be put here. Those form-classes which may stand here are the following, roughly in the order in which they normally stand in the clause, beginning with those which immediately precede the clause nucleus adverb:

1) nonspecific nouns not forming part of the clause nucleus, including subject nouns in the nominative case, when present; preceded by
2) specific nouns, including subjects in the nominative case, when present; preceded by
3) adverbs of time, manner, and place ("TMP" adverbs), either one-word adverbs or prepositional phrases, and in that order; preceded by
4) accented pronouns, personal or demonstrative.

The order of elements in this segment is not rigidly fixed, but depends on the principle of communicative importance: the more important element follows the less important one, i. e., stands nearer to the end. Nevertheless, the sequence above is a kind of neutral order to which the principle of communicative importance may induce "exceptions." The neutral order is found when the communicative weight in context of the elements present is about equal, i. e., when no word or phrase is conspicuously more important than any other. When one element or the other acquires a greater significance, then that element may easily shift to a position closer to the end of the field, in a way much like the transpositions which we observed in connection with the English infrastructure. This phenomenon is exemplified in the following sentence:

"Den Ton für dieses neue Diskussionsthema gab der CSU-Vorsitzende Strauß am politischen Aschermittwoch im bayrischen Vilshofen mit einem publizistischen Posaunenstoß: Nach Strauß wird man in der Bundesrepublik Zeuge einer 'roten Unterwanderung bei Funk und Fernsehen' " ("Via TV täglich 49,4 Verbrechen." *Die Presse* [Vienna], 24. August 1972).

The "normal" order of adverbial elements within this tagmeme was stated to be TIME + MANNER + PLACE. In this quotation, the adverb of time *am politischen Aschermittwoch* does precede the adverb of place *im bayrischen Vilshofen,* which one would expect. However, the adverb of manner *mit einem publizistischen Posaunenstoß* introduces a long indirect quotation which is the most important element in the sentence. Hence the writer of the article chose to place this adverb and the accompanying statement at the end. If we strip these adverbial prepositional phrases of all nonessential word material and rearrange them to neutralize the effect of the topicalized object *den Ton,* we can perceive both the effect of the additional communicative importance of the indirect quotation, as well as the "pull" of the fundamental sequence of elements. Compare these phrases in respect of their idiomaticity:

? er gab den Ton am Mittwoch$_{TIME}$ in Vilshofen$_{PLACE}$ mit einem Posaunenstoß$_{MANNER}$ [an]

! er gab den Ton am Mittwoch$_{TIME}$ mit einem Posaunenstoß$_{MANNER}$ in Vilshofen$_{PLACE}$ [an]

While the difference is not overwhelming, one feels that the first version above, when taken out of context, is just a bit distorted, whereas the second seems neutral, and normal in every way.

Another question which arises in connection with the adverbonominal segment is the position of the subject. The formula usually given in textbooks is that the subject of a declarative sentence, i. e., one with verb-second word order, stands immediately behind the verb when it does not precede it in initial position. What the writers of such statements have in mind are sentences like these:

die Jungen<sub>SUBJECT</sub> haben gestern Faustball gespielt

gestern haben die Jungen<sub>SUBJECT</sub> Faustball gespielt

Here the subject noun *die Jungen* alternately precedes and follows the finite auxiliary verb *haben*. Statements like the one above about the position of the subject are not wholly false, and may even be useful in the early stages of learning the language, but they do not represent the fundamental principles which govern the placing of this element. Actually, noun subjects may appear almost anywhere in the adverbo-nominal segment. Let us look at an example which supports this contention:

"(Über die große Sterblichkeit bei solchen Pestepidemien geben die Eintragungen in den kirchlichen Sterbebüchern . . . Auskunft.) So schnellte zum Beispiel bei der Peste im Jahre 1684 nach den Sterbebüchern der Pfarre Pergkirchen die Zahl der Toten bei einem jährlichen Durchschnitt von 18 auf 64 hinauf . . ." (Georg Grüll, *Bauer, Herr und Landesfürst: Sozialrevolutionäre Bestrebungen der oberösterreichischen Bauern von 1650 bis 1848* [Linz, 1963], pp. 51–52).

The clause nucleus here is *auf 64 hinaufschnellen,* the subject of the verb is *die Zahl der Toten.* This does not follow the verb *schnellte,* but is rather situated between an adverb of place, *nach den Sterbebüchern der Pfarre Pergkirchen,* and an adverb of manner, *bei einem jährlichen Durchschnitt von 18.* The elements in the adverbo-nominal tagmeme are distributed in the sequence TIME + PLACE + SUBJECT + MANNER. (The phrase *zum Beispiel* is an intersentence adverb, and hence not counted here.) Yet, if one reads this sentence in context, one finds it by no means ungrammatical or unidiomatic. This example shows that, while there is unquestionably a special grammatical relationship between the subject and the verb, this does not − in sharp contrast to English − necessarily determine or even affect its position. Whereas the subject in English has a syntactical role to play, the position of the subject in the German clause is largely, if not entirely dependent on other factors.

With this description of the adverbo-nominal tagmeme, we have raised the number of segments in the German infrastructure to four:

90

## The Modal Adverb (MDLAV)

The last two tagmemes of the clause, the modal adverbs and the unaccented personal pronouns, are distinguished by the feature that neither may bear an accent. The "modal adverb" (MDLAV), which is the fifth segment of the clause, consists of a small group of adverbs which express either the attitude of the speaker toward the situation in which he finds himself, or his feelings about the person to whom he is speaking. In English, these feelings and attitudes are often expressed, not by specific words, but by certain intonation patterns. Those adverbs which may appear in this function include: *auch, denn, doch, ja, nämlich, nicht, nur, schon,* and *wohl.* Since some of these also function as clause nucleus adverbs — in which capacity they are normally accented — it may be helpful to present examples where the two functions may be compared. (The following, including some examples, depends heavily on Schubiger 1965.)

The word *auch* as a clause nucleus adverb means 'also', but as a modal adverb 'to be sure' or, in questions, 'are you sure?' Compare these sentences in regard to the use of these adverbs:

SO sieht er auch AUS (modal adverb) 'YES, THAT'S the way he LOOKS, all right!'

SO sieht er AUCH aus (clause nucleus adverb) 'THAT'S the way HE looks, TOO!'

VERSTEHEN Sie es auch? (modal adverb) 'are you sure you UNDERSTAND it?'

VERSTEHEN Sie es AUCH? (clause nucleus adverb) 'do you UNDERSTAND it, TOO?'

verstehen SIE es AUCH? (clause nucleus adverb) 'do YOU understand it, TOO?'

In questions, the word *denn* as a modal adverb indicates surprise and interest, e. g.:

was HAST du denn da in dem KÄFIG? 'SAY, WHAT do you HAVE in the CAGE there?'

was WOLLTE sie denn? 'TELL me, WHAT did she WANT?'

was WOLLTE denn DIE? 'what did SHE want, ANYWAY?'

The last two lines are important for the relative position of modal adverbs: the unaccented pronoun *sie* precedes the modal adverb *denn*, but the accented pronoun *die*, as part of the adverbo-nominal segment because of its accent, follows it. The same considerations apply to the following pair:

bin ich denn an DEINEM Mißerfolg schuld? 'am I responsible for YOUR failure?'
bin denn ICH an deinem Mißerfolg schuld? 'am *I* responsible for your failure?'

When the unaccented personal pronoun *ich* assumes an accent, it moves into the adverbo-nominal segment which follows that of the modal adverbs.

The most frequently used modal adverb is probably *doch*, which in this function has an adversative connotation which could be translated by the phrase 'as you should know'. This is illustrated in the following exchange:

A: "WANN SCHICKEN Sie mir meine SCHREIBmaschine zurück? "

B: "Ich HABE sie Ihnen doch SCHON vor drei TAGEN zurückgeschickt!"

As a modal adverb here, *doch* follows the unaccented personal pronouns *sie* and *Ihnen*, and precedes the adverbo-nominal *schon vor drei Tagen*.

The modal adverb *ja* is virtually the contrary of *doch*. If *doch* may be roughly translated as 'as you should know', the word *ja* means approximately 'as you already know'. The contrast can be represented by the following alternative responses to a suggestion to invite some complete strangers to the speaker's house:

wir KENNEN ja nicht einmal ihre NATIONALITÄT! 'you KNOW – we DON'T even KNOW their NATIONALITY!'
wir KENNEN doch nicht einmal ihre NATIONALITÄT! 'why, WE don't even know their NATIONALITY!'

The word *ja* connotes a certain consensus, while the word *doch* suggests that the speakers are not unanimous on the point at issue.

The modal adverb *nur* is comparable to *doch* in that it connotes a kind of challenge to the hearer, one which may be either encouraging or threatening. It is especially common in imperative sentences:

(encouraging) HAB nur KEINE ANGST! 'there's NOTHING to WORRY about!'

(threatening) WARTE nur! 'JUST WAIT!!'

In questions, this tone of challenge may shade into concern:

wie KOMMST du nur nach HAUSE' 'just HOW are you GOING to get HOME?'

In declarative sentences, this concern can become a kind of speculation:

ich MUSS mich nur WUNDERN, daß er es AUShält! 'I just DON'T see HOW he STANDS it!'

It may come as a surprise to see the word *nicht* classified as a modal adverb. We have already noted that, as a clause nucleus adverb, it stands in the third segment of the clause. Moreover, in contrastive negation, it may precede any nonnuclear element, e. g.:

nicht ICH habe es verloren, sondern DU!

As a modal adverb, it usually appears in questions, as in this example:

WOLLEN Sie nicht HEUTE ABEND mit UNS ins KINO gehen?

With *nicht* as a clause nucleus adverb, the answer to this question might be:

NEIN, HEUTE ABEND will ich mit Ihnen NICHT ins Kino gehen

In this sentence, the word *nicht* has moved from the fifth segment before the adverbo-nominal elements *heute abend* and *mit uns* to the position just before the clause nucleus *ins Kino gehen*. As to its meaning, *nicht* as a modal adverb seems to be more a way of diminishing the directness of a question than a word with a specific semantic referent.

As to the remaining adverbs, *nämlich* and *wohl*, their contribution to the sentence can be fairly accurately rendered by corresponding expressions in English. The word *nämlich* may often be conveniently translated as 'you see':

er HAT nämlich HEUTE keine ZEIT 'you SEE, he DOESN'T have any TIME today'

The word *wohl*, in conjunction with the verb *werden*, commonly means 'probably':

> sie WERDEN wohl FRÜH ANkommen 'they'll PROBABLY arrive EARLY'

The word *schon* as a modal adverb is often contrasted with *wohl*, particularly in sentences containing the verb *werden* as a modal auxiliary. Whereas *wohl* suggests a kind of outer limit, *schon* connotes a kind of minimum level of effect or achievement. These adverbs may be compared in these sentences:

> ZEHN FRANKEN wird es wohl KOSTEN 'it MAY cost as much as TEN FRANCS'
> ZEHN FRANKEN wird es schon KOSTEN 'it'll cost TEN FRANCS at the LEAST'

The idea of certainty which *schon* often connotes seems to be an extension of the notion of a minimum level of performance. This idea comes out in these sentences:

> die FIRMA wird es wohl zahlen 'the FIRM will probably pay it'
> die FIRMA wird es schon zahlen 'don't worry — the FIRM will pay it'
> wir WERDEN es schon SCHAFFEN! 'DON'T WORRY — WE'LL make it!'
> ich KOMME schon! 'DON'T get EXCITED! I'M coming!'

In conclusion, we have seen that, by the use of these modal adverbs, numerous subtle shades of meaning may be conveyed. We can now add this syntactic category to the other segments described earlier:

> . . . MDLAV + AVNOM + CLNAV + NCOMP + VERB

We now take up the last tagmeme of the German infrastructure.

*The Unaccented Personal Pronoun (UPPRN)*

The last of the six fields of the German clause is that of the "unaccented personal pronoun" (UPPRN). Like the preceding segment, and as their name indicates, elements in this segment may never bear an accent. When, for reasons of emphasis, a pronoun does take an

94

accent, it moves into the fourth segment and there functions as an adverbo-nominal element. The sequence of cases in this segment is fixed: nominative, accusative, dative, and genitive. Some sentences which illustrate this distribution follow:

wann haben Sie$_{NOM}$ ihm$_{DAT}$ denn den Schlips geschenkt?

gestern habe ich$_{NOM}$ ihn$_{ACC}$ ihm$_{DAT}$ bei der Geburtstagsfeier gegeben

nie war er sich$_{DAT}$ dessen$_{GEN}$ klar bewußt, daß . . .

man hat sich$_{ACC}$ seiner$_{GEN}$ gewaltsam bemächtigt

Although the position of the unaccented personal pronouns is not problematic, we must note some exceptions to our description of the clause here, too. One of these exceptions is a relic of an older pattern of word order, but one which has not yet disappeared from the modern language. The other lies in an internal ambiguity of the language itself.

As to the former, it is possible in Standard German to place an unaccented personal pronoun, often a reflexive pronoun, not only in the sixth segment, as the examples above show, but also in a position immediately preceding the clause nucleus adverb. By the patterns which we have described, the following clause would be considered correct:

(weil) sich$_{UPPRN}$ doch$_{MDLAV}$ dieses Vorgehen$_{AVNOM}$ schon in vielen Fällen$_{AVNOM}$ nicht$_{CLNAV}$ bewährt hat$_{VERB}$

However, it is also acceptable German to place an unaccented personal pronoun immediately before the clause nucleus adverb *nicht*, though it sounds somewhat archaic there:

(weil) doch$_{MDLAV}$ dieses Vorgehen$_{AVNOM}$ schon in vielen Fällen$_{AVNOM}$ sich$_{UPPRN!}$ nicht$_{CLNAV}$ bewährt hat$_{VERB}$

Since the former is more frequently encountered, and is more idiomatic, we will take it as the norm, and be content to note that the second constitutes an exception to this pattern (cf. Dal 1962:178-9).

Another problem arises because of certain peculiarities of the morphology of the language. Except for the masculine gender, the nominative and accusative forms of the singular number, and the corresponding forms of the plural number of the personal pronouns, are identical in form:

|       | masc. | fem. | neut. | pl. |
|-------|-------|------|-------|-----|
| nom.  | er    | sie  | es    | sie |
| acc.  | ihn   | sie  | es    | sie |

Consequently, in utterances which contain a feminine or neuter singular, or plural nominative or accusative pronoun, crass misunderstandings are possible, as these examples show:

gestern hat sie ihre Schwester besucht
dann haben sie die Polizisten mit Steinen beworfen

In such cases as these, it is impossible to tell from the form of the nouns and pronouns which is the subject and which is the object. In actual speech, of course, it is always possible to avoid these few cases where the morphological and syntactical patterns might combine to create misunderstanding by the use of other constructions. For example, the sentences above could both be recast to express their content without ambiguity as follows:

gestern war sie bei ihrer Schwester zu Besuch
dann wurden die Polizisten von ihnen mit Steinen beworfen

We have here a case where two subsystems of the language cancel one another out. In accord with the practice of native speakers, we must add an amendment to the effect that, when such ambiguity becomes possible, then it is understood that the subject nominative precedes the accusative object. This means that the following sentences are open to one, and only one, interpretation — that indicated by the subscript abbreviations:

gestern hat sie$_{NOM}$ ihre Schwester$_{ACC}$ besucht
dann haben sie$_{NOM}$ die Polizisten$_{ACC}$ mit Steinen beworfen

When it is the intention of the speaker or writer to use these pronouns in the object function, i. e., in the accusative case, then the sequence must be adjusted so that the subject precedes the object, regardless of the form-class to which either belongs:

gestern hat ihre Schwester$_{NOM}$ sie$_{ACC}$ besucht
dann haben die Polizisten$_{NOM}$ sie$_{ACC}$ mit Steinen beworfen

In Chapter 11, we will return to this construction and incorporate it into the system of generative rules by which finite clauses are produced. When no such confusion is possible, as in the sentence:

gestern hat ihn seine Schwester besucht

then there is no need for using the order of these elements as an indicator of their function, i. e., for specifying that the subject must stand before the object. In such cases, the sequence of elements reflects the principle that the unaccented personal pronouns precede all other elements in the infrastructure.

We have thus completed our description of the segments of the German clause, which we have found to be six in number:

UPPRN + MDLAV + AVNOM + CLNAV + NCOMP + VERB

In the next chapter, the major areas of contrast between the infrastructures of German and English will be explored.

CHAPTER 6

THE INFRASTRUCTURES OF ENGLISH AND GERMAN: A
COMPARISON

In the preceding two chapters, a conception of the fundamental
structural base, the infrastructure, has been developed along
tagmemic lines. At this point, it will be useful to compare the results
in each case in order to ascertain what differences and similarities
between the two languages may be discerned on this level.

*General Observations*

In our analysis of English and German, we have been able to proceed
so far on the basis of one important assumption: the structure of
both languages is such that the arrangement of words in them can be
described and, to a degree, predicted, by the assignment of certain
classes of words to various syntactic categories. We can take this
approach because English and German are very much alike in respect
of the form-classes which they contain: both have morphological
categories called "nouns," "verbs," "adjectives," etc., and in most
cases, a noun in one language will have as its counterpart a noun in
the other, a verb in one language will correspond to a verb in the
other, and so forth. If we were comparing either of these languages
with, e. g., one of the American Indian languages, we would be
compelled by the basic difference in structure to devote far more
time to questions of morphology than will be necessary in this
chapter. Because English and German are composed of the same sort
of building blocks, we have been, and will be, able to ignore many
differences in morphology, and proceed to a comparison of their
syntactic categories without taking into further consideration the
form-classes of the languages as such.

The most significant point of contrast between the two languages
on the level of the infrastructure is the different position of the
verb: in English, it is surrounded by nouns and adverbs, between the
subject (SUBJ) and intraverbal adverb (ITVAV) on the one hand,
and the nominal (NOMNL) and the other adverbial tagmemes on the

other; in German, it stands at the end of the infrastructure, and is often the focus and culmination of the entire clause. This difference is important, not so much because of the two positions themselves, as because of the effect which the one-dimensional, one-directional medium of language exerts on and through them.

In Chapter 3, we noted that the system of topic and comment was based on the increase in communicative dynamism of the various elements, which was manifest by virtue of their position relative to the end of the clause, irrespective of any morphological or lexical considerations. Oversimplifying the situation for the sake of clarity, we may ask if it makes any difference whether the noun precedes the verb (typical for German) or whether the verb precedes the noun (as is usually the case in English). This leaves us with the following fundamental patterns, which have been abstracted from the infrastructures of the respective languages:

English:     (NOUN) + VERB + NOUN
German:     (NOUN) + NOUN + VERB

In Indo-European languages like English and German, the verb typically represents an activity, a process, or a condition. This activity is qualified as to when it takes place (tense), as to who is doing it (person and number), and sometimes as to how long the activity in question goes on (e. g., the English progressive verb forms). For the present purpose, we can say that these attributes contribute to the personal and dynamic character of the form-class of the verb. The noun, on the other hand, is ordinarily not related to a specific person, but stands apart as an entity outside the situation represented by the utterance as a whole; it tends toward the hypostatic and the impersonal. Moreover, the role of the noun, through its case forms, is defined by reference to the verb (cf. Sandmann 1940). If we accept these premises, we can say that, in those cases where a noun follows a verb, the tendency will be for the hypostatic and impersonal to moderate and restrain the dynamic and personal quality of the verb. Borrowing a term from electronics, we can say that the noun exerts a "damping" effect on the preceding verb. In cases where the verb follows the noun, the effect will be to deprive the noun somewhat of its neutral quality, and to make the expression in which the elements stand somewhat more lively and dynamic. No one who has ever read a page of Hegel can say that a German sentence *has* to be lively and dynamic. On the other hand, mechanisms like these are the syntactic raw materials of language, and in the hands of a gifted writer can be used with impressive results.

English and German also differ in the number of tagmemes in their infrastructures: six in German, as contrasted with seven in English. With one exception — VERB — the tagmemes of the two languages are differently constituted. In English, there is a greater tendency to take the form-class of the element as the criterion of membership in one or the other of its tagmemes. There are four tagmemes which contain only adverbs: the intraverbal adverb (ITVAV), the verb particle (VPART), the verb complement (VCOMP), and the terminal adverb (TRMAV). It is within the larger form-class of adverbs that distinctions of syntactic function are made, a principle which results in the four categories just named.

In German, there is, by and large, less of a correlation between form-class and syntactic function. There are, for example, only two tagmemes which contain adverbs exclusively, the modal adverb (MDLAV) and the clause nucleus adverb (CLNAV). Of course, adverbs appear in other tagmemes, but those tagmemes are not defined in terms of exclusive occupancy by adverbs. The nucleus complement (NCOMP), for example, may contain either nouns or adverbs, as may the adverbo-nominal (AVNOM).

There are in both languages tagmemes which contain nominal elements, and nominal elements only. In English, both the subject (SUBJ) and the nominal (NOMNL) fall into this category. In German, on the other hand, only the unaccented personal pronouns (UPPRN) share this quality. Nouns and accented pronouns in all four cases — nominative, accusative, dative, and genitive — may appear as adverbo-nominals (AVNOM) or as nucleus complements (NCOMP).

In English, the succession of tagmemes defined largely by form-class imposes a kind of *a priori* order on the elements of the clause. In particular, the fixed sequence of the postverbal adverbs — VPART, VCOMP, and TRMAV — leads to a certain basic rigidity, which, to be sure, could be overcome to some extent by the transpositions of which those elements are capable. In German, on the other hand, the composition of some tagmemes is determined somewhat differently. It was pointed out that several kinds of words and phrases could function as nucleus complements (NCOMP), yet there can be only one nucleus complement in a given infrastructure. In effect, this compels the speaker of German to make a determination of the relative importance of the various components of the content which he wants to express, and to incorporate the most important one, where possible, into a close union with the verb. This sets the nucleus complement apart from all other elements of the infrastructure, even from those of its own form-class. Because of this peculiarity of structure, the nucleus complement of German stands in greater prominence vis-à-vis the other elements of its clause than any one of the postverbal elements of English. In one important respect, however, German word order is more flexible than that of English: in the adverbo-nominal tagmeme (AVNOM), almost any sequence can be justified by reference to the context in which the sentence stands.

In regard to nominals, there is one point at which the two languages differ significantly: the role of the subject in the clause. In an earlier chapter, we alluded to the distinction between the grammatical, the syntactic, and the logical subjects, and pointed out that in English the grammatical and syntactic functions coincide with one another in one tagmeme, i. e., SUBJ. In German, on the other hand, these three functions are completely divorced from one another: the subject may appear in any tagmeme which may contain a noun or pronoun — UPPRN, AVNOM, or NCOMP; in some cases, the clause may contain no expressed subject at all. The consequences of these differences for the language teacher are mainly practical: the English-speaking student, when reading or translating German, usually approaches each independent finite clause by hunting for the subject, thus slowing down his reading speed; when writing the language, the English-speaking student often fails to avail himself of the greater facility in German for topicalization, and tends to begin every sentence with the subject — a practice which leads to grammatically correct, but unidiomatic sentences and compositions.

A final observation also relates to nouns, i. e., to the difference between specific and nonspecific nouns in German. These categories, which reflect the logical distinction between a specific member of a class of objects or a typical member — specific — and an unspecified member of the class or the class itself — nonspecific — have no functional counterpart in the syntax of English. As far as German is concerned, the distinction is crucial for the incorporation of the noun into, or its exclusion from the clause nucleus. As we noted, a specific noun may not serve as nucleus complement. This feature of German syntax is unusual, because it means that a single noun may be assigned to two different tagmemes, to the nucleus complement (NCOMP) or to the adverbo-nominal (AVNOM). To be sure, there are a number of adverbs which may appear in different tagmemes, but their assignment to one or the other is correlated with certain differences between their syntactic functions in connection with the valence of the verb, whereas the distinction between the specific and nonspecific noun is a logical feature of the noun phrase itself, and not contingent on the valence of the verb.

*The Tagmemes of English and German Compared*

After having surveyed in general terms the areas of contrast between English and German, we may conclude this chapter by examining the specific points at which the structures of the two languages may come into comparison. We will defer a study of the verb systems to the next section of this book; the chart below shows those cases where a nonverbal element in one language may correspond to a like element in the other. The numbers in the table refer to the examples which appear in the discussion which follows the table.

Points of Contrast Between Nonverbal Elements
in the German and English Infrastructures

Tagmemes of German

| Tagmemes of English | UPPRN | MDLAV | AVNOM | CLNAV | NCOMP |
|---|---|---|---|---|---|
| SUBJ | 1 | – | 2 | – | (3) |
| ITVAV | – | 4 | 5 | 6 | – |
| NOMNL | 7 | – | 8 | – | 9 |
| VPART | – | – | – | – | 10 |
| VCOMP | – | – | 11 | 12 | 13 |
| TRMAV | – | – | 14 | – | – |

As this chart indicates, there are fourteen points at which the tagmemes of the English and German infrastructures may be contrasted. This cannot be regarded as complete, because the modal adverbs of German are very often rendered in English by certain intonation patterns or with asyntactic elements. It will be somewhat simpler if we take those elements containing nouns and pronouns first. These are 1, 2, 3, 7, 8, and 9.

To begin with, the subject in English (SUBJ) may be either a noun or pronoun, forms which fall into the adverbo-nominal (AVNOM) or the unaccented personal pronoun (UPPRN) tagmemes, respectively:

1. Morgen gehen *wir* in die Stadt. — Tomorrow *we* are going down town.
2. Voriges Jahr besuchten uns *unsere Großeltern.* — Last year *our grandparents* visited us.

The third case involves the unusual situation of a noun in the nominative case functioning as a nucleus complement (NCOMP) in German.

3. Der Sache wurde nicht genügend *Rechnung* getragen. — There was not sufficient *account* taken of the matter.

The nouns *Rechnung* and *account* are in the nominative case only because of a passive voice transformation in both languages. In the infrastructure, both nouns are objects of the verb in their respective tagmemes:

IS: JEMAND der Sache nicht genügend *Rechnung*$_{ACC}$ tragen
IS: SOMEONE take not sufficient *account*$_{1NnOj}$ of the matter

In the German infrastructure, the word *Rechnung* is a nucleus complement, a role which it retains even when the infrastructure is passivized and *Rechnung* becomes the grammatical subject noun in the nominative case. As we have noted, the subject is not a syntactic category in German. When the English infrastructure is subjected to the passive voice transformation, too, we end up with the unusual situation of Example 3, where the English subject corresponds to a German nucleus complement in the nominative case. By way of demonstration, we will generate both sentences in Example 3, using the EDICT-rules described earlier:

IS: JEMAND der Sache nicht genügend Rechnung$_{ACC}$ tragen
PASV: VON JEMANDEM der Sache nicht genügend Rechnung$_{NOM}$ getragen werden

FNTZ (= PAST, PSNM): VON JEMANDEM der Sache nicht genügend Rechnung 'getragen wurde

T / FV: wurde + VON JEMANDEM der Sache nicht genügend
Rechnung getragen

T / X: der Sache + wurde + VON JEMANDEM nicht genügend
Rechnung getragen

D / EE: der Sache + wurde . . . nicht genügend Rechnung getragen

The abbreviation "D / EE" stands for the "deletion of empty
elements," those such as *JEMAND* which have purely a syntactic, but
no lexical function in a given infrastructure.

SOP: "Der Sache wurde nicht genügend Rechnung getragen."

The English infrastructure undergoes a similar series of changes:

IS: SOMEONE take not sufficient account$_{1NnOj}$ of the matter

When the passive transformation (PASV) is applied, the first noun
object *account* must be moved to the SUBJ tagmeme, and the subject *SOMEONE* made an object of the agent preposition; the resulting prepositional phrase is then shifted to the VCOMP tagmeme:

PASV: not sufficient account$_{SUBJ}$ be taken of the matter BY
SOMEONE

FNTZ (= PAST, PSNM): not sufficient account was taken of the
matter BY SOMEONE

In order for the word *account* to stand in roughly the same position
as its German counterpart *Rechnung*, i. e., in or near the comment
position, the English expression must undergo a THERE-transformation at this point. This consists of the operations T / VF&BE1
"topicalization of all verb forms up to and including the first form
of the verb BE," and I / THERE "insertion of THERE in initial
position." These operations will be studied in greater detail in
Chapter 10.

T / VF&BE1: was + not sufficient account . . . taken of the
matter BY SOMEONE

I / THERE: THERE + was + not sufficient account taken of the
matter BY SOMEONE

D / EE: THERE + was + not sufficient account taken of the
matter . . .

SOP: "There was not sufficient account taken of the matter."

It is through these transformations that a subject in English may correspond to a nucleus complement noun in German.

In the next examples, we find unaccented personal pronouns (UPPRN) in German as the equivalent of these elements in the tagmeme NOMNL in English:

7. Hast du es *ihm* gegeben? — Did you give it *to him?*

Probably the most frequent point of correspondence between English and German nouns occurs when a noun stands in the English tagmeme NOMNL and in the German AVNOM tagmeme:

8. Morgen werden wir *unsere Freunde* besuchen. — Tomorrow we are going to visit *our friends.*

A noun in the English NOMNL tagmeme may also be the counterpart of a German nucleus complement (NCOMP):

9. Anna kann *Klavier* spielen. — Anne can play *the piano.*

The following points of correspondence have to do with adverbs. Both in English and in German there are four tagmemes which may contain adverbs: in English, ITVAV, VPART, VCOMP, and TRMAV; in German, MDLAV, AVNOM, CLNAV, and NCOMP. As the chart indicated, not every tagmeme of the one language necessarily contains an element which could appear in every tagmeme of the other. Hence, we have only eight instances of syntactic correspondence to examine: those designated as 4 through 6, and as 10 through 14.

The first case of adverb correspondence is that where an intraverbal adverb (ITVAV) of English corresponds to a modal adverb (MDLAV) in German:

4. Er wird sie *wohl* morgen besuchen. — He will *probably* visit her tomorrow.

We again note in passing that the German modal adverb must often be rendered in English by intonation patterns, tag questions, and the like. These English adverbs may also appear in German as adverbonominals (AVNOM):

5. Es war *selten* besprochen worden. — It had *seldom* been discussed.

Occasionally, an intraverbal adverb may be rendered by a clause nucleus adverb (CLNAV) in German:

6. Er hat *immer* Wort gehalten. — He has *always* kept his word.

Not infrequently, the English verb particle (VPART) corresponds to a German nucleus complément (NCOMP):

10. Er kam gestern abend spät *nach Hause.* — He came *home* late yesterday evening.

The verb in German often has a separable prefix, which the verb particle (VPART) of English resembles somewhat:

Er gab ihr das Buch *zurück.* — He gave her *back* the book.

The largest class of adverbs in English is without doubt the verb complement (VCOMP). Elements in this category may be found in correspondence with elements in a number of tagmemes of German, e. e., with adverbo-nominals (AVNOM):

11. Er ging *langsam* ans Fenster. — He went *slowly* to the window.

In a few cases, an verb complement may appear in German as a clause nucleus adverb (CLNAV):

12. Er hat es *doch* getan. — He did it *anyway*.

In other cases, it may correspond to a nucleus complement (NCOMP):

13. Wir werden *nach Kalifornien* fahren. — We will drive *to California*.

The English terminal adverb (TRMAV), which is distinguished by the fact that it is normally unaccented, has no precise counterpart in German; those elements in the latter language corresponding to it usually fall into the adverbo-nominal (AVNOM) tagmeme:

14. Der Zug kam *gestern abend* spät an. — The train arrived late *yesterday evening*.

Though the infrastructures of English and German are not wholly dissimilar, one cannot dismiss the impression of numerous differences in detail. Thus far, in our review of these structures, we have ignored the verb, to which we turn in the next section.

# CHAPTER 7

## THE MORPHOLOGY OF THE ENGLISH VERB

Both in English and in German, the verb may undergo a complex series of modifications in order to signal a variety of meanings. As in the analyses in the foregoing chapters, our attention will be focused on those changes involving the generation of forms and their positions in the utterance. As a result, remarks concerning the meanings conveyed by these forms will be limited to those instances where the form or position of the verb can be explained only by reference to the semantic factor.

The changes which the lexical verb in English may undergo can be grouped under two rubrics: first, changes which a verb undergoes in order to indicate voice, etc., and which are common to finite and nonfinite verbs alike; and second, the modifications by which a neutral verb form is altered so as to fit into the larger structure of the sentence, i. e., finitization (FNTZ), infinitivization (INFZ), participialization (PRTZ), and gerundivization (GNDZ). Let us begin by considering the former group, i. e., the three common modifications to which the lexical verb of English is subject (for the following, cf. Kufner 1962:28).

### The Common Modifications of the English Verb

The form of a lexical verb in English may be altered to indicate voice, continuity of action, and relation of a prior action to the point in time suggested by the content of the utterance. Each of these involves the use of an auxiliary in conjunction with the modification of the verb form. In conformity with the principle used in other connections in this book, we will try to describe the morphology of the English verb by a series of generative rules.

The first modification which may be applied is "passivization" (PASV). This is not a rule which affects the verb alone, but one which brings with it the shift of the subject (SUBJ) into the position of the object of an agent prepositional phrase (AgPhr) in the passive sentence, and the shift of the object of the active verb into the role of the subject of the passive verb:

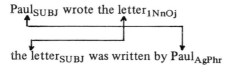

Paul$_{SUBJ}$ wrote the letter$_{1NnOj}$

the letter$_{SUBJ}$ was written by Paul$_{AgPhr}$

There is, of course, a large class of verbs in English which are intransitive; obviously, this transformation cannot be applied to them.

The passive transformation of the verb may be described as follows:

PASV: BE$_P$ + (FVF + PRT$_P$)

These symbols describe the morphological adjustments which take place in the generation of a passive verb form. The word "BE$_P$" refers to the auxiliary verb BE; because this verb is used for other purposes, it is helpful to attach a subscript "P" to indicate its origin in this transformation. The letters "FVF" mean the "first verb form" present. To be sure, this could only be the lexical verb at this point, since no other transformation has been introduced; nevertheless, we will hold to this formulation so as to maintain a parallel to other verb modifications which will be discussed presently. And finally, the form "PRT" refers to the "participle," a special form of the lexical verb; again it will be found helpful to tag this participle with a subscript "P" to show where it arose, since the participle can be introduced in another transformation as well. The parentheses mean that the two components are fused in a fashion prescribed by the morphological patterns of the language, as in these examples:

touch + PRT → touch + ed → touched
see + PRT → see + n → seen
catch + PRT → catch + ed → caught
bend + PRT → bend + ed → bent
hurt + PRT → hurt + $\emptyset$ → hurt

Thus, the first modification of the verb *watch*, which we will use as an example, produces:

BE$_P$ + (watch + PRT$_P$) → be watched

Another modification which can be applied to the verb is that which generates the socalled progressive forms of English, a change which we will call "limited duration" (LMDR). This may be produced by the following adjustment of the verb:

LMDR: $BE_L + (FVF + ING_L)$

Note, first of all, that this modification affects the verb and the verb only – unlike passivization, which requires the the rearrangement of subject and object within the infrastructure. Hence, one can distinguish between passivization (PASV), which is a transformation in the full sense of the term, and this change, which is solely a verb modification. Moreover, we again encounter the verb BE as an auxiliary, the function of which is indicated in the formula by the subscript "L." Lastly, we note that the first verb form in the series is modified by the addition of a suffix "ING," which is also tagged as to its origin by the subscript "L." Applying this formula to our example produces the expression:

$BE_L + (watch + ING_L) \rightarrow$ be watching

The third and last of the three common modifications marks the relation of a past event to a point in time in the present. This modification, familiar as the "present perfect tense," will be called "current relevance" (CRLV), and is signaled as follows:

CRLV: $HAVE_C + (FVF + PRT_C)$

As to the symbols, we know that the verb *have* may also be used as a lexical verb in English, and so it is useful to indicate its origin in this verb modification with a subscript "C." The participle is also marked in this way – as "$PRT_C$" – to distinguish it from the participle "$PRT_P$" which arises in the course of the passive voice transformation. Applied to our verb *watch*, this leads to the following change:

$HAVE_C + (watch + PRT_C) \rightarrow$ have watched

Summarizing our three modifications, we can list them as follows:

PASV:  $BE_P + (FVF + PRT_P)$
LMDR:  $BE_L + (FVF + ING_L)$
CRLV:  $HAVE_C + (FVF + PRT_C)$

The reader may have wondered why these formulas were constructed using the element "FVF" as a component. The explanation has to do with the generative principle which has been applied in several instances so far: these formulas can be applied not only to a lexical verb like *watch*, but, with some restrictions, to each other as well. The restrictions are these: first, all transformations are optional, so that the speaker can choose the combination which expresses what he wants to say; second, each transformation may be applied only once; third, the three transformations must be applied in the order given; and fourth, the letters "FVF" mean that a given transformation is to be applied to the first verb form present, whether it be the lexical verb, or an auxiliary verb introduced by a previous transformation. As a result, it is possible to generate four more modifications of the verb *watch* in addition to the three already presented. To make this procedure clear, let us review all of the possible combinations possible under these three rules:

(1) PASV:

$$\underline{BE_P + (watch + PRT_P)}$$

be   +   watched

(2) LMDR:

$$\underline{BE_L + (watch + ING_L)}$$

be   +   watching

(3) CRLV:

$$\underline{HAVE_C + (watch + PRT_C)}$$

have   +   watched

In all three of these cases, the FVF has been the lexical verb. The following show the four additional combinations which can be generated by combining two or more of these verb modifications:

(4) PASV + LMDR:

$$BE_L + (BE_P + ING_L) + (watch + PRT_P)$$

be   +   being   +   watched

110

(5) PASV + CRLV:

$$HAVE_C + \overline{(BE_P + PRT_C)} + (watch + PRT_P)$$

have   +   been   +   watched


(6) LMDR + CRLV:

$$HAVE_C + \overline{(BE_L + PRT_C)} + (watch + ING_L)$$

have   +   been   +   watching


(7) PASV + LMDR + CRLV:

$$HAVE_C + \overline{(BE_L + PRT_C)} + \overline{(BE_P + ING_L)} + (watch + PRT_P)$$

have   +   been   +   being   +   watched


It is in the last case that the use of the symbol FVF can be most easily justified. The modification for current relevance can be applied to three different verb forms: the lexical verb (Example 3), the auxiliary of the passive voice, $BE_P$ (Example 5), and the auxiliary of the modification for limited duration, $BE_L$ (Examples 6 and 7). By specifying that this transformation affects the first verb form present, one can formulate the modification as a single rule which will account for all cases. Thus, the seven verb forms above may be generated by the following three rules:

oPASV:   $BE_P + (FVF + PRT_P) \rightarrow$
oLMDR:   $BE_L + (FVF + ING_L) \rightarrow$
oCRLV:   $HAVE_C + (FVF + PRT_C)$.


*Finitization (FNTZ)*

The first verb form present after the common modifications have been applied is subject to four further changes which attend the mutation of a lexical or auxiliary verb into a finite form. First, a modal auxiliary may be added (MODL); second, the first verb form may be modified morphologically to denote a past tense (PAST); third, the first verb present may be changed to indicate the subjunctive mood (SJNC); and fourth, the first verb form present in the complete verb *must* be transformed to indicate the person and number of the grammatical subject (PSNM). Let us take up these further changes which are connected with finitization in the order listed.

In comparison with German, which has a large number of modal auxiliaries with complete conjugations, English has only five left, and these are defective: *can, may, must, shall,* and *will*. In connection with these, there are a number of points to be noted. First, *will* is often considered the auxiliary of the future tense; from the syntactic point of view, however, it behaves like any of the modals. Second, some of these alternate more or less systematically with other syntactic patterns, e. g., *can* and *be able to, must* and *to have to, will* and *be going to*, etc.; though there is a close conceptual and rhetorical affinity between these pairs of expressions, from the syntactic point of view they must be classed under two entirely different rubrics: the former are modals, and hence modifications of the verb; the latter contain infinitives, and are, therefore, complex structures which must be generated by the embedding of an infinitive into a matrix clause.

Three of the modifications of the verb consist of a change in the form of a word already present; the modification MODL consists in placing one of the five forms listed above before the first verb form which emerges from the series of common modifications described in the preceding section:

MODL: MODL + FVF . . .

This can lead to as many as eight possible combinations of verbal elements, e. g.:

LEXVB, MODL: CAN watch
LEXVB, PASV, MODL: CAN be watched
LEXVB, PASV, CRLV, MODL: CAN have been watched
LEXVB, PASV, LMDR, CRLV, MODL: CAN have been being
    watched, etc. etc.

The remaining three modifications affect the first verb form present, regardless of where it originated, i. e., whether a lexical or auxiliary verb; first, the past tense:

PAST: (FVF + PAST) + VFF . . .

112

It can be applied to a lexical verb in this way:

LEXVB, PAST: (watch + PAST) → watch +ed → watched

or to an auxiliary in like fashion:

LEXVB, PASV, PAST: $(BE_P + PAST) + (watch + PRT_P)$ → WAS watched

LEXVB, LMDR, CRLV, MODL, PAST: (CAN + PAST) + $HAVE_C$ + $(BE_L + PRT_C)$ + $(watch + ING_L)$ → COULD have been watching, etc. etc.

The modification for the subjunctive mood:

SJNC: (FVF + SJNC) + VFF . . .

is evident in the morphology of English in the third person singular of the present tense of lexical verbs, and at several points in the conjugation of the verb BE. Since the latter verb is quite irregular, it might be helpful to present the various forms resulting from these modifications in a table:

| Person and Number | BE + PSNM | BE + SJNC + PSNM | BE + PAST + PSNM | BE + PAST + SJNC + PSNM |
|---|---|---|---|---|
| 1st sg. | am | be | was | were |
| 2nd sg. | are | be | were | were |
| 3rd sg. | is | be | was | were |
| 1st pl. | are | be | were | were |
| 2nd pl. | are | be | were | were |
| 3rd pl. | are | be | were | were |

The forms with the PAST and SJNC modifications are used in Standard American English in conditions contrary to fact, e. g.:

if he *were* in charge, it would be done properly

as compared with real conditions, e. g.:

there's no doubt about it: if he *was* in charge, then it was done properly

The modification SJNC appears in American English in statements in indirect discourse after verbs of request and command, e. g.:

a letter *is* sent; cf. he asked that a letter *be* sent

An alternative pattern of expression is possible in American English, and preferred in British English:

he asked that a letter should be sent

From our point of view, however, this involves the modal modification with *shall*, about which more will be said below.

For the vast majority of verbs in English, the only point at which the modification SJNC is evident is in the third person singular; all other forms are identical with the PSNM, or the PAST + PSNM modifications of the lexical verb, e. g.:

he *appears* in person; cf. he insisted that he *appear* in person
they *appear* in person; cf. he insisted that they *appear* in person

We can summarize the observations in this section as to the modifications for the past tense (PAST), the subjunctive mood (SJNC), and for person and number (PSNM) by listing the forms for a typical verb:

| Person and Number | speak + PSNM | speak + SJNC + PSNM | speak + PAST + PSNM | speak + PAST + SJNC + PSNM |
|---|---|---|---|---|
| 1st, 2nd sg., 1st, 2nd, 3rd pl. | speak | speak | spoke | spoke |
| 3rd. sg. | speaks | speak | spoke | spoke |

The modal auxiliaries show a similar leveling of morphological contrast. Moreover, they interact with other modifications of the verb to form a "modal system" which differs from that of lexical verbs (cf. Diver 1964). The distinctions of meaning which would have to be considered here would lead us rather far afield from the question of the form of verbal elements and their distribution. It appears, on the basis of the following example, that the modification

114

SJNC cannot be applied to a modal unless the modification PAST has first been applied:

he *may* read the book if he gets permission first

but in indirect discourse after a verb of command or request:

he demanded that he *be allowed to* (? ? may, ? ? might) read it without any permission

On the basis of meaning, the verb forms *might, should,* and *would* are always potential, and therefore subjunctive. Taking this into account, as well as the fact that verb *must* lacks any other modification than PSNM, we can summarize the morphological variety of the modals thus:

| 1st, 2nd, 3rd sg., pl. of MODL | MODL + PSNM | MODL + SJNC + PSNM | MODL + PAST + PSNM | MODL + PAST + SJNC + PSNM |
|---|---|---|---|---|
| CAN | can | – | could | could |
| MAY | may | – | – | might |
| MUST | must | – | – | – |
| SHALL | shall | – | – | should |
| WILL | will | – | – | would |

The modifications described in the section above, with the restrictions noted, may be summed up in the formulas which are subsumed under the transformation of finitization (FNTZ):

oMODL: MODL + FVF . . . . →
oPAST: (FVF + PAST) + VFF . . . . →
oSJNC: (FVF + SJNC) + VFF . . . . →
+PSNM: (FVF + PSNM) + VFF . . . . .

Of all these, the common transformations as well as those connected with finitization, only one – the modification for person and number (PSNM) – is obligatory; all the others are optional.

The changes in verb forms connected with infinitivization (INFZ), participialization (PRTZ), and gerundivization (GNDZ) will be treated in the sections dealing with the syntax of those constructions.

CHAPTER 8

THE MORPHOLOGY OF THE GERMAN VERB

*The Common Modifications of the German Verb*

As in the case of the English verb, the lexical verb in German is subject to a variety of modifications, some of which are common to finite and nonfinite verbs, some only to the former of those categories. As in English, too, the common modifications of the German verb are three in number, but they are not the same ones. The first common verb modification in German is passivization (PASV), which by and large resembles its English counterpart; the second is the terminative modification (TRMV), which has affinities with current relevance (CRLV) in English; and the third and last is the addition of a modal auxiliary (MODL), which applies only to finite verbs in English, but which may occur in German in nonfinite constructions as well.

As in English, the passive voice transformation is more than a mere modification of a verb form, involving as it does the redistribution of subject and object:

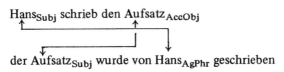

This transformation is reflected in the verb by the change of the lexical verb into its participial form, and by the addition of the auxiliary verb *werden* (W). These changes are represented in the following rule:

PASV: (LVF + PRT$_P$) + W (i. e., *werden*)

The reader may have noticed that the lexical verb is described here as "LVF," i. e., as the "last verb form"; moreover, the auxiliary verb *werden* is placed after the verb, and not before it, as is the passive auxiliary in English. A fundamental difference between the two languages is that English verbs "generate to the left," i. e., the auxiliaries are placed before the lexical verb in the generative process, whereas the verb in German "generates to the right," i. e., the auxiliaries are placed after it — hence the reference to the "last verb form" in the formula above. Applying this transformation to an example will produce the following:

(sehen + $PRT_P$) + W → gesehen werden

The next modification which may be applied to the verb in German is the terminative modification (TRMV). This signifies roughly that the action of the verb is over, or, if a point action, that it will not be repeated. As there are two auxiliaries, *haben* and *sein*, which may be used for this modification, additional specifications as to which is to be inserted under what conditions are obviously necessary to apply this modification properly; we assume that this is part of the morphology of the language, and that it lies beyond our area of concern at this time. This modification is effected as follows:

TRMV: (LVF + $PRT_T$) + H / S (i. e., *haben* or *sein*)

As applied, it produces the following forms:

(sehen + $PRT_T$) + H / S → gesehen haben
(gehen + $PRT_T$) + H / S → gegangen sein

The third and last of the common modifications is that of the modal auxiliary (MODL). As in English, this involves the addition of one of a specific class of verbs to those verb forms (VFF) already present, but with no change of the preceding form:

MODL: (LVF + $\emptyset$) + MODL

The class of modal auxiliaries is rather larger in German than in English, and includes *müssen, sollen, können, dürfen, mögen, wollen*, and *werden*. Though this last verb is sometimes regarded as the auxiliary of a future tense, it is syntactically, formally, and in some respects semantically a modal. By way of example, we may apply this modification to a verb as follows:

(sehen + $\emptyset$) + MODL → sehen können

The three common verb modifications may be summarized in the following formulas:

PASV: (LVF + $PRT_P$) + W
TRMV: (LVF + $PRT_T$) + H / S
MODL: (LVF + $\emptyset$) + MODL

117

There are certain conditions which attend the application of these transformations. First and obviously, they are optional, and as far as the passive is concerned, not all verbs can form a passive; this, again, is a feature of the lexicon of the language, and reflects the valence of the individual verb. Second, each can, under normal circumstances, be applied only once. Third, the passive, if applied at all, must be applied before the other two. But fourth, the transformations TRMV and MODL may be applied in either order: TRMV + MODL, or MODL + TRMV. The ultimate result of this peculiarity, which will be discussed in detail later in this chapter, is that there are actually two modal conjugations in German. But now, let us look at some examples to see how these rules and conditions apply:

(1) PASV:

$(\text{sehen} + \overline{\text{PRT}_P}) + \overline{\text{W}}$

gesehen    +    werden

(2) TRMV:

$(\text{sehen} + \overline{\text{PRT}_T}) + \text{H} / \text{S}$

gesehen    +    haben

(3) MODL:

$(\text{sehen} + \overline{\emptyset}) + \text{MODL}$

sehen    +    können

A variety of verbal patterns arise from various combinations of these modifications:

(4) PASV + TRMV:

$(\text{sehen} + \overline{\text{PRT}_P}) + (\overline{\text{W} + \text{PRT}_T}) + \text{H} / \text{S}$

gesehen    +    worden    +    sein

The normal form of the participle of *werden* is *geworden*; when it serves as the auxiliary of the passive voice, it loses the prefix *ge-*. This verb also takes the auxiliary *sein*.

(5) PASV + MODL:

$$(\text{sehen} + \overline{\text{PRT}_P}) + (\overline{\text{W} + \emptyset}) + \text{MODL}$$

gesehen    +    werden    +    können

Of significance here are the combinations which result when the two transformations TRMV and MODL are applied:

(6) TRMV + MODL:

$$(\text{sehen} + \overline{\text{PRT}_T}) + (\overline{\text{H} / \text{S} + \emptyset}) + \text{MODL}$$

gesehen    +    haben    +    können

(7) MODL + TRMV:

$$(\text{sehen} + \overline{\emptyset}) + (\overline{\text{MODL} + \text{PRT}_T}) + \text{H} / \text{S}$$

sehen    +    können    +    haben

It is a peculiarity of the language that the modal auxiliaries have two participial forms. When used as lexical verbs, they manifest forms which resemble those of weak verbs, e. g., *gekonnt, gemußt, gewollt*, etc. But when used as auxiliaries with another verb as lexical verb, their participial forms are identical in form to their infinitives, as in Example 7 above. The same two possibilities as in Examples 6 and 7 obtain when the passive modification is present:

(8) PASV + TRMV + MODL:

$$(\text{sehen} + \overline{\text{PRT}_P}) + (\overline{\text{W} + \text{PRT}_T}) + (\overline{\text{H} / \text{S} + \emptyset}) + \text{MODL}$$

gesehen    +    worden    +    sein    +    können

(9) PASV + MODL + TRMV:

$$(\text{sehen} + \overline{\text{PRT}_P}) + (\overline{\text{W} + \emptyset}) + (\overline{\text{MODL} + \text{PRT}_T}) + \text{H} / \text{S}$$

gesehen    +    werden    +    können    +    haben

In this way, these three common verb modifications, PASV, TRMV, and MODL, may be combined to produce six different

119

combinations of verb forms, in addition to themselves. In later sections, we will examine the two forms of the passive voice in German, and then turn our attention to the double modal conjugation of the language. But first we must review the verb modifications connected with the generation of finite forms.

*Finitization (FNTZ)*

The last verb form (LVF) to emerge from this set of common verb modifications – whether it be the lexical verb itself or any one of the auxiliary verbs – is subject to three further modifications, the result of which is the generation of a finite verb form. These three are: past tense (PAST), the subjunctive modification (SJNC), and the modification for person and number (PSNM). It is at this point that the student of German is confronted by a flexional apparatus which is much more complex than that of English. Since this feature of the language carries us across the border from the domain of syntax into the realm of morphology, we will merely indicate the various possibilities by means of a few examples.

The modification PAST may apply to any lexical verb, or to any of the various auxiliaries, producing forms like:

sehen + PAST → SAH-
spielen + PAST → SPIELT-
werden + PAST → WURD-
haben + PAST → HATT-
sein + PAST → WAR-
können + PAST → KONNT-

In like fashion, the subjunctive modification may be added to any of these verbs, too:

sehen + SJNC → SEH-
spielen + SJNC → SPIEL-
werden + SJNC → WERD-
haben + SJNC → HAB-
sein + SJNC → SEI-
können + SJNC → KÖNN-

It is also possible to apply first the PAST modification and then SJNC, in that order:

120

sehen + PAST + SJNC → SAH- → SÄH-
spielen + PAST + SJNC → SPIELT- → SPIELT-
werden + PAST + SJNC → WURD- → WÜRD-
haben + PAST + SJNC → HATT- → HÄTT-
sein + PAST + SJNC → WAR- → WÄR-
können + PAST + SJNC → KONNT- → KÖNNT-

Both PAST and SJNC are optional modifications of the verb; every completely formed finite verb must undergo the transformation PSNM for person and number. Again, the morphology of the language displays a luxuriance of forms, at least in comparison with English, a profusion which we can only suggest with a few examples, all of which are in the third person singular:

sehen +
PSNM → sieht
SJNC + PSNM → SEH- → sehe
PAST + PSNM → SAH- → sah
PAST + SJNC + PSNM → SAH- → SÄH- → sähe

spielen +
PSNM → spielt
SJNC + PSNM → SPIEL- → spiele
PAST + PSNM → SPIELT- → spielte
PAST + SJNC + PSNM → SPIELT- → SPIELT- → spielte

werden +
PSNM → wird
SJNC + PSNM → WERD- → werde
PAST + PSNM → WURD- → wurde
PAST + SJNC + PSNM → WURD- → WÜRD- → würde

haben +
PSNM → hat
SJNC + PSNM → HAB- → habe
PAST + PSNM → HATT- → hatte
PAST + SJNC + PSNM → HATT- → HÄTT- → hätte

sein +
PSNM → ist
SJNC + PSNM → SEI → sei
PAST + PSNM → WAR- → war
PAST + SJNC + PSNM → WAR- → WÄR- → wäre

können +
PSNM → kann
SJNC + PSNM → KÖNN- → könne
PAST + PSNM → KONNT- → konnte
PAST + SJNC + PSNM → KONNT- → KÖNNT- → könnte

In sum, the various transformations which may be applied to the last verb form resulting from the common verb modifications, and which constitute the clause formation transformation of finitization (FNTZ), can be represented in these formulas:

oPAST:   (LVF + PAST)
oSJNC:   (LVF + SJNC)
+ PSNM:  (LVF + PSNM)

As we have noted, the common verb modifications, coupled with these verb modifications, leave a finite verb form at the end of the clause: in effect, finite-verb-last word order (FV-L). The other two patterns, finite-verb-first (FV-1) and finite-verb-second word order (FV-2) are generated by the finite-clause transformations T / FV and T / X. The following example shows how the common verb modifications and those connected with finitization, together with the finite-clause transformations, operate conjointly to generate the sentence *Die Waren könnten schon vorher beschlagnahmt worden sein*. The infrastructure of the sentence is:

IS: JEMAND$_{NOM}$ die Waren$_{ACC}$ schon vorher beschlagnahmen

The common verb modifications which must be applied to generate the sentence are passivization (PASV), terminativization (TRMV), and modalization (MODL):

PASV: VON JMDM (= JEMANDEM) die Waren$_{NOM!}$ schon vorher beschlagnahmt werden
TRMV: ... beschlagnahmt worden sein
MODL: ... beschlagnahmt worden sein können

Now the finite verb modifications for the past tense (PAST), the subjunctive mood (SJNC), and for person and number (PSNM) are applied to the last verb form (LVF) present:

PAST: VON JMDM die Waren schon vorher beschlagnahmt worden sein KONNT-
SJNC: ... beschlagnahmt worden sein KÖNNT-

PSNM: VON JMDM die Waren schon vorher beschlagnahmt worden sein könnten

Next, the finite verb is topicalized, producing FV-1 word order:

T / FV: könnten VON JMDM die Waren schon vorher beschlagnahmt worden sein

Then, any element except a modal adverb can be topicalized:

T / X: die Waren könnten VON JMDM schon vorher beschlagnahmt worden sein

As in other cases, "empty elements" (EE), those having a syntactic function but no lexical content, are deleted:

D / EE: die Waren könnten . . . schon vorher beschlagnahmt worden sein

And finally, with standard orthography and punctuation (SOP), our sentence is generated:

SOP: "Die Waren könnten schon vorher beschlagnahmt worden sein."

This derivation shows how the common verb modifications and those of the finite clause are integrated into the system of generative rules by which sentences in German may be produced.

Before concluding this chapter, we must turn to a more detailed examination of three further facets of the verb morphology of German. The first of these has to do with the meaning of certain verb modifications, both common and finite; the second deals with some unusual features of the passive voice; and the third is the double modal conjugation which is found in German.

*Tense and Aspect in the System of Verb Modifications of German*

It is customary to speak loosely of the "tense forms" of German or English. The word *tense* is derived from the Latin word *tempus* 'time', and hence the modifications of the lexical verb which associate an action or event with a certain point in time seem to be appropriately labeled. For example, in expresssions like *wir spielten Schach* or *we played chess*, the morphemes -*t*- and -*ed* indicate that

123

the actions represented by the verb have already occurred. These verb forms cannot be used with adverbial expressions which suggest that the event in question took place in the present or in the future:

??? wir spielten morgen Schach
?? wir spielten jetzt Schach
? wir spielten heute Schach
! wir spielten gestern Schach

It follows, then, that the PAST modification of German does produce a genuine tense form, in the sense that the action represented by the verb so modified is tied to a specific point in time.

The modification "terminative" (TRMV), on the other hand, is not bound to any point in time. Thus, we can say in German:

! gestern habe ich es gelesen 'I read it yesterday'
! heute habe ich es gelesen 'I read it today'
! gerade jetzt habe ich es gelesen 'I have just now read it'
! bis morgen habe ich es gelesen 'by tomorrow I will have read it'

What these sentences have in common is the notion that the act of reading is completed – whether this took place in the past, is in the process of taking place in the present, or is supposed to take place in the future. For this reason, the modification TRMV may be regarded, not as a tense, but as an aspect – a form which indicates solely that the event represented by the verb is completed, but which does not assert that the completion occurred at a specific point in time.

It may be objected that the simple expression, e. g., *ich habe es gelesen*, without any adverbial modifiers, unmistakably refers not only to a completed action, but also to an action in the past, and consequently that the modification TRMV has not only aspectival, but also temporal meaning. This interpretation of the sentence is correct, but it is correct for "accidental" reasons. In our view, the verb form TRMV indicates the completion or end of an action; if we identify any phenomenon as the end of a larger event or action, then the entire event or action must have occurred prior to our perception of its end; hence, the TRMV modification by itself indicates a past action – for ontological reasons, as it were.

In contrast with TRMV is the unmodified form of the verb, which means simply that the action represented by the verb is continuing. Its meaning is also aspectival, and not bound to any point in time. Hence, it is possible to say:

! ich lese es heute 'I am reading it today' or 'I will read it today'
! ich lese es jetzt 'I am reading it now'
! ich lese es morgen 'I will read it tomorrow'

In the rhetorical figure known as the "praesens historicum," this verb form can be used in a description of past events, too. Because the unmarked form of the lexical verb is not tied to any time level, but indicates simply that the action of the verb is continuing, we will call it the "continuative" aspect (CNTV).

The one additional verb form to be accounted for is the past perfect or pluperfect – the form generated by a combination of the modification TRMV + PAST:

IS: ich es damals schon lesen
TRMV: . . . gelesen haben
PAST: . . . gelesen HATT-
PSNM: . . . gelesen hatte
T / FV: hatte ich es damals schon gelesen
T / X: damals hatte ich es schon gelesen
SOP: "Damals hatte ich es schon gelesen."

This clearly indicates a past event prior to another past event, for which reason we will call it the "past anterior" (PNTR).

As to the future tense, we will place the auxiliary *werden* in the category of modal auxiliaries, both syntactically and semantically. In our view, the German verb has no morphosyntactic modification corresponding to the future tense of the Romance languages or of English.

In light of the foregoing, we may regard the modifications of the German verb in the area of tense and aspect as falling into two clearly defined categories:

(1) two aspects, neutral as to tense:
"continuative" (CNTV): LEXVB + $\emptyset$ + . . .
"terminative" (TRMV): LEXVB + TRMV + . . .
(2) two tenses, neutral as to aspect:
"past" (PAST): LEXVB + PAST + . . .
"past anterior" (PNTR): LEXVB + TRMV + PAST + . . .

These four patterns of verb modification function conjointly with a series of "rhematic adverbs" (cf. Schipporeit 1971) to provide a flexible and effective means of fixing and delimiting the processes and events represented by the lexical verbs of German.

## The Forms of the Subjunctive in German

This approach to the verb forms of German furnishes us with a relatively simple interpretation of the subjunctive forms of the language. The two different patterns which may be generated in the subjunctive mood do not show tense, but aspect. To be sure, each aspect form is in turn subdivided into two variants, the socalled I and II forms, which indicate relative validity (cf. Kaufmann 1971). Just as the continuative aspect (CNTV) is the unmarked member of a pair in which the terminative (TRMV) is the marked form, so, too, is the indicative the unmarked member vis-à-vis the subjunctive forms, all of which contain the modification SJNC. Of the two variants of the subjunctive, the socalled subjunctive I and subjunctive II forms, the latter contain the modification PAST as well. These modifications may be presented in tabular form as follows:

"continuative indicative": LEXVB + PSNM (here, e. g., in the 3rd sg.) → sieht

"continuative subjunctive I": LEXVB + SJNC + PSNM → sehe

"continuative subjunctive II": LEXVB + PAST + SJNC + PSNM → sähe

"terminative indicative": LEXVB + TRMV + PSNM → gesehen hat

"terminative subjunctive I": LEXVB + TRMV + SJNC + PSNM → gesehen habe

"terminative subjunctive II": LEXVB + TRMV + PAST + SJNC + PSNM → gesehen hätte

The subjunctive II forms are normally used in irreal conditions. Both subjunctive conjugations appear in indirect discourse. In this function, the continuative aspect of the direct statement, which is in the indicative, becomes the continuative subjunctive I or II; a direct statement in the terminative indicative, or in either of the two past tenses, becomes the terminative subjunctive I or II. The choice of the I or II form in each aspect of the subjunctive is dependent on the degree of validity imputed by the speaker to the statement, with the SJNC I forms indicating relative neutrality on the part of the speaker, and the II forms, doubt or uncertainty. The relations between these two sets of forms are indicated in the following table:

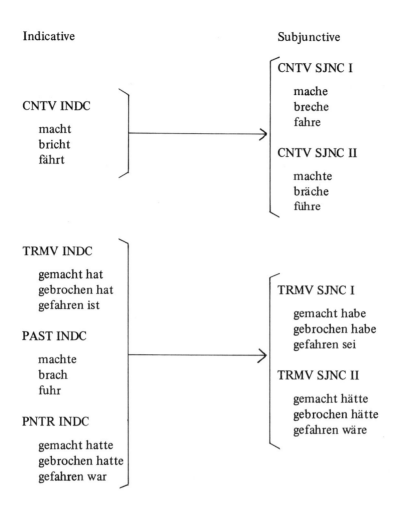

| Indicative | Subjunctive |
|---|---|

CNTV INDC

macht
bricht
fährt

CNTV SJNC I

mache
breche
fahre

CNTV SJNC II

machte
bräche
führe

TRMV INDC

gemacht hat
gebrochen hat
gefahren ist

PAST INDC

machte
brach
fuhr

PNTR INDC

gemacht hatte
gebrochen hatte
gefahren war

TRMV SJNC I

gemacht habe
gebrochen habe
gefahren sei

TRMV SJNC II

gemacht hätte
gebrochen hätte
gefahren wäre

*The Actional and Statal Forms of the Passive Voice
in German*

Whereas in English the common verb modification PASV was sufficient to account for all of the passive forms of that language, we
must note that there are not one, but two forms of the passive voice
in German. It is essential to a description of the morphology of the
German verb to show how the actional and statal forms of the passive

127

may be generated and placed in their proper position in the verb complex.

Teachers and students soon become familiar with these: the actional passive is formed with *werden*, and indicates that the action of the verb is in process; the statal forms are conjugated with *sein*, and indicate that the action of the verb has reached a resultant state or condition:

actional: die Tür wird geschlossen 'the door is being closed'
statal: die Tür ist geschlossen 'the door is (completely) closed'

Earlier grammarians, e. g., Curme (1952:298), claimed that German has a complete conjugation of the statal passive in all moods and tenses, e. g.:

es ist geschlossen
es war geschlossen
es ist geschlossen gewesen (? )
es war geschlossen gewesen (? )

and for those who believe in a future for German:

es wird geschlossen sein
es wird geschlossen gewesen sein (? )

This array of forms no longer represents modern usage, however. While all of them occur somewhere, those followed by a question mark in the synopsis above have become relatively rare. As Lederer (1969:104, n. 1) points out, the only forms in active use today are the first two in the list above: *ist geschlossen* and *war geschlossen*. If this be accepted as definitive for the scope of this conjugation, it becomes relatively simple to include the statal passive in our system of generative rules: we assume that the transformation PASV by itself will generate the actional passive; the statal passive may be formed by the subsequent application of the modification TRMV followed by the deletion of the form *worden*, the participial form of the auxiliary *werden*.

Our generative rules will normally produce actional passive forms in the following way:

IS: . . . schließen
PASV: . . . geschlossen werden
TRMV: . . . geschlossen worden sein
PSNM: . . . geschlossen worden ist

128

The rule for the formation of the statal passive assumes the modification PASV; it then prescribes the modification TRMV, followed by the deletion of *worden.* Thus the form *geschlossen war* would be generated as follows:

IS: . . . schließen
PASV: . . . geschlossen werden
TRMV: . . . geschlossen worden sein
D / *worden*: . . . geschlossen . . . sein
PAST: . . . geschlossen . . . WAR-
PSNM: . . . geschlossen . . . war

Formulated in this way, the rule will generate all, and only those forms in common use today, i. e.:

geschlossen ist (PASV + TRMV + D / *worden* + PSNM)
geschlossen war (PASV + TRMV + D / *worden* + PAST + PSNM)

Nevertheless, the other forms do appear from time to time, even in the works of modern authors, e. g.:

"Er hatte seine Frau früh verloren; sie hatte einen Kohlkopf gegessen, der mit Krähengift *gedüngt gewesen war* . . ." (Wolfdietrich Schnurre, cited in Schipporeit 1971:53; italics added).

This form may be explained as the normal form of the past anterior tense of the statal passive. Hence, a form like *gedüngt gewesen war* would be produced by the PASV modification, plus two applications of the modification TRMV, separated by the deletion of *worden.* This would take place as follows:

IS: . . . düngen
PASV: . . . gedüngt werden

This form is the actional passive; the statal passive is produced by the two following transformations:

TRMV: . . . gedüngt worden sein
D / *worden*: . . . gedüngt . . . sein

This is the base form of the statal passive; the terminative is generated by a second application of TRMV, which results in:

TRMV: . . . gedüngt . . . gewesen sein

The remaining changes affect only the last verb form:

PAST: ... gedüngt ... gewesen WAR-
PSNM: ... gedüngt ... gewesen war

As we interpret these forms, then, they represent the terminative aspect of the statal passive (e. g., *gedüngt gewesen ist*) or the past anterior tense (e. g., *gedüngt gewesen war*). They may be seldom used, but they fit in all respects into the structure of the language.

## The Concurrent and Prospicient Modal Conjugations of German

As a rule, it does not take long before the student of German discovers that sentences containing modal auxiliaries may have one of two meanings, e. g.:

Hans muß jetzt hier arbeiten
Erich soll heute zu Hause bleiben
Anna kann jetzt in Berlin studieren

The first of these means either (1) that the speaker is convinced that Hans is already at work somewhere in the vicinity, or (2) that Hans is under an obligation to perform some unspecified tasks in the area later on; on the first interpretation, Hans is already at work, on the second, his labors have not yet begun. The second sentence is also open to two interpretations: (1) the speaker believes that Erich is at home today and intends to remain there, or (2) Erich's whereabouts are not mentioned, but in any case he is under an obligation to remain at home today for a certain period of time; in the former case, Erich is already at home, in the second, he may not yet be, but is supposed to be later. In the last sentence, we note a similar ambiguity: (1) either the speaker is announcing his belief that it is possible that Anna is already a student in Berlin, or (2) that Anna is not at present a student, but that there are no apparent obstacles to her becoming one at a later time. All three of these sentences, then, are ambiguous, because they can be interpreted in two ways, which constitute the basis for our distinction between the two modal systems of German: either the modal auxiliary and the action represented by the lexical verb are felt to be in effect at the same time; or the condition represented by the modal is regarded as preceding the action denoted by the lexical verb. Those sentences in which modal and lexical verb apply simultaneously reflect the "concurrent modal conjugation," because the two verbs "run together," as it were; and those where the force of the modal is felt before that action of the lexical verb begins represent the "prospicient modal conjugation," because the subject, while in the situation described by the modal, "looks ahead" to the action of the lexical verb. For purposes of clarity, let us consider some other examples in which the lexical items are the same, or nearly so, along with their English equivalents. In these examples, the odd-numbered sentences represent the concurrent conjugation, the even-numbered the prospicent conjugation:

1) er muß heute arbeiten 'he must already be at work (around here somewhere) today'
2) er muß heute arbeiten 'he has to (go to) work today'
3) er will Arzt sein 'he claims to be a doctor'
4) er will Arzt werden 'he wants to be(come) a doctor'
5) er kann in Berlin studieren 'it is possible that he is at present a student in Berlin'
6) er kann in Berlin studieren 'he will be able to study in Berlin'
7) er soll in Berlin wohnen 'he is supposed to be living in Berlin'
8) er soll in Berlin wohnen 'he will have to live in Berlin'
9) er wird (wohl) müde sein 'he is probably tired'
10) er wird müde sein 'he will be tired' (e. g., after playing tennis)

It may come as a surprise to see *werden* included among the modal auxiliaries, since it is usually regarded as the auxiliary of a (non-existent) future tense constructed by analogy to Latin; nevertheless, by form and meaning it belongs with the other modals, because it indicates intention or probability, and hence, like them, expresses an attitude on the part of the speaker toward the events represented by the lexical verb.

If this distinction were purely semantic, one which arose out of combination of contextual factors with the lexical composition of individual sentences, one would scarcely be justified in setting up two separate "conjugations." The examples above do demonstrate that the concurrent and prospicient conjugations are identical in the continuative aspect. These two conjugations, however, have quite different patterns of formation in the terminative aspect. These arise from a peculiarity of the common verb modifications, namely, that the modification MODL can either precede or follow the modification TRMV, i. e.:

131

concurrent: LEXVB + TRMV + MODL:
  LEXVB: sehen
  TRMV: gesehen haben
  MODL: gesehen haben wollen
  PSNM, T / FV, T / X: (er) will (es) gesehen haben

prospicient: LEXVB + MODL + TRMV:
  LEXVB: sehen
  MODL: sehen wollen
  TRMV: sehen wollen haben
  PSNM, T / FV, T / X: (er) hat (es) sehen wollen

These two patterns of verb modification are the formal basis for the differing patterns represented by the concurrent and prospicient conjugations in the terminative aspect. This analysis also enables us to understand why the forms of these two conjugations are identical in the continuative aspect: one only has to remove the modification TRMV from the formulas above:

concurrent: LEXVB + . . . + MODL:
  LEXVB: sehen
  TRMV: (omitted)
  MODL: sehen wollen
  PSNM, T / FV, T / X: (er) will (es) sehen

prospicient: LEXVB + MODL + . . .:
  LEXVB: sehen
  MODL: sehen wollen
  TRMV: (omitted)
  PSNM, T / FV, T / X: (er) will (es) sehen

Since the distinction between the concurrent and the prospicient modal conjugations depends here, not on the presence or absence of any element, but on the order in which the two modifications are applied, there is no way of conveying the distinction unless both changes are present – hence, the identity of the two patterns of conjugation in the continuative aspect.

In conclusion, let us transform the ten examples above into their corresponding terminative forms. As before, the odd-numbered sentences reflect the concurrent, the even-numbered the prospicient modal conjugation:

  1) er muß heute gearbeitet haben 'he must have worked today'
  2) er hat heute arbeiten müssen 'he (has) had to work today'

3) er will Arzt gewesen sein 'he claims to have been a doctor'
4) er hat Arzt werden wollen 'he wanted to be(come) a doctor'
5) er kann in Berlin studiert haben 'it is possible that he was a student in Berlin'
6) er hat in Berlin studieren können 'he has found the means to enable him to study in Berlin'
7) er soll in Berlin gewohnt haben 'he is supposed to have lived in Berlin'
8) er hat in Berlin wohnen sollen 'he has been under an obligation to maintain residence in Berlin'
9) er wird (wohl) müde gewesen sein 'he was probably tired'
10) (a prospicient form of *werden* in the terminative aspect does not exist: ? ? ? *er hat müde sein werden*)

These examples show how the two sequences of modifications — TRMV + MODL and MODL + TRMV — generate the concurrent and prospicient modal conjugations, respectively, in the terminative aspect. We conclude this section with some brief remarks about major exceptions and points of contrast with English.

Example 10 above shows that *werden* does not form a terminative in the prospicient conjugation. Similarly, the modal *dürfen* must show the modification PAST + SJNC in the continuative aspect of the concurrent conjugation. For example, the sentence *er darf jetzt im Laboratorium arbeiten* can only mean 'he is now permitted to work in the laboratory'. The corresponding concurrent form must be:

er dürfte jetzt im Laboratorium arbeiten

which in English means 'he may be working in the laboratory now'.


*The Verb Forms of German: A Summary*

In this chapter, we have charted the possible combinations which result from the application of the three common and three finite verb modifications which exist in the language. We have seen, too, that these fall into pairs of forms, which in terms of meaning indicate the presence or absence of a feature, and which in terms of form are marked by the presence or absence of a modification. The categories and the modifications which signal them are presented in the following table:

|  | Ongoing Process (-Marked) | Resultant State (+Marked) |
|---|---|---|
| Type of Passive | actional: +PASV, xTRMV, xD / *worden* | statal: +PASV, +TRMV, +D / *worden* |
| Type of Modal | prospicient: +MODL, oTRMV | concurrent: oTRMV, +MODL |
| Aspect | continuative: xTRMV | terminative: +TRMV |
| Tense | past: xTRMV, +PAST | past anterior: +TRMV, +PAST |
| Type of Subjunctive | I forms: xPAST, +SJNC | II forms: +PAST, +SJNC |

(The signs before the abbreviations, e. g., oTRMV, xTRMV, +TRMV, indicate that the transformation is optional, prohibited, or obligatory, respectively.)

This table gives us a number of insights into the conceptual basis of the verb modifications of German. To begin with, three of the five modifications — aspect, type of passive, and tense — are signaled through the operation or exclusion of the terminative modification. This, more than any other feature of the system, suggests that the fundamental conceptual opposition which informs the system is that of ongoing process (without TRMV) versus resultant state (with TRMV). In a comparable way, the type of subjunctive is indicated by a pair of marked and unmarked forms. It is not an exaggeration to say that the German verb system, from the formal point of view, is a model of morphological symmetry.

There are some constraints on the kinds of verb forms which may actually be generated. It is therefore necessary to provide a single unitary formula which will produce all of the acceptable, and none of the unacceptable combinations of verbal elements in the language. Let us list these one by one before combining them. First, the passive modification, which must be either actional or statal:

oPASV → o(+TRMV → +D / *worden*) → . . .

This means that the passive modification itself is optional, as is that for the statal passive; however, if one opts for the statal passive, then both of the operations within the parentheses are obligatory.

Second, we may list the addition of a modal auxiliary. Modalization (MODL) involves two possibilities, which are given in this formula:

... oTRMV → +MODL → oTRMV → ...

This means that the TRMV modification is optional; if TRMV precedes MODL, a modal in the concurrent conjugation is produced, if it follows, a prospicient modal form. In third position is the modification for aspect, which is simply:

... oTRMV → ...

A form in the continuative aspect (CNTV) is produced by xTRMV, a terminative form by +TRMV.

In the area of finite modifications, we may generate either the past or the past anterior tense, using this formula:

... oTRMV → +PAST → ...

The PAST modification by itself produces a past tense form; the combination of the two − TRMV plus PAST − the past anterior tense. Modifications for mood involve the presence or absence of SJNC; however, this is applicable only in conjunction with PAST:

... oPAST → +SJNC → ...

The SJNC modification alone generates the socalled subjunctive I forms, the combination of PAST plus SJNC the subjunctive II conjugations. And lastly, every finite clause must conclude with the modification PSNM for person and number.

Combining these formulas produces the following chain of transformations:

(voice) oPASV → o(+TRMV → +D / *worden*) →
(modality) oTRMV → +MODL → oTRMV →
(aspect) oTRMV →
(tense) oTRMV → +PAST →
(mood) oPAST → +SJNC →
(finiteness) +PSNM

In this group of formulas, the modification TRMV appears no fewer than four times. It is necessary to formulate some constraint on its applicability, since the operation of more than one of these produces an unacceptable utterance, e. g.:

IS: ... lesen
   (modality)
TRMV: ¨... gelesen haben
MODL: ... gelesen haben können
   (aspect)
TRMV: ... gelesen haben können haben
   (tense)
TRMV: gelesen haben können gehabt haben
PAST: gelesen haben können gehabt HATT-
   (person and number)
PSNM: gelesen haben können gehabt hatte
SOP: ? ? ? "(Er) hatte (es) gelesen haben können gehabt."

Forms like these are meaningless, and hence must be excluded. We may eliminate these by saying that no transformation may be allowed to operate more than once, with the sole exception that TRMV may be applied twice, provided one application is in the modification for the statal passive. If this is so, we may then combine terms by removing redundant transformations; the formulas above can then be rewritten as a single formula in which all but the final transformation are optional:

$$\text{oPASV} \rightarrow \text{o(+TRMV} \rightarrow \text{+D} \,/\, worden) \rightarrow \text{oTRMV} \rightarrow \text{oMODL} \rightarrow$$
$$\text{oTRMV} \rightarrow \text{oPAST} \rightarrow \text{oSJNC} \rightarrow \text{+PSNM}.$$

This sequence of operations, with the restriction on repetition stated above, will generate all of the acceptable finite verb forms of the language, and only the acceptable ones. And with it, we conclude our study of the morphology and syntax of the German verb.

# CHAPTER 9

## THE MORPHOLOGY OF THE ENGLISH AND GERMAN
## VERB: A COMPARISON

In the two preceding chapters, the features of the modifications of English and German verbs have been catalogued and formulated in such a way as to constitute part of two systems of generative rules for the construction of utterances in the respective languages. As it happens, the structures of English and German are similar enough so that it was found possible to apply the same general patterns of formation to each. Nevertheless, differences were noted at various points, and it is these which we want to look at more closely at this time.

There are some contrasts between English and German which one may regard as relatively superficial; others reflect the most basic structural features of these languages. On several occasions we have alluded to the importance of the tagmeme VERB. To begin with, the position of this element in the infrastructure differs markedly in English and in German: in the former language, it is the third tagmeme; in the latter, the sixth and final one:

English: SUBJ ITVAV VERB NOMNL VPART VCOMP TRMAV

German: UPPRN MDLAV AVNOM CLNAV NCOMP VERB

The verb in English and German displays a comparably important contrast in regard to those modifications of it which were described in these chapters: the auxiliaries which arise in the course of the generation of the verb complex are placed before the lexical verb in English, but after it in German:

English:  AUX1 + AUX2 + AUX3 + AUX4 + LEXVB

German: LEXVB + AUX4 + AUX3 + AUX2 + AUX1

This contrast was noted at the time by remarking that the verb in English "generates to the left," i. e., that the various verb modifications are applied to the first verb form (FVF) present, whereas in German the verb "generates to the right," in that each successive modification affects the last verb form (LVF) present, either by changing its form, or by adding another element to the group of verb forms already present at that point, or by both. Thus, the arrangements of the lexical verb and its auxiliaries in English and German are in some respects mirror images of one another, as the diagram above shows.

The individual modifications have a number of points in common, but on balance are significantly different. In each language, we identified one class of verb modifications which could be applied to all four kinds of clauses, namely, the common verb modifications. Moreover, both English and German manifest a modification for the passive voice (PASV), one which is substantially the same in both: the lexical verb assumes its appropriate participial form, and an auxiliary is introduced into the verb group, the verb *be* in English, *werden* in German; in·addition, the transformation of active subject to object of the agent preposition, and active object to passive subject, occur in each.

While passivization is the first common verb modification which can be applied to a lexical verb in both English and German, the two languages diverge in respect of the following modifications. In English, the verb can be changed to express "limited duration" (LMDR), e. g., *be watching*, a modification which has no counterpart in modern standard German. Frequently German has resort to certain adverbs to express what is communicated by this feature of the English verb conjugation.

We noted that the verb system of German contained two tenses neutral as to aspect (the past and past anterior), and two aspects neutral as to tense (the continuative and the terminative). To be sure, English also contains two similar tense forms, the past and past anterior, but these can be modified by LMDR to show a continuing action, e. g.:

> John read the book while he was in the hospital (xLMDR; a completed action, separated from the present)
> John was reading the book when I came into the room (+LMDR; an uncompleted action in the past, still going on)

Bacause the German PAST is neutral as to aspect, this distinction is only implicit in the situation described by the sentence in question, as the German equivalents of the above expressions show:

Hans las das Buch, während er im Krankenhaus lag
Hans las das Buch, als ich ins Zimmer kam

The form which corresponds most closely to the TRMV modification of German is the English modification for current relevance (CRLV). This has an aspectival meaning in addition to a temporal one: the expression *John has read the book* describes a completed action (cf. the terminative of German) from the point of view of the speaker in the present, which, however, must have taken place in the past (cf. the German past tense). Because of the strong link with the present, this form cannot be used in conjunction with an adverb referring to a specific point in past time, e. g.:

? ? ? John has read the book last week
! John has read the book (already)
! John read the book last week

The first of these clashes constantly with the fully acceptable pattern of German:

! Hans hat das Buch vorige Woche gelesen
! Hans hat das Buch schon gelesen
! Hans las das Buch vorige Woche

A special case of this contrast occurs when the modifications for current relevance (CRLV) and limited duration (LMDR) are applied to the same verb form:

! John has been working on it for a year now

The use of the LMDR modification neutralizes the idea of completion, with the result that the sentence must be translated into German as:

! Hans arbeitet schon seit einem Jahre daran

The terminative aspect would be inappropriate here, since the English sentence implies that John's work is still going on. It might also be noted that the otherwise simple system of aspect and tense forms of German is supplemented by the system of "rhematic adverbs" (Schipporeit 1971). Not a few of the semantic distinctions expressed by the English verb are rendered with the help of these adverbs in German.

A significant difference arises in German in connection with the modification MODL for the modal auxiliary. This occurs in English, too, but in this language it is only a finite verb modification, whereas in German it is a common modification, one which may be applied to both finite and nonfinite forms alike. Hence, speakers of German are often at a loss for equivalents of modals in nonfinite clauses, e. g.:

German
ich kann es lesen
... um es lesen zu können
English
I can read it
? ? ? ... in order *to can read* it
! ... in order *to be able to read* it

Moreover, the modal auxiliaries of German may be inflected so as to constitute two different conjugations: the concurrent and the prospicient. These are not morphologically distinct in all their forms, however.

Other difficulties arise for speakers of English principally from two related sources: the lack of comparable forms in English for the morphologically regular German formations, and the variety of substitutes for these in rendering the meaning of the German forms in English. The fact that German has a complete flexional system of modals in two conjugations, contrasted with the modest formal resources of English in this area, means that English has had to concoct circumlocutions for many patterns which arise systematically in the course of generating verb forms with modals in German. This problem is particularly acute with *must*, which as we saw has only one form:

1) LEXVB + MODL + PSNM:
   C) er muß es lesen 'he must be reading it'
   P) er muß es lesen 'he has to read it'
2) LEXVB + MODL + PAST + PSNM:
   C) er mußte es lesen 'he had to be reading it'
   P) er mußte es lesen 'he was forced to read it'
3C) LEXVB + TRMV + MODL + PSNM:
   er muß es gelesen haben 'he must have read it'
3P) LEXVB + MODL + TRMV + PSNM:
   er hat es lesen müssen 'he has been forced to read it'
4C) LEXVB + TRMV + MODL + PAST + PSNM:
   er mußte es gelesen haben 'it was certain that he had read it'

4P) LEXVB + MODL + TRMV + PAST + PSNM:
   er hatte es lesen müssen 'he had been forced to read it'
5C) LEXVB + TRMV + MODL + PAST + SJNC + PSNM:
   er müßte es gelesen haben 'it would not seem improbable that
   he read it'
5P) LEXVB + MODL + TRMV + PAST + SJNC + PSNM:
   er hätte es lesen müssen 'he ought to have read it'

The last pattern constitutes a standard bugbear for beginning students of German:

   you should have read it → das hätten Sie lesen sollen
   you could have read it → das hätten Sie lesen können

Frequently, these are erroneously translated as:

   das sollten Sie gelesen haben ('it was alleged that you had read it'!)
   das könnten Sie gelesen haben ('you might have read it'!)

Further comparisons between English and German would lead us from the area of form and distribution even farther into considerations of meaning. In conclusion, reference is made to Diver (1963 and 1964) for the conjugational patterns of English modals and their meanings.

The main differences between the finite verb forms of English and German result from the more elaborate morphology of the latter in the modification for person and number (PSNM), a phenomenon which is sufficiently familiar to be amply illustrated by a single example:

| I speak | ich spreche |
|---|---|
| you speak | du sprichst |
| he speaks | er spricht |
| we speak | wir sprechen |
| you speak | ihr sprecht |
| they speak | sie sprechen |

In this table, the departures from the base forms *speak-* and *sprech-* are in bold-face type; the greater luxuriance of forms in German is evident. It might be added at this point that the picture above applies also to the subjunctive forms (SJNC) of each language: whereas German has a fairly complete and consistent conjugation of subjunctive forms, the English subjunctive is a fossil, the existence of which has to be reconstructed on the basis of a single contrast, i. e., that of *he speak-s* vs. *he speak-Ø* of the third person singular of the present tense, and from the more complete contrasts obtaining in the conjugation of the verb *be*.

CHAPTER 10

THE FINITE CLAUSE TYPES OF ENGLISH

Up to this point, we have described the formation of the infrastructure and the modification of the tagmeme VERB in that infrastructure, noting that one of the possible changes which the English verb could undergo was finitization (FNTZ). The next step in the formation of a finite clause involves a further set of transformations which are applied to this finitized infrastructure. These transformations are rather more complicated in English than in German, and fall into three large classes: first, those which may be called "basic transformations"; second, a group of transformations which help to solve the problem of rearranging the word material of the clause according to the principles of topic and comment, and which may hence be called "topic-comment redistribution transformations"; and third, as a special, though separate case of the latter, a series of transformations involving the introductory element *there*, a group which will be referred to as "THERE-transformations." We shall examine these groups in this order.

## *The Basic Transformations*

The basic transformations sometimes serve the general purpose of all of these transformations, namely, of bringing the sequence of syntactic elements arising from the prescriptions governing the formation of the infrastructure more into harmony with the arrangement dictated by the topic-comment principle. More frequently, these transformations have the specialized function of communicating what might be called the "structural meaning" of the utterance, e. g., the difference between a statement and a yes-no question:

John is going down town. (statement)
Is John going down town? (yes-no question)

In the following presentation, the seven transformations are arranged in order of increasing complexity. However, it should be noted that all of the finite clauses of English are generated by the application of just one rule – topicalization (T) – which is applied to one or more elements in the clause in a certain prescribed sequence (cf. in this connection Live 1967).

*Basic Transformation 1: T / TRMAV*

The first transformation which a finitized infrastructure of English may undergo is the topicalization of the terminal adverb (TRMAV), a procedure which is exemplified in the following derivation:

   IS, FNTZ: John is going down town tomorrow

The symbols "IS, FNTZ" signify that the phrase following them has been composed in accordance with the requirements specified for the formation of the infrastructure, and for the common and finite modifications of the verb.

   T / TRMAV: tomorrow John is going down town
   SOP: "Tomorrow John is going down town."

Only the terminal adverb may undergo this transformation; the topicalization of the verb complement phrase (VCPhr) *down town* leads to an unacceptable utterance:

   ? ? ? down town John is going tomorrow

– hence the specification in the symbol "T / TRMAV."

*Basic Transformation 2: T / AUX1*

In the chapter on the morphology of the verb, we discovered that the lexical verb in English might be preceded by as many as four auxiliaries:

   AUX1 + AUX2 + AUX3 + AUX4 + LEXVB

This transformation involves the topicalization of the first of these, an operation which will appear a number of times in this section. By itself, it produces two kinds of clauses: yes-no questions, and non-introduced contrary-to-fact clauses. The former is generated in the following way:

   IS, FNTZ: John is going down town tomorrow

T / AUX1: is John going down town tomorrow
SOP: "Is John going down town tomorrow? "

The rule applies whether there are one, two, three, or four auxiliaries present, e. g.:

IS, FNTZ: John could have been being watched
T / AUX1: could John have been being watched
SOP: "Could John have been being watched? "

However, when the lexical verb alone is present in the finitized infrastructure, i. e., when no auxiliaries are present, the hidden auxiliary DO, which is otherwise not expressed, is topicalized, as in this illustration:

IS, FNTZ: John goes home every weekend

If we are to topicalize the first auxiliary, we must regard the form *goes* as consisting of the morphemes *DO + go + s*. On this assumption, the rule T / AUX1 can be applied to this case as well:

T / AUX1: DO+s John go- home every weekend
SOP: "Does John go home every weekend? "

As we will see again and again in the course of this chapter, the verb BE in English departs in many cases from the patterns represented by lexical, i. e., other verbs. As an exception to the foregoing remarks about the hidden auxiliary DO, one-word forms of the verb BE behave syntactically as though they themselves were AUX1, i. e., the form of BE is topicalized rather than the expected form of the hidden auxiliary DO:

IS, FNTZ: John is at home today
T / AUX1: DO+s John be- at home today
SOP: ? ? ? "Does John be at home today? "

T / AUX1: is John at home today
SOP: ! "Is John at home today? "

Cases where the form of BE is accompanied by an auxiliary verb are treated as in the first example above:

IS, FNTZ: John has been here for a long time
T / AUX1: has John been here for a long time
SOP: "Has John been here for a long time? "

Only where we have a one-word form of BE do we have an exception to the rule prescribing the topicalization of DO.

The second clause type generated by the transformation T / AUX1 is that of nonintroduced contrary-to-fact clauses. The typical case is represented by the following derivation:

IS: SOMEONE decide this promptly
PASV: this be decided promptly BY SOMEONE
CRLV: this have been decided promptly BY SOMEONE
PAST: this had been decided promptly BY SOMEONE

We have observed that there are few morphological differences between indicative and subjunctive forms in English. Hence, the following morphological change has no visible effect, though, on the analogy of other verbs, it must be included:

SJNC: this had been decided promptly BY SOMEONE
PSNM: this had been decided promptly BY SOMEONE
T / AUX1: had this been decided promptly BY SOMEONE
D / EE: had this been decided promptly . . . .

Ordinarily this would be embedded in an independent clause, a step which we will omit for the sake of simplicity:

SOP: "Had this been decided promptly, (then . . . . )"

When a one-word lexical verb is present in this construction, it is not possible to express and topicalize the verb DO:

IS: John write the letter
PAST: John wrote (= DO+write+ed) the letter
SJNC, PSNM: John wrote (= DO+write+ed) the letter
T / AUX1: DO+ed John write- the letter
SOP: ? ? ? "Did John write the letter, (then . . . . )"

Here the speaker of English is forced to resort to an alternative structure and to insert the conjunction *if*:

I / CONJ: if + John wrote the letter
SOP: ! "If John wrote the letter, (then . . . . )"

On the other hand, when the verb is emphasized, the form of DO appears, but is not topicalized:

I / CONJ: if + John DO+ed write- the letter
SOP: ! "If John *did* write the letter, (then . . . . )"

When the verb is a one-word form of BE, it functions as before as though it were a first auxiliary, e. g.:

IS: I be in charge
PAST, SJNC, PSNM: I were in charge
T / AUX1: were I in charge
SOP: ! "Were I in charge, (then . . . . )"

However, even when emphasized, the verb BE is not preceded by the auxiliary DO, e. g.:

IS, FNTZ: I were in charge
I / CONJ: if + I were in charge
SOP: ? ? ? "If I *did* be in charge, (then . . . . )"

SOP: ! "If I *were* in charge, (then . . . . )"

This contrasts with the pattern represented by the phrase *If John DID write the letter* above, and again points up the difference between lexical verbs and BE in English.


*Basic Transformation 3: ITRGZ, T / AUX1, T / ITRG*

The two previous transformations consisted of only one operation each: the movement of a single element to the beginning of the clause. The present transformation differs from those in that the procedure of topicalization is applied to two elements, the first auxiliary and then to an interrogativized element of the infrastructure. An "interrogativized" element (ITRG) is one which has been changed from the form in which it stands in the infrastructure to that which would pose a question to which the interrogativized element would be the answer. Thus, the phrases *at home, in Boston, at the ball game,* could all be interrogativized as WHERE, the expressions *John, Aunt Sally, Mr. Magoo* as WHO or WHOM, the words *yesterday, today,* and *tomorrow* as WHEN, and so forth. It is in this interrogativized form that the element participates in the sequence of operations which constitute this basic transformation.

The result of Basic Transformation 3 is the information question, an example of which follows:

IS, FNTZ: John has written the letter

At this point, any nominal or adverbial element could be interrogativized. For reasons which will shortly become apparent, we first interrogativize an element other than the grammatical subject, namely, the object *the letter*:

ITRGZ: John has written WHAT (→ EQ)

Notice that interrogativization does not change the position of the interrogativized expression, merely its form. Notice, too, that the utterance at this stage of its derivation has the form of an emphatic question (EQ), one in which the interrogative element is not the topic, but the comment. This kind of question and its accompanying intonation pattern are often suggested by various typographical devices, e. g.:

SOP: "John has written *WHAT*?!?!"

Continuing the derivation, we note that the first element to be topicalized is the first auxiliary (AUX1):

T / AUX1: has John written WHAT (→ EQ)

Under some circumstances, this sequence, too, can be used as an emphatic question (EQ). It is only at this point, however, that the interrogativized element (ITRG) can be topicalized:

T / ITRG: WHAT has John written
SOP: "What has John written? "

As was observed in connection with Basic Transformation 2, lexical verbs without expressed auxiliaries must be regarded as containing the "hidden" auxiliary DO. In other respects, the derivation proceeds as above:

IS, FNTZ: John wrote (= DO+write+ed) the letter
ITRGZ: John wrote (= DO+write+ed) WHAT (→ EQ)
T / AUX1: DO+ed John write- WHAT (→ EQ)
T / ITRG: WHAT DO+ed John write-
SOP: "What did John write? "

We have also noted that one-word forms of the verb BE, instead of containing the hidden auxiliary DO, function as though they were first auxiliaries, as in this derivation:

IS, FNTZ: John was here yesterday
ITRGZ: John was WHERE yesterday (→ EQ)
T / AUX1: was John WHERE yesterday (→ EQ)

T / ITRG: WHERE was John yesterday
SOP: "Where was John yesterday? "

Our examples thus far have contained a noun object, *the letter*, and the predicate adverb *here*. It was suggested in passing that the subject, when interrogativized, behaves differently from such adverbs and other nominal elements. This is true, but only in the sense that the rules and patterns thus presented seem at various points to be, not incorrect or inapplicable, but redundant. The value of the generative procedure is that a properly conceived and formulated set of rules will apply ideally to all cases of the structure which it is supposed to generate. The rules used in the examples above apply both to cases where the interrogativized element is not the subject, and to those where the subject undergoes this change — hence they are of the widest possible applicability. Outside of a generative framework such as the present one, they would, to be sure, be open to the charge of being unnecessary. Let us illustrate this point with the first of three examples:

IS, FNTZ: John has written the letter
ITRGZ: WHO has written the letter

Though one might assume that the question has already been formed at this point, let us continue through the sequence of operations which were established above:

T / AUX1: has WHO written the letter ($\rightarrow$ EQ)
T / ITRG: WHO has written the letter
SOP: "Who has written the letter? "

Thus it can be seen that the changes which comprise this operation will also produce an acceptable information question when the interrogative element is the subject, even though some of the steps might seem superfluous. It should be added, on the other hand, that the emphatic question

"Has *WHO* written the letter ?!?!"

can only be understood as arising in the course of a derivation such as the one which our rules require.

When the lexical verb is not accompanied by any auxiliaries, it conforms to the T / AUX1 rule by topicalizing the hidden form DO. When, in the course of the derivation, the topicalized DO-form and the lexical verb again come into a contiguous position, the two forms reunite, as it were. This peculiarity of English verb morphology is represented in the following derivation:

IS, FNTZ: John wrote (= DO+write+ed) the letter
ITRGZ: WHO wrote (= DO+write+ed) the letter
T / AUX1: DO+ed WHO write- the letter ($\rightarrow$ EQ)

At this point, the two parts of the verb are separated by the interrogative WHO. When that form is topicalized, the two are again in a contiguous position:

T / ITRG: WHO DO+ed write- the letter ($\rightarrow$ EQ)

If the auxiliary bears an accent, it retains its separate identity in the utterance, as, e.g., in this context:

SOP: ! "(If *you* didn't write the letter, then) who *did* write the letter? !? !"

If, on the other hand, the context does not require the accenting of this auxiliary, then it is again fused with the lexical verb:

T / ITRG: WHO (DO+ed & write- $\rightarrow$ DO+write+ed $\rightarrow$) wrote the letter

which is the final stage of the derivation:

SOP: ! "Who wrote the letter? "

Again, one-word forms of the verb BE behave syntactically, not as the verb *write* above, but as if they were first auxiliaries. This also leads to an apparent redundancy of operations, one which we retain, however, for the sake of consistency. This condition is represented in the following derivation:

IS, FNTZ: John was here yesterday
ITRGZ: WHO was here yesterday
T / AUX1: ? ? ? DO+ed WHO be-here yesterday
  ! was WHO here yesterday ($\rightarrow$ EQ)
T / ITRG: WHO was here yesterday
SOP: "Who was here yesterday? "

Thus, despite a variety of attendant circumstances, we find that the important category of information questions can be generated by the morphosyntactic transformation of interrogativization (ITRGZ), followed by the topicalization of the first auxiliary (T / AUX 1) and of the interrogativized element (T / ITRG). As conditions, however, we must stipulate that one-word forms of lexical verbs be regarded as containing the hidden auxiliary DO, and that one-word forms of BE behave as though they were first auxiliaries.

*Basic Transformation 4: ITRGZ, RLTVZ; T / ITRG, RLTV*

Basic Transformation 3, just described, generated direct information questions. As speakers of English know, the indirect form of such questions often differs from the form of the question when quoted or rendered indirectly. Basic Transformation 4 generates such indirect questions, and, as we will see later in this section, relative clauses as well. As in the case of direct questions, we must distinguish between those cases where the interrogative is an element other than the grammatical subject, and those where the subject is the interrogative; furthermore, it is necessary to describe three situations in each of these categories, that where the lexical verb is accompanied by one or more auxiliaries, that where a lexical verb stands alone, and finally, that where the verb in question is a one-word form of BE.

In our analysis above, we generated the direct question:

"What has John written? "

The indirect form of this question may be derived from the same infrastructure, in the following way:

IS, FNTZ: John has written the letter
ITRGZ: John has written WHAT

If this were to become a direct question, the next step would be to topicalize the first auxiliary. From the generative point of view, however, the sole difference between direct and indirect questions is the presence of T / AUX1 in the case of the former, its absence in the latter. For the sake of clarity, we will show the place of the T / AUX1 in the derivation, indicating its absence in the case of indirect questions such as these:

T / AUX1: (omitted)
T / ITRG: WHAT John has written
SOP: "(He wants to know) what John has written."

151

This principle‘ applies also in those cases where the lexical verb is the sole form present:

IS, FNTZ: John wrote the letter
ITRGZ: JOHN wrote WHAT

If this were a direct question, we would now topicalize AUX1, and in effect split the verb into two parts, i. e.:

John DO+write+ed WHAT
T / AUX1: DO+ed John write- WHAT

However, this step is unnecessary in the generation of an indirect question:

T / AUX1: (omitted)
T / ITRG: WHAT John wrote
SOP: "(He wants to know) what John wrote."

The principle that indirect questions differ from their direct counterparts only in the absence of T / AUX1 also applies to cases where the verb is a one-word form of BE; the latter functions as though it were a first auxiliary:

IS, FNTZ: John was here yesterday
ITRGZ: John was WHERE yesterday
T / AUX1: (omitted)
T / ITRG: WHERE John was yesterday
SOP: "(He wants to know) where John was yesterday."

Where the interrogative element is the grammatical subject, our rules apply; to be sure, they might be regarded as redundant outside of this systematic framework:

IS, FNTZ: John has written the letter
ITRGZ: WHO has written the letter
T / AUX1: (omitted)

Since the interrogative element is already in initial position, the next operation, T / ITRG, accomplishes nothing, but is retained nevertheless in order to maintain a simple, consistent, and widely applicable set of rules for these patterns:

T / ITRG: WHO has written the letter
SOP: "(He wants to know) who has written the letter."

One-word forms of lexical verbs are treated in the following manner in the generation of indirect questions:

IS, FNTZ: John wrote the letter
ITRGZ: WHO wrote the letter
T / AUX1: (omitted)
T / ITRG: WHO wrote the letter
SOP: "(He wants to know) who wrote the letter."

again it was unnecessary to split the verb into a lexical component and a hidden auxiliary, i. e., into *DO+write+ed*, because T / AUX1 was omitted.

One-word forms of BE characteristically function as if they were first auxiliaries, but this peculiarity plays no great role in the generation of indirect questions, e. g.:

IS, FNTZ: John was here yesterday
ITRGZ: WHO was here yesterday
T / AUX1: (omitted)
, T / ITRG: WHO was here yesterday
SOP: "(He wants to know) who was here yesterday."

As a kind of summary, it might be helpful to compare Basic Transformations 3 and 4 at this point, so as to show how the omission of a single step, T / AUX1, can result in a variety of the differences between direct and indirect questions. In each of the groups of three below, the first example will be that of a lexical verb with an expressed auxiliary, the second, a one-word lexical verb, and the third, a one-word form of BE.

| direct question | indirect question |
|---|---|
| (Basic Transformation 3: | (Basic Transformation 4: |
| ITRGZ; T / AUX1; T / ITRG) | ITRGZ; . . . .; T / ITRG) |

### ITRG ≠ subject

| 1) What has John written? | . . . what John has written. |
|---|---|
| 2) What did John write? | . . . what John wrote. |
| 3) Where was John yesterday? | . . . where John was yesterday. |

### ITRG = subject

| 1) Who has written the letter? | . . . who has written the letter. |
|---|---|
| 2) Who wrote the letter? | . . . who wrote the letter. |
| 3) Who was here yesterday? | . . . who was here yesterday. |

153

There is another function which Basic Transformation 4 has: the generation of relative clauses. As a preliminary to the rearrangement of these clauses by topicalization, however, we have the morpho-syntactic change called "relativization" (RLTVZ). In this process, a noun or adverbial expression is transformed into its relative counter-part: *a house, the letter, those books* become *WHICH; John, Mrs. Miller, the Senator* become *WHO* or *WHOM; at the house, down town*, etc. become *WHERE*. It is also possible for the object of a preposition to be relativized, e. g., *about that book* is relativized as *about WHICH*. This has certain consequences for the patterns of topicalization which may result, as will be shown presently.

The generation of relative clauses is very similar to that of in-direct questions, and so a few representative derivations will suffice to give an idea of how these are produced. The following is a typical example in which the relativized word is not the subject:

IS, FNTZ: I wrote the letter to my friend
RLTVZ: I wrote WHICH to my friend
T / RLTV: WHICH I wrote to my friend
SOP: "( . . . the letter) which I wrote to my friend."

In this example, as well as in those which follow, the otherwise essential step of embedding will be omitted for the sake of simplic-ity, unless it is necessary to clarify the point being made by the example. In the next case, the relativized word is the subject:

IS, FNTZ: the book was returned to the library
RLTVZ: WHICH was returned to the library
T / RLTV: WHICH was returned to the library
SOP: "( . . . the book) which was returned to the library."

In English, it is possible to omit some relative elements, though there are specific limitations as to what may be deleted: first, the deleted relative element must have replaced a noun; second, it may not have been a subject noun; and third, the relative element must be contiguous with its antecedent in the matrix clause. The range of possibilities permitted by these conditions is illustrated by the following examples. First, the deleted relative element must be a noun:

IS, FNTZ: I met him in the city
RLTVZ: I met him WHERE
T / RLTV: WHERE I met him

E / RLCL (= relative clause): (we talked about it in the city) WHERE I met him

D / RLTV: . . . in the city I met him

SOP: ? ? ? "We talked about it in the city I met him."

As is evident, the deletion of the relative adverb *WHERE* leads to an unacceptable utterance. The second condition which restricts the deletion of relative elements is that the deleted element may not be a subject noun. The following derivation tests this condition:

IS, FNTZ: a topic came up frequently

RLTVZ: WHICH came up frequently

T / RLTV: WHICH came up frequently

E / RLCL: (that is a topic) WHICH came up frequently

D / RLTV: that is a topic . . . came up frequently

SOP: ? ? ? "That is a topic came up frequently."

When the relativized noun is not the subject in its clause, and is contiguous to its antecedent when embedded, then deletion is optional, as in this case:

IS, FNTZ: we discussed a topic frequently

RLTVZ: we discussed WHICH frequently

T / RLTV: WHICH we discussed frequently

E / RLCL: (that is a topic) WHICH we discussed frequently

SOP: ! "That is a topic which we discussed frequently."

D / RLTV: (that is a topic) . . . we discussed frequently

SOP: ! "That is a topic we discussed frequently."

Both clause patterns are acceptable, the more complete form tending toward the style of the written language, the form with deletion inclining a bit toward the colloquial.

In the foregoing examples and in our discussion of them, each relativized expression has been a single unit. It is a feature of English structure that some syntactic units containing a relative element can be split in the process of generation. This occurs in the case of prepositional phrases which contain a relative element as the object of the preposition. The following derivation will show what options are open to the speaker in connection with this pattern:

IS, FNTZ: we have heard a great deal about a young man

RLTVZ: we have heard a great deal about WHOM

The next step is either (1) the topicalization of the syntactic element in which the relative form stands, i. e., *about WHOM*, or (2) the topicalization of the relative form itself, i. e., *WHOM*:

>T / RLTV: (1) about WHOM are have heard a great deal
>(2) WHOM we have heard a great deal about

Upon embedding, this leads to two different patterns:

>E / RLCL: (1) (that is a young man) about WHOM we have heard a great deal
>(2) (that is a young man) WHOM we have heard a great deal about
>SOP: (1) ! "That is a young man about whom we have heard a great deal."
>(2) ! "That is a young man whom we have heard a great deal about."

The first of these clauses is not subject to any further modification. In the case of the second, however, it is possible to develop it further by the deletion of the relative pronoun, since it fulfils all three conditions, i. e., it is a noun, it is not the subject, and it stands in contiguous position to its antecedent — even though it is only part of a syntactic element:

>E / RLCL: (2) (that is a young man) WHOM we have heard a great deal about
>D / RLTV: (that is a young man) . . . we have heard a great deal about
>SOP: ! "That is a young man we have heard a great deal about."

It must be stressed that the deletion of a relativized object of a preposition is possible only when it has been separated from its preposition by topicalization, and contiguous with its antecedent in the matrix clause.

Traditionally, purists have objected to this kind of deletion. In practice, however, many if not most speakers of English appear to subscribe to the dictum attributed to Winston Churchill, namely, that a preposition is a bad word to end a sentence with. As far as our generative analysis is concerned, these structures seem in every respect to arise systematically through rules which apply to related structures, so that one cannot say that there is any reason to regard them as distortions or aberrations of the language.

In an earlier chapter, we identified as part of the infrastructure of English the tagmeme containing the intraverbal adverbs (ITVAV), and noted that the lexical items comprising that tagmeme could be divided into restrictive and nonrestrictive intraverbal adverbs. The criterion by which this distinction was established was partly semantic and partly syntactical. As to their meaning, all of these words, e. g., *hardly, scarcely, only, seldom, never, rarely,* etc. shared a privative or restrictive connotation, but more conspicuous and easier to define was the effect which they induced on their clause when they were topicalized: as the formulas above suggest, these restrictive intraverbal adverbs (RSAV) can be topicalized if, and only if, their topicalization is preceded by that of the first auxiliary. This feature of English structure is demonstrated in the following examples:

IS, FNTZ: I have seldom heard such nonsense

Notice that the restrictive intraverbal adverb *seldom* follows the first auxiliary, as required by the rules for the formation of the infrastructure. Now, if that adverb is topicalized, an unacceptable utterance results:

T / RSAV: seldom I have heard such nonsense
SOP: ? ? ? "Seldom I have heard such nonsense."

This step is possible, but only after the topicalization of the first auxiliary:

T / AUX1: have I seldom heard such nonsense
T / RSAV: seldom have I heard such nonsense
SOP: ! "Seldom have I heard such nonsense."

The topicalization of the first auxiliary follows the pattern noted earlier for one-word forms of lexical verbs, in connection with which the hidden auxiliary DO comes into play:

IS, FNTZ: John seldom went (= DO+go+ed) home on weekends
T / AUX1: DO+ed John seldom go- home on weekends
T / RSAV: seldom DO+ed John go- home on weekends
SOP: ! "Seldom did John go home on weekends."

In like fashion, the conditions attending the use of one-word forms of BE apply here, too:

IS, FNTZ: John was seldom in the dorms on weekends
T / AUX1: was John seldom in the dorms on weekends
T / RSAV: seldom was John in the dorms on weekends
SOP: ! "Seldom was John in the dorms on weekends."

Thus, the rule T / AUX1 follows the patterns identified earlier in every way.

### Basic Transformation 6: AVBLZ / FF&AUX1; T / AV&AUX1

With Basic Transformation 6, we encounter a phenomenon which is quite common in spoken English, a finite clause pattern which we shall call the "confirmative correlative sentence." This occurs most often in conversations, where it serves to indicate the second party's agreement with the previous utterance, as in this exchange:

A: "John has gone down town this morning."
B: "So he has."

The phrase *So he has* is correlated with A's statement, in that it indicates B's support or confirmation of it.

Since this transformation generates a confirmation of a preceding utterance, it can only be produced within a specific context. Hence, the context utterance must be relied on to show what the infrastructure of the confirmative correlative sentence must have contained. This observation leads us to the following procedure: first, a context utterance must be postulated:

CONTEXT: "John has gone down town this morning."

On the basis of this context, the following finitized infrastructure may be assumed:

IS, FNTZ: he has gone down town this morning

What now happens is that every element in this infrastructure which follows the first auxiliary (FF&AUX1) is reduced by the morphosyntactic process of adverbialization (AVBLZ) to the particle *SO*:

AVBLZ / FF&AUX1: he has SO

The final step in the derivation is the topicalization of this adverbial form which stands for the word material which followed the first auxiliary (AV&AUX1), i. e., the form *SO*:

158

T / AV&AUX1: SO he has
SOP: "So he has."

As in most of the other transformations in this section, a one-word form of a lexical verb contains the hidden auxiliary DO. The following derivations illustrates a confirmative correlative sentence with such a verb form:

CONTEXT: "John plays the piano well."
IS, FNTZ: he plays (= DO+play+s) the piano well

At this point, everything following the first auxiliary *DO+s* is adverbialized:

AVBLZ / FF&AUX1: he DO+s SO
T / AV&AUX1: SO he DO+s
SOP: "So he does."

Not surprisingly, one-word forms of the verb BE function, not as the lexical verb above, but as though they were first auxiliaries. This is exemplified in the following derivation:

CONTEXT: "John's name is among the winners."
IS, FNTZ: it is among the winners
AVBLZ / FF&AUX1: it is SO
T / AV&AUX1: SO it is
SOP: "So it is."

Because of the influence of the context in the case of these confirmative correlative sentences, we have passed beyond the limits of syntax in English, and are clearly entering into the area of context or discourse grammar. On the other hand, the beginnings such a grammar may be found in the patterns of deletion, substitution, and topicalization such as those above, and those to be discussed in the following sections of this chapter (cf. also Gunter 1966).

*Basic Transformation 7: AVBLZ / FF&AUX1; T / AUX1;
T / AV&AUX1*

As a glance at this caption reveals, the difference between Basic Transformations 6 and 7 is the presence in the latter of T / AUX1, the topicalization of the first auxiliary, in the sequence of generative procedures. Basic Transformation 7 produces a similar, yet distinc-

159

tive kind of sentence, on which we may call the "comparative correlative sentence." This kind of sentence is "correlative" in that it appears in relation with another utterance which constitutes a context for it; it is "comparative" in that it extends the general content of the context utterance to another person or entity, thus creating a kind of comparison. The following is an example of an affirmative comparative sentence:

A: "Fred is going to the movies this evening."
B: "So is John."

We can explain the brief statement *So is John* in much the same way as we analyzed the confirmative correlative sentences generated by Basic Transformation 6: by the adverbialization (AVBLZ) of the forms (FF) following the first auxiliary (&AUX1). On the other hand, an additional step is clearly required, because the grammatical subject *John* is preceded by the finite verb, i. e., the auxiliary *is*. This difference is accounted for by the incorporation of T / AUX1 into the derivation, which takes place as follows:

CONTEXT: "Fred is going to the movies this evening."
IS, FNTZ: John is going to the movies this evening, too

Here, everything following the first auxiliary *is* is reduced to the adverb *SO*:

AVBLZ / FF&AUX1: John is SO

At this point, the first auxiliary is topicalized:

T / AUX1: is John SO

And finally, the adverb is also topicalized:

T / AV&AUX1: SO is John
SOP: "So is John."

The rationale for these Basic Transformations, 6 as well as 7, must be looked for in the topic-comment principle which, mediately or immediately, underlies so many of these syntactic variants. In both cases, the first element is the topic, the last, the comment. The comment in the context becomes the topic of the correlative sentence:

160

|  | context | | response | |
|---|---|---|---|---|
|  | topic | comment | topic | comment |
| confirmative: | John is SO | → | SO John | is |
| comparative: | Fred is SO | → | SO is | John |

It is because the hearer interprets them in light of this principle that the sequences *so John is* and *so is John* have a structural meaning, one which allows the hearer to reduce the bulk of his response to the subject and verb plus the adverb *SO*, and which allows him either to confirm the context utterance by commentizing the verb *is*, or to relate another entity to the context utterance by commentizing the entity to be compared, in the example, the word *John*.

Again, one-word lexical verbs and one-word forms of BE require special mention. As to the former, the lexical verb again manifests the hidden auxiliary DO when topicalized:

CONTEXT: "John reads Latin."
IS, FNTZ: Fred reads (= DO+read+s) Latin, too
AVBLZ / FF&AUX1: Fred DO+s SO
T / AUX1: DO+s Fred SO
T / AV&AUX1: SO DO+s Fred
SOP: "So does Fred."

One-word forms of BE function as though they were first auxiliaries:

CONTEXT: "John was sick yesterday."
IS, FNTZ: Fred was sick yesterday, too
AVBLZ / FF&AUX1: Fred was SO
T / AUX1: was Fred SO
T / AV&AUX1: SO was Fred
SOP: "So was Fred."

All of the examples of comparative correlative clauses presented above were affirmative in character. When the context utterance contains a negative adverb, certain adjustments must be made in the adverb which represents the word material followed by the first auxiliary (AV&AUX1). Whereas, in the case of affirmative sentences, this material with the adverb *too* is reduced to the form *SO*, in negative comparative correlative sentences the combination of the word material present, including the negative adverb and the form *either*, result in the word *NEITHER*. This change is exemplified in the following derivation:

CONTEXT: "John hasn't left yet."
IS, FNTZ: Fred hasn't left yet, either

Notice that the negative adverb here is enclitic to the first auxiliary; in the following step, however, it fuses with the other elements in the word *NEITHER*:

AVBLZ / FF&AUX1: Fred has+n't . . . either →
  Fred has NEITHER
T / AUX1: has Fred NEITHER
T / AV&AUX1: NEITHER has Fred
SOP: "Neither has Fred."

In like fashion, one-word lexical verbs and one-word forms of BE manifest their typical patterns of generation. First, the former:

CONTEXT: "John doesn't read Latin."
IS, FNTZ: Fred doesn't read Latin, either

Note here that the first auxiliary is already present, because of the negative adverb which is enclitic to it:

AVBLZ / FF&AUX1: Fred does+n't . . . either →
  Fred does NEITHER
T / AUX1: does Fred NEITHER
T / AV&AUX1: NEITHER does Fred
SOP: "Neither does Fred."

One-word forms of BE function like first auxiliaries, even as to the prescription that the negative adverb is enclitic to the first auxiliary:

CONTEXT: "John isn't here today."
IS, FNTZ: Fred isn't here today, either
AVBLZ / FF&AUX1: Fred is+n't . . . either →
  Fred is NEITHER
T / AUX1: is Fred NEITHER
T / AV&AUX1: NEITHER is Fred
SOP: "Neither is Fred."


*The Seven Basic Transformations: A Summary*

With this, the series of seven basic transformations comes to a close. As a summary, we list below the various procedures by which

162

the sentences patterns generated by them were produced, doing so in such a way as to throw their differences and similarities into relief. The various steps are indicated in the following table.

| Basic Transformation | – – – Z | T / AUX1 | T / – – – |
|---|---|---|---|
| Ø (zero): untopicalized statements; indirect yes-no questions . . | – – – | – – – | – – – |
| 1: topicalized statements . . . | – – – | – – – | T / TRMAV |
| 2: direct yes-no questions; non-introduced contrary-to-fact clauses . . . . . . . | – – – | T / AUX1 | – – – |
| 3: direct information questions . | ITRGZ | T / AUX1 | T / ITRG |
| 4a: indirect information questions | ITRGZ | – – – | T / ITRG |
| 4b: relative clauses . . . . . | RLTVZ | – – – | T / RLTV |
| 5: statements with topicalized restrictive intraverbal adverbs . | – – – | T / AUX1 | T / RSAV |
| 6: confirmative correlative sentences. . . . . . . . . | AVBLZ / FF&AUX1 | – – – | T / AV&AUX1 |
| 7: comparative correlative sentences. . . . . . . . | AVBLZ / FF&AUX1 | T / AUX1 | T / AV&AUX1 |

The table shows, first of all, that a specific clause type may be generated by one, two, or three operations on a finitized infrastructure. In the first column are the morphosyntactic "Z-rules," specifying certain patterns of reduction of word material in the infrastructure. The second column shows the topicalization of the first auxiliary, where applicable. In the last column, additional topicalizations of nonverbal elements are indicated. These basic transformations by no means exhaust the changes which may be made in an infrastructure which has been finitized like those above. For a different set of transformations, we turn to those related to the redistribution of word material according to the principles of topic and comment.

## Topic-Comment Redistribution Transformations

In the preceding section, we noted how the basic transformations seem to shift various elements from within the infrastructure to the important topic position at the beginning of the clause. All of these transformations had the common feature of relating the clause more closely to the larger context of the discourse by placing a linking element in the topic position; the clearest example of this is the relative clause. The topic-comment redistribution transformations have a related, yet different function, one which arises chiefly from the rigidity of the English infrastructure. It requires little imagination to conceive of cases where the placement of lexical items required by the fundamental structure of the language – i. e., the infrastructure – might conflict with the communicative priorities imposed by the context as reflected in the topic-comment principle. The transformations to which we now turn are ways by which the speaker can redistribute the components of the infrastructure so that the finished utterance conforms more closely to the arrangement called for by the context. These transformations fall into three classes: first, those which contains forms of the verb BE; second, those containing lexical verbs, a category which is further subdivided into those with one-word lexical verbs, and those with expressed auxiliaries. We will treat each one of these groups in this order.

### TCR-Transformations with BE

These transformations may occur when the verb BE is followed by either an adjective or an adverb as a verb complement – in more familiar terminology, a predicate adjective or a predicate adverb. The operations involved are, as before, topicalization, first applied to FV+FF, i. e., the entire complex of elements beginning with the finite verb (FV) and extending to the end of the infrastructure, and then to the postverbal adjective (PVAJ) or postverbal adverb (PVAV). These combinations are identified in the following diagrams.

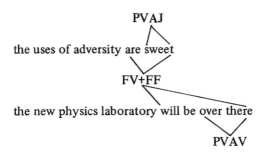

PVAJ

the uses of adversity are sweet

FV+FF

the new physics laboratory will be over there

PVAV

The actual redistribution of these elements is shown in these derivations:

IS, FNTZ: the uses of adversity are sweet

At this point, the entire phrase consisting of the finite verb and everything following it is topicalized:

T / FV+FF: are sweet the uses of adversity

In the next step, a part of this phrase — the postverbal adjective — is again topicalized:

T / PVAJ: sweet are the uses of adversity
SOP: "Sweet are the uses of adversity."

The next example illustrates this procedure as applied to a postverbal adverb, and, in addition, shows that these rules apply to verb complexes containing auxiliaries, too:

IS, FNTZ: the new physics laboratory will be over there
T / FV+FF: will be over there the new physics laboratory
T / PVAV: over there will be the new physics laboratory
SOP: "Over there will be the new physics laboratory."

As a result of these transformations, the position of subject and predicate adjective or adverb has been reversed, so as to conform to the arrangement according the topic and comment — a sequence which is in turn suggested by the content and context of the utterances themselves.

Cases where finitized infrastructures containing one-word forms of lexical verbs are not numerous, but some are quite familiar. Again we may interpret these as modifications of the infrastructure by successive acts of topicalization applied to specific elements. A typical case, with its relevant elements indicated, is the following:

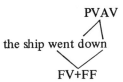

This infrastructure is modified, much like those examples containing the verb BE, by the topicalization, first of the phrase FV+FF, and then of the postverbal adverb (PVAV):

IS, FNTZ: the ship went down
T / FV+FF: went down the ship
T / PVAV: down went the ship
SOP: "Down went the ship."

A variety of familiar expressions may be analyzed as being generated by this pattern of transformation, e. g.:

IS, FNTZ: the weasel goes pop
T / FV+FF: goes pop the weasel
T / PVAV: pop goes the weasel
SOP: "Pop goes the weasel!"

It is clear that the effect of this transformation is to place the subject in the comment position, i. e., in final or near-final position. If the subject is a pronoun, however, it lacks, by virtue of its character as a surrogate for a noun, sufficient communicative importance to stand as comment in this kind of sentence, particularly when communicative importance is regarded as the justification for substantial rearrangements in word order. In many cases, the role of comment passes by default, as it were, to other elements, not infrequently the verb. If we pronominalize the subject of the example used above, *the ship went down*, we have the finitized infrastructure:

IS, FNTZ: it went down

For purposes of illustration, let us apply the same series of transformations to this as to the original infrastructure:

T / FV+FF: went down it
T / PVAV: down went it
SOP: ? ? ? "Down went it."

The pronoun *it* in this sentence is so clearly subordinate in communicative importance to other elements that the sentence sounds awkward and badly formed — although the sequence of syntactic elements is exactly the same as in the original phrase, *down went the ship*. In cases like the one under consideration, the English language admits of an alternative pattern of distribution which is achieved by the omission of the transformation T / FV+FF in the generation of the utterance. This applies to the example above in the following way:

IS, FNTZ: it went down
T / FV+FF: (omitted)
T / PVAV: down it went
SOP: ! "Down it went!"

The same sequence of transformations, applied to an infrastructure with a noun subject, generates an utterance of questionable acceptability:

IS, FNTZ: the ship went down
T / VF+FF: (omitted)
T / PVAV: down the ship went
SOP: ? "Down the ship went."

The varying degrees of acceptability of these four utterances:

! down went the ship
? ? ? down went it
! down it went
? down the ship went

depends directly on the coincidence of the most significant lexical item with the comment position. English has evolved a simple way of getting the more important word into this crucial position: by giving the speaker the option of topicalizing FV+FF or of omitting this step in the generation of the utterance. We close this section with another example of this kind, one which has a pronoun subject:

IS, FNTZ: we go away
- (1) T / FV+FF: go away we
  T / PVAV: away go we
  SOP: ? ? ?  "Away go we."
- (2) T / FV+FF: (omitted)
  T / PVAV: away we go
  SOP: !  "Away we go!"

Compared with the verb *go*, the pronoun *we* is so lacking in importance that it cannot possibly serve as the comment.

### TCR-Transformations with Lexical Verbs: Lexical Verbs with Auxiliaries

Without doubt the transformations involving lexical verbs with auxiliaries are the most important TCR-transformations to be discussed in this section, not only because they occur frequently, but also because a full control of idiomatic English is impossible without the ability to use them properly and effectively. In addition to the terms used in the preceding sections of this chapter, we must now introduce a new concept which is of crucial importance in the generation of these structures: the first form of BE (BE1) in the complex of forms which arises in the course of the modification of the verb. At times, BE1 will also be the finite verb (FV); at other times, a verb other than BE will have this function. These possibilities are illustrated in the following sentences:

FV BE1      FF&BE1                                        FV+FF

a man *has been standing there for some time*

In this sentence, the form *has* is the finite verb (FV); the word *been*, however, is the first form of BE (BE1); the phrase *standing there for some time* comprises the forms following BE1 (FF&BE1).

It is often the case that the first form of BE is at the same time the finite verb, as in this sentence:

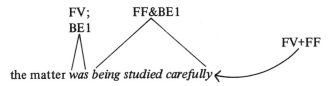

FV;
BE1

FF&BE1

FV+FF

the matter *was being studied carefully*

The word *was* is both FV and BE1; as it happens, there is another form of BE in the sentence, i. e., *being*, but it plays no independent syntactic rule. The expression *being studied carefully* includes the forms following BE1 (FF&BE1). These terms – BE1, AUX1, FF&BE1, and FV+FF – are all involved in various ways in the transformations which have as their object the redistribution of topic and comment. We will discover that the structures which we are about to analyze are generated by the selective topicalization of the phrase FV+FF, of the postverbal adverb (PVAV), and of the forms following the first form of BE which is present in the phrase following FV (FF&BE1). (The treatment of these structures here owes much to Sundby 1970:83 ff.).

The following finitized infrastructure is not untypical of the kind of expression which these patterns of topicalization apply to:

IS, FNTZ: a man in a blue suit was standing in the doorway

The segments of this infrastructure which are affected by this kind of transformation are the following:

the postverbal adverb (PVAV): *in the doorway*
the finite verb, along with the forms which follow it (FV+FF):
*was standing in the doorway*
the first form of BE present in the complex of verb forms (BE1):
*was*
the forms which follow the first form of BE (FF&BE1): *standing in the doorway*

By various patterns of topicalization, it is possible to modify this infrastructure in order to produce three different sequences of elements in which different elements serve as topic. In the first, the postverbal adverb may be topicalized:

IS, FNTZ: a man in a blue suit was standing in the doorway
(1) T / PVAV: in the doorway a man in a blue suit was standing
SOP: "In the doorway, a man in a blue suit was standing."

The remaining sequences require the prior topicalization of the entire verb phrase FV+FF:

169

IS, FNTZ: a man in a blue suit was standing in the doorway

(2) T / FV+FF: was standing in the doorway a man in a blue suit

At this point, two further options emerge. As the first, the postverbal adverb may be topicalized:

(2a) T / PVAV: in the doorway was standing a man in a blue suit
SOP: "In the doorway was standing a man in a blue suit."

Another possibility, perhaps the most common, would be to topicalize all of the forms following the first form of BE:

(2b) T / FF&BE1: standing in the doorway was a man in a blue suit
SOP: "Standing in the doorway was a man in a blue suit."

By means of these patterns of topicalization, the infrastructure with which we started can be made to yield three additional arrangements of its word material:

IS, FNTZ: *a man in a blue suit*$_T$ was standing *in the doorway*$_C$
1: *in the doorway*$_T$ a man in a blue suit was *standing*$_C$
2a: *in the doorway*$_T$ was standing *a man in a blue suit*$_C$
2b: *standing in the doorway*$_T$ was *a man in a blue suit*$_C$

By virtue of these transformations, each of the major syntactic elements can serve both as topic (T) and as comment (C). It is apparent that this feature of English syntax compensates in large measure for the rigidity which obtains in the order of elements in the infrastructure.

One of the distinguishing characteristics of the verb in the sentence above is the presence of one form of BE, a form which derives from the modification LMDR ("limited duration"): *stand* → *BE stand+ING*. A form of BE may also be introduced into the complex of verb forms through the modification PASV ("passive voice"), as in this sentence:

a resistance to inflation must be added to this

This sentence would be generated as follows:

IS: SOMEONE add a resistance to inflation to this
PASV: a resistance to inflation BE added to this BY SOMEONE
MODL, PSNM: a resistance to inflation must be added to this BY SOMEONE

170

D / EE: a resistance to inflation must be added to this . . .
SOP: "A resistance to inflation must be added to this."

The segments of the sentence which are important for these transformations are the same as before:

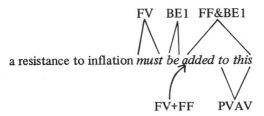

The various TCR-transformations are then applied as in the case of the former example:

IS, FNTZ: a resistance to inflation must be added to this
(1) T / PVAV: to this a resistance to inflation must be added
SOP: "To this, a resistance to inflation must be added."

The two remaining possibilities require the topicalization of the phrase including and following the finite verb:

(2) T / FV+FF: must be added to this a resistance to inflation

As before, the postverbal adverb may now be topicalized:

(2a) T / PVAV: to this must be added a resistance to inflation
SOP: "To this must be added a resistance to inflation."

The last possible arrangement arises from the topicalization of all of the elements following the first form of BE which is present. The verb complex here is *must be added*; in it, *be* is the first (and only) form of BE. This means that *must* and *be* retain their position, but that everything which follows them in the infrastructure is topicalized:

(2b) T / FF&BE1: added to this must be a resistance to inflation
SOP: "Added to this must be a resistance to inflation."

By means of these TCR-transformations, virtually all of the major syntactic elements in sentences of this kind may occupy the topic and comment positions.

In the foregoing analyses, we have modified the infrastructures containing lexical verbs plus their auxiliaries by three patterns of topicalization:

IS, FNTZ:
(1) T / PVAV
(2a) T / FV+FF + T / PVAV
(2b) T / FV+FF + T / FF&BE1

Under certain conditions, one or the other of these possibilities must be excluded. We can identify four such situations which limit the possibilities for topic-comment redistribution by the patterns described above.
The first of these specifies that, when the verb is transitive, and in the active voice, particularly when the object is expressed, then Pattern 2a, i. e., T / FV+FF + T / PVAV, is excluded. This is exemplified in the following derivation:

IS, FNTZ: a man in a blue suit was smoking a cigarette in the doorway

(1) T / PVAV: in the doorway a man in a blue suit was smoking a cigarette
SOP: ! "In the doorway, a man in a blue suit was smoking a cigarette."

(2) T / FV+FF: was smoking a cigarette in the doorway a man in a blue suit

(2a) T / PVAV: in the doorway was smoking a cigarette a man in a blue suit
SOP: ? ? ? "In the doorway was smoking a cigarette a man in a blue suit."

(2b) T / FF&BE1: smoking a cigarette in the doorway was a man in a blue suit
SOP: ! "Smoking a cigarette in the doorway was a man in a blue suit."

A second condition specifies that, when the verb is in the passive voice, and when the postverbal adverb is the instrumental object of the verb, i. e., the agent prepositional phrase, then that adverb cannot be topicalized. This excludes both Patterns 1 and 2a; only Pattern 2b is admissible here. This condition is exemplified by the following derivation:

IS: the committee also examine the candidate's last income tax return

PASV: the candidate's last income tax return be also examined by the committee

PAST, PSNM: the candidate's last income tax return was also examined by the committee

(1) T / PVAV: by the committee the candidate's last income tax return was also examined

SOP: ? ? ? "By the committee, the candidate's last income tax return was also examined."

(2) T / FV+FF: was also examined by the committee the candidate's last income tax return

(2a) T / PVAV: by the committee was also examined the candidate's last income tax return

SOP: ? ? ? "By the committee was also examined the candidate's last income tax return."

(2b) T / FF&BE1: also examined by the committee was the candidate's last income tax return

SOP: ! "Also examined by the committee was the candidate's last income tax return."

It is evident that the agent prepositional phrase is felt to be different from other adverbial prepositional phrases.

According to the third condition, when the auxiliaries contain two forms of BE, then Pattern 2a, T / FV+FF + PVAV, is excluded. This can be seen in the following derivation:

IS, FNTZ: the candidate's last income tax return is also being examined in this investigation

(1) T / PVAV: in this investigation the candidate's last income tax return is also being examined

SOP: ! "In this investigation, the candidate's last income tax return is also being examined."

(2) T / FV+FF: is also being examined in this investigation the candidate's last income tax return

(2a) T / PVAV: in this investigation is also being examined the candidate's last income tax return

SOP: ? ? ? "In this investigation is also being examined the candidate's last income tax return."

(2b) T / FF&BE1: also being examined in this investigation is the candidate's last income tax return
SOP: ! "Also being examined in this investigation is the candidate's last income tax return."

As the fourth and final condition, we note that, when there is no form of BE among the auxiliaries, then Pattern 2 b, T / FV+FF + T / FF&BE1, is excluded by definition; however, the application of these procedures is shown in the following example:

IS, FNTZ: the family of Fleetwood had lived at the village manor

(1) T / PVAV: at the village manor the family of Fleetwood had lived
SOP: ! "At the village manor, the family of Fleetwood had lived."

(2) T / FV+FF: had lived at the village manor the family of Fleetwood

(2a) T / PVAV: at the village manor had lived the family of Fleetwood
SOP: ! "At the village manor had lived the family of Fleetwood."

(2b) T / FF&BE1: lived at the village manor had the family of Fleetwood
SOP: ? ? ? "Lived at the village manor had the family of Fleetwood."

These four conditions are summarized in the following table:

| Condition | 1<br>T / PVAV<br>only | 2a<br>T / FV+FF<br>+ T / PVAV | 2b<br>T / FV+FF<br>+ T / FF&BE1 |
|---|---|---|---|
| transitive verb in active voice with expressed object | + | ... | + |
| transitive verb in passive voice with expressed agent prepositional phrase | ... | ... | + |
| verb complex contains two forms of BE | + | ... | + |
| verb complex contains no forms of BE | + | + | ... |

These four conditions serve to limit the opportunity for the redistribution of the lexical material of the utterance according to the requirements of the topic-comment organization of the utterance.

## THERE-Transformations

Closely related to the TCR-transformations is a group of sentence patterns with very similar features, one which is distinguished by the insertion of the element THERE in the course of their derivation. All of these share the characteristic of semantic or communicative imbalance which obtained among those described in the preceding section: the material at the beginning of the infrastructure is much more important than that at the end of it. In sentences which have undergone the THERE-transformation, the significant information has been moved to the end of the utterance, while the resulting "communicative vacuum" at the beginning is filled by the element THERE.

There is a difference betwenn THERE-transformations and TCR-transformations which is of the highest importance. Whereas the TCR-transformations led to utterances which might be called "terminal" sequences, in that they could not be further modified by any of the other transformations presented in this chapter, the THERE-transformations are under no such limitations. After the prescribed THERE-transformations have been performed, it is open to the speaker to submit the sequence of elements which has been generated to any one of the first six basic transformations described in the first part of this chapter. This means that any fully generated THERE-clause may be transformed into a yes-no question, or into a relative clause, just as if it were a finitized infrastructure. We will inspect some examples of these further derivations in the course of the following exposition.

The transformations by which sentences with THERE are generated differ slightly from those used to produce TCR-transformations: in THERE-transformations, it is possible to topicalize either the entire complex of the lexical verb and its auxiliaries (VFF), or those up to and including the first form of BE (VFF+BE1). For reasons of simplicity of presentation, we will divide the patterns which comprise this set of transformations into two groups: those which apply when the main verb is BE; and those

175

which obtain when the verb in the infrastructure is a lexical verb. Our analysis begins with the former category — those sentences with infrastructures containing BE.

One restriction which attaches to these is that there can be no predicate noun following BE; the number of possible predicate adjectives and adverbs is, in practice, quite limited. In many cases there is no predicate element present at all, so that we may speak of a "zero-predicate." These conditions are exemplified in the following derivations. The first shows how a zero-predicate may be treated:

IS: some reason for it BE $\emptyset$
CRLV: some reason for it HAVE been $\emptyset$
MODL: some reason for it MUST HAVE been $\emptyset$
PSNM: some reason for it must have been $\emptyset$

The first step in the reorganization of this palpably unbalanced sequence is to topicalize all the verb forms up to and including the first form of BE which happens to be present; in this instance, this is tantamount to the entire complex of verb forms:

T / VFF+BE1: must have been some reason for it $\emptyset$

The next step is to insert the element THERE at the beginning of the sequence:

I / THERE: THERE must have been some reason for it $\emptyset$
SOP: "There must have been some reason for it."

The same transformations can be applied to sentences with predicate expressions which indicate location or position:

IS, FNTZ: many prominent politicians will be at the meeting
T / VFF+BE1: will be many prominent politicians at the meeting
I / THERE: THERE will be many prominent politicians at the meeting
SOP: "There will be many prominent politicians at the meeting."

As was noted earlier, sentences like the one above can be further subjected to the first six of the seven basic transformations described at the beginning of this chapter. To illustrate this feature, we will apply them to this sentence, changing it where necessary to make it lexically compatible with the structure under consideration. First, the terminal adverb may be topicalized (Basic Transformation 1):

T / TRMAV: at the meeting THERE will be many prominent politicians

SOP: "At the meeting, there will be many prominent politicians."

Second, it would be possible to transform the sentence into a yes-no question (Basic Transformation 2):

T / AUX1: will THERE be many prominent politicians at the meeting

SOP: "Will there be many prominent politicians at the meeting? "

Basic Transformation 3 produces information questions:

ITRGZ: THERE will be WHO at the meeting
T / AUX1: will THERE be WHO at the meeting
T / ITRG: WHO will THERE be at the meeting
SOP: "Who will there be at the meeting? "

Basic Transformation 4 can generate a relative clause:

RLTVZ: THERE will be many prominent politicians WHERE
T / RLTZ: WHERE THERE will be many prominent politicians
SOP: "(It will be a meeting) where there will be many prominent politicians."

Statements with topicalized restrictive intraverbal adverbs (RSAV) are produced by Basic Transformation 5:

(THERE have rarely been any prominent politicians at these meetings)
T / AUX1: have THERE rarely been any prominent politicians at these meetings
T / RSAV: rarely have THERE been any prominent politicians at these meetings
SOP: "Rarely have there been any prominent politicians at these meetings."

Confirmative correlative sentences, produced by Basic Transformation 6, can also be derived from THERE-clauses:

CONTEXT: "There will be many prominent politicians at the meeting."
AVBLZ / FF&AUX1: THERE will SO
T / AV&AUX1: SO THERE will
SOP: "So there will."

Of all the basic transformations, only the seventh cannot be applied to the output of a THERE-transformation.

A great number of THERE-clauses contain lexical verbs. There are several conditions which must be fulfilled, however, before an infrastructure with a lexical verb may be transformed into a THERE-clause. First, the infrastructure may contain only an intransitive verb, or a transitive verb in the passive voice. Second, the intransitive verb must be a verb of manifestation, one which expresses the manner in which the subject appears, e. g., *appear, arise, come, float, fly, follow, go, hang, lie, stand,* etc. And third, there must be a kind of "imbalance" in the infrastructure such that the more important element stands near the beginning, the less important toward the end; not infrequently, this means that the verb is the last, or nearly the last element in the infrastructure; quite often the subject is a nonspecific noun.

The THERE-transformations which may apply to infrastructures containing lexical verbs fall into three classes: (1) those where the auxiliaries present contain one form of the verb BE; (2) those where they contain no form of BE at all; and (3) those where two forms of BE are to be found among the auxiliaries. Beginning with the first group, we find that either of the two operations may precede the insertion of THERE: either all of the verb forms present may be topicalized (T / VFF), or only those preceding and including the first (in this instance, the only) form of BE (T / VFF+BE1). This means that any finitized infrastructure in which the auxiliaries contain one form of BE can be modified as a THERE-clause in two ways. These are illustrated in the following derivations:

IS, FNTZ: a time when these questions will no longer be of importance is coming

It is clear that the subject, with its long relative clause attached — *a time when these questions will no longer be of importance* — overwhelms the verb phrase *is coming*; hence, some form or readjustment in the order of elements in this infrastructure is called for. This can be accomplished, first, by a topicalization of all verb forms (T / VFF), followed by the insertion of THERE:

T / VFF: is coming a time when etc.
I / THERE: THERE is coming at time when etc.
SOP: "There is coming a time when these questions will no longer be of importance."

It would also be possible to modify the finitized infrastructure by topicalizing the verb forms preceding and including the first form of BE:

T / VFF+BE1: is a time when etc. coming
I / THERE: THERE is a time when etc. coming
SOP: "There is a time when these questions will no longer be of importance coming."

This sequence could stand as an acceptable utterance in English. However, it is considered a stylistic flaw to allow a lexical verb to be separated from its auxiliary by too many intervening elements, such as the relative clause here. Thus, whereas it is both grammatically and stylistically acceptable to say:

there is a time for that coming

the same structure, with a long relative clause in place of *for that*, sounds cumbersome and confusing, e. g.:

? there is a time when the question of women's rights will no longer be discussed as intensively as before coming

For this reason, it would have been prudent, after embedding, to commentize the relative clause, i. e., to move it to the end of the infrastructure. The resulting sentence would read:

SOP: "There is a time coming when these questions will no longer be of importance."

Cases of this kind will be considered under the rubric of embedding in a later chapter.

Both of these patterns of derivation may be applied to transitive verbs in the passive voice which contain only one form of BE among their auxiliaries, e. g.:

IS, FNTZ: a surprisingly large number of cases of smallpox have been reported

(1) T / VFF: have been reported a surprisingly large number of cases of smallpox
I / THERE: THERE have been reported a surprising large number of cases of smallpox
SOP: "There have been reported a surprisingly large number of cases of smallpox."

179

(2) T / VFF+BE1: have been a surprisingly large number of cases
of smallpox reported
I / THERE: THERE have been a surprisingly large number of
cases of smallpox reported
SOP: "There have been a surprisingly large number of cases of
smallpox reported."

The question may again be raised as to the rationale of these
sequences of syntactic elements. The effect of the element THERE
is to detopicalize the sentence, so that we have a gradual increase in
the communicative value of its component phrases:

there have been reported *a surprisingly large number of cases of
smallpox* $_C$

In this sentence, the concept of "reporting" is subordinated to the
item of new information which the sentence as a whole has been
conceived to convey. For this reason, the pattern of T / VFF +
I / THERE is often found where a list of things is to be presented,
e. g.:

! there have been reported in the past week three cases of smallpox, two of diphtheria, and one of scarlet fever

We have here another way in which the relatively rigid infrastructure
of English can be made to yield to the communicative priorities of
the context. So strong is this tendency that one of the most deeply
rooted principles of English word order, namely, that the syntactical
subject precedes the lexical verb, finds its sole exception here in
these TCR- and THERE-transformations.

The second of the three classes of THERE-clauses comprises
those in which no form of BE occurs among the auxiliaries. It is
obvious from this condition that the transformation T / VFF+BE1
cannot apply. The following is an example of this derivation with an
infrastructure with an intransitive verb:

IS, FNTZ: a time when these questions will no longer be of
importance will come
T / VFF: will come a time when etc.
I / THERE: THERE will come a time when etc.
SOP: "There will come a time when these questions will no longer
be of importance."

This transformation cannot apply to transitive verbs in the passive voice, since the passive transformation introduces a form of BE into the complex of verb elements. The third and last class of THERE-transformations contains those in which the auxiliaries of the verb contain two forms of BE. By virtue of this condition, all such finitized infrastructures must be transitive verbs in the passive voice, since only the modifications LMDR and PASV introduce BE into the verb complex. The two patterns of transformation are exemplified below:

IS, FNTZ: severe cases of smallpox were being reported almost daily

(1) T / VFF: were being reported severe cases of smallpox almost daily

I / THERE: THERE were being reported severe cases of smallpox almost daily

SOP: "There were being reported severe cases of smallpox almost daily."

(2) T / VFF+BE1: were severe cases of smallpox being reported almost daily

I / THERE: THERE were severe cases of smallpox being reported almost daily

SOP: "There were severe cases of smallpox being reported almost daily."

The greater the number of auxiliaries, and the less important the subject, the more awkward the first of these two constructions is; the second will produce acceptable utterances without regard to those factors:

IS, FNTZ: cases of smallpox have been being reported almost daily this winter

(1) T / VFF: have been being reported cases of smallpox almost daily this winter

I / THERE: THERE have been being reported cases of smallpox almost daily this winter

SOP: ? "There have been being reported cases of smallpox almost daily this winter."

The sentence, while not incorrect, sounds clumsy. On the other hand, the following can be accepted without hesitation:

(2) T / VFF+BE1: have been cases of smallpox being reported almost daily this winter

I / THERE: THERE have been cases of smallpox being reported almost daily this winter

SOP: ! "There have been cases of smallpox being reported alsmost daily this winter."

It is probable that the acceptability of the former pattern (with T / VFF) depends to an unusual extent on the circumstances of context and content. It is also very likely that we are approaching here the structural limits of the language.

In conclusion, we may summarize the various transformations which accompany the insertion of the element THERE. The possibilities described in this section are given in tabular form below:

| Condition | T / VFF<br>+ I / THERE | T / VFF+BE1<br>+ I / THERE |
|---|---|---|
| BE as verb in infrastructure | ... | + |
| LEXVB with 1 form of BE among AUXX | + | + |
| LEXVB with no form of BE among AUXX | + | ... |
| LEXVB with 2 forms of BE among AUXX | +(? ) | + |

*Extraposition and Intraposition*

At several points it has been observed that the relative rigidity of the English infrastructure has made patterns of word-order adjustment like the TCR- and THERE-transformations virtually indispensable. In particular, the fixed position of the subject (SUBJ) in clause-initial position, and the medial position of the object nouns and pronouns (NOMNL) may in many cases conflict with the communicative priorities of the context. It is not surprising, therefore, that English has evolved additional syntactic devices for bringing word order and context into closer harmony. Extraposition (EXPOS) and intraposition (INPOS) are treated here, not as special sets of rules, but as exceptions to the rules which we have established regarding the order of elements in the infrastructure. The word "extraposition" has been used with different meanings by Jacobs and Rosenbaum (1968:171 ff.) and Langendoen (1969:25, 59 ff.); in this discussion, we will use it to mean the movement of an element

182

originating in the NOMNL tagmeme to the end of the infrastructure. The contrasting term "intraposition" signifies here the movement of a verb complement adverb or phrase (VCOMP) or a terminal adverb (TRMAV) to a position in the interior of the infrastructure immediately preceding the lexical verb (LEXVB). These processes are indicated in the following diagram:

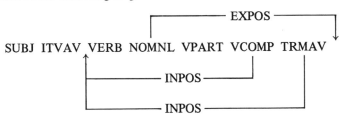

In the following discussion, we will try to illustrate these adjustments in word order with examples from various sources.

As to extraposition, this becomes necessary because the noun object not infrequently surpasses the adverbial elements which normally follow it – VPART, VCOMP, and TRMAV – in importance, as in this sentence:

"I wish we could drop into the Potomac all those obsolescent conservatives who are still preoccupied with MacArthur" (Kevin Phillips, *New York Times Magazine*, 17 May 1970).

Although a subordinate clause, the part of the sentence which we are concerned with here is:

we could drop into the Potomac all those obsolescent conservatives who are still preoccupied with Mac Arthur

The infrastructure behind this clause, with its elements stripped of adjectival modifiers, is:

IS: we drop those conservatives into the Potomac

Here the verb (VERB) is *drop; those conservatives* is a nominal (NOMNL); and *into the Potomac* a verb complement (VCOMP), to be specific, a verb complement phrase (VCPhr). Not only does this conform to the order of tagmemes as defined in our description of the English infrastructure, the reverse order of the two postverbal elements would be unacceptable:

? ? ? we could drop into the Potomac those conservatives

183

And yet, this is precisely the order of elements which we find in the original quotation above. It is the greater communicative importance of the noun object phrase which encourages the speaker to extrapose that element to the end of the clause: using the number of words in each syntactic element as a rough index of its communicative value, we note that the verb complement phrase *into the Potomac* has three words, whereas the noun phrase *all those obsolescent conservatives who are still preoccupied with MacArthur* has ten. To be sure, the normal or expected order would also be acceptable:

> ! we could drop all those obsolescent conservatives who are still preoccupied with MacArthur into the Potomac

However, because the phrase *into the Potomac* is now in the comment position, this arrangement suggests that the destination is a least as important as the lengthy noun phrase, and the semantic weight and relative position of the two elements are not in equilibrium. By extraposition, the noun phrase can be shifted into the comment position, so that the sentence – despite the fact that the sequence of its elements conflicts with the order of tagmemes in the infrastructure – now appears well balanced:

> !! we could drop into the Potomac all those obsolescent conservatives who are still preoccupied with MacArthur

This is in fact the sequence we find in the quotation.

We detect the same tendencies in the following example:

> "But he has also tried to impose upon the stories a thematic unity which he deduces from a letter, not previously reprinted, which Conrad wrote in 1901 to the New York Times to correct what he believed to be a misunderstanding about *The Inheritors*" ("Conrad in Fashion," [London] *Times Literary Supplement*, No. 3565, 25 June 1970, p. 674).

The phrases which we are concerned with here are dependent upon the verb *impose*, which stands in an infinitive construction in the sentence. The infrastructure behind this part of the sentence, with adjectival modifiers removed, would be:

> IS: he impose a unity upon the stories

The phrase *a unity* is a noun object (NOMNL), the expression *upon the stories* a verb complement phrase (VCPhr). Again, the reverse order of these elements as they stand would be unacceptable:

? ? ? he has imposed upon the stories a unity

Only because the semantic weight of the noun *unity* has been increased by the attachment of a lengthy and complex chain of relative clauses does this sequence of elements sound correct; indeed, so great is the disparity in communicative potential between the noun phrase and the verb complement phrase that the normal or predicted sequence, in this context, sounds awkward:

> ? he has imposed a thematic unity which he deduces from a letter, not previously reprinted, which Conrad wrote in 1901 to the *New York Times* to correct what he believed to be a misunderstanding about *The Inheritors* upon the stories

The writer here has elected to extrapose the noun phrase because of its greater communicative importance. This adjustment also serves the purpose of bringing the key words in each tagmeme, *unity* and *stories*, somewhat closer to the verb *impose*, so that the reader has all of the clues to the syntactic plan required by the valence of that verb close to the beginning of the clause.

A comparable operation serves to remove adverbs from their positions at or near the end of the infrastructure, as the case may be — and to place them immediately before the lexical verb. This procedure, called "intraposition," is well illustrated in the following passage:

> " ' these words . . . . thou shalt teach them diligently to thy children . . . . '
> Diligently to thy children . . . Gumbril remembered his own childhood; they had not been very diligently taught to him" (Aldous Huxley, *Antic Hay*, Perennial Library P30 [New York: Harper and Row, 1965] p. 4).

The words *teach* and *diligently* appear twice in this passage; in the one case, the adverb precedes the verb, in the other, it follows it. In the first instance, the infrastructure would be:

IS1: thou teach thy children the words diligently

and in the second:

IS2: SOMEONE not teach Gumbril the words very diligently

In the first case, the second noun object (2NnOj) has been extraposed; in the second, the adverb phrase *very diligently*, a verb complement adverb (VcAdv), has been intraposed. To illustrate how these sentences may be derived, as well as the specific procedures of extra- and intraposition, we will generate each, beginning with the former:

IS1: thou teach thy children the words diligently

As before, the final modifications are made in the infrastructure; first, the preposition *to* is placed before the second noun object (2NnOj); then, the object phrase is commentized to the end of the NOMNL tagmeme; and finally, the first noun object (1NnOj) is pronominalized:

I / PRP: thou teach to thy children the words diligently
C / OjPhr: thou teach the words to thy children diligently
PRNMZ / 1NnOj: thou teach them to thy children diligently

The verb modifications then follow; the archaic pronoun and verb forms do not affect the syntax of the sentence:

MODL, PSNM: thou shalt teach them to thy children diligently

And in conclusion, the phrase from the NOMNL tagmeme, *to thy children* — even though it is the second and not the first noun object — is extraposed:

EXPOS: thou shalt teach them diligently to thy children

The second derivation differs in that it involves intraposition instead of extraposition; the infrastructure in this case is:

IS2: SOMEONE not teach Gumbril the words very diligently

Both noun objects in the NOMNL tagmeme are pronominalized, with the resulting changes of position:

PRNMZ / 1NnOj: SOMEONE not teach him the words very diligently
I / Prp: SOMEONE not teach to him the words very diligently
C / OjPhr: SOMEONE not teach the words to him very diligently
PRNMZ / 1NnOj: SOMEONE not teach them to him very diligently

After the infrastructure has achieved its final form, the verb modifications are applied:

PASV: they not be taught to him very diligently BY SOMEONE

186

CRLV: they not have been taught to him very diligently BY
SOMEONE

When the modification for person and number (PSNM) is applied,
the negative adverb is placed behind the first auxiliary:

PAST, PSNM: they had not been taught to him very diligently
BY SOMEONE

At this point, empty elements may be deleted:

D / EE: they had not been taught to him very diligently

From the context, it is clear that the word *him* is to be emphasized;
indeed, it is used in an implicitly contrastive way. To be sure, it
would be possible to extrapose the second noun object phrase *to
him*, which would produce:

EXPOS: they had not been taught very diligently to him

But Huxley has chosen to intrapose the verb complement adverb
phrase (VcAdv) *very diligently*, placing it before the lexical verb,
irrespective of the number of auxiliaries present:

INPOS: they had not been very diligently taught to him

The effect of this it to fuse adverb and verb into a single concept, as
the context would imply; the other pattern, with extraposition,
would seem to suggest that the words had in fact been taught to him
though not very diligently. The latter sequence does not convey this
impression. These sentences, then, exemplify both the procedure
and rationale of extra- and intraposition.

Not only the verb complement adverb or phrase, but also the
terminal adverb (TRMAV) may be intraposed, as in this example:

"(Seven million people . . . . ) Millions of them are now sleeping
in an empested atmosphere" (ibid., p. 61).

The infrastructure underlying this sentence would be:

IS: millions of them sleep in an empested atmosphere now

The only further modifications relate to the verb forms:

LMDR, PSNM: millions of them are sleeping in an empested
atmosphere now

The sequence dictated by the infrastructure gives the terminal
adverb (TRMAV) *now* a prominence not justified by the context;

topicalization, an alternative adjustment in word order, does not seem appropriate in this context, either:

> T / TRMAV: now millions of them are sleeping in an empested atmosphere

Huxley has elected to intrapose the adverb before the lexical verb, retaining its semantic contribution to the thought of the sentence, while denying it any syntactic prominence:

> INPOS: millions of them are now sleeping in an empested atmosphere

This sentence, and the other preceding it, indicate the adjustments in position which are called extraposition and intraposition, and give some idea of their reason of being in the disposition of sentence elements in actual discourse.

In regard to these transformations, we have left the area of sentence grammar, which is the intended province of this book, and have crossed the boundary separating it from text or discourse grammar. To continue in this direction would unduly enlarge the scope of the work. However, since it has also been our ambition to present a system of rules which account for the position of words in English and German sentences, one last observation must be added to the foregoing discussion. In an earlier part of this chapter, we included the topicalization of the terminal adverb in our list of basic transformations. For reasons which lie beyond the obligatory structures of English, and which have their origin in considerations of style, a number of other elements may also be placed at the beginning of the utterance. Some examples, all from Huxley's novel, follow: the original position of the topicalized elements in the infrastructures of their respective sentences (here italicized) is indicated by ellipsis points (. . .):

> *in the great windows opposite,* young David stood . . . like a cock, crowing on the dunghill of a tumbled giant (p. 3)
> *an atheist and an anti-clerical of the strict old school* he was . . . (p. 4)
> *on the opposite side of the chapel* two boys were grinning . . . and whispering to one another behind their lifted Prayer Books (p. 6)
> *with a sigh of disgusted weariness,* Gumbril looked at his papers . . . (p. 11)

> *to his friend Shearwater* he gave half a million ... for physiolo-
> gical research (p. 14)
> *gauzily* the distance faded ... to a soft, rich indistinctness (p. 37)
> *discreetly,* he looked ... at his watch (p. 41)

These rearrangements reflect the literary intention of the author rather than the structures of the language, and hence fall under the rubric of text grammar.

CHAPTER 11

## THE FINITE CLAUSES OF GERMAN

As does English, so, too, does German have two groups of transformations. The first changes the finitized infrastructure so as to produce yes-no questions, relative clauses, and the like, much as the basic transformations of English. The second group, however, has no distinct and separate function, but serves as an extension of the first for certain special purposes. The basic transformations are fewer in number than their English counterparts. As we have observed elsewhere, the pattern of word order which is "normal" for German was verb-last word order (FV-L), the sequence of elements which results from the common verb modifications and those connected with finitization. With an exception to be discussed presently, FV-L word order is used in all dependent finite clauses, i. e., in relative clauses, and in those subordinate clauses which are introduced by a conjunction. As an example of this feature of German, we may generate a clause with several verb modifications to show how these changes automatically produce certain patterns of word order:

IS: die Versammlung den Vorschlag nicht zur Kenntnis nehmen

In this infrastructure, the verb (VERB) *nehmen*, together with the nucleus complement (NCOMP) *zur Kenntnis,* comprises the clause nucleus (CN). The word *nicht*, as a clause nucleus adverb (CLNAV), immediately precedes it. Both the subject, *die Versammlung*, and the accusative object, *den Vorschlag*, are adverbo-nominals (AVNOM). It would now be possible to apply several common and finite verb modifications to this infrastructure, e. g.:

PASV: der Vorschlag von der Versammlung nicht zur Kenntnis genommen werden
MODL: der Vorschlag von der Versammlung nicht zur Kenntnis genommen werden sollen
PAST: . . . genommen werden SOLLT-
SJNC: . . . genommen werden SOLLT-
PSNM: der Vorschlag von der Versammlung nicht zur Kenntnis genommen werden sollte

This sequence could, without further modification, form a nominal clause:

SOP: "(Ich meine aber, daß) der Vorschlag von der Versammlung nicht zur Kenntnis genommen werden sollte."

If, however, the verb modifications above had included the modification TRMV ("terminative"), a situation would have arisen which constitutes the sole exception to the rule that the output of the series of verb modifications may be regarded as finite-verb-last word order (FV-L). We recapitulate, with this change:

IS: die Versammlung den Vorschlag nicht zur Kenntnis nehmen
PASV: der Vorschlag von der Versammlung nicht zur Kenntnis genommen werden
MODL: ... genommen werden sollen
TRMV: ... genommen werden sollen haben
PAST: ... genommen werden sollen HATT-
SJNC: ... genommen werden sollen HÄTT-
PSNM: der Vorschlag von der Versammlung nicht zur Kenntnis genommen werden sollen hätte

Teachers of German will recognize this as the familiar "double infinitive construction," i. e., a situation where the verb complex contains two verb forms which appear to be unmodified — *werden* and *sollen* — though the latter has the function here of a participle. When two such forms appear in the verb complex as the result of the patterns of generation described in the chapter on verb morphology, then the finite verb does not remain at the end of the clause, but moves to a position between the clause nucleus adverb (CLNAV) and the nucleus complement (NCOMP) — in this example, between *nicht* and *zur Kenntnis*:

SOP: "(Ich bin der Meinung, daß) der Vorschlag von der Versammlung nicht hätte zur Kenntnis genommen werden sollen."

Though this rule reflects the pattern of Standard German, it must be noted that there is no little dialectal variation in such situations. It is not unusual to hear sentences in Austria like:

das ist ein Roman, den ich schon lange lesen hätte sollen

instead of the sequence ... *hätte lesen sollen.*

With the exception just discussed, then, finite-verb-last word order is generated by the modification of the verb, without any

191

further change or adjustment of position. The next transformation which may occur in the development of a finite clause is the topicalization of the finite verb (T / FV). Returning to our earlier example, this takes place as follows:

> IS, FNTZ: Der Vorschlag von der Versammlung nicht zur Kenntnis genommen werden sollen hätte
> T / FV: hätte der Vorschlag von der Versammlung nicht zur Kenntnis genommen werden sollen

This pattern would appear in a yes-no question:

> SOP: "Hätte der Vorschlag von der Versammlung nicht zur Kenntnis genommen werden sollen? "

It is in connection with the last of the three patterns, verb-second word order (FV-2), that one of the most conspicuous features of German syntax becomes evident: the almost unlimited potential for topicalization. It is possible at this point in a derivation to topicalize any element except a modal adverb (MDLAV), even the finite verb. We pick up the thread of our exposition with the example of verb-first word order cited above:

> T / FV: hätte der Vorschlag von der Versammlung nicht zur Kenntnis genommen werden sollen

The most likely candidates for topicalization at this stage are nominal and adverbial elements, e. g.:

> T / X: der Vorschlag hätte von der Versammlung nicht zur Kenntnis genommen werden sollen

or, in an appropriate context:

> T / X: von der Versammlung hätte der Vorschlag nicht zur Kenntnis genommen werden sollen

Not only can these elements undergo this transformation, but even verbal elements may be topicalized. The following citations indicate the wide range of possibilities for verbal elements and related forms:

> lexical verb (neutral form): " Entbrennen wird der Disput jedoch vor allem an dem Rechenschaftsbericht des bisherigen Vorsitzenden . . . ." ("Angeblich proletarisch," *Der Spiegel*, 14 Jan. 1974, p. 28).
> participle: "Ausgelöst wurde das Dilemma durch den Stellen-

wechsel von . . . ." ("Große Schlacht," *Der Spiegel,* 14 Jan. 1974, p. 32).

participle plus auxiliary: "Geglaubt haben wird sie's kaum!" (Agricola 1969-1970:1133).

Non-verbal elements closely associated with the verb form can also accompany the latter in its movement to the topic position:

"Nicht einigen konnten sich die Unterhändler über die Bezahlung der 'waiting time' — jener Zeit, in der die Arbeiter sich waschen und umkleiden" ("England vor dem Stillstand," *Der Spiegel,* 14 Jan. 1974, p. 62).

"Ausführlicher diskutieren wollen wir den zweiten Punkt der unter 1.1.3 genannten Gesichtspunkte" (Schwarze 1972:16).

When justified by the context, even single syntactic elements can be split by topicalization, e. g., the element *eine ganze Menge Theorien* in the sentence:

"Theorien gibt es eine ganze Menge" (Agricola 1969-1970: 1133).

This would be generated in the following way:

IS: es eine ganze Menge Theorien geben
PSNM: es eine ganze Menge Theorien gibt
T / FV: gibt es eine ganze Menge Theorien

Since it is the intention of the speaker that the topic be *Theorien* and the comment *eine ganze Menge,* it is necessary to split this single syntactic element in the final topicalization:

T / X: *Theorien*$_T$ gibt es *eine ganze Menge*$_C$

There is one more instance of this transformation which must be mentioned: it is possible to topicalize an already topicalized finite verb, provided it is a lexical verb, and not an auxiliary. This appears in the following sentence:

"Rauchen zum Beispiel tat er auch nicht" (Dürrenmatt, cited in Erben 1972:§198).

The phrase *zum Beispiel* is an intersentence adverb, an asyntactic element, and can be ignored. The remaining expression, *rauchen tat er auch nicht,* would be generated as follows:

IS: er auch nicht rauchen

The word *er* is an unaccented personal pronoun (UPPRN), and *rauchen* the verb (VERB); *nicht* is a clause nucleus adverb (CLNAV), which is modified by the adverb *auch*, so that *auch nicht* is a single syntactic element which occupies that tagmeme. The verb is next subjected to the modifications PAST and PSNM:

PAST: er auch nicht raucht-
PSNM: er auch nicht rauchte

After the modification of the verb is complete, the finite verb is topicalized:

T / FV: rauchte er auch nicht

At this point, it would be possible to topicalize the pronoun *er*:

T / X: er rauchte auch nicht

But the speaker's intention is clearly to make the concept of 'smoking' the topic, and *auch nicht* the comment. Since the form *rauchte* is the finite verb, it can only be topicalized if some other form assumes the important role of the finite verb, so that the FV-2 pattern is not distorted or destroyed. In this situation, the appropriate form of *tun* is introduced, and the retopicalized lexical verb reverts to the neutral form:

T / X: rauchen TAT er auch nicht
SOP: "Rauchen tat er auch nicht."

While the verb *tun* is widely used as an auxiliary in the dialects, this is the one case where it is not only admissible, but required, in Standard German.

To summarize, the basic transformations of German are three in number, if we count verb-last word order, which is, strictly speaking, the output of the verb modification phase of sentence generation. There is an exception to verb-last word order, namely, that the finite verb at this stage moves from final position to a point between the clause nucleus adverb (CLNAV) and the nucleus complement (NCOMP), when the complex of verb forms contains two which have the neutral form, regardless of their function. The second transformation is the topicalization of the finite verb, whether it be a lexical verb or an auxiliary. And the third is the topicalization of any element except one of the modal adverbs (MDLAV).

In the immediately preceding discussion of topicalization, especially in connection with the generation of verb-second word order, we accepted as our major premise the condition that the contexts in which these sequences would be produced would call for the placement of one of several syntactic elements in the topic position. We must also consider what happens when the context exerts no such attraction on the various elements which may be present — when the speaker must topicalize something in order to produce the required pattern of FV-2 word order, but where no element seems to fit the communicative role of topic. In cases of this kind, a dummy topic may be introduced: the pronoun *es*. The pronoun itself here serves no purpose other than to occupy the topic position, so that another element may stand elsewhere in the utterance, usually closer to the end, where it not infrequently functions as comment. This construction is often found in announcements such as the following, where the entire phrase is, in effect, the comment:

es spricht heute abend Professor Meyer

The finitized infrastructure which lies behind this sequence is:

IS, FNTZ: heute abend Professor Meyer spricht

The order of elements in the adverbo-nominal tagmeme (AVNOM) is motivated by the greater importance of who is speaking — *Professor Meyer* — in comparison with the somewhat lesser significance of when he is speaking — *heute abend*. Verb-first word order is generated by the topicalization of the finite verb:

T / FV: spricht heute abend Professor Meyer

At this juncture it would be possible to topicalize either *heute abend* or *Professor Meyer*, or even *spricht* in an unusual context. However, both adverb and noun are items of new information which the sentence has been created to convey, and hence it would contradict their communicative function as comment elements to place them at the beginning. In situations of this kind, the dummy topic ES may be inserted:

I / ES: ES spricht heute abend Professor Meyer
SOP: "Es spricht heute abend Professor Meyer."

This use of ES is not uncommon in connection with the socalled subjectless passives. For example, the finitized infrastructure:

IS, FNTZ: heute abend getanzt wird

must first be modified by the topicalization of the finite verb:

T / FV: wird heute abend getanzt

Either the adverb *heute abend* or the participle *getanzt* could now be topicalized. If, for reasons of context, the speaker or writer does not choose to do so, the dummy topic ES may then be inserted:

I / ES: ES wird heute abend getanzt
SOP: "Es wird heute abend getanzt."

This use of ES as a dummy topic may be distinguished from other uses of the word by virtue of the fact that it is not present in the infrastructure, and hence can only stand in topic position, not medially. For this reason, the following sentence is impossible:

? ? ? heute abend wird es getanzt

ES can only function as a dummy topic when no other element in the infrastructure can, in a given context, assume this function.

The various types of interrogative and relative clauses require no special treatment, since they also reflect the familiar patterns of verb-first, verb-second, and verb-last word order. We have already observed that yes-no questions (*Entscheidungsfragen*) are generated by the topicalization of the finite verb, e. g.:

IS, FNTZ: Hans gestern abend ins Theater gegangen ist
T / FV: ist Hans gestern abend ins Theater gegangen
SOP: "Ist Hans gestern abend ins Theater gegangen? "

Information questions (*Ergänzungsfragen*) require, first, the change of one element in the infrastructure into the appropriate interrogative expression, and, ultimately, its topicalization:

IS, FNTZ: Hans gestern abend ins Theater gegangen ist
ITRGZ: Hans WANN ins Theater gegangen ist
T / FV: ist Hans WANN ins Theater gegangen
T / ITRG: WANN ist Hans ins Theater gegangen
SOP: "Wann ist Hans ins Theater gegangen? "

Indirect questions are characterized by the omission of the T / FV transformation from the derivation. As far as yes-no questions are concerned, these require the special conjunction *ob*:

IS, FNTZ: Hans gestern abend ins Theater gegangen ist
T / FV: (omitted)

SOP: "(Er fragte mich, ob) Hans gestern abend ins Theater gegangen ist."

The same principle applies to information questions:

IS, FNTZ: Hans gestern abend ins Theater gegangen ist
ITRGZ: Hans WANN ins Theater gegangen ist
T / FV: (omitted)
T / ITRG: WANN Hans ins Theater gegangen ist
SOP: "(Er fragte mich,) wann Hans ins Theater gegangen ist."

Relative clauses closely resemble indirect information questions in the way in which they are generated. As in English, one element in the infrastructure is transformed into the appropriate relative form, which is then topicalized:

IS, FNTZ: er mir das Buch geborgt hat
RLTVZ: er mir WELCHES geborgt hat
T / RLTV: WELCHES er mir geborgt hat
SOP: "(Das ist das Buch,) das (welches) er mir geborgt hat."

Both indirect questions and relative clauses are distinguished by the absence of any transformation affecting the position of the finite verb.

In addition to the patterns of topicalization just de-scribed — which are comparable to the basic transformations of English — there are two further modifications of the finitized infra-structure which may occur in German. One of these arises from an ambiguity present in the morphology of the language. The nomina-tive and accusative cases of nouns and pronouns are identical in two of the three genders — the feminine and the neuter — and in the plural; only the masculine has different forms for these cases: *er*, the nominative, contrasts with *ihn*, the accusative, but *sie* and *es* could be in either case. For this reason, it is possible for a situation to arise where the hearer or reader might not be able to tell whether a given noun or pronoun was the subject or the object of the verb, as, e. g., in this sentence:

gestern hat sie ihre Schwester besucht

the phrases *sie* and *ihre Schwester* could be either nominative or accusative, to judge by the form alone, and hence one could inter-pret this sentence to mean either 'yesterday she visited her sister' or 'yesterday her sister visited her'. Because of this ambiguity in the

197

system of nominal and pronominal forms, a convention has arisen which specifies that, in such cases as the one above, the reader is to assume that the nominative precedes the accusative, so that only the first of the two interpretations can be regarded as correct. On the other hand, it might easily happen that, in a given case, the functions of noun and pronoun might be reversed, e. g., that the pronoun would be in the accusative case, but the noun phrase in the nominative:

sie$_{ACC}$ ihre Schwester$_{NOM}$ gestern besuchen

This sequence correctly reflects the fundamental distribution of elements in the infrastructure, in which unaccented personal pronouns (UPPRN) constitute the first tagmeme, regardless of whether the pronoun in question is an accusative object or a nominative subject. It is thus not at all out of the ordinary for a pronoun object to precede a noun subject. In light of the convention referred to above, the question then arises as to how the speaker or writer is to order these elements so that the completed utterance reflects the content which he wishes to convey. The solution is to be found in an additional topicalization which precedes that of the finite verb, a modification in sequence which will be called "pre-FV topicalization." This specifies that, in those cases where the subject and object cannot, by their form, be identified as to function, and where, by the operation of other rules, the object precedes the subject, that subject element must be topicalized before the topicalization of the finite verb. This operation will be abbreviated as "T / SJ" in the derivations which follow.

The case above, then, would be treated as follows. The finitized infrastructure underlying the sentence is:

IS, FNTZ: sie$_{ACC}$ ihre Schwester$_{NOM}$ gestern besucht hat

In order to reverse the sequence of nominative subject noun and accusative object pronoun, the pre-FV transformation T / SJ must be applied to that noun:

T / SJ: ihre Schwester$_{NOM}$ sie$_{ACC}$ gestern besucht hat

The remaining transformations are then carried out as before.

T / FV: hat ihre Schwester$_{NOM}$ sie$_{ACC}$ gestern besucht
T / X: gestern hat ihre Schwester$_{NOM}$ sie$_{ACC}$ besucht
SOP: "Gestern hat ihre Schwester sie besucht."

Because of the additional transformation T / SJ, the order of elements now conforms to the convention that the subject must precede the object when their respective functions are not clear from their form. Whereas this modification is obligatory in order to prevent the kind of misunderstanding just mentioned, the topicalization of the grammatical subject before that of the finite verb is optional in other cases where pronoun objects and noun subjects appear in the infrastructure. The sentence:

trotzdem hörte ihm Paul nicht zu

may be generated as follows:

IS, FNTZ: ihm Paul trotzdem nicht zuhörte
T / FV: hörte ihm Paul trotzdem nicht zu
T / X: trotzdem hörte ihm Paul nicht zu
SOP: "Trotzdem hörte ihm Paul nicht zu."

It would also be possible to topicalize the grammatical subject *Paul* before topicalizing the finite verb, a step which would lead to a different arrangement of the elements of that clause:

IS, FNTZ: ihm Paul trotzdem nicht zuhörte
T / SJ: Paul ihm trotzdem nicht zuhörte
T / FV: hörte Paul ihm trotzdem nicht zu
T / X: trotzdem hörte Paul ihm nicht zu
SOP: ! "Trotzdem hörte Paul ihm nicht zu."

The difference between the two sequences is not easy to define — one senses in the latter case an overtone of contrast not present in the former.

In the subject were the pronoun, however, the dative object *Paul* could not be topicalized. This reversal of roles is exemplified in the following derivations; first, the one without T / SJ:

IS, FNTZ: $er_{NOM}Paul_{DAT}$ trotzdem nicht zuhörte
T / FV: hörte er Paul trotzdem nicht zu
T / X: trotzdem hörte er Paul nicht zu
SOP: ! "Trotzdem hörte er Paul nicht zu."

IF we now apply the pre-FV topicalization rule T / SJ to the noun *Paul* — here a dative object — we generate an unacceptable utterance:

IS, FNTZ: er$_{NOM}$ Paul$_{DAT}$ trotzdem nicht zuhörte
T / SJ (i. e., *Paul*): Paul$_{DAT}$ er $_{NOM}$ trotzdem nicht zuhörte
T / FV: hörte Paul er trotzdem nicht zu
T / X: trotzdem hörte Paul er nicht zu
SOP: ? ? ? "Trotzdem hörte Paul er nicht zu."

The range of possibilities which arise in connection with pre-FV topicalization of the subject is summarized in the following group of sentences:

! trotzdem hörte ihm Paul nicht zu (without T / SJ)
! trotzdem hörte Paul ihm nicht zu (T / SJ optional)
! trotzdem hörte er Paul nicht zu (without T / SJ).
? ? ? trotzdem hörte Paul er nicht zu

Not only can the basic patterns of the German finite clause be augmented by pre-FV topicalization, but they may also be modified by an additional topicalization which follows that of the finite verb — a procedure which we will call "post-FV topicalization." This rule states that two elements may be topicalized after the topicalization of af finite verb; and that one may be a noun; and that when such a noun is topicalized, it must be so after the accompanying adverb. Thid enables us to describe post-FV topicalization as the optional topicalization of an adverb (T/AV). This situation can be seen in the following example:

"Scipio, nach der Zerstörung Carthagos, rief aus: . . ." (Marie Luise Kaschnitz, "Fortschritt," *Engelsbrücke: Römische Betrachtungen*, Fischer-Bücherei 820 [Frankfurt: Fischer, 1967], p. 145).

Here, the two elements *Scipio* and *nach der Zerstörung Carthagos* precede the verb in that order. The reverse order, however, would be unacceptable:

? ? ? nach der Zerstörung Carthagos Scipio rief aus . . . .

The patterns of the language require in such cases that the adverb be topicalized before the noun:

IS, FNTZ: Scipio nach der Zerstörung Carthagos DAS ausrief

The DAS here is a dummy element standing for the direct quotation.

T / FV: rief Scipio nach der Zerstörung Carthagos DAS aus
T / AV: nach der Zerstörung Carthagos rief Scipio DAS aus

200

T / X: Scipio nach der Zerstörung Carthagos rief DAS aus
SOP: "Scipio, nach der Zerstörung Carthagos, rief . . . aus: . . . "

There are also cases of post-FV topicalization where both the elements involved are adverbs, e. g.:

"Heute nacht, im Traum, sagte mir jemand, was ich aber schon wußte, . . ." (Marie Luise Kaschnitz, ibid., p. 162).

This sentence would be generated according to our rules as follows:

IS, FNTZ: mir jemand DAS heute nacht im Traum sagte
T / FV: sagte mir jemand DAS heute nacht im Traum
T / AV: im Traum sagte mir jemand DAS heute nacht
T / X: heute nacht im Traum sagte mir jemand DAS
SOP: "Heute nacht, im Traum, sagte mir jemand, . . . ."

There seems to be little difference between this sequence of elements and the reverse:

! im Traum, heute nacht, sagte mir jemand, . . . . .

The first element in each case is perceptibly of greater importance, whereas the second has the effect of a mere parenthetical expression:

heute nacht (es war im Traum) sagte mir jemand, . . . .
im Traum (es war heute nacht) sagte mir jemand, . . . .

These groups of adverbs thus constitute a kind of expanded compound topic, although the communicative priority of the first element in each is apparent.

We may summarize our discussion of these supplementary patterns of pre- and post-FV topicalization by generating a sentence which, if not stylistically elegant, nevertheless has the virtue of exemplifying all of the possibilities for topicalization which exist for finite clauses in German:

IS, FNTZ: ihn seine Frau gestern abend zum ersten Mal seit dem Unfall im Krankenhaus gesehen hat
(→ FV-L word order)
(1) T / SJ: seine Frau ihn gestern abend zum ersten Mal seit dem Unfall im Krankenhaus gesehen hat
(→ FV-L word order)

(2) T / FV: hat seine Frau ihn gestern abend zum ersten Mal seit dem Unfall im Krankenhaus gesehen
(→ FV-1 word order)

(3) T / AV: im Krankenhaus hat seine Frau ihn gestern abend zum ersten Mal seit dem Unfall gesehen
(→ FV-2 word order)

(4) T / X: gestern abend im Krankenhaus hat seine Frau ihn zum ersten Mal seit dem Unfall gesehen
(→ FV-2 word order)

SOP: "Gestern abend, im Krankenhaus, hat seine Frau ihn zum ersten Mal seit dem Unfall gesehen."

The finitized infrastructure which underlies this sentence has been modified four times: (1) pre-FV topicalization of the grammatical subject — here optionally, and not obligatorily; (2) normal topicalization of the finite verb (T / FV) to produce FV-1 word order; (3) post-FV topicalization of an adverbial element; and (4) normal topicalization of the topic element proper (T / X). It is by this process of bringing specific syntatic elements in a certain sequence to the beginning of the clause that we can modify the finitized infrastructure to generate the various finite clause patterns of German.

# CHAPTER 12

## THE FINITE CLAUSES OF ENGLISH AND
## GERMAN: A COMPARISON

The transformations which have been described in the two preceding chapters constitute the third stage in the generation of a finite clause. In each of the two preceding stages — the assignment of syntactical elements to their proper place in the infrastructure, and the modification of the verb — certain significant differences between the two languages were noted, differences which also contribute to the contrasts which obtain between the finished finite clauses of English and German. In the English infrastructure, the verb occupied a medial position, whereas in German, it stood as the last element. In the system of verb modifications, it was shown that the English verb distributes its auxiliaries to the left, while the German verb "generates to the right," as it was put. Both of these differences carry forward to the third stage, the modification of the finitized infrastructure, which we are considering in this section.

When we look at the transformations which may be applied to these finitized infrastructures in English and in German from the broadest point of view, we note two fundamental features in common, and two points at which the structures of the languages differ. They are alike in that all of the various finite clause types in each are produced by the operation of only one rule — topicalization — in conjunction, to be sure, with the morphosyntactic transformations of interrogativization (ITRGZ), relativization (RLTVZ), and, in English, adverbialization (AVBLZ). English and German also resemble one another in that the series of topicalizations by which the finite clauses of the respective language are generated apply in specified order to both verbal elements and to elements not part of the verb phrase. They differ in that the verbal component which is topicalized is, in the basic transformations of English, the first auxiliary (AUX1), whereas in German it is the finite verb (FV), irrespective of whether that element is an auxiliary or a lexical verb, or — referring now to another peculiarity of English — a form of the the verb *sein* 'be'. The second difference lies in the range of nonverbal forms which can be topicalized: in English, only two kinds of adverbs may be shifted to initial position as part of the basic transformations of that language, the terminal adverb (TRMAV) and the restrictive intraverbal adverb (RSAV); in German, any element may be topicalized except modal adverbs (MDLAV) — indeed, under certain circumstances, even the lexical verb may be topicalized a second time. In both languages, interrogativized (ITRG) and relativized (RLTV) elements can be — under some circumstances, must be — topicalized as well.

Thus, the differences and similarities between the finite clauses of English and those of German can be in large measure explained by reference to these features: the difference in the position of the VERB tagmeme in the infrastructure; the difference in the position of the auxiliaries arising in the phase of verb modification; and the extent of topicalization, and its application to both verbal and nonverbal elements. Because the finite clauses are the foundation on which all the larger syntactic structures are built — every acceptable utterance which can stand alone must contain at least one — a control of these structures is of the greatest importance in language learning. For this reason, a detailed comparison of these clauses in the two languages is clearly called for. Moreover, as the clause types of English are more numerous and complex, such a comparison can best be made by listing the transformations in that language and indicating their equivalents in German.

*The Basic Transformations of English and their German Equivalents*

The first of the basic transformations of English was that by which the terminal adverb (TRMAV) was topicalized:

    IS, FNTZ: John is leaving for Vienna tomorrow
    T / TRMAV: tomorrow John is leaving for Vienna
    SOP: "Tomorrow John is leaving for Vienna."

The equivalent of this expression in German is produced by the topicalization of a nonverbal element applied to verb-first word order:

    IS, FNTZ: Hans morgen nach Wien abreist
    T / FV: reist Hans morgen nach Wien ab
    T / X: morgen reist Hans nach Wien ab
    SOP: "Morgen reist Hans nach Wien ab."

As we have already observed, topicalization of nonverbal elements like *tomorrow* in the example above is limited to these terminal adverbs (and restrictive intraverbal adverbs, to be discussed below), whereas the range of choice in German is much wider.

Basic Transformation 2 in English involves the topicalization of the first auxiliary (AUX1), a procedure which in English generates yes-no questions and conditions contrary-to-fact:

    IS, FNTZ: he has found the book
    T / AUX1: has he found the book
    SOP: "Has he found the book? "

If the verb is in the subjunctive — a condition not always evident from its form alone — then this transformation can produce conditions contrary-to-fact, e. g.:

    IS: he find the book
    CRLV: he HAVE found the book
    PAST: he HAVE+ED found the book
    SJNC, PSNM: he had found the book
    T / AUX1: had he found the book
    SOP: "Had he found the book, (he would have told us.)"

In German, it is the finite verb which is topicalized. When this finite form is the auxiliary, the resulting utterance resembles its English counterpart:

    IS, FNTZ: er das Buch gefunden hat
    T / FV: hat er das Buch gefunden
    SOP: "Hat er das Buch gefunden? "

The similarity also extends to contrary-to-fact conditions:

    IS; er das Buch finden
    TRMV: er das Buch gefunden haben
    PAST: er das Buch gefunden HATT-
    SJNC: er das Buch gefunden HÄTT-
    PSNM: er das Buch gefunden hätte
    T / FV: hätte er das Buch gefunden
    SOP: "Hätte er das Buch gefunden, (so hätte er es uns gesagt)."

When the verb form in the finitized infrastructure in English is a one-word lexical verb form, the hidden auxiliary DO is topicalized:

IS, FNTZ: he found (= DO+find+ED) the book
T / AUX1: DO+ED he find- the book
SOP: "Did he find the book?"

This has no counterpart in German (although the verb *tun* 'do' can sometimes serve as an auxiliary), where the finite verb is topicalized whether it is the auxiliary verb or not:

IS, FNTZ: er das Buch fand
T / FV: fand er das Buch
SOP: "Fand er das Buch?"

The third variable related to the movement of the first auxiliary in English occurs in connection with one-word forms of the verb BE, which, contrary to what one would expect in light of the preceding pattern with DO, behaves as though it were a first auxiliary:

IS, FNTZ: he is at home today
T / AUX1: is he at home today
SOP: "Is he at home today?"

Because the first auxiliary is always a finite verb, in this case German displays a pattern much like that of English:

IS, FNTZ: er heute zu Hause ist
T / FV: ist er heute zu Hause
SOP: "Ist er heute zu Hause?"

These comparisons indicate that in two cases the resulting sequences of English and German, though generated by different rules, are nevertheless markedly similar in structure; in one case, however, there is a significant contrast:

    lexical verb plus expressed auxiliary:
has he found the book
hat er das Buch gefunden
    one-word form of lexical verb
*did he find* the book
*fand er* das Buch
    one-word form of BE
is he at home today
ist er heute zu Hause

Of the three cases resulting from variant patterns of formation of the English verb, only the second, that involving one-word forms of lexical verbs, conflicts with a comparable pattern of German.

The third basic transformation of English generated information questions, and was characterized by the change of one element in the infrastructure to the appropriate interrogative form, and then, after the topicalization of the first auxiliary, that of the interrogative element. Because of the variant patterns of distribution of auxiliaries with lexical verbs, and of one-word forms of lexical verbs and of BE, we again have three cases to consider here. In addition, we noted that it makes a difference whether the interrogativized element was the subject, or an element other than the subject. As a result of these two sets of variables, we have no fewer than six cases in English to compare with German. As before, it is perhaps simpler to take those cases first in which the interrogative element is not the subject.

Where the lexical form is accompanied by an auxiliary verb, the patterns of the two languages are not wholly dissimilar:

IS, FNTZ: John has written the letter
ITRGZ: John has written WHAT
T / AUX1: has John written WHAT
T/ITRG: WHAT has John written
SOP: "What has John written? "

So as not to complicate this comparison of German and English, we will ignore the matter of emphatic questions here. A corresponding derivation in German would be:

IS, FNTZ: Hans den Brief geschrieben hat
ITRGZ: Hans WAS geschrieben hat
T / FV: hat Hans WAS geschrieben
T / ITRG: WAS hat Hans geschrieben
SOP: "Was hat Hans geschrieben? "

As it happens, the order of elements is the same in both cases; the sequence of operations in English – ITRGZ, T / AUX1, and T / ITRG – is very close to that of German – ITRGZ, T / FV, and T / ITRG.

When the verb in English is a one-word form of a lexical verb, the two languages diverge:

IS, FNTZ: John wrote (= DO+write+ED) the letter
ITRGZ: John wrote (= DO+write+ED) WHAT
T / AUX1: DO+ED John write- WHAT
T / ITRG: WHAT DO+ED John write-
SOP: "What did John write? "

In German, the splitting of the verb and the appearance of a hidden auxiliary does not take place:

IS, FNTZ: Hans den Brief schrieb
ITRGZ: Hans WAS schrieb
T / FV: schrieb Hans WAS
T / ITRG: WAS schrieb Hans
SOP: "Was schrieb Hans?"

On the other hand, when the verb form in question in English is a one-word form of BE, the two languages again display a parallel in regard to the formation of this pattern:

IS, FNTZ: John was here yesterday
ITRGZ: John was WHERE yesterday
T / AUX1: was John WHERE yesterday
T / ITRG: WHERE was John yesterday
SOP: "Where was John yesterday?"

The same pattern can be generated in German thus:

IS, FNTZ: Hans gestern hier war
ITRGZ: Hans gestern WO war
T / FV: war Hans gestern WO
T / ITRG: WO war Hans gestern
SOP: "Wo war Hans gestern?"

Of these three cases, only that involving one-word forms of the lexical verb displays a form markedly contrasting with that of German, at least in respect of the transformations which we are considering in this chapter.

When the interrogativized word is the subject, however, even this contrast is removed — because of the capacity of the English auxiliary DO to recombine with its lexical component when the two are contiguous. This is reviewed in the following derivation:

IS, FNTZ: John wrote (= DO+write+ED) the letter
ITRGZ: WHO wrote (= DO+write+ED) the letter
T / AUX1: DO+ED WHO write- the letter
T / ITRG: WHO DO+ED write- the letter

Unless the question is emphatic, e. g.:

SOP: "Who *did* write the letter?"

the first auxiliary and the lexical form recombine:

SOP: "Who wrote the letter?"

The corresponding derivation in German produces a virtually identical pattern:

IS, FNTZ: Hans den Brief schrieb
ITRGZ: WER den Brief schrieb
T / FV: schrieb WER den Brief
T / ITRG: WER schrieb den Brief
SOP: "Wer schrieb den Brief?"

In the other two cases, that in which a lexical verb is accompanied by an auxiliary, and that where the verb is a one-word form of BE, the derivations do not differ from those where the interrogative is an element other than the subject.

Before summarizing the results of this comparison, let us examine the indirect information questions, which in English are produced by Basic Transformation 4. These are generated in both languages by the same rules, i. e., by interrogativization (ITRGZ) and the subsequent topicalization of the interrogative form (T / ITRG). Since no verb form is topicalized in either language, the irregularities occasioned by the hidden auxiliary DO or one-word forms of BE do not arise. The one aspect deserving of attention is the redundancy of the T / ITRG rule when the subject is the interrogative element, e. g.:

IS, FNTZ: John has written the letter
ITRGZ: WHO has written the letter
T / AUX1: (omitted)
T / ITRG: WHO has written the letter

Strictly speaking, this step is unnecessary here, because nothing is changed by it. We include it so that we can use one set of rules to derive any and all of these patterns.

SOP: "(He wants to know) who has written the letter."

A comparable situation may arise in German:

IS, FNTZ: Hans den Brief geschrieben hat
ITRGZ: WER den Brief geschrieben hat
T / FV: (omitted)
T / ITRG: WER den Brief geschrieben hat
SOP: "(Er möchte wissen,) wer den Brief geschrieben hat."

A comparison of the various patterns of direct and indirect informations questions which arise from Basic Transformations 3 and 4 with their counterparts in German will show where the differences and similarities between these output-sequences lie. This comparison is presented in the following table, in which the divergent patterns are italicized.

| *direct* | *indirect* |
|---|---|
| English: BT 3, i. e., ITRGZ; T / AUX1; T / ITRG; and German: ITRGZ; T / FV; T / ITRG | English: BT 4, and German: both ITRGZ; . . . . ; T / ITRG |

ITRG ≠ subject

| | |
|---|---|
| What has John written? | . . . what John has written |
| Was hat Hans geschrieben? | . . . was Hans geschrieben hat. |
| *What did John write?* | . . . what John wrote. |
| *Was schrieb Hans?* | . . . was Hans schrieb. |
| Where was John yesterday? | . . . where John was yesterday. |
| Wo war Hans gestern? | . . . wo Hans gestern war. |

ITRG = subject

| | |
|---|---|
| Who has written the letter? | . . . who has written the letter. |
| Wer hat den Brief geschrieben? | . . . wer den Brief geschrieben hat. |
| Who wrote the letter? | . . . who wrote the letter. |
| Wer schrieb den Brief? | . . . wer den Brief schrieb. |
| Who was here yesterday? | . . . who was here yesterday. |
| Wer war gestern hier? | . . . wer gestern hier war. |

In these twelve pairs of cases, only one betrays a contrast which arises as the result of the generation of a type of finite clause, i. e., that between *what did John write?* and *was schrieb Hans?* To be sure, all of the pairs of indirect questions are characterized by a contrast as to the position of the verb, but this difference reflects the position of the modified verb in the infrastructure, and not the transformations under consideration here. We conclude that the patterns of formation of these information questions, and, indeed, of yes-no questions as well, are very similar, the most conspicuous difference being the presence of the hidden auxiliary DO in English, or, to describe the same feature in different terms, the effect of the topicalization of the first auxiliary (T / AUX1) in English and that of the finite verb (T / FV) in German.

There is no specific syntactic pattern in German which corresponds to Basic Transformation 5 in English, a pattern which involves the topicalization of a restrictive intraverbal adverb (RSAV). Nevertheless, this kind of clause is of more than casual interest because it constitutes an unusual parallel to the familiar pattern of verb-second word order in German. The operations which give rise to Basic Transformation 5 in English appear in the following derivation:

IS, FNTZ: I have seldom read such a boring book
T / AUX1: have I seldom read such a boring book
T / RSAV: seldom have I read such a boring book
SOP: "Seldom have I read such a boring book!"

A comparable sequence of elements is generated in German by the usual transformations which produce verb-second word order:

IS, FNTZ: ich selten ein so langweiliges Buch gelesen habe
T / FV: habe ich selten ein so langweiliges Buch gelesen
T / X: selten habe ich ein so langweiliges Buch gelesen
SOP: "Selten habe ich ein so langweiliges Buch gelesen!"

The similarity of the two sequences is all the more striking because it occurs so rarely:

seldom have I read such a boring book
selten habe ich ein so langweiliges Buch gelesen

Whereas the pattern is quite normal for German, it appears in English only when a restrictive intraverbal adverb is present which can be topicalized.

Basic Transformation 6, by which confirmative correlative sentences are generated, has no corresponding syntactic pattern in German. The English structure is exemplified by the following derivation:

CONTEXT: "John has gone down town this morning."
IS, FNTZ: he has gone down town this morning
AVBLZ / FF&AUX1: he has SO
T / AV&AUX1: SO he has
SOP: "So he has."

211

This pattern is generated by the adverbialization of all elements which follow the first auxiliary (AVBLZ / FF&AUX1), by which procedure they are reduced to the adverb SO, which is then topicalized (T / AV&AUX1). The response by a native speaker of German in a situation like the one above might vary widely, and depends on other circumstances. Following the utterance:

CONTEXT: "Hans ist heute morgen in die Stadt gegangen."

one could say *ich weiß* 'I know' or *das stimmt* 'that is correct' or *allerdings* 'indeed' or nothing at all.

In regard to Basic Transformation 7, that by which comparative correlative sentences, both affirmative and negative, are generated, we must again acknowledge that German has no sentence patterns which specifically correspond to it. There are, however, certain charateristic turns of speech which occur in roughly the same circumstances. As to the English patterns, the affirmative form of the comparative correlative sentence is exemplified in the following derivation:

CONTEXT: "John is going to the movies this evening."
IS, FNTZ: Fred is going to the movies this evening, too
AVBLZ / FF&AUX1: Fred is SO
T / AUX1: is Fred SO
T / AV&AUX1: SO is Fred
SOP: "So is Fred."

That pattern in German which corresponds most closely to this kind of clause makes use of the adverb *auch* 'also'. Using this device, we can construct the following derivation:

CONTEXT: "Hans wird heute abend ins Kino gehen."
IS, FNTZ: Fritz heute abend auch ins Kino gehen wird

The word *auch* functions here as a clause nucleus adverb (CLNAV), in which capacity it stands immediately before the clause nucleus *ins Kino gehen*. It is also important to note that *Fritz* and *auch* are the only two strongly accented words in the clause, a factor which, as we will soon discover, is crucial for the development of this expression. The derivation continues:

T / FV: wird Fritz heute abend auch ins Kino gehen
T / X: Fritz wird heute abend auch ins Kino gehen

Since this utterance follows another which contains — except for the

212

accented elements *Fritz* and *auch* — exactly the same lexical items, these items in common are redundant, and may be deleted as empty elements:

D / EE: Fritz (wird heute abend) auch (ins Kino gehen)
SOP: "Fritz auch."

We may thus regard the expressions *so is Fred* and *Fritz auch* as semantically and rhetorically comparable, although they are generated in quite different ways.

In like fashion, the negative comparative correlative sentence may be related to corresponding expressions in German, i. e., through the derivation:

CONTEXT: "John is not going to the movies this evening."
IS, FNTZ: Fred is not going to the movies this evening, either
AVBLZ / FF&AUX1: Fred is not . . . either → Fred is NEITHER
T / AUX1: is Fred NEITHER
T / AV&AUX1: NEITHER is Fred
SOP: "Neither is Fred."

In German, the essential idea is rendered by the clause nucleus adverbs *auch nicht*, e. g.:

CONTEXT: "Hans wird heute abend nicht ins Kino gehen."
IS, FNTZ: Fritz heute abend auch nicht ins Kino gehen wird
T / FV: wird Fritz heute abend auch nicht ins Kino gehen
T / X: Fritz wird heute abend auch nicht ins Kino gehen
D / EE: Fritz (wird heute abend) auch nicht (ins Kino gehen)
SOP: "Fritz auch nicht."

As in the case of the affirmative comparative correlative sentences, *neither is Fred* and *Fritz auch nicht* convey the same general idea in their respective contexts, but are not syntactic equivalents. English uses a special transformation in these instances, whereas German again applies the basic pattern of topicalization leading to verb-second word order, supplemented by selective deletion.


*The Topic-Comment-Redistribution (TCR) Transformations*
*and their Equivalents in German*

In the preceding section, we noted that English contains more numerous and relatively more complex patterns of finite clauses than does German, and that the latter language could in many cases generate formally and semantically comparable utterances by using the familiar sequence of operations for the generation of FV-2 word order. The reason that so many different kinds of sentences can be produced by so few operations lies in the much wider range of nonverbal elements which may be topicalized by the rule T / X. This formula applies to the topic-comment-redistribution transformations as well: whereas the lexical material of the finitized infrastructure is rearranged according to the specific patterns which are grouped under this label, German has no such group of transformations, but can produce roughly equivalent utterances by means of the patterns of topicalization which comprise the basic finite clause transformations of the language. This means that our comparison in this section ist not so much one of structures which are more or less alike in the two languages, but rather is an analysis of the way in which the simple, but powerful structural patterns of German can be manipulated to produce roughly the same sequence of elements as the more complex, but rigid TCR-transformations of English.

In our discussion of these structures, we identified four patterns: the basic sequence as defined by the infrastructure and subsequent verb modifications, and three transformations of it. As we noted at the time, the function of syntactical variants of this kind is to allow those elements which, in a given context, function as topic and comment to stand in or near initial and final position without destroying or distorting the syntactical relations which obtain among these and other elements in the uttterance. It is a simple matter to place the topic at the beginning of an utterance and the comment at the end; but it has to be done in a way consistent with the patterns which define and convey the internal lines of dependency of the language in question, so that the utterance does not lose its structural meaning.

The basic sequence, i. e., the finitized infrastructure, which we used as our example was the following:

a man in a blue suit was standing in the doorway

This could be achieved in German by topicalizing the grammatical subject:

ein Mann in einem blauen Anzug stand im Eingang

The first transformation of this basic sequence in English involved the topicalization of the postverbal adverb (PVAV):

214

in the doorway, a man in a blue suit was standing
im Eingang stand ein Mann in einem blauen Anzug

It is true, of course, that the order of subject and verb in German is the reverse of that in the English example; yet, the last accented element in the English sentence is *suit*. Using capital letters to indicated the accented elements, the sentence would be pronounced thus:

in the DOORWAY, a MAN in a BLUE SUIT was standing

It is characteristic of verbs of manifestation like *stand* that they are unaccented, particularly when an indefinite reference like *a man in a blue suit* is present (cf. Firbas 1964); a modified version of this sentence without a verb of manifestation would be accented differently, i. e.:

in the DOORWAY, a MAN in a BLUE SUIT was SHOUTING

As far as the two sentences under comparison are concerned, then, they may be regarded as equivalent in terms of the placement of topic and comment as the first and last accented elements, respectively, though not identical in structure.

There is another transformation of English which resembles the German in both respects: the distribution of topic and comment, and the order of their syntactic elements:

in the doorway was standing a man in a blue suit
im Eingang stand ein Mann in einem blauen Anzug

In this case, the parallel is complete.

The last transformation of the basic English sequence can be duplicated in German only be an additional step. The English sentence is:

standing in the doorway was a man in a blue suit

The infrastructure of the German equivalent would be:

IS, FNTZ: im Eingang ein Mann in einem blauen Anzug stand

We note here that, since both elements *im Eingang* and *ein Mann in einem blauen Anzug* are in the adverbo-nominal field (AVNOM), that element with the greater communicative value may be placed closer to the end. The derivation continues:

T / FV: stand im Eingang ein Mann in einem blauen Anzug

215

Instead of topicalizing either of the two adverbo-nominals, it is possible to maintain the prominent initial position of the verb by inserting the dummy topic ES:

I / ES: ES stand im Eingang ein Mann in einem blauen Anzug
SOP: "Es stand im Eingang ein Mann in einem blauen Anzug."

Both the distribution of elements and the pattern of accentuation are almost exactly parallel in the two sentences:

STANDING in the DOORWAY was a MAN in a BLUE SUIT
es STAND im EINGANG ein MANN in einem BLAUEN ANZUG

By using its own structural devices, German can arrange and distribute the various lexical items of its sentences in virtually the same order as that produced by the TCR-transformations of English.

*THERE-Transformations and their Equivalents in German*

The third category of finite sentence patterns in English is that of the THERE-transformations, those introduced by the dummy adverb *there*, e. g.:

there was once upon a time a king, . . . .
es war einmal ein König, . . . .
there came over her a deep feeling of peace
es kam sie ein tiefer Friede an
there are guests coming today
es kommen heute Gäste
there has been a new plan developed
es hat sich ein neuer Plan entwickelt

As the German equivalents of these sentence suggest, the dummy topic *es* may often be used in a way comparable to that in which *there* is employed. In both languages, the effect is that of "detopicalization," i. e., of diminishing the significance of the first position in the sentence, and of shifting the attention of the hearer to a point farther along in the utterance.

# CHAPTER 13

## EMBEDDING

The clauses which have been described in the foregoing chapters are all finite clauses, both dependent and independent. The distinction between these two categories has important consequences for the way in which a grammar constructed on generative principles is conceived. For that reason, we must give some thought to the general features of languages like English and German.

It is common knowledge that these languages contain certain form-classes or kinds of words, categories which at one time were called *partes orationis*. These include verbs, nouns and pronouns, adjectives and adverbs, prepositions and conjunctions, and sometimes interjections. Interjections may, in many cases, be treated as asyntactic elements; prepositions and conjunctions are "function-words" which link other syntactic elements together; a pronoun is a noun which has been partially stripped of its lexical individuality. This process of elimination leaves us with four major classes of words: verbs, nouns, adjectives, and adverbs. It is in the nature of English and German that all important semantic content must be expressed in one or more of these form-classes (cf. Sandmann 1929).

To be sure, these form-classes also have certain syntactic characteristics: adverbs, for example, modify adjectives or other adverbs, and cannot function as the subject or object of a verb — a role reserved to nouns (and pronouns). Adjectives modify nouns; in some cases they may also serve as a special kind of noun, e. g., *das Schöne, das Wahre, das Gute*. Ultimately, all of these — nouns, adjectives, and adverbs — are oriented toward the verb; the various patterns of this orientation have been described earlier from the point of view of that element as its syntactic valence. Summarizing briefly, then, we note that the four major form-classes are not only specialized for the expression of certain kinds of semantic content, but also that these classes have certain syntactic roles to play in the sentence.

These observations are relevant to the concept of embedding because dependent clauses, both finite and nonfinite, have a relationship to the independent finite clause which is analogous to the relationship between noun, adjective, and adverb, on the one hand,

and the verb on the other. Stating the case another way, we can say that some dependent clauses are nominal in character, some are adjectival, and some adverbial. The specific correlations between dependent clause types and the various word-classes are presented in the following table.

| Form-Class | Correlative Finite-Clause Structure | Correlative Nonfinite-Clause Structure |
|---|---|---|
| verb | independent finite clause | — — — |
| noun | noun clauses<br>1) *daß*-clauses<br>2) indirect questions<br>  a) yes-no (with *ob / whether*)<br>  b) information (with ITRG) | infinitive;<br>gerundive |
| adjective | relative clause | adjectival participial clause |
| adverb | subordinate (adverbial) clause | adverbial participial clause |

This table reveals a number of interrelationships between clause types. To begin with, the independent finite clause has the same priority vis-à-vis all dependent clause types as the verb vis-à-vis nouns, adjectives, and adverbs: just as there can be no infrastructure without a verb, neither can there be an acceptable sentence without an independent finite clause. Moreover, dependent clauses can be either nominal, adjectival, or adverbial in character, i. e., a clause may have the same syntactic function within another infrastructure as a single noun, adjective, or adverb. It is this quality which is the key to the process of embedding: a dependent clause — either finite or nonfinite — is embedded by assuming the function of an element in its matrix clause. The assumption of function may be partial or complete: if it is partial, it assumes the function of the matrix element by attaching itself to that element — this is called "clause-element-restricting embedding"; the total assumption of function — called "clause-element-replacing embedding" — involves the total displacement by the embedded clause of an element in the matrix clause. All dependent finite clauses are embedded by attaching the embedded clauses to an element in the matrix clause, i. e., by clause-element-restricting embedding; nonfinite clauses (except when in apposition) are embedded by replacing an element in the matrix clause by the embedded clause. In the presentation to follow, the various patterns of embedding which arise in connection with finite clauses will be studied; the embedding of nonfinite clauses will be discussed in subsequent chapters as part of the analysis of those constructions.

One of the most familiar patterns of embedding involves the relative clause. This kind of clause is adjectival in character; relative clauses may be thought of as modifying their antecedents. Thus, the relative clause in the following sentence qualifies or modifies its antecedent, *the letter*:

the letter which I received this morning is lying on the table

As in other cases, our analysis proceeds by establishing the infrastructure and defining the intervening steps by which that infrastructure becomes the sentence whose syntactic structure we want to explicate. The two infrastructures in this sentence are:

IS1: the letter lie on the table
IS2: I receive the letter this morning

The position of the various elements is determined by the rules for the formation of the infrastructure. Throughout the remainder of this book, we will follow the practice of generating the dependent clause first, and then embedding it in its matrix clause:

IS2: I receive the letter this morning

As this sequence is destined to become a relative clause, the modifications appropriate to that function are applied:

RLTVZ: I receive WHICH this morning

Next, the verb is modified:

PAST, PSNM: I received WHICH this morning
T / RLTV: WHICH I received this morning

This clause is now ready to be embedded. Relative clauses, like all finite clauses, are clause-element-restricting, and so the procedure of embedding consists of attaching the newly generated relative clause to its antecedent in the matrix infrastructure, which at this point has not yet undergone any changes:

> IS1: the letter lie on the table
> E / IS2: the letter + WHICH I received this morning + lie on the table

(The plus sign "+" indicates a clause boundary.) After embedding, it would be possible to commentize the embedded clause, an operation which would remove it from its position following its antecedent to the end of the matrix clause, e. g.:

> C / 2: the letter . . . lie on the table + WHICH I received this morning

This change would also have the effect of isolating the dependent clause from any further movement in the generation of the sentence. However, the commentizing of relative clauses is far less common in English than in German, in part because English relative pronouns are few in number (*which, that, who,* and *whom*), and hence often leave the identity of their antecedent in doubt; moreover, certain peculiarities of German word order also tend to encourage commentization, peculiarities which we will examine below. Hence, we will omit this operation (C / 2) at this point, and proceed after embedding (E / 2) to the modification of the verb of the matrix clause:

> LMDR: the letter + WHICH I received this morning + BE lying on the table
> PSNM: the letter + WHICH I received this morning + is lying on the table

This series of transformations has generated the sentence which we wanted to analyze:

> SOP: "The letter which I received this morning is lying on the table."

It would now be possible to apply any of the finite clause transformations to this sequence, to create, e. g., a yes-no question:

> T / AUX1: is the letter + WHICH I received this morning + lying on the table

SOP: "Is the letter which I received this morning lying on the table? "

or perhaps one of the TCR-transformations, e. g.:

T / AUX1+FF: is lying on the table the letter + WHICH I received this morning
T / FF&BE1: lying on the table is the letter + WHICH I received this morning
SOP: "Lying on the table is the letter which I received this morning."

In general, the embedding of relative clauses in German follows much the same pattern as in the English example above. In practice, however, the commentization of the embedded clause is far more common, for reasons which have to do with the otherwise unrelated feature of verb position in the infrastructure. Let us approach this question by studying the following sentence:

er hat die Geldbörse, die ich gestern in dem Laden, der an der Ecke steht, verlor, gefunden

Even a simple sentence like this is difficult to understand at first glance because each clause envelopes its dependent clause completely, with the result that the three lexical verbs appear in a group at the end. Yet it is completely grammatical, as the following derivation will show. It consists of the three infrastructures:

IS1: er die Geldbörse finden
IS2: ich die Geldbörse in dem Laden verlieren
IS3: der Laden an der Ecke stehen

As in the English example, the derivation begins with the "most dependent" clause:

IS3: der Laden an der Ecke stehen
RLTVZ: WELCHER an der Ecke stehen
PSNM: WELCHER an der Ecke steht
T / RLTV: WELCHER an der Ecke steht

This clause is now embedded in its matrix clause:

IS2: ich die Geldbörse in dem Laden verlieren

Embedding consists of attaching the relative clause to its antecedent in the matrix clause:

E / 3: ich die Geldbörse in dem Laden + WELCHER an der Ecke steht + verlieren

We will pass over the possibility of commentizing the relative clause at this point, but will return to it presently. The following modifications apply to the second infrastructure:

PAST, PSNM: ich die Geldbörse in dem Laden + WELCHER an der Ecke steht + verlor

RLTVZ: ich WELCHE in dem Laden + WELCHER an der Ecke steht + verlieren

T/RLTV: WELCHE ich in dem Laden + WELCHER an der Ecke steht + verlor

This complex is in turn embedded in the matrix clause of IS2:

IS1: er die Geldbörse finden

E / 2: er die Geldbörse ++ WELCHE ich in dem Laden + WELCHER an der Ecke steht + verlor ++ finden

Next, the verb is modified; since IS1 is the independent finite clause, i. e., the "main clause" of the sentence, relativization (RLTVZ) does not take place:

TRMV, PSNM: er die Geldbörse ++ WELCHE ich in dem Laden + WELCHER an der Ecke steht + verlor ++ gefunden hat

T / FV: hat er die Geldbörse ++ WELCHE ich in dem Laden + WELCHER an der Ecke steht + verlor ++ gefunden

T / X: er hat die Geldbörse ++ WELCHE ich in dem Laden + WELCHER an der Ecke steht + verlor ++ gefunden

In the derivation, the forms WELCHER, etc. are used to designate the relative pronoun because the more customary *der / die / das* has other common functions, and hence its use might lead to confusion. However, in the final stage of the derivation, SOP, it is open to the speaker to substitute the more idiomatic forms, if desired:

SOP: "Er hat die Geldbörse, die ich in dem Laden, der an der Ecke steht, verlor, gefunden."

In this fashion, one type of the famous German "Schachtelsatz" may be generated. The tendency today, however, is to place one clause after another; this is accomplished by commentizing each relative clause after embedding. In other respects, the derivation in the same:

IS3: der Laden an der Ecke stehen
RLTVZ: WELCHER an der Ecke stehen
PSNM: WELCHER an der Ecke steht
T / RLTV: WELCHER an der Ecke steht

IS2: ich die Geldbörse in dem Laden verlieren
E / 3: ich die Geldbörse in dem Laden + WELCHER an der Ecke
steht + verlieren
C / 3: ich die Geldbörse in dem Laden verlieren + WELCHER an
der Ecke steht
PAST, PSNM: ich die Geldbörse in dem Laden verlor + WEL-
CHER an der Ecke steht
RLTVZ: ich WELCHE in dem Laden verlieren + WELCHER an
der Ecke steht
T/RLTV: WELCHE ich in dem Laden verlor + WELCHER an
der Ecke steht

IS1: er die Geldbörse finden
E / 2: er die Geldbörse ++ WELCHE ich in dem Laden verlor +
WELCHER an der Ecke steht ++ finden
C / 2: er die Geldbörse finden ++ WELCHE ich in dem Laden
verlor + WELCHER an der Ecke steht
TRMV, PSNM: er die Geldbörse gefunden hat ++ WELCHE ich in
dem Laden verlor + WELCHER an der Ecke steht
T / FV: hat er die Geldbörse gefunden ++ WELCHE ich in dem
Laden verlor + WELCHER an der Ecke steht
T / X: er hat die Geldbörse gefunden ++ WELCHE ich in dem
Laden verlor + WELCHER an der Ecke steht
SOP: !! "Er hat die Geldbörse gefunden, die ich in dem Laden
verlor, der an der Ecke steht."

It is obvious that the sentence, organized in this way, is easier to
grasp, since each clause is completed before the next one begins; the
change has been achieved by commentizing each relative clause
(C / 3, C / 2) after embedding. This strategy, which in part accounts
for Nietzsche's fluid style, represents the tendency in modern German, where not outweighed by other considerations arising from the
context.

There is another possibility open to the speaker of German in
connection with the placement of relative clauses. This is exemplified by the following sentences, which contain the same lexical
items:

(1) er hat in einem Geschäft die Geldbörse gefunden, die ich gestern verlor

(2) die Geldbörse, die ich gestern verlor, hat er in einem Geschäft gefunden

The difference between these two sentences lies in the treatment of the relative clause: in the first, it was commentized after embedding, as in the previous example; in the second, it has been topicalized, along with its antecedent. Both strategies are open to the speaker; his choice will depend upon his communicative intent in the situation in which the sentence is uttered. The derivation proceeds as follows:

IS2: ich die Geldbörse gestern verlieren
RLTVZ: ich WELCHE gestern verlieren
PAST, PSNM: ich WELCHE gestern verlor
T / RLTV: WELCHE ich gestern verlor

IS1: er in einem Geschäft die Geldbörse finden
E / 2: er in einem Geschäft die Geldbörse + WELCHE ich gestern verlor + finden

Here a choice must be made: to commentize or not to commentize. If one opts for this transformation, a later topicalization of the relative clause and its antecedent is out of the question. For purposes of the example, we will carry out this change here:

C / 2: er in einem Geschäft die Geldbörse finden + WELCHE ich gestern verlor
TRMV, PSNM: er in einem Geschäft die Geldbörse gefunden hat + WELCHE ich gestern verlor
T / FV: hat er in einem Geschäft die Geldbörse gefunden + WEL-CHE ich gestern verlor
T / X: er hat in einem Geschäft die Geldbörse gefunden + WEL-CHE ich gestern verlor
SOP: (1) "Er hat in einem Geschäft die Geldbörse gefunden, die ich gestern verlor."

By commentizing after embedding, we have produced the first of these two sentences. By passing over this option, however, one can topicalize the relative clause, along with its antecedent, at the stage represented by the rule T / X. This means that, after embedding, the derivation would continue as follows:

E / 2: er in einem Geschäft die Geldbörse + WELCHE ich gestern
    verlor + finden
TRMV, PSNM: er in einem Geschäft die Geldbörse + WELCHE
    ich gestern verlor + gefunden hat
T / FV: hat er in einem Geschäft die Geldbörse + WELCHE ich
    gestern verlor + gefunden

By embedding, the relative clause was attached to its antecedent, *die
Geldbörse*; when this element is topicalized, the relative clause
accompanies it:

T / X: die Geldbörse + WELCHE ich gestern verlor + hat er in ei-
    nem Geschäft gefunden
SOP: (2) "Die Geldbörse, die ich gestern verlor, hat er in einem
    Geschäft gefunden."

In sentences containing dependent finite clauses, the speaker will be
required to make decisions constantly whether to commentize, to
topicalize, or to do neither. The decision he makes will determine
the position of the clause in the completed sentence. If he elects to
commentize, it will be at the end:

er hat in einem Geschäft die Geldbörse gefunden, die ich gestern
verlor

If he decides to topicalize, it will be in initial position:

die Geldbörse, die ich gestern verlor, hat er in einem Geschäft
gefunden

If he does neither, it will lie in the interior of the sentence:

er hat die Geldbörse, die ich gestern verlor, in einem Geschäft
gefunden

His decision will depend on the communicative requirements of the
situation in which the sentence is composed.

    Other kinds of dependent finite clauses follow the same general
pattern of embedding, with the chief difference that, in place of an
antecedent in the matrix clause, a dummy element is found. This
occurs, e. g., in noun clauses, where the element THAT in English
and DAS in German appears in the infrastructure of the matrix
clause. Thus the sentence:

he said that he was departing tomorrow

has the infrastructures:

IS1: he say THAT
IS2: he depart tomorrow

First, the dependent clause is generated:

LMDR, PAST, PSNM: he was departing tomorrow

It is then embedded by being attached to the dummy element THAT:

E / 2: he say THAT + he was departing tomorrow

At this point, a morphosyntactic change, "conjunctionalization" (CJNLZ), takes place, by which the dummy element THAT / DAS is transformed into one of three kinds of clause-introductory forms:

|                                  | THAT →    | DAS →    |
|----------------------------------|-----------|----------|
| indirect statement:              | THAT      | DAß      |
| indirect yes-no question:        | WHETHER   | OB       |
| indirect information question:   | Ø         | Ø        |

Since the dependent clause in this example is an indirect statement, the dummy element THAT becomes (or remains) the conjunction THAT:

CJNLZ: he say + THAT he was departing tomorrow

Once the dependent clause is embedded, the matrix clause may be generated:

PAST, PSNM: he said + THAT he was departing tomorrow
SOP: "He said that he was departing tomorrow."

The generation of the German equivalent of this sentence follows the same procedure:

IS2: er morgen abfahren
PSNM: er morgen abfährt

IS1: er DAS sagen
E / 2: er DAS + er morgen abfährt + sagen
CJNLZ: er + DAß er morgen abfährt + sagen

In German, one normally commentizes noun clauses after verbs of saying:

C / 2: er sagen + DAß er morgen abfährt
TRMV, PSNM: er gesagt hat + DAß er morgen abfährt
T / FV: hat er gesagt + DAß er morgen abfährt
T / X: er hat gesagt + DAß er morgen abfährt
SOP: "Er hat gesagt, daß er morgen abfährt."

In the case of indirect yes-no questions, THAT (or DAS) becomes WHETHER (OB). With indirect information questions, the dummy element disappears in conjunctionalization, as in these sentences:

he asked me where I had lived
er wollte wissen, wo ich gewohnt hatte

The English sentence would be generated thus:

IS2: I live THERE
CRLV: I HAVE lived THERE
ITRGZ: I HAVE lived WHERE
PAST, PSNM: I had lived WHERE
T / ITRG: WHERE I had lived

IS1: he ask me THAT
E / 2: he ask me THAT + WHERE I had lived

Since a clause-introductory element, *where*, is already present, the dummy element THAT is deleted:

CJNLZ: he ask me ∅ + WHERE I had lived
PAST, PSNM: he asked me ∅ + WHERE I had lived
SOP: "He asked me where I had lived."

The German sentence is produced in much the same way:

IS2: ich DORT wohnen
TRMV: ich DORT gewohnt HABEN
ITRGZ: ich WO gewohnt HABEN
PAST, PSNM: ich WO gewohnt hatte
T / ITRG: WO ich gewohnt hatte

IS1: er DAS wissen
E / 2: er DAS + WO ich gewohnt hatte + wissen
CJNLZ: er ∅ + WO ich gewohnt hatte + wissen

227

C / 2: er ∅ wissen + WO ich gewohnt hatte
MODL: er ∅ wissen wollen + WO ich gewohnt hatte
PAST, PSNM: er ∅ wissen wollte + WO ich gewohnt hatte
T / FV: wollte er ∅ wissen + WO ich gewohnt hatte
T / X: er wollte ∅ wissen + WO ich gewohnt hatte
SOP: "Er wollte wissen, wo ich gewohnt hatte."

Dependent finite clauses of an adverbial character – usually called "subordinate clauses" – differ from noun clauses in that the dummy element in the matrix clause is one of several adverbs, and in that there is a greater number of subordinating conjunctions which may be chosen. The following example shows how these are embedded:

we will visit the museum when we have time

The infrastructures which underlie this sentence are:

IS1: we visit the museum THEN
IS2: we have time

The subordinate clause requires only one modification:

PSNM: we have time

This is then embedded by attaching it to its antecedent adverb, as though it were a relative clause:

IS1: we visit the museum THEN
E / 2: we visit the museum THEN + we have time

Conjunctionalization, in this construction, involves the selection of a subordinating conjunction lexically compatible with the dummy element THEN and the other words in the sentence, and placing it between the dummy element and the embedded clause:

CJNLZ: we visit the museum THEN + WHEN we have time

The matrix clause is now modified:

MODL, PSNM: we will visit the museum THEN + WHEN we have time

As a rule, the dummy element is deleted when not accented:

D / EE: we will visit the museum + WHEN we have time
SOP: "We will visit the museum when we have time."

That sequence is also subject to several combinations of topicalization and deletion, some of which were referred to in the section on extra- and intraposition. These would yield the following sentences:

(then) when we have time, we will visit the museum
when we have time, (then) we will visit the museum

As these patterns depend to a preponderant extent on the influence of the context, no rules (other than topicalization and deletion) have been formulated to make the manner of their generation explicit. They are adduced for the sake of completeness, and to provide structures comparable to those generated in German by patterns which are normal for that language.

The German equivalent of the sentence above would be produced in a similar fashion:

wir werden das Museum besuchen, wenn wir Zeit haben

The infrastructures contained in this sentence are:

IS1: wir das Museum DANN besuchen
IS2: wir Zeit haben

The generation proceeds as follows, beginning with IS2:

PSNM: wir Zeit haben

By embedding, this phrase is placed after the dummy adverb DANN:

IS1: wir das Museum DANN besuchen
E / 2: wir das Museum DANN + wir Zeit haben + besuchen

Conjunctionalization here introduces a lexically compatible subordinating conjunction between the dummy element and the dependent clause:

CJNLZ: wir das Museum DANN + WENN wir Zeit haben + be-
ᵤuchen

One of several possibilities for the further development of this sequence would be to commentize the dependent clause at this point:

C / 2: wir das Museum DANN besuchen + WENN wir Zeit haben
MODL, PSNM: wir das Museum DANN besuchen werden +
WENN wir Zeit haben
T / FV: werden wir das Museum DANN besuchen + WENN wir
Zeit haben

T / X: wir werden das Museum DANN besuchen + WENN wir Zeit haben

Dummy elements are normally deleted, except when accented:

D / EE: wir werden das Museum besuchen + WENN wir Zeit haben

SOP: "Wir werden das Museum besuchen, wenn wir Zeit haben."

Without deletion, the following sentence might be produced; the adverb is added to make the construction idiomatic:

"Wir werden das Museum erst *dann* besuchen, wenn wir Zeit haben."

As in the case of relative clauses, there are, in general, two options: commentization or topicalization. We have performed the former in the example above; now let us explore the latter. This option effectively precludes commentization, and hence we must return to the step which precedes it:

CJNLZ: wir das Museum DANN + WENN wir Zeit haben + besuchen

MODL, PSNM: wir das Museum DANN + WENN wir Zeit haben + besuchen werden

T / FV: werden wir das Museum DANN + WENN wir Zeit haben + besuchen

At this point, a number of combinations of topicalization and deletion emerge. For one thing, the entire adverb phrase may be topicalized:

T / X: DANN + WENN wir Zeit haben + werden wir das Museum besuchen

SOP: "Dann, wenn wir Zeit haben, werden wir das Museum besuchen."

The dummy adverb, if unaccented, might be deleted:

D / EE: WENN wir Zeit haben + werden wir das Museum besuchen

SOP: "Wenn wir Zeit haben, werden wir das Museum besuchen."

And yet, the syntactic resources of the German language have still not been exhausted. In the analysis of finite clauses, it was pointed out that one could topicalize an adverb (T / AV) between the steps

T / FV and T / X. This sequence of transformations can be applied here:

> T / FV: werden wir das Museum DANN + WENN wir Zeit haben
> + besuchen
> T / AV: DANN werden wir das Museum + WENN wir Zeit haben
> + besuchen
> T / X: WENN wir Zeit haben + DANN werden wir das Museum
> besuchen
> SOP: "Wenn wir Zeit haben, dann werden wir das Museum be-
> suchen."

To recapitulate, these two infrastructures can produce a variety of sentence patterns:

> wir werden das Museum besuchen, wenn wir Zeit haben
> wir werden das Museum (erst) dann besuchen, wenn wir Zeit
> haben
> wenn wir Zeit haben, werden wir das Museum besuchen
> dann, wenn wir Zeit haben, werden wir das Museum besuchen
> wenn wir Zeit haben, dann werden wir das Museum besuchen

All five of these (more might have been adduced) have been generated solely by the application of the EDICT-rules of commentization, topicalization, and deletion, applied to certain elements in certain sequences.

We close this chapter with a description of a kind of relative clause which appears only in German — the socalled indefinite relative clause. This is exemplified by the following sentence:

> er hat nicht angerufen, was mich überraschte

The difference between this and a normal relative clause can be seen from an inspection of the infrastructures:

> IS1: er nicht anrufen
> IS2: mich DAS überraschen

The element DAS in IS2 refers to the entire clause of IS1, which is its antecedent. With this qualification, the derivation proceeds substantially as in the case of normal relative clauses:

> IS2: mich DAS überraschen

There is a special form of the relative pronoun for this function:

RLTVZ: mich WAS überraschen
PAST, PSNM: mich WAS überraschte
T / RLTV: WAS mich überraschte

As with normal relative clauses, the indefinite relative clause is placed immediately behind its antecedent, which here, however, is the entire independent clause:

IS1: er nicht anrufen
E / 2: er nicht anrufen + WAS mich überraschte

The derivation then proceeds:

TRMV, PSNM: er nicht angerufen hat + WAS mich überraschte
T / FV: hat er nicht angerufen + WAS mich überraschte

Since the antecedent of the indefinite relative clause is the entire matrix clause, and not a single element in it, it cannot be topicalized:

T / X: WAS mich überraschte + hat er nicht angerufen
SOP: ? ? ? "Was mich überraschte, hat er nicht angerufen."

Only an element in the matrix clause may be topicalized:

T / X: er hat nicht angerufen + WAS mich überraschte
SOP: ! "Er hat nicht angerufen, was mich überraschte."

Because its antecedent is the entire clause, this is an example of clause-restricting embedding, a subcategory of clause-element-restricting embedding. The distinction between normal and indefinite relative clauses is reflected in German syntactically in the position of the clause, and morphologically in the special form of the relative pronoun.

# CHAPTER 14

## THE INFINITIVE IN ENGLISH

In an earlier chapter, in the discussion of the patterns of verb modification, it was stated that an infrastructure could be modified in order to produce a number of different types of clauses, five in number: finite clauses, infinitives, adjectival and adverbial participial clauses, and gerundives. Just as the finite clauses which we have been considering in the previous chapters are generated by several transformations grouped under the general label of finitization (FNTZ), so, too, are infinitives produced by two operations on the infrastructure which comprise the procedure called "infinitivization" (INFZ): (1) the word *for* is placed in front of the subject (SUBJ), which is then transformed into the objective case; and (2) the word *to* is inserted before the first verb form present, whether a lexical verb or an auxiliary. For example, the infrastructure:

IS1: John call Mary

becomes, by infinitivization:

INFZ / 1: for John to call Mary

If the subject of the infrastructure were a pronoun, e. g.:

IS2: he call Mary

then the subject pronoun *he* would be changed to the objective case:

INFZ / 2: for him to call Mary

It is sometimes stated that phrases like *to call Mary* are infinitives, too, but as we shall see, these expressions are only parts of infinitives, from which segments have been deleted in the process of generating the utterance. Such phrases reflect only the surface structure of an utterance, not its infrastructure.

As far as the verb itself is concerned, there are no special modifications peculiar to the process of infinitivization, as there were in the case of the finite transformation. However, of the eight forms made theoretically possible by the lexical verb in combination with the three common verb modifications, two do not appear in modern usage. The following can be generated by the common verb modification rules plus infinitivization:

for him
LEXVB, INFZ: to watch
LEXVB, PASV, INFZ: to be watched
LEXVB, LMDR, INFZ: to be watching
LEXVB, CRLV, INFZ: to have watched
LEXVB, PASV, LMDR, INFZ: ? *to be being watched*
LEXVB, PASV, CRLV, INFZ: to have been watched
LEXVB, LMDR, CRLV, INFZ: to have been watching
LEXVB, PASV, LMDR, CRLV, INFZ: ? *to have been being watched*

The fifth and the last of these, while not egregiously wrong, are avoided by those who favor a clear and direct style. It is probably the repetition of the two forms of the verb BE which makes these patterns sound awkward. Hence, the generative rules for the common verb modifications may be emended to allow for the recommended deletion of the element BE + ING, i. e., *being*, after another form of the verb BE when the infinitivization of the verb is effected. In the case of the passive voice transformation, the subject and object of the active verb become the instrumental object, i. e., agent prepositional phrase, and the subject, respectively, of the passive verb, as in this case:

IS: she reject him
PASV: he be rejected by her
INFZ: for him to be rejected by her

Turning now from the form of the infinitive to its function as an element in a clause, we noted in the discussion of clause types at the beginning of the preceding chapter that dependent clauses are analogous in function to nouns, adjectives, and adverbs. It was also observed that the English infinitive is fundamentally an infrastructure which has been transformed into a noun — a characteristic which it shares with the gerundive. But the infinitive differs from the gerundive in three important respects: first, whereas the gerundive can, in a suitable lexical context, replace any other noun, the embedding of the infinitive into its matrix clause is subject to a number of conditions and restrictions; second, in some cases the infinitive enters in to a partial fusion with the matrix clause; and third, the infinitive can in some cases split and be redistributed in a fashion similar to the transformations which were found in the preceding chapters to apply to the finite clause. These conditions have as their consequence the fact that constructions involving the infinitive are among the most complex in the English language.

As we have observed on several occasions, the verb BE in English often diverges from the syntactic patterns which are characteristic of other verbs. This is true when the infinitive accompanies that verb, too, for which reason the first section in this chapter will treat those constructions in which the infinitive appears in matrix clauses which contain BE. Then we will examine those cases where the verb of the matrix clause is a verb other than BE, i. e., a lexical verb. Finally, in a third section, we will look at a number of other syntactic situations involving the use of this structure.

### The Infinitive in Matrix Clauses with BE

The first two syntactic situations under this rubric have to do with cases where the infinitive and a nominal element are linked by the verb BE. Here and in the sequel we shall represent such situations by means of abbreviations which will indicate the essential structure of the entire sequence of elements. The letters "INF" stand for 'infinitive', of course, and "NOM" refers to a 'nominal'.

### 1. NOM + BE + INF

This construction is exemplified by the following phrase:

the orders were for the passengers to remain in their seats

This can be analyzed as follows:

IS1: the orders BE + INF
IS2: the passengers remain in their seats

The generation of the sentence takes place by the following steps:

INFZ / 2: for the passengers to remain in their seats

The hallmark of the English infinitive is that the subject is preceded by *for* and the first verb form present by *to*. Embedding takes place by the replacement of the element INF in the matrix clause with the infinitivized infrastructure:

E / 2: the orders BE + for the passengers to remain in their seats

It remains only to complete the generation of the matrix clause, IS1, which takes place in the usual way:

PAST, PSNM: the orders were + for the passengers to remain in their seats

Since there are no further changes to be made, this sequence constitutes the output of the generative process:

SOP: "The orders were for the passengers to remain in their seats."

However, when these transformations have been completed, the output sentence can still be subjected to Basic Transformations 1 through 7. For example, the first auxiliary can be topicalized to form a yes-no question:

T / AUX1: were the orders for the passengers to remain in their seats
SOP: "Were the orders for the passengers to remain in their seats? "

## 2. INF + BE + NOM

This construction can give rise to two different sequences involving the same lexical items:

for parents to give their children greater freedom is the tendency today
it is the tendency today for parents to give their children greater freedom

It will thus be necessary, not only to show how the clauses in these sentences are generated from their respective infrastructures, but also to indicate the subsequent transformations which can be applied in order to produce both variants above. The infrastructures are:

IS1: INF + BE the tendency today
IS2: parents give their children greater freedom

As before, we begin with the infinitive:

INFZ / 2: for parents to give their children greater freedom

This is now embedded in the clause which is the matrix clause:

E / 2: for parents to give their children greater freedom + BE the tendency today

The verb of IS1 can now be finitized:

PSNM: for parents to give their children greater freedom + is the tendency today
SOP: "For parents to give their children greater freedom is the tendency today."

When we consider this sentence in comparison with the other one, which we will now attempt to generate, we note that the infinitive in the utterance above is the first element in the matrix clause. Given its greater semantic weight, it is understandable that, in the course of the development of the language, some means might have arisen of shifting this infinitive to, or at least closer to, the comment position at the end of the utterance. When this happens, the element IT is inserted into the slot left vacant by the movement of the infinitive to serve as a dummy subject. This sequence of operations can be applied to dependent finite clauses as well, e. g.:

it is understandable that this has arisen

reflects the infrastructures:

IS1: THAT + BE understandable
IS2: this arise

and the sentence above would be generated:

CRLV, PSNM: this has arisen
E / 2: THAT + this has arisen + BE understandable
CJNLZ: THAT this has arisen + BE understandable
C / 2: . . . BE understandable + THAT this has arisen
I / IT: IT + BE understandable + THAT this has arisen
FNTZ / 1: IT + is understandable + THAT this has arisen
SOP: "It is understandable that this has arisen."

The same transformations can be applied to the infinitive embedded in its matrix clause in the sequence:

for parents to give their children greater freedom + BE the tendency today

First, the infinitive is commentized:

C / INF: ... BE the tendency today + for parents to give their children greater freedom

Then the element IT is inserted in place of the commentized infinitive:

I / IT: IT + BE the tendency today + for parents to give their children greater freedom

Finally, the matrix verb is modified:

PSNM: IT + is the tendency today + for parents to give their children greater freedom

By these changes, we have generated the second of those clauses which reflect the basic structure INF + BE + NOM:

SOP: "It is the tendency today for parents to give their children greater freedom."

It might be added at this point that this sequence is subject to further modification by the basic transformations. For example, the first auxiliary may be topicalized to form a yes-no question:

T / AUX1: is it the tendency today for parents to give their children greater freedom
SOP: "Is it the tendency today for parents to give their children greater freedom? "

## 3. INF + BE + INF

The next syntactic pattern involving the infinitive and the verb BE is that in which both the subject and the nominal or predicate noun are infinitives. The following utterances reflect this structure:

he was a fool to expect results
the Assyrians were the first to use chariots
Bill is a good person to know
that sonata is a difficult piece for her to play

The surface structure of these sentences bears no clear relation to the pattern in the caption of this section, an observation which means that these utterances can be generated only through extensive transformations. The first of these sentences reflects a combination of three infrastructures:

238

IS1: INF2 + BE + INF3
IS2: he expect results
IS3: he be a fool

The latter infrastructures are infinitivized, and then embedded in IS1:

INFZ / 2: for him to expect results
INFZ / 3: for him to be a fool

The pattern of embedding is clause-element-replacing, i. e., the infinitivized infrastructures simply take the place of the elements labeled "INF" in the matrix clause:

IS1: INF2 + BE + INF3
E / 2,3: for him to expect results + BE + for him to be a fool

As in the case in the preceding section, the subject infinitive is commentized:

C / 2: . . . + BE + for him to be a fool ++ for him to expect results

At this point, something unusual happens, something which is unique to these infinitive constructions: the subject of the commentized infinitive is retopicalized to fill the slot left vacant by the commentization of the whole structure:

T / $SJ_2$: him + BE + for him to be a fool ++ for . . . to expect results

This change is sometimes referred to in other theories of syntax as "subject-raising." It has been identified by comparison in a large number of cases and is required by the sense of the utterance. The justification for its being considered a pattern in English thus depends on its extensive use and wide utility in the analysis of this and related constructions. As a result of this transformation, the sequence of elements begins with *him + BE*. We noted in our analysis of the English infrastructure that the tagmeme SUBJ normally preceded the tagmemes ITVAV and VERB. Because this sequence of forms − SUBJ (+ ITVAV) + VERB − is so deeply rooted in the structure of English and in the consciousness of its speakers, it is understandable that any initial sequence of elements could, and indeed, will be interpreted by the native speaker as being SUBJ + VERB, even though the nominal element is not the grammatical subject of that verb, but another element which has been moved to that position by the application of other transformations. This reinterpretation of these two initial elements as subject and verb compels a change in the form of these elements, a change which we incorporate into 'our set of rules as "subjectivization" (SJCTZ). Through it, the nominal element, whatever its provenience, is transformed into the nominative or subjective case, though it retains its number; by so doing it becomes the pseudosubject (PSJ) of the matrix clause. In the present case, the infinitive subject *him* becomes *he*; this change is expressed as follows:

SJCTZ: he + BE + for him to be a fool ++ for . . . to to expect results

When the matrix verb is finitized, it conforms in both person and number to the pseudosubject, just as though it were a subject of its own clause:

PAST, PSNM: he + was + for him to be a fool ++ for . . . to expect results

This change has still further consequences for the remaining elements of the utterance. Because of the loss of the object of the preposition *for*, the parallel between the two infinitives has been obscured, and hence the expression *for him* (from IS3), which also refers to the person represented by the pronoun *he*, is deleted. Furthermore, after *was*, the verb phrase *to be* is redundant, and it, too, is deleted. These changes lead to the following deletions (indicated, in this case, by parentheses):

D / EE: he + was + (for him to be) a fool ++ for . . . to expect results

As a general rule, a preposition in English must be followed by a noun or pronoun object; thus, when by the operation of this or another transformation, a preposition loses its object, it is deleted:

D / EE: he + was + . . . a fool ++ (for) . . . to expect results

The remaining elements constitute the utterance which it was our aim to generate:

SOP: "He was a fool to expect results."

The second sentence:

the Assyrians were the first to use chariots

can be derived in the same way. Its component infrastructures are the following:

IS1: INF2 + BE + INF3
IS2: the Assyrians use chariots
IS3: the Assyrians be the first

As before, the first step is to infinitivize the two infrastructures which are to be embedded:

INFZ / 2: for the Assyrians to use chariots
INFZ / 3: for the Assyrians to be the first
IS1: INF2 + BE + INF3
E / 2,3: for the Assyrians to use chariots + BE + for the Assyrians to be the first

Next, the initial infinitive, INF2, is commentized:

C / 2: ... + BE + for the Assyrians to be the first ++ for the Assyrians to use chariots

Now the subject of the commentized infinitive is topicalized:

T / $SJ_2$: the Assyrians + BE + for the Assyrians to be the first ++ for ... to use chariots

By subjectivization (SJCTZ), the phrase *the Assyrians* is transformed into the subjective case and becomes the pseudosubject of BE:

SJCTZ: the Assyrians + BE + for the Assyrians to be the first ++ for ... to use chariots

Then the verb of the matrix clause can be modified:

PAST, PSNM: the Assyrians + were + for the Assyrians to be the first ++ for ... to use chariots

Now the redundant elements in INF3 and the superfluous preposition in INF2 are deleted:

D / EE: the Assyrians + were + ...... the first ++ ...... to use chariots

This, of course, is our output sentence:

SOP: "The Assyrians were the first to use chariots."

A third case illustrates the principle that the object of an infinitive may also become a pseudosubject; this construction appears in the following sentence:

Bill is a good person to know

This reflects the infrastructures:

IS1: INF2 + BE + INF3
IS2: SOMEONE know Bill
IS3: SOMEONE know a good person

Infinitivization and embedding take place as in the examples above:

INFZ / 2: for SOMEONE to know Bill
INFZ / 3: for SOMEONE to know a good person
E / 2,3: for SOMEONE to know Bill + BE + for SOMEONE to know a good person
C / 2: ... + BE + for SOMEONE to know a good person ++ for SOMEONE to know Bill

At this point, the object of INF2 — not the subject, as in the two previous examples — is topicalized:

T / $OJ_2$: Bill + BE + for SOMEONE to know a good person ++ for SOMEONE to know ...

In order to function as a pseudosubject, the word *Bill* must undergo subjectivization:

SJCTZ: Bill + BE + for SOMEONE to know a good person ++ for SOMEONE to know ...

The verb in the matrix clause is now finitized:

PSNM: Bill + is + for SOMEONE to know a good person ++ for SOMEONE to know ...

As in the other cases of this construction, the infinitive INF3 loses its subject and verb; deletion of the subject of IS2 is optional:

D / EE: Bill + is + . . . . . . a good person ++ (for SOMEONE) to know . . .
SOP: "Bill is a good person (for someone) to know."

The following is a further example of a sentence with the infinitive object as pseudosubject:

that sonata is a difficult piece for her to play

242

This sentence would be generated in the following way:

IS1: INF2 + BE + INF3
IS2: she play that sonata
IS3: she play a difficult piece
INFZ / 2: for her to play that sonata
INFZ / 3: for her to play a difficult piece
E / 2,3: for her to play that sonata + BE + for her to play a difficult piece

C / 2: ... + BE + for her to play a difficult piece ++ for her to play that sonata

T / OJ$_2$: that sonata + BE + for her to play a difficult piece ++ for her to play ...

SJCTZ: that sonata + BE + for her to play a difficult piece ++ for her to play ...

PSNM: that sonata + is + for her to play a difficult piece ++ for her to play ...

D / EE: that sonata + is + . . . . . . a difficult piece ++ for her to play ...

SOP: "That sonata is a difficult piece for her to play."

On the basis of these examples, we may hazard some generalizations about the constraints on these constructions. To begin with, the subjects of the two infinitives must be identical. However, if INF3 (which occupies the NOMNL tagmeme in IS1: INF2 + BE + INF3) contains BE, then the subject of INF3 is topicalized, as in the first two examples:

T / SJ$_2$: ... + BE + for him to be a fool$_{INF3}$ ++

for *him* to expect results$_{INF2}$

T / SJ$_2$: ... + BE + for the Assyrians to be the first$_{INF3}$

++ for *the Assyrians* to use chariots$_{INF2}$

On the other hand, if the verb in INF3 is a lexical verb (and it must be the same lexical verb as that of INF2), then the object of INF2 may be topicalized:

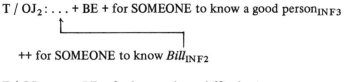

T / OJ$_2$: ... + BE + for SOMEONE to know a good person$_{INF3}$

++ for SOMEONE to know *Bill*$_{INF2}$

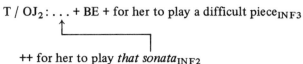

T / OJ$_2$: ... + BE + for her to play a difficult piece$_{INF3}$

++ for her to play *that sonata*$_{INF2}$

By these criteria, the two forms of the construction INF + BE + INF may be distinguished. It should be added that the prohibition against the topicalization of elements from a commentized infrastructure finds its sole exception in these infinitive constructions.

*4. INF + BE + ∅*

This pattern resembles one of the THERE-transformations in that it also displays a "zero-predicate," i. e., no element follows the verb BE in its infrastructure. This is one of the most widely used of the several structures involving BE and the infinitive, although its presence is often concealed by deletion. The output of this transformation consists of sentences which contain the sequence *BE (for ... ) to ...*, e. g.:

it is for her to read these books
she is to read these books
these books are for her to read

It is characteristic of utterances of this kind that they connote obligation, responsibility, purpose, and in some cases, instrumentality. From the formal point of view, these sentences may be analyzed as containing two infrastructures, e. g.:

IS1: INF + BE + ∅
IS2: she read these books

The generation of these sentences begins in a manner not unlike that of other clauses, i. e., with the infinitivization (INFZ), embedding (E), and commentization (C) of the infinitive clause:

INFZ / 2: for her to read these books
E / 2: for her to read these books + BE + ∅
C / 2: ... + BE + ∅ ++ for her to read these books

At this point, three possibilities emerge as to what may fill the slot left vacant by the commentizing of the infinitive. For one thing, the dummy element IT may be inserted in the place of that element:

I / IT: IT + BE + $\emptyset$ + for her to read these books

Then the verb of the matrix clause is modified:

PSNM: IT + is + $\emptyset$ + for her to read these books
SOP: "It is for her to read these books."

This utterance has a connotation of contrast, as if to say that it was her obligation, and not someone else's to study the volumes in question.

There is a second possibility which the speaker may avail himself of after commentization – he may retopicalize the subject of the infinitive:

T / SJ$_2$: her + BE + $\emptyset$ + for ... to read these books

This element must now be modified by subjectivization (SJCTZ) to conform to the morphological patterns typical of the sequence of subject and verb:

SJCTZ: she + BE + $\emptyset$ + for ... to read these books
PSNM: she + is $\emptyset$ + for ... to read these books

Surplus prepositions must be deleted:

D / EE: she + is + $\emptyset$ + . . . . . . to read these books
SOP: "She is to read these books."

A third possibility is to retopicalize, not the subject, but the object of the infinitive. After commentizing, the derivation would proceed as follows:

T / OJ$_2$: these books + BE + $\emptyset$ + for her to read . . .
SJCTZ: these books + BE + $\emptyset$ + for her to read . . .
PSNM: these books + are + $\emptyset$ + for her to read
SOP: "These books are for her to read."

Thus, the three sequences:

it is for her to read these books
she is to read these books
these books are for her to read

are all derived from the same infrastructures by the same set of transformations, the only difference being the element which is placed in the slot made vacant by the commentization of the embedded infinitive: the dummy topic IT; the infinitive subject *her* > *she*; or the infinitive object *these books*. All three present the same lexical material, organized differently in regard to topic and comment, and have the general connotation of obligation, responsibility, or purpose.

To be sure, there some limiting conditions which apply to these constructions. First, when the infinitive clause contains no object, then it is obviously not possible to retopicalize that element, e. g., when the verb is intransitive. Thus, the structure:

for them to leave tomorrow + BE + $\emptyset$

can only yield the following utterances:

it is for them to leave tomorrow
they are to leave tomorrow

Moreover, when the object stands in such a relation to the verb that the two represent a single concept or action, then the object cannot be retopicalized, e. g., the structure:

for him to call the office immediately + BE + $\emptyset$

can, by the patterns above, the changed in three different ways:

! it is for him to call the office immediately
! he is to call the office immediately
? ? ? the office is for him to call immediately

The phrase *to call the office* represents, in most contexts, a single and unitary action, so that the retopicalization of the object phrase *the office* would separate lexical items which are meaningful only in close conjunction with one another. As a result, the last sentence above would sound natural only in a very rare or unusual context.

The structure INF + BE + $\emptyset$ also occurs in a number of structures which have been interpreted as infinitives modifying nouns (cf. Nilsen 1968:91 ff.):

he gave us bread to eat
there are several questions (for us) to consider
the truck is John's to take care of

Our interpretation of these infinitives which supposedly modify nouns is, in effect, that they are the last remains of the relative clauses in which they stand, the existence of which has been concealed by the deletion of redundant elements. Thus, the first may be derived from a combination of three infrastructures, one of which is the structure INF + BE + $\emptyset$ under consideration here:

IS1: he give us bread
IS2: INF3 + BE + $\emptyset$
IS3: we eat bread

The generation of the sentence proceeds as follows:

INFZ / 3: for us to eat bread
E / 3: for us to eat bread ++ BE + $\emptyset$
C / 3: . . . + BE + $\emptyset$ ++ for us to eat bread
T / OJ, SJCTZ: bread + BE + $\emptyset$ ++ for us to eat . . .
PAST, PSNM: bread + was + $\emptyset$ ++ for us to eat . . .

This sequence is now subject to the basic transformation by which relative clauses are generated:

RLTVZ, T / RLTV: WHICH + was + $\emptyset$ + for us to eat . . .

It is as a relative clause that this sequence is embedded into the independent clause, IS1:

E / 2: he give us bread ++ WHICH + was + $\emptyset$ + for us to eat . . .

Now the matrix clause is formed:

PAST, PSNM: he gave us bread ++ WHICH + was + $\emptyset$ + for us to eat . . .

At this point, the relative pronoun plus the verb are deleted (cf. König & Nickel 1970:71); the phrase *for us* need not be deleted, but duplicates the pronoun *us* of the independent clause, and hence is redundant:

D / EE: he gave us bread ++ . . . + . . . + (for us) to eat . . .
SOP: "He gave us bread (for us) to eat."

These deletions, incidentally, manifest a characteristic which is common in the case of complex sentences: the deleted material is often in the center of the utterance, at the farthest remove from the initial topic and final comment positions.

The next sentence, *there are several questions (for us) to consider*, reflects the infrastructures:

IS1: several questions BE + $\emptyset$
IS2: INF3 + BE + $\emptyset$
IS3: we consider several questions

What is different here is that the presence of a zero-predicate in IS1 forces us to a THERE-transformation. Apart from this, the generation of the sentence proceeds as in the example above:

INFZ / 3: for us to consider several questions
E / 3: for us to consider several questions ++ BE + $\emptyset$
C / 3: . . . BE + $\emptyset$ ++ for us to consider several questions
T / $OJ_3$, SJCTZ: several questions + BE + $\emptyset$ ++ for us to consider . . .
PSNM: several questions + are + $\emptyset$ ++ for us to consider . . .
RLTVZ, T / RLTV: WHICH + are + $\emptyset$ ++ for us to consider . . .

This relative clause is now embedded in IS1:

E / 2: several questions +++ WHICH + are + $\emptyset$ ++ for us to consider . . . +++ BE + $\emptyset$
PSNM: several questions +++ WHICH + are + $\emptyset$ ++ for us to consider . . . +++ are + $\emptyset$

At this point, a THERE-transformation must be applied:

T / VFF+BE1: are + several questions +++ WHICH + are + $\emptyset$ ++ for us to consider . . . + $\emptyset$
I / THERE: THERE are + several questions +++ WHICH + are + $\emptyset$ ++ for us to consider . . . + $\emptyset$

As before, the relative pronoun and the verb following it are deleted; the phrase *for us* may be deleted optionally:

D / EE: THERE are + several·questions +++ . . . + . . . + $\emptyset$ ++ (for us) to consider . . . + $\emptyset$
SOP: "There are several questions (for us) to consider."

The last of the three sentences again differs in the composition of the independent clause. The infrastructures present in the sentence *the truck is John's to take care of* are:

IS1: the truck BE John's truck
IS2: INF3 + BE + $\emptyset$
IS3: John take care of the truck

The role of the infinitive clause (IS3) is the same here as in the others above:

INFZ / 3: for John to take care of the truck
E / 3: for John to take care of the truck + BE + $\emptyset$
C / 3: . . . + BE + $\emptyset$ ++ for John to take care of the truck

In this case, it is the subject of the infinitive which is retopicalized:

T / SJ$_3$, SJCTZ: John + BE + $\emptyset$ ++ for . . . to take care of the truck

The matrix clause, IS2, is finitized:

PSNM: John + is + $\emptyset$ ++ for . . . to take care of the truck

This expression is now embedded in IS1 as a relative clause:

RLTVZ: John + is + $\emptyset$ ++ for . .,. to take care of WHICH
T / RLTV: WHICH John + is + $\emptyset$ ++ for . . . to take care of . . .
E / 2: the truck BE John's truck +++ WHICH John + is + $\emptyset$ ++ for . . . to take care of . . .

At this point, the independent clause, IS1, is finitized:

PSNM: the truck is John's truck +++ WHICH John + is + $\emptyset$ ++ for . . . to take care of . . .

Again, those elements which merely duplicate others are deleted:

D / EE: the truck is John's . . . +++ . . . + . . . + $\emptyset$ ++ . . . . . . to take care of . . .
SOP: "The truck is John's to take care of."

In all three of these complex sentences, the structure *INF + BE + $\emptyset$* serves as a hidden, yet indispensable element in the development of the terminal utterance.


## 5. *INF + BE + ADJ*

We turn now to those structures in which an infinitive stands as subject of the verb BE, which in turn is followed by what in traditional terminology would be a predicate adjective, but what for us would be a verb complement. For reasons which are suggested by the sentences below, the utterances which reflect this basic pattern can be further subdivided into three groups:

(5a) for him to call her + was pointless
! IT was pointless + for him to call her
? ? ? he + was pointless + . . . to call her
? ? ? she + was pointless + for him to call . . .
    (5b) for him to call her + was easy
! IT was easy + for him to call her
? ? ? he + was easy + . . . to call her
! she + was easy + for him to call . . .
    (5c) for him to call her + was clever of him
! IT was clever of him + for him to call her
! he + was clever (of him) + . . . to call her
? ? ? she + was clever of him + for him to call . . .

In the preceding section, we noted that there were three possibilities for further modification after an infinitive had been commentized: first, the dummy element IT could be inserted in the place of the infinitive; second, the subject of the infinitive could be topicalized and subjectivized; and third, the object of the infinitive could undergo these changes.

These three changes have been applied to each of the infinitive constructions above, and, as the output sequences show, with differing results in each case. In the case of 5a, only the insertion of IT in place of a commentized infinitive yields an acceptable utterance. In the sentences under 5b, IT-insertion produces an acceptable utterance, as does the topicalization of the infinitive object. And in 5c, IT-insertion again results in an acceptable utterance, and so does the topicalization of the infinitive subject, in contrast to 5b. On the basis of these differences, we can postulate three classes of adjectives which are relevant to the construction INF + BE + ADJ.

In the first instance (5a), the adjective *pointless* in fact modifies the entire infinitive, its subject and object, as well as the action in which they are joined. In the second group (5b), the adjective really modifies the action of the verb in conjunction with its object: it is the act of calling her which is easy, and it is irrelevant to the construction who the caller is. And in the last example (5c), the adjective most narrowly modifies the subject of the infinitive, a relationship which is underscored by the fact that the adjectives of this group are followed by a prepositional phrase with *of*, the object of which is identical to the subject of the infinitive, e. g.:

250

| | kind | |
| it was | considerate | of him + for him to call her |
| | rude | |
| | boorish | |
| | ill-advised | |

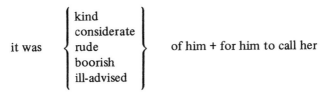

The transformations by which the various patterns are generated resemble those which obtained for the structure INF + BE + ∅ in the preceding section: after the embedding of the infinitive and the modification of the verb in the matrix clause, then follow commentization of the infinitive and the filling of the vacant slot by IT, by the subject of the infinitive, or by its object, as the case may be. As an example of the second category (5b), it may be instructive to consider a well-known sentence (Chomsky 1964:66):

John is easy to please

This reflects the two infrastructures:

IS1: INF2 BE easy
IS2: SOMEONE please John

As in the other examples, we begin by infinitivizing and embedding the second infrastructure:

INFZ / 2: for SOMEONE to please John
E / 2: for SOMEONE to please John + BE easy

The infinitive is then commentized:

C / 2: BE easy + for SOMEONE to please John

At this point, it would be possible to insert IT and delete the empty phrase *for SOMEONE*, thus producing one acceptable arrangement of these lexical items:

I / IT: IT + BE easy + for SOMEONE to please John
PSNM: IT + is easy + for SOMEONE to please John
D / EE: IT + is easy + . . . to please John
SOP: "It is easy to please John."

However, the speaker, after commentizing the infinitive, may also elect to retopicalize its object:

T / OJ$_2$: John + BE easy + for SOMEONE to please . . .

Subjectivization and finitization of the matrix verb follow:

SJCTZ: John + BE easy + for SOMEONE to please . . .
PSNM: John + is easy + for SOMEONE to please . . .

Deletion of dummy elements is optional, though customary:

D / EE: John + is easy + . . . to please . . .
SOP: "John is easy to please."

If the object of the infinitive were a pronoun, i. e., if *John* were *him*, then subjectivization would be more visible. There would then be a clear contrast between:

IT + is easy + for SOMEONE to please *him*
*he* + is easy + for SOMEONE to please . . .

There are other problematic constructions which can be interpreted as reflecting the third of these three kinds of clauses which we have described above (5c). These include brief social formulae like the following:

(it was very) kind of you to come
how kind of you to come (cf. Coppieters 1969:196)

These represent variant transformations of the same infrastructures, along with varying patterns of deletion. The infrastructures in question are:

IS: INF + BE very kind of you
IS2: you come

The generation of the sentences proceeds as before:

INFZ / 2: for you to come
E / 2: for you to come + BE very kind of you

At this point, the infinitive is commentized and IT inserted:

C / 2: . . . BE very kind of you + for you to come
I / IT: IT + BE very kind of you + for you to come
PAST, PSNM: IT + was very kind of you + for you to come

The first utterances are produced by varying patterns of deletion:

D / EE: (IT was very) kind of you + (for you) to come
SOP: "It was very kind of you to come."
    "Kind of you to come."

The second sentence above has the form of an indirect question, and hence some element must be interrogativized (Basic Transformation 4):

ITRGZ: IT + was HOW kind of you + for you to come

The syntactic element containing the interrogative expression is now topicalized:

T / ITRG: HOW kind of you + IT + was . . . + for you to come

Again, deletion of the communicatively less important elements completes the transformation:

D / EE: HOW kind of you + (IT + was . . . + for you) to come
SOP: "How kind of you to come!"


## 6. NOM + BE + ADJ + PREP + INF

As the formula in the caption indicates, the infinitive in this construction has the function of the object of a preposition. There is only one preposition in English which can have an infinitive as its object, i. e., *for*. Since this also precedes the subject of the infinitive itself, we must first establish its presence after certain adjectives by adverting to cases where it has ordinary nouns as its object:

the troops were ready for combat
the men are anxious for a signal
John was eager for acceptance

When an infinitive is present, this preposition is sometimes conspicuous by its absence:

the troops were ready to start
the troops were ready for the battle to start

the men are anxious to be fed
the men are anxious for their comrades to be fed

John was eager to meet Dr. Smith
John was eager for his wife to meet Dr. Smith

These contrasts are again to be explained through the process of deletion. There are a number of peculiarities which arise in connection with this construction, however, for which reason it will be helpful to trace the derivation of a few sentences in some detail.

As an example, let us take the last pair of sentences just cited. The infrastructures which underlie them are:

IS1: John BE eager for INF2
IS2a: John meet Dr. Smith
IS2b: his wife meet Dr. Smith

Taking the first of the two sentences, i. e., that with IS2a, we infinitivize and embed the infrastructure as in other cases of this kind:

INFZ / 2a: for John to meet Dr. Smith
E / 2a: John BE eager for + for John to meet Dr. Smith

We notice that the preposition *for* appears twice in the structure above: once as an element of the matrix clause, and once as the sign of the subject of the infinitive (an adaptation from Wagner 1968:90). Next, the matrix clause is modified:

PAST, PSNM: John was eager for + for John to meet Dr. Smith

Since the infinitive subject *John* simply repeats the subject of the matrix verb, that phrase can be deleted:

D / EE: John was eager for + for . . . to meet Dr. Smith

As a result of this deletion, three prepositions stand in contiguity with one another, *for* + *for* . . . *to*. On the principle that objectless prepositions constitute an anomaly, the first two of these are deleted (cf. Hathaway 1967:216). In the sequel, this will be included in the deletion process without special justification:

D / EE: John was eager . . . + . . . . . . to meet Dr. Smith
SOP: "John was eager to meet Dr. Smith."

The second of the two sentences which we have elected to analyze differs from the one above only in that the subject of the infinitive is different in the two cases. In other respects, its derivation follows, up to the point of deletion, the same path:

INFZ / 2b: for his wife to meet Dr. Smith
E / 2b: John BE eager for + for his wife to meet Dr. Smith
FNTZ / 1 (= PAST, PSNM): John was eager for + for his wife to meet Dr. Smith

Since the subject of the infinitive contains different information, it is not deleted here; the objectless preposition *for*, on the other hand, is dropped:

D / EE: John was eager . . . + for his wife to meet Dr. Smith
SOP: "John was eager for his wife to meet Dr. Smith."

In light of these analyses, we are now in a position to interpret another familiar example of this construction (cf. Chomsky 1964:66):

John is eager to please

In light of the foregoing, this must reflect:

IS1: John BE eager for + INF2
IS2: John please SOMEONE

The derivation proceeds as follows:

INFZ / 2: for John to please SOMEONE
E / 2: John BE eager for + for John to please SOMEONE
FNTZ / 1 (= PSNM): John is eager for + for John to please SOMEONE

At this point, the infinitive subject *John* may be deleted as a repetition of the subject of the matrix verb, its object *SOMEONE* as an empty element, and the preposition *for* because it has lost its object in both instances:

D / EE: John is eager . . . + . . . . . . to please . . .
SOP: "John is eager to please."

It is thus apparent that sentence and its counterpart, *John is easy to please*, reflect different structures within the category of infinitive constructions (cf. also Lees 1960a).


## The Infinitive in Matrix Clauses with LEXVB

In the foregoing description of infinitive constructions, the one factor which was held constant was that the verb of the matrix clause was BE. In the discussion which follows, that key verb is a lexical verb. Here, too, it is possible to discern several ways in which the infinitive may be related to the verb of the matrix clause. For one thing, it may function as the grammatical subject. Or again, it may stand after the verb of the matrix clause, in which case it displays several different patterns of fusion and linkage with that verb. We shall consider these two syntactic situations separately.

## 1. INF + LEXVB (+ OBJ)

When the infinitive is the subject of a lexical verb, it retains its character as a noun, though its function and relationship may be masked by a variety of subsequent modifications. The following sentences are not atypical of this condition:

it astonished me to hear that
I was astonished to hear that

Both of these sentences are derived from the same pair of infrastructures, namely:

IS1: INF astonish me
IS2: I hear that

The procedure by which the sentences above are generated is substantially the same as that used in connection with infinitives with BE: the infinitive clause is first generated separately, and then embedded in the matrix clause:

INFZ / 2: for me to hear that
E / 2: for me to hear that + astonish me

This sequence is susceptible of modification in two ways. The infinitive may be commentized, and then the element IT inserted as a dummy subject:

C / 2: astonish me + for me to hear that
I / IT: IT astonish me + for me to hear that
FNTZ / 1: IT astonished me + for me to hear that

Since the object of the matrix verb *me* and the subject of the infinitive *me* refer to the same person, the latter may be deleted as a repetition of the former; the objectless preposition *for* is also unnecessary:

D / EE: IT astonished me + . . . . . . to hear that
SOP: "It astonished me to hear that."

To be sure, this is not the only sentence which can be derived from these infrastructures. Because the verb of the matrix clause in the sequence:

for me to hear that + astonish me

256

is transitive, and the infinitive, in effect, a noun subject, the modification for the passive voice may be applied:

PASV: I be astonished by + for me to hear that

When finitized, this yields:

PAST, PSNM: I was astonished by + for me to hear that

As before, the subject of the infinitive, *me*, merely repeats the subject of the matrix verb, and hence may be dropped; the objectless prepositions *by* and *for* are also deleted:

D / EE: I was astonished . . . + . . . . . . to hear that
SOP: "I was astonished to hear that."

In the example above, the lexical verb *astonish* was followed by an object. It is also possible for infinitives to be subjects of intransitive verbs, in which case, of course, passivization is impossible. The following sentence illustrates this condition:

it remains (for us) to inquire into his reasons

This reflects the infrastructures:

IS1: INF2 remain
IS2: we inquire into his reasons

The pattern of generation is the same as in the preceding example:

INFZ / 2: for us to inquire into his reasons
E / 2: for us to inquire into his reasons + remain
C / 2: . . . remain + for us to inquire into his reasons
I / IT: IT remain + for us to inquire into his reasons
FNTZ / 1 (= PSNM): IT remains + for us to inquire into his reasons

Deletion of the infinitive subject *(for) us* is optional:

SOP: "It remains (for us) to inquire into his reasons."


## 2. *INF + LEXVB + ∅*

The examples above represent the function of the infinitive as subject of the lexical verb in a relation which is characteristic of the vast majority of such cases. There is a special category of verb in

English, however, whose valence is such that it is followed by a zero-object, one to which a somewhat different series of transformations may be applied. These verbs fall into two syntactic and semantic classes:

I: seem, appear
II: happen

The treatment of these verbs resembles that of the zero-predicates examined in the preceding section, i. e., INF + BE + ∅, in that here, too, the infinitive is commentized, and its subject then retopicalized and subjectivized. These constructions are reflected in the sentences below:

she seems to be rich
he happens to be poor

As to the former, it contains two infrastructures:

IS1: INF2 seem
IS2: she be rich

The second of these is infinitivized and embedded as follows:

INFZ / 2: for her to be rich
E / 2: for her to be rich + seem

This infinitive is now commentized, and its subject retopicalized:

C / 2: ... seem + for her to be rich
T / $SJ_2$: her + seem + for ... to be rich

By subjectivization, the subject of the infinitive now becomes the pseudosubject of the matrix verb:

SJCTZ: she seem + for ... to be rich

The matrix verb is then modified, and the objectless preposition deleted:

PSNM: she seems + for ... to be rich
D / EE: she seems + ... ... to be rich
SOP: "She seems to be rich."

By way of comparison, it should be noted that verbs like *seem* may also take dependent finite clauses as subjects. With this adjustment, the infrastructures above would also generate the sentence:

it seems that she is rich

This would be produced by the following steps:

IS1: THAT seem
IS2: she be rich
FNTZ / 2: she is rich
E / 2: THAT + she is rich + seem
CJNLZ: THAT she is rich + seem
C / 2: ... seem + THAT she is rich
I / IT: IT seem + THAT she is rich
FNTZ / 1: IT seems + THAT she is rich
SOP: "It seems that she is rich."

By the same sets of procedures, the infrastructures:

IS1: INF2 happen − − − THAT happen
IS2: he be poor

can be transformed into the sentences:

he happens to be poor
it happens that he is poor

There are a number of similar patterns of expression which may be interpreted as variants of these structures. One of these has to do with the presence of a mere adjective after a verb of Class I, e. g., *seem*. This condition was exemplified some years ago in a discussion of the following expression:

the book seems to be interesting (Chomsky 1957:15)

At that time it was pointed out that this expression was superficially identical in structure to others like:

the child seems to be sleeping

and yet the verb *to be* could be eliminated in the former case, though not in the latter:

! the book seems interesting
? ? ? the child seems sleeping

The reason has less to do with the verb *seem* − though that, too, is involved − than with the different functions of the verb *to be* in the two sentences. The former is derived from the two infrastructures below in the following way:

IS1: INF2 seem
IS2: the book be interesting
INFZ / 2: for the book to be interesting
E / 2: for the book to be interesting + seem
C / 2: ... seem + for the book to be interesting
T / SJ$_2$: the book + seem + for ... to be interesting
SJCTZ: the book seem + for ... to be interesting
FNTZ / 1 (= PSNM): the book seems + for ... to be interesting
D / EE: the book seems + . . . . . . (to be) interesting
SOP: "The book seems (to be) interesting."

The second of the two sentences is derived from the infrastructures:

IS1: INF2 seem
IS2: the child sleep

Before infinitivization, the verb is modified to show limited duration, a common verb modification:

LMDR: the child be sleeping
INFZ / 2: for the child to be sleeping

From this point on, the derivation is the same as in the case above:

E / 2: for the child to be sleeping + seem
C / 2: ... seem + for the child to be sleeping
T / SJ$_2$: the child + seem + for ... to be sleeping
SJCTZ: the child seem + for ... to be sleeping
FNTZ / 1: the child seems + for ... to be sleeping

At this point, the objectless preposition *for* is deleted. However, the deletion of the phrase *to be* is impossible, because it is not the lexical verb in its infrastructure, but only part of it: it is an auxiliary, linked to the lexical verb as part of the modification LMDR:

D / EE: the child seems + . . . . . . to be sleeping
SOP: "The child seems to be sleeping."

These examples indicate that the verb BE may be relatively freely deleted when it is the main verb in an infinitive clause; as an auxiliary, however, it has an indispensable communicative role to play, and must be retained.

In another case, too, the verb *seem* appears to be followed by an adjective, so that the formula of the caption LEXVB + ∅ would not appear to be justified. This occurs in sentences like:

the plane seems certain to be late
for the plane to be late seems certain

A different, though evidently related sentence is:

for the plane to be late seems to be certain

Another form of this utterance, one sometimes heard, but one which does not seem entirely acceptable to the ear of the author, is the sequence:

? it seems to be certain for the plane to be late

As in other cases of this kind, our concern is to explain these syntactic variants in a way which shows their relation to one another as organic developments of their component infrastructures. The key to the interpretation of these sentences lies in the realization that there are two infinitives which are involved here, not just one. On this hypothesis, the infrastructures in question would be:

IS1: INF2 seem
IS2: INF3 be certain
IS3: the plane be late

The derivation proceeds as follows:

INFZ / 3: for the plane to be late
E / 3: for the plane to be late + be certain
INFZ / 2: for + for the plane to be late + to be certain

It is essential to the interpretation of this structure to recognize that the subject of the infinitive *for INF to be certain* is also an infinitive, namely, *for the plane to be late*. Moreover, there is an alternative at this point which is crucial for the further development of these structures: it is possible to commentize the infinitive subject and to replace it in the matrix infinitive with IT. For the moment, we will disregard this possibility, but return to it after the sequence of elements in its present form has been fully transformed. The next step is to embed the structure under discussion, and then to finitize the matrix clause:

E / 2: for + for the plane to be late + to be certain ++ seem
C / 2: . . . seem ++ for + for the plane to be late + to be certain

As before, the subject of the commentized infinitive — here the embedded infinitive — is retopicalized:

T / SJ$_3$: for the plane to be late ++ seem ++ for . . . to be certain
SJCTZ: for the plane to be late + seem ++ for . . . to be certain
FNTZ / 1: for the plane to be late + seems ++ for . . . to be certain

We observed in the discussion of the examples which immediately preceded this analysis that the elements *to be,* when not part of an auxiliary verb, may be deleted:

D / EE: for the plane to be late + seems ++ . . . . . . (to be) certain
SOP: "For the plane to be late seems (to be) certain."

Let us now return to that point in the derivation where the two infinitives stood alone, the one embedded in the other:

for + for the plane to be late + to be certain

Again and again in these constructions, we note the potentiality for any full infrastructure to be commentized; this alternative is available to the speaker here, too:

C / 3: for . . . to be certain + for the plane to be late

After this step, the derivation proceeds as before:

E / 2: for . . . to be certain + for the plane to be late ++ seem

In this step, the infinitive complex is commentized:

C / 2: . . . seem ++ for . . . to be certain + for the plane to be late

There are two possibilities which arise at this point: as the first, IT may be inserted, in which case the derivation proceeds as follows:

I / IT: IT seem ++ for . . . to be certain + for the plane to be late
FNTZ / 1: IT seems ++ for . . . to be certain + for the plane to be late
D / EE: IT seems ++ . . . . . . (to be) certain + for the plane to be late
SOP: ? "It seems (to be) certain for the plane to be late."

The second option open to the speaker after the commentizing of the infinitive is the retopicalization of the subject of the infinitive. The subject of INF2, *for INF to be certain,* is the entire infinitive clause INF3, *for the plane to be late,* and we have already seen that this leads to the acceptable sequence:

for the plane to be late seems (to be) certain

In infinitive constructions of this kind, the subject of INF3 — in this example, *the plane* — may also be topicalized and become the pseudosubject of the verb *seem* in IS1. This operation takes place as follows:

T / $SJ_3$: the plane ++ seem ++ for ... to be certain + for ... to be late

SJCTZ: the plane seem ++ for ... to be certain + for ... to be late

PSNM: the plane seems ++ for ... to be certain + for ... to be late

At this point, the objectless prepositions and the redundant verb phrase *to be* from INF2 are deleted:

D / EE: the plane seems ++ ...... certain + ...... to be late

SOP: "The plane seems certain to be late."

Sentences like this one convey the impression that *seem* and other verbs of its kind may be followed by an adjective, much as a predicate adjective follows the verb BE. As the foregoing analysis indicates, however, this pattern of surface structure may be interpreted as reflecting the multiple embedding of infinitives, with substantial deletions. We will discover later in this chapter that this occurs in other constructions as well.

In a not altogether different way, certain complex sentence patterns containing verbs in Class II may be explained, e. g., the sentences:

that he has escaped happens to be true
it happens to be true that he has escaped

These two utterances reflect the infrastructures:

IS1: INF2 happen
IS2: THAT be true
IS3: he escape

From the sentences as they stand, it is clear that the third infrastructure is a dependent finite clause:

FNTZ / 3
CRLV: he have escaped
PSNM: he has escaped

IS2: THAT be true
E / 3: THAT + he has escaped + be true
CJNLZ: THAT he has escaped + be true
INFZ / 2: for + THAT he has escaped + to be true

The speaker may elect here to commentize the dependent clause. We will pass over this opportunity, but return to it as soon as the present derivation has been realized:

IS1: INF2 happen
E / 2: for + THAT he has escaped + to be true ++ happen
C / 2: . . . happen ++ for + THAT he has escaped + to be true

Now the subject of the infinitive — in this case, the entire dependent finite clause — is retopicalized:

T / SJ$_3$: THAT he has escaped ++ happen ++ for . . . to be true
SJCTZ: THAT he has escaped + happen ++ for . . . to be true
FNTZ / 1: THAT he has escaped + happens ++ for . . . to be true
D / EE: THAT he has escaped + happens ++ . . . . . . to be true
SOP: "That he has escaped happens to be true."

For the generation of the second of these two sentences, we return to the point at which the dependent finite clause from IS3 lay embedded in INF2:

for + THAT he has escaped + to be true

The step which was omitted was the commentization of the dependent clause, which is now carried out:

C / 3: for . . . to be true + THAT he has escaped

It is in this form that the infinitive INF2 is embedded in IS1:

IS1: INF2 happen
E / 2: for . . . to be true + THAT he has escaped ++ happen

This infinitive complex is in turn commentized:

C / 2: . . . happen ++ for . . . to be true + THAT he has escaped

We insert IT into the slot left vacant by the commentized infinitive:

264

I / IT: IT happen ++ for . . . to be true + THAT he has escaped

FNTZ / 1: IT happens ++ for . . . to be true + THAT he has escaped

In contrast to the verbs of Class I, the expression *to be* cannot be deleted in the case of *happen*:

D / EE: IT happens ++ . . . . . . to be true + THAT he has escaped

SOP: "It happens to be true that he has escaped."

Thus, these expressions can be explained and analyzed on the assumption of multiple embedding in infinitives which are the subjects of verbs. In their underlying structure, these constructions reflect the basic syntactic pattern of INF + LEXVB + $\emptyset$.


## 3. LEXVB + INF

In all of the constructions which we have examined so far, the infinitive has functioned as a noun, although, to be sure, a complex one: it has been found to be relatively independent within the matrix clause, retaining its integrity as a single syntactic unit, at least up to the point where its subject or object was retopicalized and subjectivized. When we turn to those constructions in which the infinitive follows a lexical verb, we encounter a different set of conditions. In some cases, the infinitive retains its character as a noun; in others, it becomes a kind of verb complement. In some cases, the range of noun which can serve as the subject of the infinitive is restricted by the matrix verb; in others, it is not. In some cases, the matrix verb can undergo passivization, though not in others. On the basis of these three variables, we can identify five different ways in which the infinitive can be related to its matrix verb. The five types which evolve from this view reflect the five sets of conditions which are imposed by the valence of the matrix verb on the infinitive. In the following analysis, we shall consider them one by one.


### Type A Infinitive Constructions

In this construction, the subject of the infinitive must be the same as that of the matrix verb:

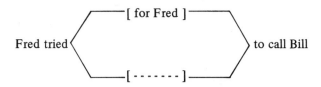

As the square brackets indicate, the subject phrase *for Fred* must be deleted. Moreover, the infinitive *for Fred to call Bill* has become simply an adjunct to the verb, because it cannot become the subject of the matrix verb when the latter is in the passive voice:

PASV: ? ? ?  for Fred to call Bill + was tried by Fred

This is perhaps the simplest of the infinitive constructions. Other examples of Type A verbs are: *forget, fail, deserve, demand, have (to), consent, agree, offer, refuse, decline, propose, swear, pledge,* etc.


*Type B Infinitive Constructions*

In the case of these verbs, the subject of the infinitive may or may not be the same as that of the matrix verb:

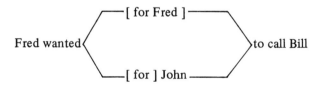

As the square brackets indicate, when the subjects of the infinitive and matrix verb are identical, the entire infinitive phrase, including the preposition *for*, must be deleted; when they are different, only the element *for* must be deleted. The infinitive with a Type B verb is merely a verb complement, as it cannot, as any noun could, become the subject of the matrix verb when the verb has been transformed into the passive voice:

PASV: ? ? ?  for John to call Bill + was wanted by Fred

In connection with the potential for passivization, it should be noted that both the Type A verb *try* and the Type B verb *want* may undergo this transformation when they have nouns as objects, e. g.:

Type A: Fred has already tried that approach → ! That approach has already been tried by Fred

Type B: the law wants him → ! he is wanted by the law

The labels "Type A, B, etc." refer thus to only one aspect of the valence of the matrix verb, i. e., the way in which it influences the form of the infinitive associated with it.

As far as the verbs of Type B are concerned, the two instances of the verb *dare* in the sentences below might be construed as constituting two different syntactic constructions:

Fred dared to swim out to the boat

Fred dared John to swim out the boat

It is true that the meaning of the verb *dare* is different in each of these sentences: in the former, it refers to a spirit of boldness or courage which its subject, Fred, possesses; in the latter, it refers to an act of provocation directed by Fred at the subject of the infinitive, John, an act which has as its aim the testing of John to see whether he, John, has these qualities. The first sentence implies unmistakably that Fred has these qualities of boldness and courage; as far as the second is concerned, he could be an utter coward. On the basis of this difference, one could regard the verb *dare* as being, in a sense, two verbs, which have meanings which correlate with different syntactic constructions. This point could be made in connection with many verbs of the language, and their proper and idiomatic use depends upon the speaker's being aware of the distinction. However, our concern here is with word placement, with whether a given word or syntactic element is present, and if so, what position it can occupy or be moved to, and under what circumstances. Though the difference in meaning in the sentences above certainly exists, it is not sufficient to establish two syntactic classes of verbs. Other examples of Type B verbs are: *like, promise, prepare*, etc.


## Type C Infinitive Constructions

As in the case of Type B, the subject of the infinitive in this type of construction may be either the same as, or different from the subject of the matrix verb:

267

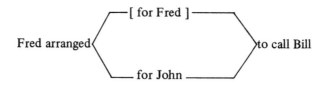

Fred arranged ⟨ [ for Fred ] / for John ⟩ to call Bill

As the brackets indicate, the entire infinitive subject phrase, including the preposition *for*, is deleted when the two subjects are identical; nothing is deleted when they are different. Another characteristic of this construction is the role of the infinitive within the matrix clauses: whereas in Type A and B constructions the infinitive has been fused to the matrix verb as a verb complement, in Type C constructions it retains its original quality of noun. This means that the infinitive, as a syntactic unit, can become the subject of the matrix verb when the latter is in the passive voice. This takes place in the following way:

IS1: Fred arrange INF2
IS2: John call Bill
INFZ / 2: for John to call Bill
E / 2: Fred arrange + for John to call Bill

Here the passive voice transformation, one of the common verb modifications, may be applied:

PASV: for John to call Bill + be arranged by Fred
PAST, PSNM: for John to call Bill + was arranged by Fred

This is an acceptable, if not exactly elegant English sentence:

SOP: "For John to call Bill was arranged by Fred."

Because the communicatively more important infinitive has, by the normal process of passivization, been shifted to the beginning of the utterance, it is not surprising that a device has evolved for moving it to the comment position where it, in most contexts, would belong. In this kind of construction, the infinitive, after passivization, could be commentized thus:

C / 2: ... be arranged by Fred + for John to call Bill

The element IT can now be inserted in the slot left vacant by the commentized infinitive:

268

I / IT: IT be arranged by Fred + for John to call Bill
PAST, PSNM: IT was arranged by Fred + for John to call Bill
SOP: "It was arranged by Fred for John to call Bill."

There is an important subclass of Type C constructions, the socalled *verba dicendi* or verbs of saying, which differ from the pattern above in two ways: first, with infinitives, these are almost always used in the passive voice — indeed, there are in some cases no active forms in common use; and second, after commentization of the infinitive, the vacant slot is filled, not by IT, but by retopicalization of the subject of the infinitive. These two characteristics can be seen in the following sentence:

John was said by Fred to have called Bill

On the basis of the foregoing analysis, it is not difficult to see that this was generated as follows:

IS1: Fred say INF2
IS2: John call Bill

Before infinitivization, the verb is modified to show current relevance:

CRLV: John have called Bill
INFZ / 2: for John to have called Bill
E / 2: Fred say + for John to have called Bill
PASV: for John to have called Bill + be said by Fred

This subject infinitive is now commentized:

C / 2: . . . be said by Fred + for John to have called Bill

At this point, the change characteristic of this subtype takes place — the retopicalization of the subject of the infinitive:

T / $SJ_2$: John + be said by Fred + for . . . to have called Bill

This element is transformed by subjectivization into the pseudo-subject of the matrix verb:

SJCTZ: John be said by Fred + for . . . to have called Bill
PAST, PSNM: John was said by Fred + for . . . to have called Bill
D / EE: John was said by Fred + . . . . . . to have called Bill
SOP: "John was said by Fred to have called Bill."

As we can see from this derivation, the corresponding structure in the active voice would be the unidiomatic expression:

? ? ? Fred said for John to have called Bill

To be sure, if the tense of the verb in the infinitive is changed, a sequence appears which is acceptable:

! Fred said for John to call Bill

But the verb *said* here is not a verbum dicendi, but a Type B verb. This sentence does not mean 'Fred said that John called Bill', rather it means that 'Fred gave orders to the effect that John should call Bill'. The verb *say*, when used with an infinitive, can only be regarded as a true verbum dicendi in the passive voice.

This discontinuity between the active and passive forms of the same infrastructure is illustrated by the following sentence, which contains the oft-used idiom *be supposed to*:

a guard was supposed to be on duty

The corresponding active form of this sentence is no longer completely acceptable:

? ? ? someone supposed (for? ) a guard to be on duty

If one were moved to use the verb *suppose* as a verb of saying in the active voice, the dependent clause would almost certainly be a dependent finite clause, a *that*-clause:

! someone supposed that a guard was on duty

Yet the passive sentence is derived from the same infrastructures as the active one containing the infinitive, and in the same way:

IS1: SOMEONE suppose INF2
IS2: a guard be on duty
INFZ / 2: for a guard to be on duty
E / 2: SOMEONE suppose + for a guard to be on duty
PASV: for a guard to be on duty + be supposed by SOMEONE
C / 2: ... be supposed by SOMEONE + for a guard to be on duty
T / $SJ_2$: a guard + be supposed by SOMEONE + for ... to be on duty
SJCTZ: a guard be supposed by SOMEONE + for ... to be on duty
PAST, PSNM: a guard was supposed by SOMEONE + for ... to be on duty

D / EE: a guard was supposed ... + ...... to be on duty
SOP: "A guard was supposed to be on duty."

This shows that constructions of this kind have become fixed and isolated within the larger structure of the language, to the extent that they cannot be retransformed into the active voice at the pleasure of the speaker – at least not without a substantial change of meaning.

The other difference between the two subgroups of Type C infinitives appears in connection with the filling of the empty slot caused by the commentization of the infinitive. In the case of "regular" Type C verbs, it was the element IT which was inserted; in the case of the verba dicendi, it was, as we have just noted, the subject of the infinitive which took the place of that commentized element. This comparison throws these contrasts into relief:

"regular"
! IT was arranged by Fred + for John to call Bill
? ? ? John + was arranged by Fred + for ... to call Bill
*verbum dicendi*
? ? ? It + was said by Fred + for John to have called Bill
! John + was said by Fred + for ... to have called Bill

These verbs of saying and reporting are not infrequently encountered in relatively complex constructions, which may be composed of two, three, or even more infrastructures. The sentence, for example:

they felt it advisable to attend college (after Coppieters 1969:302)

consists of a chain of embedded infinitives which follow the verb *feel*; the infrastructures reflected by the sentence are:

IS1: they feel INF2
IS2: INF3 be advisable
IS3: SOMEONE attend college

The derivation proceeds from the "most dependent" infrastructure to that in which it is itself embedded, in the following way:

INFZ / 3: for SOMEONE to attend college
E / 3: for SOMEONE to attend college + be advisable

At this point, IS2 is infinitivized:

INFZ / 2: for + for SOMEONE to attend college + to be advisable

The embedded infinitive may now be commentized, and the vacant slot filled by IT:

C / 3: for . . . to be advisable + for SOMEONE to attend college
I / IT: for IT to be advisable + for SOMEONE to attend college

This infinitive is in turn embedded in its matrix clause, IS1:

E / 2: they feel ++ for IT to be advisable + for SOMEONE to attend college
FNTZ / 1 (= PAST, PSNM): they felt ++ for IT to be advisable + for SOMEONE to attend college

At this point, empty elements may be deleted; IT is retained, however, because it stands for the commentized infinitive of IS3:

D / EE: they felt ++ . . . IT . . . advisable + . . . to attend college
SOP: "They felt it advisable to attend college."

This already involved derivation is subject to yet a further complication: the use of the passive voice in the verb of saying. This appears in the sentence:

it was found necessary to make a new entrance for heavy traffic
(Coppieters 1969:301)

Behind this utterance stand three infrastructures:

IS1: SOMEONE find INF2
IS2: INF3 be necessary
IS3: SOMEONE make a new entrance for heavy traffic

For reasons of simplicity of presentation, in all but the last stages of the derivation, we will abbreviate IS3 as "SOMEONE make etc." The sentence above would then be generated thus:

INFZ / 3: for SOMEONE to make etc
E / 3: for SOMEONE to make etc + be necessary

This complex is in turn infinitivized:

INFZ / 2: for + for SOMEONE to make etc + to be necessary

The embedded infinitive from IS3 is now commentized, but IT is not inserted, as it will be placed in the sentence at a later point:

C / 3: for . . . to be necessary + for SOMEONE to make etc

This sequence is now embedded in IS1:

> E / 2: SOMEONE find ++ for . . . to be necessary + for SOMEONE to make etc.

Here the verb of saying, *find*, is passivized, and its object, the infinitive complex of IS3 + IS2, becomes the subject of the passive verb:

> PASV: for . . . to be necessary + for SOMEONE to make etc ++ be found by SOMEONE

Here, again, the infinitive is commentized, and the empty slot filled by the dummy element IT:

> C / 2: . . . be found by SOMEONE ++ for . . . to be necessary + for SOMEONE to make etc
> 
> I / IT: IT + be found by SOMEONE ++ for . . . to be necessary + for SOMEONE to make etc

The verb of IS1 is now finitized, and empty elements deleted:

> FNTZ / 1 (= PAST, PSNM): IT was found by SOMEONE ++ for . . . to be necessary + for SOMEONE to make a new entrance for heavy traffic
> 
> D / EE: IT was found . . . ++ . . . . . . . . necessary + . . . to make a new entrance for heavy traffic
> 
> SOP: "It was found necessary to make a new entrance for heavy traffic."

These examples serve to convey some idea of the prevalence, importance, and complexity of these structures containing verbs of saying in English.

## Type D Infinitive Constructions

In this and the following types of infinitive constructions, there is not only an infinitive which follows the matrix verb, but another noun as well:

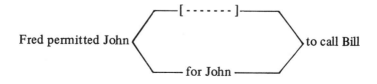

Fred permitted John / [ - - - - - - - ] \ to call Bill / for John \

The additional noun is a second noun object, and this must be identical to the noun in the subject phrase of the infinitive. The infinitive is also a true noun, not a verb complement, and as such can become the subject of the matrix verb in the passive voice. There are two obligatory deletions which apply to verbs of this type: in the active voice, the subject of the infinitive must be deleted; in the passive, the second noun object. Thus, the sentence above, as the penultimate stage in a derivation, would be generated in this way:

IS1: Fred permit John INF2
IS2: John call Bill
INFZ / 2: for John to call Bill
E / 2: Fred permit John + for John to call Bill
FNTZ / 1 (= PAST, PSNM): Fred permitted John + for John to call Bill

Here the subject of the infinitive, *John*, as well as the preposition *for*, which has thereby become objectless, are deleted:

D / EE: Fred permitted John + . . . . . . to call Bill
SOP: "Fred permitted John to call Bill."

Because the infinitive is a first noun object, it can become the subject of the matrix verb in the passive voice:

IS1: Fred permit John INF2
IS2: John call Bill
INFZ / 2: for John to call Bill
E / 2: Fred permit John + for John to call Bill                    .

Now the matrix verb is passivized:

PASV: for John to call Bill + be permitted John by Fred
FNTZ / 1: for John to call Bill + was permitted John by Fred

Here, the derivation may proceed in several directions. First, after deletion of the second noun object, the sequence as it stands constitutes an acceptable utterance:

D / EE: for John to call Bill + was permitted . . . by Fred
SOP: "For John to call Bill was permitted by Fred."

A more idiomatic form of this sentence can be achieved by commentizing the infinitive after passivization, and then retopicalizing its subject, thereby making it the pseudosubject of the matrix verb:

274

PASV: for John to call Bill + be permitted John by Fred

C / 2: . . . be permitted John by Fred + for John to call Bill

T / SJ$_2$: John + be permitted John by Fred + for . . . to call Bill

SJCTZ: John be permitted John by Fred + for . . . to call Bill

FNTZ / 1 (= PAST, PSNM): John was permitted John by Fred + for . . . to call Bill

As stated above, when the verb is in the passive voice, it is the second noun object which is deleted:

D / EE: John was permitted . . . by Fred + . . . . . . to call Bill

SOP: "John was permitted by Fred to call Bill."

There is yet a third possibility when the matrix verb is in the passive voice: after the commentization of the infinitive, the dummy element IT may be inserted in the vacant slot. This development proceeds as follows:

PASV: for John to call Bill + be permitted John by Fred

C / 2: . . . be permitted John by Fred + for John to call Bill

I / IT: IT be permitted John by Fred + for John to call Bill

FNTZ / 1 (= PAST, PSNM): IT was permitted John by Fred + for John to call Bill

D / EE: IT was permitted . . . by Fred + for John to call Bill

SOP: "It was permitted by Fred for John to call Bill."

There are relatively few verbs which may take Type D constructions: *permit, allow, forbid, prohibit*. Often they appear in sentences which have a restrictive or privative meaning, especially the latter two. As a further and final example, we may take the sign which appears in New York City subway cars:

passengers are forbidden to ride between cars

Our analysis of this utterance assumes the existence of the infrastructures:

IS1: SOMEONE forbid passengers INF2

IS2: passengers ride between cars

This can be made to yield the three variant patterns in the passive voice described above; the derivation begins as follows:

INFZ / 2: for passengers to ride between cars

E / 2: SOMEONE forbid passengers + for passengers to ride between cars

PASV: for passengers to ride between cars + be forbidden passengers by SOMEONE

PSNM: for passengers to ride between cars + is forbidden passengers by SOMEONE

By deletion of the second noun object and the empty instrumental phrase, the sequence itself can become an acceptable utterance:

D / EE: for passengers to ride between cars + is forbidden . . . . . .

SOP: "For passengers to ride between cars is forbidden."

If, on the other hand, the infinitive is commentized, then either the element IT or the subject of the infinitive may be placed in the empty slot before the verb:

C / 2: . . . be forbidden passengers by SOMEONE + for passengers to ride between cars

At this point, one can insert IT, which as an artificial element is incorporated into the derivation without need of subjectivization:

I / IT: IT be forbidden passengers by SOMEONE + for passengers to ride between cars

FNTZ / 1 (= PSNM): IT is forbidden passengers by SOMEONE + for passengers to ride between cars

As before, the second noun object and the empty agent phrase are deleted:

D / EE: IT is forbidden . . . . . . + for passengers to ride between cars

SOP: "It is forbidden for passengers to ride between cars."

The third possibility is to fill the vacant slot by retopicalizing the subject of the commentized infinitive:

PASV: for passengers to ride between cars + be forbidden passengers by SOMEONE

C / 2: . . . be forbidden passengers by SOMEONE + for passengers to ride between cars

T / SJ$_2$: passengers + be forbidden passengers by SOMEONE + for . . . to ride between cars

SJCTZ: passengers be forbidden passengers by SOMEONE + for . . . . to ride between cars

FNTZ / 1 (= PSNM): passengers are forbidden passengers by SOMEONE + for . . . to ride between cars

Three elements are now deleted: the second noun object of the matrix verb, *passengers,* as is required of Type D infinitives in the passive voice; the empty element *SOMEONE,* the subject of the matrix verb in the active voice, and its instrumental object in the passive; and the objectless prepositions *by* and *for*:

D / EE: passengers are forbidden ... ... + ... ... to ride between cars

SOP: "Passengers are forbidden to ride between cars."

*Type E Infinitive Constructions*

Like Type D verbs, those of Type E are also accompanied by an additional noun, one which must be identical with the subject of the infinitive:

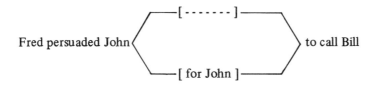

There are two differences, however. First, the subject of the infinitive must be deleted after Type E verbs – it is only to be regarded as present because all infinitives must have subjects, and because its presence is implied by the sense of these constructions. This leads to the second difference: the infinitive following a Type E verb is not a noun, but a verb complement. Thus, the object following the verb is a first noun object, one which can become the subject of the matrix verb in the passive voice. Thus, the passive voice would change the sentence above to read:

John was persuaded by Fred [for John] to call Bill

This would be generated as follows:

IS1: Fred persuade John INF2
IS2: John call Bill

First, the infinitive clause is formed, and then embedded:

INFZ / 2: for John to call Bill
E / 2: Fred persuade John + for John to call Bill

277

When the matrix verb is passivized, however, the infinitive retains its position and function as verb complement; it is the first noun object *John* which becomes the subject of the matrix verb:

PASV: John be persuaded by Fred + for John to call Bill

FNTZ / 1 (= PAST, PSNM): John was persuaded by Fred + for John to call Bill

After the obligatory deletion of the infinitive subject and its preposition, the sentence is complete:

D / EE: John was persuaded by Fred + . . . . . . to call Bill

SOP: "John was persuaded by Fred to call Bill."

It is evident that Type D and Type E constructions manifest identical surface structures at several points. In the active voice, for example, they seem to be identical, though as the subscript labels indicate, they are not:

Type D (infinitive = 1NnOj): $Fred_{SJ_{in}}$ forbade $John_{2NnOj}$ + for $John_{SJ_i}$ to call Bill

Type E (infinitive = VCOMP): $Fred_{SJ_m}$ urged $John_{1NnOj}$ + for $John_{SJ_i}$ to call Bill

In the passive voice, however, a Type E infinitive cannot become the subject of its matrix verb:

Type D: ! for John to call Bill + was forbidden (John) by Fred

Type E: ? ? ? for John to call Bill + was urged (John) by Fred

On the other hand, the first noun object of a Type E verb can become the subject of the matrix verb in the passive. What appears to be the same structure in connection with Type D verbs, however, actually represents a different derivation entirely: the commentization of the infinitive and the retopicalization of its subject:

Type D: $John_{SJ_i}$ was forbidden ($John_{2NnOj}$) by Fred $_{SJ_m}$ + for . . . to call Bill

Type E: $John_{1NnOj}$ was urged by $Fred_{SJ_m}$ + for $John_{SJ_i}$ to call Bill

The difference in deep structure between these expressions becomes apparent on the surface when IT is inserted in the place of a commentized infinitive:

Type D: ! IT was forbidden (John) by Fred + for John to call Bill
Type E: ? ? ? IT was urged John by Fred + for John to call Bill

Hence, despite superficial similarities, these verbs must be regarded as representing different types with different valences. Other examples of Type E verbs include: *urge, advise, convince, tell, encourage, ask, persuade, teach, induce, entreat, force, authorize, license, compel,* etc.

This type of infinitive construction can also be used to explain another peculiar feature of English. The formation of the passive voice with verbs of designation and appointment has been regarded as an anomaly in some treatments of English grammar, in that the second noun object, in our terminology, becomes the subject of the passive verb, instead of the first noun object (cf. Fillmore 1965:13,34; Jacobs & Rosenbaum 1968:145). This contrast is exemplified in these pairs of sentences:

Pattern 1:

$Fred_{SJ}$ gave $John_{2NnOj}$ the $book_{1NnOj} \rightarrow PASV$: the $book_{1NOj}$

was given to $John_{2NnOj}$ by $Fred_{SJ}$

Pattern 2:

$Fred_{SJ}$ appointed $John_{2NnOj}$ $chairman_{1NnOj} \rightarrow PASV$: $John_{2NnOj}$

was appointed $chairman_{1NnOj}$ by $Fred_{SJ}$

In light of the analysis of the infinitive constructions of Type E presented in this section, the second of these is susceptible of an alternative explanation. It is very likely that verbs of designation and appointment are in fact Type E verbs, in connection with the verb of the infinitive, *to be,* has been deleted. Thus, the example of Pattern 2 above can be analyzed as follows:

$Fred_{SJ_m}$ appointed $John_{1NnOj}$ + [for John] to be chairman

We have seen a number of constructions in which the verb *to be* has been deleted; this may be interpreted as another:

Fred appointed John + [for John] . . . chairman

As a Type E verb, the infinitive is unaffected by the passive voice transformation:

John was appointed by Fred + [for John] to be chairman

or, with the placement of the instrumental phrase after the infinitive:

John was appointed + [for John] to be chairman + by Fred

In this way, the pattern in question can be related to the infinitive constructions, and the passive transformation can thereby be simplified.

## Miscellaneous Constructions Containing the Infinitive

In addition to the two groups of constructions described above — infinitives with BE and those with LEXVB — there are several others in which the infinitive is combined with other syntactic elements. These are examined one by one in the sections which follow.

### 1. "in order" + INF

In English, the infinitive may follow the prepositional expression *in order (to)* In this capacity, it presents few problems. However, this construction can be confused with other uses of the infinitive because of the ever-present tendency toward the deletion of empty elements — those which have a syntactic, but little or no semantic function, e. g., SOMEONE — and of redundant elements — those which have already appeared once in the utterance. The expression *in order (to)* is itself sometimes deleted as self-understood. The examples which follow illustrate the effects of these phenomena on the surface structure of sentences containing *in order (to)*.

The following sentence can be understood only be restoring the deleted elements:

John acted quickly to save the ship

With the deleted elements restored (in parentheses), this would read:

John acted quickly (in order + for John) to save the ship

Not infrequently, this kind of deletion occurs in sentences in which the matrix verb is in the passive voice:

a purchase is required to win a prize

This is to be construed as reflecting the two infrastructures:

IS1: SOMEONE require a purchase in order + INF2
IS2: SOMEONE win a prize

The second of these is infinitivized, and then embedded in the matrix clause:

INFZ / 2: for SOMEONE to win a prize
E / 2: SOMEONE require a purchase in order + for SOMEONE to win a prize

The matrix verb is passivized and then given its final modification as a finite verb:

PASV: a purchase be required by SOMEONE in order + for SOMEONE to win a prize
PSNM: a purchase is required by SOMEONE in order + for SOMEONE to win a prize

Then the various empty elements, including *in order*, are deleted:

D / EE: a purchase is required . . . . . . + . . . to win a prize
SOP: "A purchase is required to win a prize."

Sometimes even more elements are deleted, as in this sentence:

this car is priced to sell

In actuality, this is generated in the same way as the sentence above; it contains the two infrastructures:

IS1: SOMEONE price this car in order + INF2
IS2: SOMEONE sell this car

The derivation is as follows:

INFZ / 2: for SOMEONE to sell this car
E / 2: SOMEONE price this car in order + for SOMEONE to sell this car

The matrix clause is passivized:

PASV: this car be priced by SOMEONE in order + for SOMEONE to sell this car
PSNM: this car is priced by SOMEONE in order + for SOMEONE to sell this car

Now the empty and redundant elements are deleted:

D / EE: this car is priced . . . . . . + . . . to sell . . .
SOP: "This car is priced to sell."

Wherever an infinitive seems to express purpose, it is likely that the expression *in order (to)* has been deleted.

## 2. NOUN (+ PREP) + INF

There are a number of cases in English where an infinitive appears to be directly attached to a noun, e. g.:

his eagerness to avenge the insult
their readiness to forgive
time for us to eat
time to eat

These may be construed in a manner comparable to those cases where an infinitive follows an adjective; as the caption to this section suggests, the infinitives above are in fact objects of the preposition *for*, which, being objectless, is always deleted. The existence of this preposition is revealed when a noun is substituted for the infinitives in these examples:

his eagerness for vengeance
their readiness for forgiveness
time for lunch

Thus, the phrases *time for us to eat* and *time to eat* can be restored as follows:

time for + for us to eat SOMETHING
time for + for SOMEONE to eat SOMETHING

The objectless preposition *for* is deleted, as are the empty elements. This yields:

time . . . + for us to eat . . . → time for us to eat
time . . . + . . . . . . to eat . . . → time to eat

The infrastructures of the embedded infinitives are *we eat SOME-THING* and *SOMEONE eat SOMETHING*, respectively.

CHAPTER 15

THE INFINITIVE IN GERMAN

As in English, the transformation of a neutral verb form into an infinitive represents a partial change of the infrastructure in which it stands into a noun. The rule for the formation of the German infinitive has two parts:

INFZ →
1) I / zu: . . . VFF + zu + LVF
2) D / SJ: ( (SJ) ) . . . VERB

As these formulas indicate, the infrastructure is modified in infinitivization, first, by the placing of zu before the last verb form present after the common verb modifications have been applied, and second, by the deletion of the grammatical subject. In regard to the latter step, it should be noted that we have here a significant contrast between English and German: whereas the subject of the English infinitive is retained (though it may be subsequently deleted for other reasons), the subject of the German infinitive is suppressed by virtue of the INFZ transformation itself. Some examples may make this difference clearer:

IS: he visit his uncle
INFZ: for him to visit his uncle

IS: er seinen Onkel besuchen
INFZ: ( (er) ) seinen Onkel zu besuchen

Though the German infinitive is functionally a noun, it retains some characteristics of a verb. It can, for example, undergo certain of the common verb modifications: it may be passivized (PASV), and in addition may have applied to it either the modification for the terminative aspect (TRMV) or for the modal auxiliary (MODL) — but not both. Thus, an infinitive may appear with as many as six different patterns of verb modifications (nonverbal elements are omitted in the following synopsis):

LEXVB only: lesen → INFZ: zu lesen
LEXVB + PASV: gelesen werden → INFZ: gelesen zu werden

LEXVB + TRMV: gelesen haben → INFZ: gelesen zu haben
LEXVB + MODL: lesen können → INFZ: lesen zu können
LEXVB + PASV + TRMV: gelesen worden sein → INFZ: gelesen worden zu sein
LEXVB + PASV + MODL: gelesen werden können → INFZ: gelesen werden zu können

Unlike the finite verb, the infinitive cannot accept the modifications TRMV and MODL, both at the same time, in either order:

LEXVB + TRMV + MODL: gelesen haben können → INFZ: ? gelesen haben zu können
LEXVB + MODL + TRMV: lesen können haben → INFZ: ? ? lesen können zu haben
LEXVB + PASV + TRMV + MODL: gelesen worden sein können → INFZ: ? ? ? gelesen worden sein zu können
LEXVB + PASV + MODL + TRMV: gelesen werden können haben → INFZ: ? ? ? ? gelesen werden können zu haben

The forms of the infinitive are thus not altogether very complicated. The complexities attending the infinitive have for the most part to do with the way in which it is combined with finite verbs, a topic to which the following sections will be devoted.

The ways in which the German infinitive may be combined with other syntactic elements are not wholly unlike the patterns which were found to exist in English. Infinitive constructions in German may be divided into four groups: the first, those in which the infinitive is the grammatical subject in its matrix clause; the second, those in which it functions as the expansion of the lexical verb; the third, those where the infinitive serves as the object of a preposition; and fourth and finally, those constructions where the infinitive is closely linked to a noun or adjective. In the following discussion, we will examine each of these groups of infinitive constructions in the order given above.

*The Infinitive as Subject of Its Matrix Verb*

The infinitive can be the subject of the verb *sein*, in conjunction with a noun, an adjective, or with a zero-complement. It may also serve as subject of various types of lexical verbs. We will look at each of these constructions in the discussion which follows.

## 1. $INF_{SJ}$ + $NCOMP_{NOUN}$ + sein

This construction, in which the infinitive is the subject of the verb *sein* accompanied by a nucleus complement in the form of a noun, is exemplified by the following utterances:

das Gerät in Ordnung zu halten war seine Aufgabe
seine Aufgabe war, das Gerät in Ordnung zu halten
seine Aufgabe war es, das Gerät in Ordnung zu halten
es war seine Aufgabe, das Gerät in Ordnung zu halten

All four of these sentences are derived from the two infrastructures:

IS1: INF + seine Aufgabe sein
IS2: er das Gerät in Ordnung halten

In the generation of the sentences above, the first step is to infinitivize the second of the two infrastructures:

INFZ / 2: ( (er) ) das Gerät in Ordnung zu halten

It must be emphasized again that one of the major differences between English and German is the obligatory deletion of the subject of the German infinitive. Although it may reappear in the surface structure in certain cases — to be examined below — in most instances it is present only by implication. For this reason, the verb modification of infinitivization (INFZ) includes not only the insertion of *zu* before the last verb form, but also the deletion of the subject of the infinitive. This element is indicated in the derivation by double parentheses, i. e., "( (er) )," and is automatically deleted in the last stage of the derivation, unless specific conditions call for its retention.

Once the infrastructure in question has been infinitivized, it is embedded in the structure of the matrix clause:

E / 2: ( (er) ) das Gerät in Ordnung zu halten + seine Aufgabe sein

The next step is to modify the verb of the matrix clause, here by finitization (FNTZ); the specific modification is for the past tense (PAST) and for person and number (PSNM):

FNTZ / 1 (= PAST, PSNM): ( (er) ) das Gerät in Ordnung zu halten + seine Aufgabe war

As with all complex structures, there is a tendency here for the infinitive to move to the end of the clause because of its greater communicative value. Hence, there are few contexts in which the sequence above – though grammatical – would be regarded as idiomatic; the following might not be considered by a native speaker as wholly unacceptable:

(er bestritt heftig, daß) das Gerät in Ordnung zu halten seine Aufgabe war

In this and all following derivations, each construction will be carried through the sequence of transformations from verb-last to verb-second word order. It will be taken for granted that the reader will keep in mind that verb-last and verb-first word order have certain specific uses, i. e., as dependent finite clauses and as yes-no questions, respectively. In the derivations which follow, we will, for the most part, generate independent finite clauses, because it is in connection with these that the interaction of language structure and topic-comment organization is most apparent. This part of the derivation, then, continues as follows:

T / FV: war + ( (er) ) das Gerät in Ordnung zu halten + seine Aufgabe

At this point, the relatively wide latitude as to what can be topicalized in German opens up two possibilities:

T / X: ( (er) ) das Gerät in Ordnung zu halten + war seine Aufgabe
SOP: "Das Gerät in Ordnung zu halten war seine Aufgabe."

or the alternative:

T / X: seine Aufgabe war + ( (er) ) das Gerät in Ordnung zu halten
SOP: "Seine Aufgabe war, das Gerät in Ordnung zu halten."

These transformations generate the first two of the four sentence patterns which we must account for. In order to produce the remaining two, we must return to that point at which the infinitive was embedded:

E / 2: ( (er) ) das Gerät in Ordnung zu halten + seine Aufgabe sein

It is open to the speaker here to move the infinitive to the end of the clause; thereupon, the element ES takes the place of the commentized infinitive, and becomes the pseudosubject of the matrix verb:

286

C / 2: . . . seine Aufgabe sein + ( (er) ) das Gerät in Ordnung zu
halten
I / ES: ES seine Aufgabe sein + ( (er) ) das Gerät in Ordnung zu
halten

From this point on, the derivation proceeds as above:

FNTZ / 1 (= PAST, PSNM): ES seine Aufgabe war + ( (er) ) das
Gerät in Ordnung zu halten
T / FV: war ES seine Aufgabe + ( (er) ) das Gerät in Ordnung zu
halten

Here, again, there are two possibilities for topicalization:

T / X: seine Aufgabe war ES + ( (er) ) das Gerät in Ordnung zu
halten
SOP: "Seine Aufgabe war es, das Gerät in Ordnung zu halten."

or:

T / X: ES war seine Aufgabe + ( (er) ) das Gerät in Ordnung zu
halten
SOP: "Es war seine Aufgabe, das Gerät in Ordnung zu halten."

These procedures have generated the remaining two of the four sentences which we wanted to account for. It might be added that, once the infinitive has been commentized and ES inserted, it is no longer possible to topicalize it or any of its elements in these constructions:

T / X: ( (er) ) das Gerät in Ordnung zu halten + war ES seine
Aufgabe
SOP: ? ? ? "Das Gerät in Ordnung zu halten war es seine Aufgabe."

The commentized infinitive is no longer part of the clause being transformed, its place having been taken by ES, and hence does not further enter into the development of its matrix clause.

When the infinitive stands as subject or nucleus complement of the verbs *sein, heißen,* and a few other verbs, it is possible under certain conditions to delete the infinitive marker *zu.* As a rule, the more closely related a single element is to the verb, the more likely that *zu* will be absent from the expression. When no nonverbal element precedes the verb, *zu* is almost always deleted; when two or more nonverbal elements accompany the verb, it is very probable that *zu* will be retained. Other things being equal, the tendency to delete *zu* is greater in sentence-initial position than elsewhere. The following phrases and sentences exemplify these conditions and limitations.

In initial position, *zu* is generally deleted when the infinitivized verb is accompanied by no other elements (several of the following examples are taken from Duden Grammatik 1973: 559 ff. and from Helbig & Buscha 1974:576):

> ! irren ist menschlich
> ? zu irren ist menschlich

but:

> ! zu kommen ist ratsam

When a single nonverbal element is present, and that element is a nucleus complement, it is likely that *zu* will be deleted:

> CN (= clause nucleus): Klavier spielen
> ! Klavier spielen macht Spaß
> ? Klavier zu spielen macht Spaß
> CN: ein Tier quälen
> ! ein Tier quälen ist böse
> ? ein Tier zu quälen ist böse

When the nonverbal element is an element other than the nucleus complement, both possibilities, the one with, the other without *zu*, are equally acceptable in most cases:

> ! sich beherrschen ist nicht immer leicht
> ! sich zu beherrschen ist nicht immer leicht

> ! für ihn kochen muß ein besonderes Vergnügen sein
> ! für ihn zu kochen muß ein besonderes Vergnügen sein

When two or more nonverbal elements are present, the tendency is to retain *zu*, although again the peculiarities of a given context may outweigh this factor:

> ? den Gästen gefällig sein war sein Bestreben
> ! den Gästen gefällig zu sein war sein Bestreben

The following may be regarded as a more or less typical case:

> "( . . . durch seine Biographie österreichisch vorbelastet . . . ) Deswegen aber zu sagen, Persönlichkeit und Denken des Mannes seien von diesen Jahren in Österreich stark bestimmt, hieße zur

falschen Harfe greifen" ("Ein Christ bei der Wintersaat: Zum 70. Geburtstag von Karl Rahner," *Die Presse* [Vienna], 5 March 1974).

The long infinitive *deswegen . . . zu sagen, Persönlichkeit und Denken des Mannes seien von diesen Jahren in Österreich stark bestimmt* calls for the presence of *zu* to indicate its syntactic function within the sentence. (The word *aber* is an intersentence adverb). On the other hand, the function of the short infinitive *zur falschen Harfe greifen* is fairly clear in this context; hence, there is no compelling reason to split a clause nucleus with *zu*. It must be emphasized again that considerations of context play an unusually important role here.

## 2. $INF_{SJ} + NCOMP_{AJ} + sein$

The constructions which fall under this rubric can be subdivided into two groups, of which the first is represented by the following sentences:

(a) dieses Buch zu verstehen ist leicht
    leicht ist, dieses Buch zu verstehen
(b) es ist leicht, dieses Buch zu verstehen
    leicht ist es, dieses Buch zu verstehen
(c) dieses Buch ist leicht zu verstehen

All of these sentences are derived from the two infrastructures:

IS1: INF2 leicht sein
IS2: JEMAND dieses Buch verstehen

As before, the derivation begins with the infinitivization of the second infrastructure:

INFZ / 2: ( (JEMAND) ) dieses Buch zu verstehen

This is then embedded:

E / 2: ( (JEMAND) ) dieses Buch zu verstehen + leicht sein

At this point, the infinitive could be commentized and its place taken by ES. For the moment, we will pass over this step, and continue the derivation by modifying the verb in the matrix clause by finitization:

FNTZ / 1 (= PSNM): ( (JEMAND) ) dieses Buch zu verstehen +
leicht ist
T / FV: ist + ( (JEMAND) ) dieses Buch zu verstehen + leicht

Here the opportunities for topicalization are two in number:

T / X: leicht ist + ( (JEMAND) ) dieses Buch zu verstehen
SOP: "Leicht ist, dieses Buch zu verstehen."

or:

T / X: ( (JEMAND) ) dieses Buch zu verstehen + ist leicht
SOP: "Dieses Buch zu verstehen ist leicht."

These transformations have produced the sentences under (a) above.

The remaining sentences which it is our aim to account for are
generated by the commentization of the infinitive and its replacement by ES. These changes take place immediately after embedding:

E / 2: ( (JEMAND) ) dieses Buch zu verstehen + leicht sein
C / 2: . . . leicht sein + ( (JEMAND) ) dieses Buch zu verstehen

The element ES serves as a surrogate in the matrix clause for the
commentized infinitive, and becomes the pseudosubject of that
clause:

I / ES: ES leicht sein + ( (JEMAND) ) dieses Buch zu verstehen

Once this has been completed, the derivation proceeds with the
modification of the matrix clause:

FNTZ / 1 (= PSNM): ES leicht ist + ( (JEMAND) ) dieses Buch zu
verstehen
T / FV: ist ES leicht + ( (JEMAND) ) dieses Buch zu verstehen

Again, two possibilities emerge:

T / X: ES ist leicht + ( (JEMAND) ) dieses Buch zu verstehen
SOP: "Es ist leicht, dieses Buch zu verstehen."

or:

T / X: leicht ist ES + ( (JEMAND) ) dieses Buch zu verstehen
SOP: "Leicht ist es, dieses Buch zu verstehen."

These operations generate the sentences under (b) above.

The last sentence we must account for is:
dieses Buch ist leicht zu verstehen

For this, we must return to that point at which the infinitive is embedded:

E / 2: ( (JEMAND) ) dieses Buch zu verstehen + leicht sein

At this point, it is possible to commentize the infinitive and to retopicalize the object of the infinitive *dieses Buch*:

C / 2: . . . leicht sein + ( (JEMAND) ) dieses Buch zu verstehen
T / $OJ_2$ : dieses Buch + leicht sein + ( (JEMAND) ) . . . zu verstehen

This transformation is subject to certain constraints. For one thing, the object in question must be an accusative object: dative or genitive objects cannot undergo this transformation. For another, the subject of the infinitive may not have an implicit connection with, or reference to, another element in the sentence; empty elements such as *JEMAND* fulfil this condition completely. When these conditions are met, the infinitive object may be inserted into the empty slot of the matrix clause, becoming, by subjectivization, the pseudosubject of that clause. This morphosyntactic transformation, in German, means that the element is changed from the accusative to the nominative case:

SJCTZ: dieses Buch leicht sein + ( (JEMAND) ) . . . zu verstehen

At this point, the matrix verb is modified, and the derivation proceeds as in the previous examples:

FNTZ / 1 (= PSNM): dieses Buch leicht ist + ( (JEMAND) ) . . . zu verstehen
T / FV: ist dieses Buch leicht + ( (JEMAND) ) . . . zu verstehen
T / X: dieses Buch ist leicht + ( (JEMAND) ) . . . zu verstehen
SOP: "Dieses Buch ist leicht zu verstehen."

In this fashion, the sentence under (c) above has been generated.

At the beginning of this section, it was stated that constructions with infinitive subjects and adjectival nucleus complements with *sein* could be divided into two groups. In the foregoing discussion we have analyzed the first of these. The second is exemplified by the following sentence patterns:

(a) ihm die Schallplatte zum Geburtstag zu schenken war nett von dir

(b) es war nett von dir, ihm die Schallplatte zum Geburtstag zu schenken

(c) nett war es von dir, ihm die Schallplatte zum Geburtstag zu schenken

These sentences reflect the infrastructures:

IS1: INF2 nett von dir sein
IS2: du ihm die Schallplatte zum Geburtstag schenken

It is of the greatest significance that the subject of the second infrastructure *du* is, in contrast to the preceding examples, not an empty element, but one which refers to the same person as the pronoun *dir* in the matrix clause. As will be shown, the effect of this difference is to exclude the commentization of the infinitive and the retopicalization of the infinitive verb's object. In other respects, the generation of these sentences proceeds as in the case of the first group:

INFZ / 2: ( (du) ) ihm die Schallplatte zum Geburtstag zu schenken

E / 2: ( (du) ) ihm die Schallplatte zum Geburtstag zu schenken + nett von dir sein

In a moment, we will return to this point to commentize the infinitive and to insert ES; for the present, we will omit this step:

FNTZ / 1 (= PAST, PSNM): ( (du) ) ihm die Schallplatte zum Geburtstag zu schenken + nett von dir war

T / FV: war + ( (du) ) ihm die Schallplatte zum Geburtstag zu schenken + nett von dir

T / X: ( (du) ) ihm die Schallplatte zum Geburtstag zu schenken + war nett von dir

SOP: "Ihm die Schallplatte zum Geburtstag zu schenken war nett von dir."

This accounts for the sentence labeled (a) above. The remaining patterns presuppose the commentization of the infinitive and the insertion and subjectivization of ES. These changes take place immediately after the embedding of the infinitive:

C / 2: . . . nett von dir sein + ( (du) ) ihm die Schallplatte zum Geburtstag zu schenken

I /ES: ES nett von dir sein + ( (du) ) ihm die Schallplatte zum Geburtstag zu schenken

From this point on, the derivation proceeds as before:

FNTZ / 1 (= PAST, PSNM): ES nett von dir war + ( (du) ) ihm die Schallplatte zum Geburtstag zu schenken

T / FV: war ES nett von dir + ( (du) ) ihm die Schallplatte zum Geburtstag zu schenken

The two sentences, the derivation of which we want to explain, are produced at this point by the topicalization of different elements, i. e., either:

T / X: ES war nett von dir + ( (du) ) ihm die Schallplatte zum Geburtstag zu schenken

SOP: "Es war nett von dir, ihm die Schallplatte zum Geburtstag zu schenken."

or it is possible to split the element *nett von dir* and topicalize the adjective alone, a procedure which implies a certain contrast:

T / X: nett war ES von dir + ( (du) ) ihm die Schallplatte zum Geburtstag zu schenken

SOP: "Nett war es von dir, ihm die Schallplatte zum Geburtstag zu schenken."

Because the subject of the infinitive has a point of reference within the matrix clause, it is not possible to commentize the infinitive and insert the accusative object in its place. As the following derivation shows, these changes lead to an unacceptable utterance:

E / 2: ( (du) ) ihm die Schallplatte zum Geburtstag zu schenken + nett von dir sein

C / 2: ... nett von dir sein + ( (du) ) ihm die Schallplatte zum Geburtstag zu schenken

T / OJ$_2$: die Schallplatte + nett von dir sein + ( (du) ) ihm ... zum Geburtstag zu schenken

SJCTZ: die Schallplatte nett von dir sein + ( (du) ) ihm ... zum Geburtstag zu schenken

FNTZ / 1: die Schallplatte nett von dir war + ( (du) ) ihm ... zum Geburtstag zu schenken

T / FV: war die Schallplatte nett von dir + ( (du) ) ihm ... zum Geburtstag zu schenken

T / X: die Schallplatte war nett von dir + ( (du) ) ihm ... zum Geburtstag zu schenken

SOP: ? ? ? "Die Schallplatte war nett von dir, ihm zum Geburtstag zu schenken."

293

Because of the link between the elements *nett von dir* of the matrix clause and the suppressed subject *du* of the infinitive clause, this line of development is prohibited.

## 3. INF$_{SJ}$ + ∅ + sein

Whereas in the two constructions just described the verb *sein* was accompanied by an adjective or noun as nucleus complement, the present structure is characterized by the absence of such an element. For this reason, we may speak of this syntactical structure as having a "zero-complement." The subtypes which share this feature are in turn differentiated by various patterns involving the presence or absence of an element of the infinitive clause in the structure dominated by the matrix verb. We begin with a case which is particularly troublesome to speakers of English, because it contains no expressed noun subject:

> an Flucht war nicht zu denken

This reflects the infrastructures:

> IS1: INF2 + ∅ sein
> IS2: JEMAND an Flucht nicht denken

The derivation begins with the infinitive:

> INFZ / 2: ( (JEMAND) ) an Flucht nicht zu denken
> E / 2: ( (JEMAND) ) an Flucht nicht zu denken + ∅ sein

Once the infinitive is embedded, the matrix verb is modified, and the derivation continues as in other cases:

> FNTZ / 1 (= PAST, PSNM): ( (JEMAND) ) an Flucht nicht zu denken + ∅ war
> T / FV: war + ( (JEMAND) ) an Flucht nicht zu denken + ∅

It is permissible here to topicalize an element from within the commentized infinitive clause:

> T / X: an Flucht + war ( (JEMAND) ) . . . nicht zu denken
> SOP: "An Flucht war nicht zu denken."

It would also be possible, after T / FV, to insert the dummy topic ES:

294

T / X: ES war + ( (JEMAND) ) an Flucht nicht zu denken + $\emptyset$
SOP: "Es war an Flucht nicht zu denken."

In the example above, the verb in the infinitive clause was intransitive. In those cases where the infinitivized verb is a transitive one, and where it is accompanied by an accusative object, this infinitive object must be transformed by subjectivization into the pseudosubject of the matrix verb. Once this step has been taken, the derivation proceeds as before. These changes are illustrated by the derivation of the following familiar sentence:

Hunde sind an der Leine zu führen

This reflects the infrastructures:

IS1: INF2 + $\emptyset$ sein
IS2: JEMAND Hunde an der Leine führen

The output sentence is derived as follows:

INFZ / 2: ( (JEMAND) ) Hunde an der Leine zu führen
E / 2: ( (JEMAND) ) Hunde an der Leine zu führen + $\emptyset$ sein

At this point, the infinitive object *Hunde* is topicalized and subjectivized:

T / OJ$_2$: Hunde + ( (JEMAND) ) ... an der Leine zu führen + $\emptyset$
sein
SJCTZ: Hunde + ( (JEMAND) ) ... an der Leine zu führen + $\emptyset$
sein

The derivation continues with the word *Hunde* as the pseudosubject of the matrix clause:

FNTZ / 1 (= PSNM): Hunde + ( (JEMAND) ) ... an der Leine zu
führen + $\emptyset$ sind
T / FV: sind Hunde + ( (JEMAND) ) ... an der Leine zu führen
+ $\emptyset$
T / X: Hunde sind + ( (JEMAND) ) ... an der Leine zu führen
+ $\emptyset$
SOP: "Hunde sind an der Leine zu führen."

## 4. INF$_{SJ}$ + scheinen, beginnen, anfangen, aufhören, etc.

The relationship of the infinitive to verbs of the kind listed in the caption is substantially the same as that described in the preceding section: the infinitive is the subject of the verb, but by a secondary change, an element in the infinitive clause is transferred to the domain of the verb of the matrix clause, and by subjectivization becomes the pseudosubject of the latter. In the case of *sein*, it was the object of the infinitive which became the subject of the matrix verb; in the case of the verbs above, it is the subject of the infinitive which is removed from that clause to the domain of the matrix clause. As the first example, let us analyze the sentences:

er fing zu singen an
er fing an zu singen

The infrastructures underlying both utterances are these:

IS1: INF2 + anfangen
IS2: er singen

The sentences above are generated in the following way:

INFZ / 2: ( (er) ) zu singen
E / 2: ( (er) ) zu singen + anfangen

Here, the subject of the infinitive *er* is shifted from the domain of the infinitive, and becomes, by subjectivization, the grammatical subject of the matrix verb *anfangen*:

SJCTZ: er + ( ( . . . ) ) zu singen + anfangen

As pseudosubject, *er* determines the number and person of the matrix verb when the latter is finitized:

FNTZ / 1 (= PAST, PSNM): er + ( ( . . . ) ) zu singen + anfing

The derivation then runs to its conclusion in the customary fashion:

T / FV: fing er + ( ( . . . ) ) zu singen + an
T / X: er fing + ( ( . . . ) ) zu singen + an
SOP: "Er fing zu singen an."

This series of changes has produced one of the sentence patterns which we wanted to generate. For the second of these, we must return to the point referred to above, at which the subject of the infinitive became the pseudosubject of the matrix verb:

SJCTZ: er + ( ( . . . ) ) zu singen + anfangen

The verb *anfangen* contains the separable prefix *an-*, and this can cause problems of communicative priority, as, for example, when a lengthy infinitive phrase is enclosed within the frame constituted by, e. g., the subject and verb on the one hand, and the separable prefix on the other:

er fing – zu singen – an

For this reason, the speaker or writer may wish to avail himself of the opportunity to commentize the infinitive:

C / 2: er . . . anfangen + ( ( . . . ) ) zu singen

From this point on, the derivation proceeds as usual for finite clauses:

FNTZ / 1 (= PAST, PSNM): er . . . anfing + ( ( . . . ) ) zu singen
T / FV: fing er . . . an + ( ( . . . ) ) zu singen
T / X: er fing . . . an + ( ( . . . ) ) zu singen
SOP: "Er fing an zu singen."

A good rule of thumb for the commentization of the infinitive is: the longer the infinitive, the more likely it will be commentized.

As the caption of this section indicates, one of the verbs which can enter into this kind of construction is *scheinen*. There are numerous instances in German in which we encounter this verb when it is followed, not by an infinitive, but solely by an adjective, e. g.:

er scheint heute fröhlich

Cases of this kind constitute no exception to the generative patterns elaborated in this section; rather, the verb *zu sein* has been deleted as redundant. The complete sentence, on this interpretation, is in actuality:

er scheint heute fröhlich zu sein

and is derived from these infrastructures as follows:

IS1: INF2 scheinen
IS2: er heute fröhlich sein
INFZ / 2: ( (er) ) heute fröhlich zu sein
E / 2: ( (er) ) heute fröhlich zu sein + scheinen

When the matrix verb *scheinen* is finitized, the subject of the infinitive, *er*, becomes the subject of that matrix verb:

SJCTZ: er + ( ( . . . ) ) heute fröhlich zu sein + scheinen
FNTZ / 1: er + ( ( . . . ) ) heute fröhlich zu sein + scheint
T / FV: scheint er + ( ( . . . ) ) heute fröhlich zu sein
T / X: er scheint + ( ( . . . ) ) heute fröhlich zu sein

Here, the redundant element *zu sein* may be optionally deleted:

D / EE: er scheint + ( ( . . . ) ) heute fröhlich (zu sein)
SOP: "Er scheint heute fröhlich (zu sein)."

Seen from this perspective, then, single adjectives like *fröhlich* may be regarded as the remnants of infinitive clauses containing *sein*.

## 5. *INF$_{SJ}$ + LEXVB*

The infinitive may not only serve as the subject of special classes of verbs like those considered above, but it may also stand in that function in connection with other lexical verbs. One of its most frequent uses is that of subject of verbs like *sich gelingen, sich schicken, sich ziemen, sich gehören,* etc. The following sentences are typical of constructions of this kind:

seinen Namen zu erfahren gelang mir nicht
es gelang mir nicht, seinen Namen zu erfahren

These sentences are derived from the following infrastructures:

IS1: mir INF2 nicht gelingen
IS2: ich seinen Namen erfahren

The derivations take the following course:

INFZ / 2: ( (ich) ) seinen Namen zu erfahren
E / 2: mir + ( (ich) ) seinen Namen zu erfahren + nicht gelingen

At this point, the writer could commentize the infinitive — a step which we will omit here but return to presently:

FNTZ / 1 (= PAST, PSNM): mir + ( (ich) ) seinen Namen zu erfahren + nicht gelang
T / FV: gelang mir + ( (ich) ) seinen Namen zu erfahren + nicht

The most likely candidate for topicalization here is the infinitive itself:

T / X: ( (ich) ) seinen Namen zu erfahren + gelang mir nicht
SOP: "Seinen Namen zu erfahren gelang mir nicht."

After embedding, it is open to the speaker to commentize the infinitive; in constructions of this kind, ES must be inserted into the slot left vacant by the commentized infinitive, because some element must play the role, as it were, of the grammatical subject. Since ES has the form and function of a pronoun in the nominative case − whatever its origin − it moves to a position just before the dative pronoun *mir*:

C / 2: mir . . . nicht gelingen + ( (ich) ) seinen Namen zu erfahren
I /ES: ES mir nicht gelingen + ( (ich) ) seinen Namen zu erfahren

The development from this stage on follows the usual patterns, e. g., for finite verbs:

FNTZ / 1 (= PAST, PSNM): ES mir nicht gelang + ( (ich) ) seinen Namen zu erfahren
T / FV: gelang ES mir nicht + ( (ich) ) seinen Namen zu erfahren

Here, one could topicalize *mir*, or more probably:

T / X: ES gelang mir nicht + ( (ich) ) seinen Namen zu erfahren
SOP: "Es gelang mir nicht, seinen Namen zu erfahren."

The presence of *es* in a sentence containing an infinitive is frequently a sign that that infinitive has been commentized. Indeed, many expressions virtually require this transposition so that the infinitive, which is often the most important syntactic unit in the utterance, may occupy the comment position. Thus, in the following sentences, the infinitive is the subject of the verb, yet because of the communicative priority of the infinitive, the second of the two is more idiomatic than the first, though both are acceptable in suitable contexts:

länger zu warten hätte keinen Sinn
es hätte keinen Sinn, länger zu warten

Thus, the speaker would, in all probability, avail himself of the opportunity to make this change in the position of the infinitive. For the sake of the example, the latter sentence would be generated thus:

IS1: INF2 keinen Sinn haben
IS2: JEMAND länger warten
INFZ / 2: ( (JEMAND) ) länger zu warten
E / 2: ( (JEMAND) ) länger zu warten + keinen Sinn haben
C / 2: . . . keinen Sinn haben + ( (JEMAND) ) länger zu warten
I / ES: ES keinen Sinn haben + ( (JEMAND) ) länger zu warten
FNTZ / 1 (= PAST, SJNC, PSNM): ES keinen Sinn hätte +
 ( (JEMAND) ) länger zu warten
T / FV: hätte ES keinen Sinn + ( (JEMAND) ) länger zu warten
T / X: ES hätte keinen Sinn + ( (JEMAND) ) länger zu warten
SOP: "Es hätte keinen Sinn, länger zu warten."

Another variant of those constructions in which the infinitive is
the grammatical subject of a lexical verb arises when the matrix verb
is in the passive voice. Thus, the sentence:

ich war erstaunt, ihn wieder zu sehen

contains the following infrastructures:

IS1: mich INF2 erstaunen
IS2: ich ihn wieder sehen

The sentence above is generated by the following operations:

INFZ / 2: ( (ich) ) ihn wieder zu sehen
E / 2: mich + ( (ich) ) ihn wieder zu sehen + erstaunen

The infinitive is now commentized and its place in the matrix clause
filled by ES, which, as an unaccented personal pronoun, moves to its
specified place in the UPPRN tagmeme:

C / 2: mich . . . erstaunen + ( (ich) ) ihn wieder zu sehen
I / ES: ES mich erstaunen + ( (ich) ) ihn wieder zu sehen

Since the verb *erstaunen* is transitive, with an accusative object, it is
possible for it to be passivized:

PASV: ich durch ES erstaunt werden + ( (ich) ) ihn wieder zu
 sehen

The verb in the matrix clause is then further modified: first, to form
the terminative aspect (TRMV), followed by the deletion of *worden*
to become the statal passive; then by the past modification (PAST)
to turn the verb complex into the past anterior tense; and finally for
person and number (PSNM):

300

TRMV: ich durch ES erstaunt
    worden sein
D / *worden*: ich durch ES erstaunt
    sein
PAST: ich durch ES erstaunt WAR-
PSNM: ich durch ES erstaunt war

( (ich) )
ihn
wieder
zu
sehen

From this point on, the derivation follows the pattern for finite clauses:

T / FV: war ich durch ES erstaunt + ( (ich) ) ihn wieder zu sehen
T / X: ich war durch ES erstaunt + ( (ich) ) ihn wieder zu sehen

As will be seen in the following section, too, there is a marked tendency to delete prepositional phrases containing surrogate elements like ES for the infinitive when the relation between the matrix clause and the infinitive is clear; hence, *durch ES* may be deleted:

D / EE: ich war . . . erstaunt + ( ( . . . ) ) ihn wieder zu sehen
SOP: "Ich war erstaunt, ihn wieder zu sehen."

When accented for reasons of emphasis, *durch ES* appears in the surface structure as *dadurch*:

SOP: "Ich war *dadurch* erstaunt, ihn wieder zu sehen."

### The Infinitive as Expansion of Its Matrix Verb

The infinitive constructions which were discussed in the first part of this chapter shared the characteristic that, as nouns, they had the function of grammatical subject in their respective matrix clauses. As has been observed in several places in this book, the subject in German is not a syntactic element, as it is in English, but merely an element which has a relation of morphological correspondence with its verb. The grammatical subject of German may thus stand in several tagmemes. When we turn to the infinitive as the "expansion" of its matrix verb, we imply a number of things by that phrase. First, the infinitive is no longer the subject of its matrix verb, but is rather a kind of object. Second, the precise syntactic role of the infinitive depends upon whether it functions as the nucleus complement (NCOMP) of the matrix verb, or whether it occupies the much less prominent position of an adverbo-nominal (AVNOM) in the matrix clause. For reasons of clarity of presentation, we will begin our discussion of these functions with the latter group.

### 1. The Infinitive as Adverbo-Nominal (AVNOM)

As an adverbo-nominal, the infinitive retains its essential characteristic as a noun to a greater degree than in any other construction of which it is a part. It has this role in the following sentence:

> er hat es sich zur Aufgabe gemacht, den Roman zu übersetzen

Underlying this sentence are the infrastructures:

> IS1: er sich INF2 zur Aufgabe machen
> IS2: er den Roman übersetzen

In the first infrastructure, the phrase *zur Aufgabe machen* is the clause nucleus; since there can be only one nucleus complement in a given infrastructure, and since the infinitive is a noun, albeit a special kind of noun, then by a process of elimination it must stand in the only other tagmeme in which a noun can stand, i. e., the adverbo-nominal tagmeme (AVNOM). As we will see presently, it is obligatory after embedding to commentize the infinitive and to replace it in the matrix clause with the element ES. These changes will be introduced at the proper place in the derivation, which begins as in previous instances involving the infinitive as follows:

> INFZ / 2: ( (er) ) den Roman zu übersetzen
> E / 2: er sich + ( (er) ) den Roman zu übersetzen + zur Aufgabe machen

At this point, the infinitive must be commentized:

> C / 2: er sich ... zur Aufgabe machen + ( (er) ) den Roman zu übersetzen

Because ES has the form of a pronoun and is in the accusative case, it takes its position among the unaccented personal pronouns (UPPRN) between the nominative and dative pronouns:

> I / ES: er ES sich zur Aufgabe machen + ( (er) ) den Roman zu übersetzen

From this point to the end of the derivation, the usual pattern for finite verbs is followed:

FNTZ / 1 (= TRMV, PSNM): er ES sich zur Aufgabe gemacht hat + ( (er) ) den Roman zu übersetzen

T / FV: hat er ES sich zur Aufgabe gemacht + ( (er) ) den Roman zu übersetzen

T / X: er hat ES sich zur Aufgabe gemacht + ( (er) ) den Roman zu übersetzen

SOP: "Er hat es sich zur Aufgabe gemacht, den Roman zu übersetzen."

A variant of this construction occurs with verbs which may take accusative objects, often reflexive pronouns, e. g.:

ich weigerte mich, weiter mitzuarbeiten
er rühmt sich, viel geleistet zu haben
sie befleißigt sich jetzt, höflich zu sein (after Erben 1972: §594)

Because an accusative object is already present, the infinitive cannot be construed as having that function. In light of the fact that these verbs may take nominals in the genitive case as additional objects, we may regard these infinitives as also having that function. Thus, in the sentence:

die Polizei hat ihn beschuldigt, das Geld gestohlen zu haben

the infinitive is to be construed as a genitive object, preceded by the element DES in the matrix clause. The infrastructures represented in this example would be:

IS1: ihn die Polizei DES + INF2 beschuldigen
IS2: er das Geld stehlen

The derivation proceeds, for the most part, is in earlier examples; the common verb modification TRMV is applied to IS2, which is then infinitivized:

TRMV: er das Geld gestohlen haben
INFZ / 2: ( (er) ) das Geld gestohlen zu haben
E / 2: ihn die Polizei DES + ( (er) ) das Geld gestohlen zu haben + beschuldigen

As in almost all of these cases, the embedded infinitive is commentized; the element ES is inserted in its place:

C / 2: ihn die Polizei DES . . . beschuldigen + ( (er) ) das Geld gestohlen zu haben

I / ES: ihn die Polizei DES + ES beschuldigen + ( (er) ) das Geld gestohlen zu haben

At this point, the modification of the matrix verb takes place:

TRMV: ihn die Polizei DES + ES beschuldigt haben + ( (er) ) das Geld gestohlen zu haben

PSNM: ihn die Polizei DES + ES beschuldigt hat + ( (er) ) das Geld gestohlen zu haben

T / FV: hat ihn die Polizei DES + ES beschuldigt + ( (er) ) das Geld gestohlen zu haben

T / X: die Polizei hat ihn DES + ES beschuldigt + ( (er) ) das Geld gestohlen zu haben

As a rule, the element DES + ES is deleted; the suppressed infinitive subject also disappears:

D / EE: die Polizei hat ihn . . . beschuldigt + ( ( ) ) das Geld gestohlen zu haben

SOP: "Die Polizei hat ihn beschuldigt, das Geld gestohlen zu haben."

When the infinitive is deleted in a specific context, the ES is expressed; however, it combines with DES to form the pronoun *dessen*:

X: "Er soll das Geld gestohlen haben? "

Y: "Die Polizei hat ihn dessen beschuldigt."

## 2. The Infinitive as Nucleus Complement (NCOMP)

The identification of the role of the infinitive as nucleus complement of its matrix verb is based on its significance within the matrix clause as well as its position in those constructions in which it functions as an expansion of a verb. It is awkward to rely exclusively on positional and distributional criteria in regard to this question, because the infinitive is normally commentized. The following sentences are examples of this kind of construction:

wir haben ihm versprochen, die Ausstellung zu besuchen

wir haben ihm empfohlen, die Ausstellung zu besuchen

The first of these can be analyzed as containing the infrastructures:

IS1: wir ihm INF2 versprechen
IS2: wir die Ausstellung besuchen

The second, on the other hand, deviates from this pattern in one important respect:

IS1: wir ihm INF2 empfehlen
IS2: er die Ausstellung besuchen

The two sentences are thus structurally and lexically identical with two exceptions: the matrix verbs *versprechen* and *empfehlen*, on the one hand; and the subjects of the second infrastructure in each example, *wir* and *er* in the first and second sentence, respectively. The attempt has been made (by Lindgren 1964; 1966; 1967) to use the latter as an ordering principle in establishing the various categories in which the infinitives of German may be classified. It is quite true that the two sentences which we are considering, while identical in regard to surface structure, are nevertheless recognizably different in meaning: in the former, we have promised him that *we* are going to visit the exhibition; in the latter, we have recommended to him that *he* attend that exposition. Because the subjects of infinitives are obligatorily deleted in German in constructions of this kind, one must have recourse to the meanings of the various lexical items if one is to understand what content they are intended to convey. Lindgren's observations are valid and important for the proper use of these verbs, but it is unnecessary to incorporate the distinction between those cases where the subject of the matrix verb refers to the same person or entity as the subject of the infinitive — as in the case of *versprechen* — and those where the object of the matrix verb and the subject of the infinitive do so — as with *empfehlen* — into a system of generative rules according to which the various syntactic elements of the utterance are arranged and distributed.

However, for the sake of the example, we will derive both of the sentences above. The first may be generated as follows:

INFZ / 2: ( (wir) ) die Ausstellung zu besuchen
E / 2: wir ihm + ( (wir) ) die Ausstellung zu besuchen + versprechen

Commentization of the infinitive is optional, but customary; as a rule of thumb, one can say that the longer the infinitive, the more likely it is that it will be moved to the end of the matrix clause. In any case, careful writers of German today tend to avoid the

"Schachtelsatz" of clauses within clauses, and try to arrange them in a connected series. When the infinitive is a nucleus complement, ES is inserted, but is deleted unless the infinitive itself is deleted:

C / 2: wir ihm . . . versprechen + ( (wir) ) die Ausstellung zu besuchen

I / ES: wir ES ihm versprechen + ( (wir) ) die Ausstellung zu besuchen

FNTZ / 1 (= TRMV, PSNM): wir ES ihm versprochen haben + ( (wir) ) die Ausstellung zu besuchen

T / FV: haben wir ES ihm versprochen + ( (wir) ) die Ausstellung zu besuchen

T / X: wir haben ES ihm versprochen + ( (wir) ) die Ausstellung zu besuchen

D / EE: wir haben . . . ihm versprochen + ( ( . . . . ) ) die Ausstellung zu besuchen

SOP: "Wir haben ihm versprochen, die Ausstellung zu besuchen."

In contexts where the infinitive is understood, it becomes redundant and is therefore deleted; in such cases, however, ES is retained:

X: "Sie werden die Ausstellung besuchen? "
Y: "Wir haben es ihm versprochen."

Either ES or the infinitive must be present.

The second of the two sentences, despite the differences which we have adverted to, is generated in precisely the same fashion:

INFZ / 2: ( (er) ) die Ausstellung zu besuchen

E / 2: wir ihm + ( (er) ) die Ausstellung zu besuchen + empfehlen

C / 2: wir ihm . . . empfehlen + ( (er) ) die Ausstellung zu besuchen

I / ES: wir ES ihm empfehlen + ( (er) ) die Ausstellung zu besuchen

FNTZ /1 (= TRMV, PSNM): wir ES ihm empfohlen haben + ( (er) ) die Ausstellung zu besuchen

T / FV: haben wir ES ihm empfohlen + ( (er) ) die Ausstellung zu besuchen

T / X: wir haben ES ihm empfohlen + ( (er) ) die Ausstellung zu besuchen

D / EE: wir haben . . . ihm empfohlen + ( ( . . . ) ) die Ausstellung zu besuchen

SOP: "Wir haben ihm empfohlen, die Ausstellung zu besuchen."

In light of the foregoing comparison, it is possible to see why in some cases superficially identical sentences are not always equally acceptable. The difference between the following pair can only be explained by reference to the infinitive, to the patterns of deletion which apply to it, and to the valence of the lexical items *kennen* and *kommen*:

! ich glaube ihn schon zu kennen
? ? ? ich glaube ihn bald zu kommen (cf. Lindgren 1966:156)

The infrastructure of the matrix clause in both cases is:

IS1: ich INF2 glauben

The infinitive underlying the infinitive is, in the first sentence:

IS2: ich ihn schon kennen

but in the second:

IS2: er bald kommen

In the former, the word *ihn* is the object of *kennen*; in the latter, an inadmissible transformation has taken place, by which the pronoun *er* has been changed into the accusative case to serve as an expressed subject of the infinitive on the model of Finnish grammar, in Lindgren's case, or of infinitive constructions in indirect discourse in Classical Greek and Latin. Because of our requirement that the subject of the infinitive be deleted, and because *glauben* is one of those verbs where the subjects of the matrix verb and the infinitive must refer to the same person, and, finally, because *kommen* cannot take an accusative object, the native speaker of German judges the second of the two sentences to be unacceptable.

This construction may also appear with the matrix verb in the passive voice, as in this sentence:

es wurde erwogen, die beiden Waggons zu bergen (cited by Lindgren 1967:73)

This is based on the infrastructures:

IS1: JEMAND INF2 erwägen
IS2: JEMAND die beiden Waggons bergen

The derivation proceeds as follows:

INFZ / 2: ( (JEMAND) ) die beiden Waggons zu bergen

E / 2: JEMAND + ( (JEMAND) ) die beiden Waggons zu bergen + erwägen

Again, the infinitive is commentized, and ES inserted in its place:

C / 2: JEMAND . . . erwägen + ( (JEMAND) ) die beiden Waggons zu bergen

I / ES: ES JEMAND erwägen + ( (JEMAND) ) die beiden Waggons zu bergen

The verb *erwägen* is transitive, with an expressed object; hence, it can be passivized:

PASV: ES von JEMANDEM erwogen werden + ( (JEMAND) ) die beiden Waggons zu bergen

PAST, PSNM: ES von JEMANDEM erwogen wurde + ( (JEMAND) ) die beiden Waggons zu bergen

T / FV: wurde ES von JEMANDEM erwogen + ( (JEMAND) ) die beiden Waggons zu bergen

T / X: ES wurde von JEMANDEM erwogen + ( (JEMAND) ) die beiden Waggons zu bergen

D / EE: ES wurde . . . erwogen + ( ( . . . ) ) die beiden Waggons zu bergen

SOP: "Es wurde erwogen, die beiden Waggons zu bergen."

## 3. Quasi-Modal Infinitive Constructions

There is a subtype of this construction — more precisely, several subtypes which have certain features in common — in which the matrix verbs in some ways resemble modal auxiliary verbs. We have already dealt with the latter class of verb — *dürfen, können, mögen, müssen, sollen, wollen,* and *werden* — by incorporating them into the system of verb modification; thus, sentences of the type:

seine Kinder haben in der Schule Deutsch sprechen müssen
er hatte nach Italien fahren wollen
das hätten Sie nicht tun sollen

have already been analyzed and described in Chapter 8, and hence do not require separate treatment here.

There are four other patterns of infinitive formation which resemble these modal auxiliaries to varying degrees. Because of their similarity to that class of verbs, these will be referred to as "quasi-

modal infinitive constructions," or simply "quasi-modals." The four
types are exemplified by the sentences below:

Type A
wir haben etwas anderes zu tun bekommen
IS1: wir INF2 bekommen
IS2: wir etwas anderes tun
das haben wir ihnen deutlich zu verstehen gegeben
IS1: wir ihnen INF2 geben
IS2: sie das deutlich verstehen

Type B
wir haben ihn in Köln kennengelernt
IS1: wir INF2 lernen
IS2: wir ihn in Köln kennen
er hat mich lachen gemacht
IS1: er mich INF2 machen
IS2: ich lachen

Type C
das hat er nicht zu tun brauchen
IS1: er INF2 brauchen
IS2: er das nicht tun

Type D
ich habe ihn kommen sehen
IS1: ich ihn INF2 sehen
IS2: er kommen

There are quite a few verbs which may be used as Type A quasi-
modals; in addition to those in the examples above, the verbs *pflegen, meinen, wissen, verstehen, haben*$_A$, and *vermögen* may be mentioned. The number of quasi-modals of Types B, C, and D, in the
other hand, is quite small: the only verbs which are distributed in
these categories are: *brauchen, fühlen, haben*$_B$, *heißen, helfen, hören, lassen, lehren, lernen, machen,* and *sehen.*
  If we take the NCOMP-infinitives described at the beginning of
this section and the modal auxiliaries proper as the end-points of a
spectrum of formal variation, it is clear that the four patterns represented by these quasi-modals occupy positions at various points
between the two extremes. All of these categories – the NCOMP-
infinitives, the quasi-modals, and the regular modal auxiliaries – may
be defined generatively by reference to three factors: first, whether

the embedded infinitive has been commentized; second, whether the element *zu* has been deleted; and third, whether the participle has reassumed the form of the infinitive, i. e., stands in the socalled double infinitive construction. The relevant combinations of these three factors are presented in the table below. The numbers in parentheses identify constructions which are referred to in the discussion which follows the table.

Patterns of Infinitive Formation Among
NCOMP-Infinitives, Quasi-Modals,
and Modal Auxiliaries

| Construction | C / INF? | D / *zu*? | PRT > INF? |
|---|---|---|---|
| NCOMP-Infinitive | almost always (1) | never | never |
| Type A Quasi-Modal, e. g., *geben* | usually not (2) | never | never |
| Type B Quasi-Modal, e. g., *machen* | never (3) | always (3) | never |
| Type C Quasi-Modal, only *brauchen* | never | Standard German: never (5); Colloquial German: = Type D | always (4) |
| Type D Quasi-Modal, e. g., *sehen* | never | always (6) | always |
| Modal Auxiliary Verbs | never | always | always |

With this table as guide, we now turn to the details of some of the differences between these classes of verbs. To begin with, the distinction between NCOMP-infinitives and Type A quasi-modals is virtually one of degree rather than one of kind: in the case of the former group, the infinitive is far more likely to be commentized than in the latter. Nevertheless, there is a perceptible difference in acceptability, as these examples show:

(1) !! wir haben versucht, etwas anderes zu tun
   (NCOMP-infinitive with C / INF)
   ! wir haben etwas anderes zu tun versucht
   (NCOMP-infinitive without C / INF)
(2) ? wir haben bekommen, etwas anderes zu tun
   (Type A quasi-modal with C / INF)
   ! wir haben etwas anderes zu tun bekommen
   (Type A quasi-modal without C / INF)

Though not great, the difference is nevertheless perceptible.

Type A and Type B quasi-modals differ in two respects. As to the first, the infinitive may be commentized in some cases of Type A quasi-modals, but it can never be so in Type B constructions, as this example shows:

(3) ? ? ? wir haben gelernt, ihn in Köln (zu) kennen (with C / INF)
   ! wir haben ihn in Köln kennengelernt (without C / INF)

The second difference, as the sentences above suggest, is the absence of the infinitive marker *zu*: this must be deleted in Type B quasi-modal constructions.

The verb *brauchen* is the sole member of the class labeled Type C quasi-modal infinitive constructions. It differs from Type B constructions in that its participle assumes the form of its infinitive, i. e., it requires the socalled double infinitive construction:

(4) ? ? ? das hat er nicht zu tun gebraucht
   ! das hat er nicht zu tun brauchen

There is, however, some variation in regard to the deletion of *zu*: in Standard German, this element is not deleted; it is often conspicuous by its absence in colloquial German, however:

(5) ! das hat er nicht zu tun brauchen
   ? das hat er nicht tun brauchen

311

In the latter case, this verb has, in effect, merged with those of Type D.

It is in connection with the deletion of *zu* that Type D quasi-modals may be distinguished from *brauchen*: in the latter category, *zu* is always deleted:

(6) ? ? ? ich habe ihn zu kommen sehen
! ich habe ihn kommen sehen

Type D quasi-modals may be distinguished from regular modal auxiliaries, first, by virtue of certain morphological characteristics common to the latter: a present tense which resembles the Germanic preterite in endings and vowel gradation, e. g., *er will* but *wir wollen, ich darf* but *wir dürfen*, etc. Moreover, in the present system of syntax, the regular modals are inserted as modifications of the verb, whereas quasi-modals are treated as infinitives derived from separate infrastructures embedded in a matrix clause.

In the course of the foregoing presentation, it was observed that there were eleven verbs in common use in modern German which can be treated as quasi-modals of Types B, C, or D. Whereas some of these can be labeled as one type or the other without difficulty, others manifest some variation in their patterns of use and formation. The reasons for this lack of uniformity are doutbless partly structural or synchronic and partly historical. In those cases where it is a question as to whether the infinitive can be commentized, considerations of communicative priority may play a role. In those instances where the variant feature is the form of the participle, there is often a long history of dialectal variation which suggests that the reason for the variation in question may lie so far back in the history of the language that the functional justification may no longer be recoverable. Our aim here, then, is to ascertain the range of variation, and to offer such reasons as may be found for the different patterns which we encounter among the quasi-modals.

As the table above indicates, Type B quasi-modals are characterized, first, by the deletion of *zu*, and second, by the normal form of the participle, i. e., they do not manifest the double infinitive construction. The verbs *machen* and *haben*$_B$ conform to this description. It should be noted that the verb *haben*, as a Type A quasi-modal, means 'to have the duty, responsibility of', e. g.:

wir hatten gestern viel zu tun
hier habe ich zu befehlen

As a Type B quasi-modal, on the other hand, it means 'to maintain the state, condition of':

> er hatte viel Geld daheim liegen
> sie hatte einen großen Behälter in der Küche stehen

The remaining verbs which may be grouped under the rubric of Type B quasi-modals are *lehren* and *lernen*, as the following examples show (cf. Duden Hauptschwierigkeiten 1965:412, 414):

> er hat ihn reiten gelehrt
> er hat reiten gelernt

When the embedded infinitive contains a relatively large number of lexical items, however, there is a tendency to commentize it, in which case the element *zu* is not deleted. This means that these verbs then have the function of Type A quasi-modals. The following sentences patterns exemplify this contingency:

> ? ? er hat mich die Haustür immer sorgfältig schließen gelehrt
> ! er hat mich gelehrt, die Haustür immer sorgfältig zu schließen

To be sure, in some cases, the verb *lernen* may be used as a Type A verb without commentization of the verb, particularly in relative and subordinate clauses, e. g.:

> "Die Spannungen, denen man hier ausgesetzt ist, sind nicht die gewohnten, nicht die, *aus denen wir unsere Kraft zu schöpfen gelernt haben*" (Marie Luise Kaschnitz, *Engelsbrücke: Römische Betrachtungen*, Fischer Bücherei 820 [Frankfurt: Fischer, 1967], p. 7).

The italicized relative clause in this passage might also be written as a Type A quasi-modal with commentized infinitive:

> (Spannungen,) aus denen wir gelernt haben, unsere Kraft zu schöpfen

In a case of this kind, stylistic considerations may have lain behind the author's choice: the sentence as it stands has a weight and concentration which would be diffused by commentizing the infinitive and placing clause after clause.

As was pointed out, *brauchen* is the only example in the language of a Type C quasi-modal. Moreover, it was observed that it sometimes merges with quasi-modals of Type D in colloquial German by the additional deletion of *zu*.

The remaining six verbs basically belong to the class of Type D quasi-modals. Of these, *sehen* and, in most instances, *lassen* conform to the pattern of this group. The remaining verbs show some variation as to form and function. The verbs *heißen* and *helfen* normally function as Type D quasi-modals, with infinitive participles and without *zu*:

er hat mich kommen heißen
er hat mir waschen helfen

When the embedded infinitive is relatively long, however, there is again a tendency to use these verbs as Type A quasi-modals with commentized infinitives, e. g.:

? ? er hat ihn das Zimmer auf der Stelle verlassen heißen
! er hat ihn geheißen, das Zimmer auf der Stelle zu verlassen

? ? er hat mir das Auto waschen helfen
! er hat mir geholfen, das Auto zu waschen

It should perhaps be pointed out in connection with these cases, where uncertainty seems at times to prevail, that the structure of the language itself contributes to the confusion. When, as the result of the normal process of finitization, the embedded infinitive comes to stand at the end of the utterance, it is impossible to tell whether the infinitive has been commentized or not. Thus, the sentence:

er half mir das Auto (zu) waschen

could be construed as having either a commentized or an uncommentized infinitive, and the presence or absence of *zu* would be correlated with the former and the latter conditions, respectively. To make this point clear, especially since sentences of this kind are often adduced as evidence of syntactic variation, let us generate both possibilities. The infrastructures reflected in the sentence above are:

IS1: er mir INF2 helfen
IS2: ich das Auto waschen

The generation begins in the fashion so often observed — with the infinitivization of the second of these:

INFZ / 2: ( (ich) ) das Auto zu waschen
E / 2: er mir + ( (ich) ) das Auto zu waschen + helfen

At this point, the derivation may take either of two courses: either the infinitive may be commentized; or the element *zu* may be deleted and, when the matrix verb is finitized, the participle assume the form of the infinitive. Let us take the former alternative first, and then return to the latter:

C / 2: er mir . . . helfen + ( (ich) ) das Auto zu waschen
FNTZ / 1 (= PAST, PSNM): er mir half + ( (ich) ) das Auto zu waschen
T / FV: half er mir + ( (ich) ) das Auto zu waschen
T / X: er half mir + ( (ich) ) das Auto zu waschen
SOP: "Er half mir, das Auto zu waschen."

The second possibility arises immediately after embedding, and begins thus:

D / *zu*: er mir + ( (ich) ) das Auto . . . waschen + helfen
FNTZ / 1 (= PAST, PSNM): er mir + ( (ich) ) das Auto waschen + half
T / FV: half er mir + ( (ich) ) das Auto waschen
T / X: er half mir + ( (ich) ) das Auto waschen
SOP: "Er half mir das Auto waschen."

Thus, pairs of utterances like:

er half mir, das Auto zu waschen
er half mir das Auto waschen

are not simply variants of one another, as is sometimes claimed (Duden Grammatik 1973:561), but constitute different patterns of generation which in turn reflect different combinations of circumstances which may obtain in different contexts. It is for this reason that all of the examples in this section have been placed in the terminative aspect (i. e., present perfect tense): whereas the two sentences above might be construed as syntactically identical, the presence of the participial form in clause-final position enables us to determine immediately whether the infinitive has been commentized:

er hat mir geholfen, das Auto zu waschen (with C / INF)
er hat mir das Auto waschen helfen (without C / INF)

The verbs *fühlen, hören,* and, again, *helfen* manifest yet another variation from the pattern of Type D quasi-modals: the participles of these verbs may either stand in the normal form, i. e., with the *ge*-prefix, or they may have the form of the infinitive. Thus, both sentences in the pairs below must be regarded as acceptable, though the former in each case is considered to be more idiomatic (Duden Hauptschwierigkeiten 1965:240, 294, 304):

!! er hat das Fieber kommen fühlen
!? er hat das Fieber kommen gefühlt
!! ich habe ihn nicht kommen hören
!? ich habe ihn nicht kommen gehört
!! ich habe ihm waschen helfen
!? ich habe ihm waschen geholfen

These may be regarded as instances of true syntactic and morphological variation. The range of variation of these quasi-modals described in the foregoing remarks is summarized in this table:

Range of Variation Among
Quasi-Modal Verbs

| Quasi-Modal | "Normal" Type | Range of Variation | | |
|---|---|---|---|---|
| | | when C / INF | when D / zu | when PRT ≠ INF |
| machen | B | – | – | – |
| haben$_B$ | B | A | – | – |
| lehren | B | A | – | – |
| lernen | B | A | – | – |
| brauchen | C | – | D | – |
| sehen | D | – | – | – |
| lassen | D | – | – | B |
| heißen | D | A | – | – |
| fühlen | D | – | – | B |
| hören | D | – | – | B |
| helfen | D | A | – | B |

316

A last note might be added concerning a quasi-modal construction which might not, at first glance, seem to fit into any of the categories above. This is exemplified by the sentence:

er fühlte sich durch meine Bemerkung beleidigt

The verb *fühlen* is often found accompanied by a reflexive pronoun and an adjective or participle. This participle is in fact the last visible remnant of an infinitivized verb. The sentence above may be analyzed as containing the following infrastructures:

IS1: er sich INF2 fühlen
IS2: ich ihn durch meine Bemerkung beleidigen

The essential step in the generation of this sentence is the modification of the infinitive by the transformations for the passive:

PASV: er von mir durch meine Bemerkung beleidigt werden

Since a state is described by the clause, and not a process, the statal passive is generated by the common verb modification for the terminative aspect, followed by the deletion of *worden*:

TRMV: er von mir durch meine Bemerkung beleidigt worden sein
D / *worden*: er von mir durch meine Bemerkung beleidigt . . . sein

This sequence is then infinitivized and embedded in IS1:

INFZ / 2: ( (er) ) von mir durch meine Bemerkung beleidigt zu sein
E / 2: er sich + ( (er) ) von mir durch meine Bemerkung beleidigt zu sein + fühlen

The infinitive marker *zu* is deleted because *fühlen* is a Type D quasi-modal:

D / *zu*: er sich + ( (er) ) von mir durch meine Bemerkung beleidigt . . . sein + fühlen

Now the matrix clause undergoes modification:

FNTZ / 1 (= PAST, PSNM): er sich + ( (er) ) von mir durch meine Bemerkung beleidigt sein + fühlte
T / FV: fühlte er sich + ( (er) ) von mir durch meine Bemerkung beleidigt sein
T / X: er fühlte sich + ( (er) ) von mir durch meine Bemerkung beleidigt sein

317

The various empty elements present may now be deleted: the phrase *von mir* is implied in the word *meine*; the auxiliary *sein* is redundant in this context:

> D / EE: er fühlte sich + ( ( . . . ) ) . . . durch meine Bemerkung beleidigt . . .
> SOP: "Er fühlte sich durch meine Bemerkung beleidigt."

Thus, the construction of *sich fühlen* with a participle is merely a special case of *fühlen* as a Type D quasi-modal. Constructions with an adjective in place of the participle differ only in that the verb *sein* has been deleted. Thus, the sentence:

> ich fühle mich krank

reflects the infrastructures:

> IS1: ich mich INF2 fühlen
> IS2: ich krank sein

In other respects, it is generated as in the preceding example:

> INFZ / 2: ( (ich) ) krank zu sein
> E / 2: ich mich + ( (ich) ) krank zu sein + fühlen
> D / *zu*: ich mich + ( (ich) ) krank . . . sein + fühlen
> PSNM: ich mich + ( (ich) ) krank sein + fühle
> T / FV: fühle ich mich + ( (ich) ) krank sein
> T / X: ich fühle mich + ( (ich) ) krank sein
> D / EE: ich fühle mich + ( ( . . . ) ) krank . . .
> SOP: "Ich fühle mich krank."

## 4. PREP + INF + LEXVB

Constructions in which the infinitive is the object of a preposition which is closely associated with a verb are numerous in German, e. g.:

> es geht darum, eine neue Regierung zu bilden
> es diente dazu, die Tür offen zu halten
> er bat mich (darum), ihm das Buch zu borgen
> er riet uns (dazu), dieses Museum zu besuchen

In all of these cases, the matrix verb is regularly accompanied by a preposition which may take either an ordinary noun or an infinitive as its object. Those in parentheses may be deleted under conditions to be discussed presently. When the object of one of these prepositions is a noun, the combination of preposition plus noun is normally not commentized:

! er hat uns zu einem Besuch dieses Museums geraten

? ? er hat uns geraten zu einem Besuch dieses Museums (colloquial, but substandard)

When an infinitive is the object of the preposition, the infinitive is commentized, but the preposition remains in the matrix clause. The element ES then becomes the object of the preposition, and the combination appears in the surface structure as a compound with *da-*, e. g., *zu + ES* becomes *dazu, mit + ES* becomes *damit*, etc. These changes are illustrated in the following derivation:

IS1: er uns zu + INF raten
IS2: wir dieses Museum besuchen
INFZ / 2: ( (wir) ) dieses Museum zu besuchen
E / 2: er uns zu + ( (wir) ) dieses Museum zu besuchen + raten

At this point, the infinitive is commentized and ES inserted in its place:

C / 2: er uns zu . . . raten + ( (wir) ) dieses Museum zu besuchen
I / ES: er uns zu ES raten + ( (wir) ) dieses Museum zu besuchen

The remainder of the derivation affects the matrix verb, except for the change in the form of the prepositional compound at the last stage of generation:

FNTZ / 1 (= TRMV, PSNM): er uns zu ES geraten hat + ( (wir) ) dieses Museum zu besuchen
T / FV: hat er uns zu ES geraten + ( (wir) ) dieses Museum zu besuchen
T / X: er hat uns zu ES geraten + ( (wir) ) dieses Museum zu besuchen
SOP: "Er hat uns dazu geraten, dieses Museum zu besuchen."

There is one additional question to consider in connection with this kind of construction: the possibility of deleting the prepositional compound, e. g., *dazu* in the example above. In the examples at the beginning of this section, two prepositional compounds were enclosed in parentheses, two not. The enclosed elements may be optionally deleted, the others may not be. The principles by which some are retained and others deleted are not altogether clear, but it is possible to make out two factors which may be relevant here. First, the prepositional compound may be deleted when the verb of the matrix clause has the function of a verb of saying, so that the infinitive then reproduces the content of what was said, as in these sentences:

sie haben uns (dazu) überredet, mitzukommen
ich kann mich (daran) nicht erinnern, die Dame je gesehen zu haben

On the other hand, when it is a question of other kinds of relationships, e. g., instrumentality, the prepositional compound is normally not deleted, e. g.:

! ich habe mich daran gewöhnt, früh aufzustehen
? ? ? ich habe mich . . . gewöhnt, früh aufzustehen

! man ist dabei, eine neue Firma zu gründen
? ? ? man ist . . ., eine neue Firma zu gründen

As to the second factor, compounds with *zu* seem to be deleted more frequently than those with other prepositions, regardless of their communicative role in the sentence, perhaps because of the presence of the element *zu* in the infinitive itself, which might cause the preposition to be felt as redundant. Thus, one would expect the infinitive marker *zu* to be retained in cases like these, although it may be deleted:

er hat mich (dazu) bewogen, das Haus zu verkaufen
besondere Umstände haben mich (dazu) gezwungen, das Haus zu verkaufen

*The Infinitive as Object of a Preposition*

To be sure, the construction just discussed in the preceding section had to do with the infinitive in close relationship to a preposition; however, the defining factor in that structure was the presence of a lexical verb on which the preposition was dependent. The constructions to be examined in this section fall into two groups: those in which an adjective is closely associated with the preposition, on which the infinitive is in turn dependent; and those where the infinitive is the object of the prepositions *ohne, statt,* or *um* in the matrix clause.

320

## 1. ADJ + PREP + INF

This construction appears in the following sentences:

sie ist (darüber) froh, in die Berge fahren zu können
er war nicht (damit) zufrieden, gewonnen zu haben
ich bin weit (davon) entfernt, ihm zu glauben
er erklärte sich (dazu) bereit, ihm zu helfen

These constructions are similar to those in which the infinitive and preposition accompany a lexical verb in a valence bond, in the sense that here, too, the infinitive is the object of a preposition which is then commentized, after which the vacant slot is filled by the element ES; this element is then fused with the preposition in the form *da-*, e. g., *über* + *ES* becomes *darüber*, etc.

The last of the sentences above is particularly instructive, not only because it contains an infinitive as object of a preposition, but also because it contains two embedded infinitives, and hence gives some idea of the complexity of these constructions. The sentence:

er erklärte sich (dazu) bereit, ihm zu helfen

would be generated as follows:

IS1: er sich INF2 erklären
IS2: er zu + INF3 bereit sein
IS3: er ihm helfen

These are joined to form the sentence above in the following way:

INFZ / 3: ( (er) ) ihm zu helfen
E / 3: er zu + ( (er) ) ihm zu helfen + bereit sein

This is now infinitivized, and then embedded into the next infrastructure:

INFZ / 2: ( (er) ) zu + ( (er) ) ihm zu helfen + bereit zu sein
E / 2: er sich ++ ( (er) ) zu + ( (er) ) ihm zu helfen + bereit zu sein ++ erklären

The infinitive from IS3, because of its communicative importance, is commentized, and the element ES inserted in its place:

C / 3: er sich + ( (er) ) zu . . . bereit zu sein + erklären ++ ( (er) ) ihm zu helfen
I / ES: er sich + ( (er) ) zu ES bereit zu sein + erklären ++ ( (er) ) ihm zu helfen

321

Finally, the independent clause may be formed:

FNTZ / 1 (= PAST, PSNM): er sich + ( (er) ) zu ES bereit zu sein
+ erklärte ++ ( (er) ) ihm zu helfen

T / FV: erklärte er sich + ( (er) ) zu ES bereit zu sein ++ ( (er) )
ihm zu helfen

T / X: er erklärte sich + ( (er) ) zu ES bereit zu sein ++ ( (er) )
ihm zu helfen

Several elements are now deleted, for various reasons: the suppressed
subjects of the infinitives; the redundant verb *zu sein*; the expression *zu ES*, which is realized as *dazu* in the surface structure, from
which it may be optionally deleted:

D / EE: er erklärte sich + ... (dazu) bereit ... ++ ... ihm zu
helfen

SOP: "Er erklärte sich (dazu) bereit, ihm zu helfen."

Again the question of the deletion of the prepositional compound
arises. This element is almost always present when the infinitive is
not actually present, but is understood, e. g.:

er erklärte sich dazu bereit

It is also retained in cases of contrast or emphasis, e. g.:

er wollte wissen, ob sein Onkel dazu bereit wäre, ihm mit einer
beträchtlichen Summe zum Studium zu verhelfen

This sentence might be freely translated as: 'he wanted to know if
his uncle was prepared to support his university education to the
extent of granting him a substantial sum of money'. The element
*dazu* alerts the hearer to the coming infinitive, and conveys the
notion 'to the extent of'.

## 2. ohne, statt, um + INF

In addition to those cases above, the prepositions *ohne, statt,* and
*um* may take infinitives as objects, independently of any other
syntactic elements such as verbs or adjectives, e. g.:

ohne länger zu warten
statt uns zu besuchen
um ihm zu helfen

The preposition stands in the matrix clause; the infinitive is generated separately, and then embedded; thus the sentence:

ohne länger zu warten ging sie nach Hause

would be generated as follows:

IS1: sie ohne + INF nach Hause gehen
IS2: sie länger warten
INFZ / 2: ( (sie) ) länger zu warten
E / 2: sie ohne + ( (sie) ) länger zu warten ++ nach Hause gehen
FNTZ / 1: sie ohne + ( (sie) ) länger zu warten ++ nach Hause
    ging
T / FV: ging sie ohne + ( (sie) ) länger zu warten ++ nach Hause
T / X: ohne + ( (sie) ) länger zu warten ++ ging sie nach Hause
SOP: "Ohne länger zu warten ging sie nach Hause."

The infinitive with these prepositions constitutes a single syntactic unit, in most cases an adverbo-nominal which can be topicalized at the stage T / X, as in the example above.

### The Infinitive with Adjective and Noun

These two constructions are alike in that the infinitive appears to be immediately connected to the adjective or noun, with no intervening function word such as a preposition.

### 1. ADJ + INF

There are a few adjectives in German which are used primarily or exclusively as predicate adjectives — in our terminology as nucleus complements (NCOMP) with *sein* — for example, *gewohnt, müde, satt; gewillt, willens*. As has been pointed out, the infinitive is basically a noun, and hence it may be regarded as standing in the genitive case. Indeed, in certain instances, when the infinitive has been commentized, the element ES — which is, after all, the genitive singular neuter pronoun in Middle High German — is inserted into the vacant slot. This is exemplified in these sentences:

er ist es gewohnt, viel allein zu sein
ich bin es müde, das immer wieder zu sagen
seine Eltern sind es satt, ihn immer wieder zu ermahnen

The first of these would be generated as follows:

IS1: er gewohnt + INF sein
IS2: er viel allein sein

The first step is to infinitivize the second infrastructure:

INFZ / 2: ( (er) ) viel allein zu sein
E / 2: er gewohnt + ( (er) ) viel allein zu sein + sein
C / 2: er gewohnt . . . sein + ( (er) ) viel allein zu sein

Because ES has the form of a personal pronoun, it takes its position in that tagmeme (UPPRN):

I / ES: er ES gewohnt sein + ( (er) ) viel allein zu sein
FNTZ / 1: er ES gewohnt ist + ( (er) ) viel allein zu sein
T / FV: ist er ES gewohnt + ( (er) ) viel allein zu sein

The element ES reveals its peculiar function here by virtue of the fact that it cannot be topicalized:

T / X: ES ist er gewohnt + ( (er) ) viel allein zu sein
SOP: ? ? ? "ES ist er gewohnt, viel allein zu sein."

The most likely candidate for topicalization is *er*:

T / X: er ist ES gewohnt + ( (er) ) viel allein zu sein
SOP: ! "Er ist es gewohnt, viel allein zu sein."

The elements *willens* and *gewillt* differ from *satt, müde,* and *gewohnt* in that they require the deletion of ES:

? ? ? er ist es willens, es zu bezahlen
! er ist willens, es zu bezahlen

There are so few of these, however, that they may hardly be considered a separate category.

## 2. NOUN + INF

This construction, which occurs frequently in German, is exemplified by these sentences:

sie hat die *Möglichkeit*, dieses Jahr in Deutschland zu studieren
die Künstler hatten damals den *Mut*, sich von jeder Konvention
    loszusagen

ich habe nur den einen *Wunsch,* möglichst schnell von hier weg-
zukommen

der Gemeinderat hat den *Beschluß* gefaßt, entsprechende Ent-
schädigungen zu zahlen

es ist natürlich kaum jemandem zumutbar, die Innenstadt zu besuchen, wenn er vor der *Alternative* steht, entweder unzuläng-
liche öffentliche Verkehrsmittel zu benützen oder stundenlang
auf Parkplatzjagd zu gehen

In each of these cases, a noun in the matrix clause — italicized
above — stands for and represents the infinitive which follows, e. g.,
the *Möglichkeit* in the first sentences is precisely that of studying in
Germany this year. In light of this observation, we may regard these
nouns as standing in apposition (represented by the sign "=") to the
infinitive elements which follow them. Thus, the first sentence
would be generated as follows:

IS1: sie die Möglichkeit = INF haben
IS2: sie dieses Jahr in Deutschland studieren
INFZ / 2: ( (sie) ) dieses Jahr in Deutschland zu studieren
E / 2: sie die Möglichkeit = ( (sie) ) dieses Jahr in Deutschland zu
studieren + haben

The infinitive may be commentized, but ES ist not inserted:

C / 2: sie die Möglichkeit . . . haben + ( (sie) ) dieses Jahr in
Deutschland zu studieren
FNTZ / 1: sie die Möglichkeit hat + ( (sie) ) dieses Jahr in
Deutschland zu studieren
T / FV: hat sie die Möglichkeit + ( (sie) ) dieses Jahr in Deutsch-
land zu studieren
T / X: sie hat die Möglichkeit + ( (sie) ) dieses Jahr in Deutsch-
land zu studieren
SOP: "Sie hat die Möglichkeit, dieses Jahr in Deutschland zu
studieren."

As the nouns in the examples above all imply a certain content — *Möglichkeit, Wunsch, Beschluß,* etc. — it may be helpful to
regard this construction as a form of indirect discourse. This in turn
suggests that there might be a transformational relationship between
utterances like:

```
der Gemeinderat hat beschlossen          )  (   Entschädigungen
                                         )  (
der Gemeinderat hat den Beschluß gefaßt )  (   zu zahlen
```

To explore this possibility, however, would take us across the boundary between syntax and morphology, and unduly complicate the picture of generative syntax which has been drawn in the preceding pages. (For a development of this idea in English, cf. Lees 1960b.)

CHAPTER 16

THE INFINITIVE CONSTRUCTIONS OF ENGLISH AND
GERMAN: A COMPARISON

When we approach the infinitive constructions of English and German, we encounter structures of greater complexity than the infrastructures which were compared in Chapter 6, or the finite clauses
compared in Chapter 12. Because the patterns of infinitive constructions are more varied, it is not surprising that the differences
between the two languages in this regard are more numerous, and
that where similarities can be identified, it is less the larger patterns
which are alike than specific constructions which, as if by accident,
manifest a formal resemblance or a comparable function. It is these
considerations which have determined the organization of this chapter. After an examination of those areas where the two languages
display certain general differences and similarities, we will turn to
specific patterns which are roughly comparable in structure, in communicative function, or in both, and study them as features of those
constructions which are likely to lead the native speaker of one
language onto false paths in his attempt to use the other.

As to general areas of contrast between German and English, it
has been pointed out that the most striking difference between the
infinitives of the two languages was the retention of the subject in
English and its deletion in German. Its effects are most visible in
connection with the English construction LEXVB + INF, where a
good part of the problem was to establish the patterns of retention
and deletion of the subject of the infinitive when this element was
joined to its matrix verb. We were compelled to set up no fewer than
five types of infinitive constructions, in large measure to account for
variations arising out of this structural feature. In German, on the
other hand, this was completely unnecessary, because in that language the subject of the infinitive is deleted in the process of infinitivization. Thus, this distinction, which appears at the stage of clause
formation, continues to make its presence felt through subsequent
transformations of structures in which the infinitive is a component
element.

The second general difference between English and German is the greater prominence in the former language of infinitive structures with the verb BE. To be sure, there are comparable structures in German which may only occur with *sein*, but these are fewer in number and play a less distinctive role in the structure of that language than BE in English. This verb is often used in contexts in which a German would be likely to use another verb altogether.

This observation leads directly to the third and last general difference, namely, that even where infinitive constructions may be similar in form, the semantic areas covered by the verbs which may appear in them may be quite different. For example, there is a general formal similarity in the treatment of infinitives as expansions of a lexical verb, a similarity which results in a variety of patterns according to which these infinitives may be embedded: these are the constructions designated as LEXVB + INF in English and as $INF_{NCOMP}$ + LEXVB in German. The five types of infinitive constructions in English bear a certain superficial formal resemblance to the NCOMP-infinitives and quasi-modals of German. Yet, the number of such verbs in German is far smaller, and covers a smaller semantic area — preponderantly the areas of cognition, sensation, mode of action, etc. — than the verbs subsumed under the five types of infinitive constructions of English, which come from a much broader spectrum of the language. Hence, though the structures as such may be more or less similar, the lexical items which characteristically appear in them come from quite different sectors of the vocabulary.

With these general differences in mind, then, we turn to the examination of eleven constructions in connection with which the languages manifest either striking contrasts or superficial, but partial similarities, such that speakers of one language might be likely to make mistakes in learning and using the other.

### 1. Eng. NOM + BE + INF vs. Grm. LEXVB

This structure is exemplified in English by the sentence:

the orders were for everyone to take his seat

Patterns of this kind are rare in German, the usual equivalent being a verb of saying in place of BE, or an expression which replaces both the noun and the verb BE. The sentence above, for example, might be rendered:

der Befehl lautete, Platz zu nehmen

es wurde $\left\{\begin{array}{l}\text{befohlen,} \\ \text{gebeten,} \\ \text{ersucht,}\end{array}\right\}$ Platz zu nehmen

Examples of this construction would thus be variously rendered by lexical items appropriate to the specific context in which the expression appeared.

## 2. Eng. *INF + BE + NOM vs. GRM. INF$_{SJ}$ + NCOMP$_{NOUN}$ + sein*

These constructions result in utterances which are fairly close in syntactic form, though the compulsory deletion of the subject of the infinitive may compel the speaker to resort to other structures when that element is crucial to the thought to be expressed. Thus, these sentences are parallel in structure:

(for me) to see him again was a source of great joy for me
( (ich) ) ihn wiederzusehen war mir eine große Freude

The expressed subject of the English infinitive forces the speaker of German to use a dependent finite clause here:

for his parents to see him again was a source of great joy for me
daß ihn seine Eltern wiedersehen konnten, war mir eine große Freude

In addition, the element IT or ES may replace a commentized dependent clause, either finite or infinitive:

IT was a source of great joy for me . . .
to see him again
for his parents to see him again
ES war mir eine große Freude . . .,
ihn wiederzusehen
daß ihn seine Eltern wiedersehen konnten

To be sure, it would be possible to replace all of these infinitive clauses in both languages with dependent finite clauses, a step which would remove them from the context in which we are considering them altogether, however.

## 3. Eng. INF + BE + INF vs. Grm. INF + INF + heißen

This is one of those cases where BE in English is usually rendered by a verb other than *sein* in German. Where two infinitives are linked by the verb BE in English, German in many cases uses *heißen*:

to be human is to be mortal
Mensch sein heißt sterben müssen

There is no exact German equivalent for constructions like:

he was a fool to expect results

which was analyzed as reflecting the structure:

for him to expect results + was + for him to be a fool

It is possible, in colloquial German, to use the preposition *um* as a loose connective element to produce an utterance which resembles the surface structure of the sentence above, i. e.:

er war ein Trottel, um positive Ergebnisse zu erwarten

This sentence does not contain the two infinitives which are present in the English structure under consideration. Moreover, this usage is frowned upon by grammarians and writers on German style (e. g., by Killinger & Doppler 1950:122).

## 4. Eng. INF + BE + $\emptyset$ vs. Grm. $INF_{SJ}$ + $\emptyset$ + sein

In English, this construction generates three different patterns of surface structure:

IS1: INF + BE + $\emptyset$
IS2: John read these books
INFZ / 2, E / 2, C / 2: BE $\emptyset$ + for John to read these books
    (1) I / IT, FNTZ / 1: IT is $\emptyset$ + for John to read these books
SOP: "It is for John to read these books."
    (2) T / $SJ_2$, SJCTZ, FNTZ / 1, D / EE: John is $\emptyset$ + ..... to read these books
SOP: "John is to read these books."
    (3) T / $OJ_2$, SJCTZ, FNTZ / 1: these books are $\emptyset$ + for John to read ...
SOP: "These books are for John to read."

330

These utterances are generated, after the commentization of the infinitive, by the insertion of IT (1), by the retopicalization of the subject of the infinitive (2), or of its object (3). In the construction in German which most closely corresponds to the English structure, the infinitive is not commentized, and hence ES cannot be inserted, nor the subject nor the object of the infinitive moved to its place. What happens in German is that the object of the infinitive, by subjectivization, becomes the pseudosubject of *sein*, as in this example:

IS1: INF2 + ∅ + sein
IS2: JEMAND diese Bücher lesen
INFZ / 2: ( (JEMAND) ) diese Bücher zu lesen
E / 2: ( (JEMAND) ) diese Bücher zu lesen + ∅ sein
T / $OJ_2$: diese Bücher ( (JEMAND) ) . . . zu lesen + ∅ sein
SJCTZ: diese Bücher + ( (JEMAND) ) . . . zu lesen + ∅ sein
FNTZ / 1: diese Bücher + ( (JEMAND) ) . . . zu lesen + ∅ sind
T / FV: sind diese Bücher + ( (JEMAND) ) . . . zu lesen + ∅
T / X: diese Bücher sind + ( (JEMAND) ) . . . zu lesen + ∅
SOP: "Diese Bücher sind zu lesen."

Given the similarity of these derivations, it is not accidental that the sentences:

these books are for John to read
diese Bücher sind zu lesen

are similar in surface structure. In regard to the English construction, it is also possible to passivize the infinitive when no subject is expressed; nevertheless, the English sentence is still a close semantic equivalent of the German expression:

! these books are to read
! these books are to be read
! diese Bücher sind zu lesen

The utterance:

John is to read these books

is normally expressed in German with the aid of a modal auxiliary:

Hans soll diese Bücher lesen

Under this rubric, we identified three classes of adjective in English, according to the potential of each for the retopicalization of the subject or object of the embedded infinitive, e. g.:

$$
\text{for him to do that + was} \quad
\begin{cases}
(1) & \text{pointless} \\
(2) & \text{easy} \\
(3) & \text{clever of him}
\end{cases}
$$

The parallel constructions in German are:

$$
\text{das zu tun + war} \quad
\begin{cases}
(1) & \text{zwecklos} \\
(2) & \text{leicht} \\
(3) & \text{raffiniert von ihm}
\end{cases}
$$

In each instance, the infinitive in both languages may be commentized at some point in the derivation and replaced by IT or ES:

$$
\text{IT + was} \quad
\begin{cases}
(1) & \text{pointless} \\
(2) & \text{easy} \\
(3) & \text{clever of him}
\end{cases}
\quad \text{+ for him to do that}
$$

$$
\text{ES + war} \quad
\begin{cases}
(1) & \text{zwecklos} \\
(2) & \text{leicht} \\
(3) & \text{raffiniert von ihm}
\end{cases}
\quad \text{+ das zu tun}
$$

But is is impossible in German to retopicalize the subject of the infinitive, as can be done in English with adjectives of the third category like *clever*, e. g.:

! he + was clever (of him) + . . . to do that
? ? ? er + war raffiniert (von ihm) + ( ( . . . ) ) das zu tun

On the other hand, English and German are alike in that the object of the infinitive may be retopicalized when the adjective present belongs to the second category exemplified by *easy* and *leicht*, e. g.:

! that + was easy + for him to do . . .
! das + war leicht + ( (er) ) . . . zu tun

The reader may recall the frequently cited example of this construction:

John is easy to please

As was noted in Chapter 14, the underlying structure of this sentence is:

(for SOMEONE) to please John + is easy

which has, as the foregoing discussion explains, the following variants:

IT + is easy + (for SOMEONE) to please John

and, of course:

John + is easy + (for SOMEONE) to please . . .

Only two of these have counterparts in German:

! Hans zu gefallen + ist leicht
! ES + ist leicht + Hans zu gefallen

The retopicalization of the infinitive object in German is possible only when that object is an accusative object, e. g.:

das zu zeigen + ist leicht
das + ist leicht + . . . zu zeigen

The verb *gefallen*, however, takes a dative object, for which reason the sentence:

? ? ? Hans + ist leicht + . . . zu gefallen

is unacceptable. Moreover, it is more usual to retopicalize impersonal objects than those representing persons, like *Hans*.

It must be added that there is a construction which superfically resembles the unacceptable utterance above, i. e.:

! Hans ist nicht zu gefallen

Despite their apparent similarity, however, the underlying structures are not the same. The infinitive in this sentence is the subject of *sein* as in the preceding example, but here we have a zero-complement rather than an adjective as nucleus complement. The word *nicht* is a clause nucleus adverb in the embedded infinitive clause, not a nucleus complement of the matrix clause. Moreover, the noun *Hans* is not a pseudosubject in the nominative case, but merely a topicalized element which retains its form and function as a dative object. The sentence may be generated as follows:

IS1: INF2 + $\emptyset$ + sein
IS2: JEMAND dem Hans nicht gefallen

We attach the article to the noun *Hans* to show its case.

INFZ / 2: ( (JEMAND) ) dem Hans nicht zu gefallen
E / 2: ( (JEMAND) ) dem Hans nicht zu gefallen + ∅ sein
FNTZ / 1: ( (JEMAND) ) dem Hans nicht zu gefallen + ∅ ist
T / FV: ist + ( (JEMAND) ) dem Hans nicht zu gefallen + ∅
T / X: dem Hans ist + ( (JEMAND) ) ... nicht zu gefallen + ∅
SOP: "(Dem) Hans ist nicht zu gefallen."

*6. Eng. . . . + BE + ADJ + PREP + INF vs. Grm. ADJ + PREP + INF + sein*

These constructions are not altogether dissimilar, as the examples below indicate:

he is ready (for) $\begin{cases} \text{(for him) to leave} \\ \text{for us to leave} \end{cases}$

er ist (dazu) bereit, abzufahren

The chief difference here is the dummy object *da-* in the compound *dazu*, which may be retained in some cases. In English, objectless prepositions like *for* are always deleted.

*7. Eng. INF + LEXVB (+ OBJ) vs. Grm. INF$_{SJ}$ + LEXVB*

There are a number of verbs in German which characteristically take infinitives as subjects, which are as a rule commentized and replaced by ES:

es zu erfahren + gelang mir
ES + gelang mir + es zu erfahren

Constructions of this kind are not unknown in English, e. g.:

to find that out + surprised me
IT + surprised me + to find that out

It is also possible to transform the sentence into the passive voice, in which case the infinitive becomes the object of the instrumental preposition *by*:

I was surprised (by) + to find that out

When the object of the active verb in German is in the accusative, the same transformation is possible:

das zu erfahren + überraschte mich →
ich war (durch + INF) überrascht (worden) + das zu erfahren

When the object is in the dative case, as with *gelingen*, this kind of construction is inadmissible.

## 8. Eng. INF + LEXVB + ∅ vs. Grm. $INF_{SJ}$ + anfangen, scheinen, etc.

The verbs *seem* and *scheinen* enter into virtually identical constructions, the distinguishing characteristic of which is that the subject of the infinitive becomes the pseudosubject of the matrix verb. This change takes place in German as well — indeed, this is the one construction in the language in which the subject of the infinitive appears in the surface structure. Thus the sentences:

he seems to be cheerful today
er scheint heute fröhlich zu sein

both reflect the parallel structures:

for him to be cheerful today + seem
( (er) ) heute fröhlich zu sein + scheinen

This pattern applies to *seem, appear,* and *happen* in English; in German *aufhören, anfangen, beginnen, scheinen,* and a few others appear in this construction. The English counterparts of these verbs (other than *scheinen*) either take other nonfinite forms in place of the German infinitive, e. g.:

er hörte auf zu singen (with infinitive)
he stopped singing (with gerundive)

or follow one or the other of the patterns subsumed under the rubric LEXVB + INF, e. g., *begin*:

( (er) ) zu singen + anfangen → er fing an zu singen
he began + (for him) to sing (= Type A infinitive construction)

## 9. Eng. LEXVB + INF vs. Grm. INF_NCOMP + LEXVB

These structures are the most varied which the two languages manifest: as the reader will recall, five types of infinitive constructions were found to exist in English, and in German there were four patterns of quasi-modals which were postulated in addition to the NCOMP-infinitives. In English, the main variable was the presence of the subject of the infinitive; in German, the criteria by which these groups of verbs were distinguished were the tendency toward the commentization of the infinitive, the form of the participle when present, and the deletion of *zu*.

In addition, those verbs which were in the main responsible for these variant patterns of infinitive formation in German were few in number, though there are large numbers of verbs which may enter into normal NCOMP-infinitive constructions; furthermore, they were semantically and structurally akin to the modal auxiliaries, for which reason they were labeled "quasi-modals." Those English verbs which may be followed by infinitives are distributed among the five types of infinitive constructions which were identified; they did not fall into any specific semantic categories. Because these groups of verbs have so few characteristics in common, a comparison of them, feature by feature, would only lead into a maze of detail. Hence, these structures must be studied individually within the context of the structural patterns of the language in question.

## 10. Eng. in order + INF vs. Grm. ohne, statt, um + INF

The chief difference between the two languages in respect of these constructions lies in the fact that the English phrase *in order* is the only preposition which may take an infinitive as object, whereas *ohne, statt,* and *um* may do so in German:

in order + (for him) to do it
um + es zu tun

The objects of the English prepositions *instead of* and *without* are gerundives in such cases:

instead of + taking the train
statt + mit dem Zug zu fahren

without + waiting any longer
ohne + länger zu warten

The preposition *um* cannot be deleted as *in order* can in English:

he came (in order) to visit his friend
er kam, um seinen Freund zu besuchen
(but: ? ? ? er kam, seinen Freund zu besuchen)

## 11. Eng. *NOUN (+ PREP) + INF vs. Grm. NOUN + INF*

In regard to the constructions which fall under this rubric, we noted that infinitives which appear to follow English nouns immediately are in fact objects of the preposition *for*, which, when objectless, must be deleted. Thus the phrase:

we have no time to eat now

actually reflects the structure:

we have no time (for + for us) to eat (SOMETHING) now

In the case of German, it seemed more compatible with the form and meaning of such constructions to regard the infinitive as standing in apposition to the noun, particularly since the latter often, though by no means always, postulates a general category or rubric of which the infinitive describes the specific case:

die Möglichkeit, nach Dänemark zu fahren
der Versuch, die Tür aufzumachen
die neue Art, Theater zu spielen

In many cases, this construction comes close to a kind of indirect discourse, where the noun represents the verb of saying and the infinitive the content of what is said, e. g.:

die Absicht, hier zu bleiben
der Wunsch, eine Reise zu machen
der Plan, diese Straße in eine Fußgängerzone zu verwandeln

# CHAPTER 17

## THE PARTICIPIAL CONSTRUCTIONS OF ENGLISH

In the chapter dealing with the infinitive, we saw that the infrastructure could be partially transformed into a species of noun. In the pages to follow, we will see how English and German infrastructures may be changed into complex adjectival and adverbial constructions called participles. As these are dependent clauses, they must be embedded in matrix clauses, where, as adverbs, they modify the matrix verb, or, as adjectives, a specific noun in the matrix clause.

Not only do participial clauses have two functions — adjectival and adverbial — they have two forms: attributive and absolute. An attributive participle must be adjectival in function, and is incorporated into the matrix clause by clause-element-restricting embedding. It is thus attached to a specific noun, and becomes part of the syntactic element of which that noun is the chief component. These attributive adjectival participles may, by procedures to be described in this chapter, be placed either before or after the noun they modify; the former are called "prenominal," the latter "postnominal" attributive adjectival participles. These are illustrated by the following sentences:

> the ballots *counted yesterday* were placed in a vault (attributive adjectival postnominal)
> the *hastily counted* ballots were examined by the committee (attributive adjectival prenominal)

Absolute participles are not embedded by being attached to any specific noun, though absolute adjectival participles may refer fairly unambiguously to a specific noun, and indeed, should be placed near it. Rather, they are brought into the matrix clause by clause-element-replacing embedding. The distinguishing characteristic of absolute participles is thus a relatively high degree of syntactic independence, as these examples show:

> the election reports, *containing many errors,* confused the situation completely (absolute adjectival)
> the election reports arrived late, *confusing the situation completely* (absolute adverbial)

It is possible to contrive cases where the difference between an attributive adjectival postnominal and an absolute adjectival participle is minimal, e. g.:

the ballots *marked improperly* were examined by the committee
(attributive postnominal)
the ballots, *marked improperly*, were examined by the committee
(absolute postnominal)

In cases of this kind, only the punctuation pattern (and the pauses in the spoken language) indicate the syntactic role of the participle.

The change which we will call "participialization" (PRTZ) is simple: it consists of the addition of the element -ING to the first verb form present, whether that verb form be an auxiliary or a lexical verb; and in addition, of the deletion of the grammatical subject, although this latter operation is subject to certain conditions which will be considered later. By way of example, let us consider the following sentence:

the man watching the entrance is a detective

We regard this as composed of two infrastructures, namely:

IS1: the man be a detective
IS2: the man watch the entrance

The second of these is modified by participialization as follows:

PRTZ: (the man) watching the entrance

As the output sentence suggests, this is to be incorporated into the matrix clause by means of clause-element-restricting embedding: it is placed immediately after the noun to which it refers, and with which it shares a common element:

E / 2: the man + (the man) watching the entrance + be a detective

The matrix verb is then modified:

FNTZ / 1 (= PSNM): the man + (the man) watching the entrance + is a detective

When the subject of the embedded clause is identical to the noun which the participial clause is attached to, the noun subject of the participial clause is deleted as redundant:

D / EE: the man + ( . . . ) watching the entrance + is a detective
SOP: "The man watching the entrance is a detective."

339

This example presents the process of participialization in its simplest form: the modification of the first verb form present by the addition of -ING; the deletion of the subject; and the embedding of the adjectival participial clause by placing it immediately after the noun it modifies.

These steps are made more complicated by a number of factors. To begin with, the lexical verb of any infrastructure is subject to as many as three common verb modifications before it could be participialized: that of the passive voice (PASV), that for current relevance (CRLV), and that for limited duration (LMDR). The various combinations which may arise under the rules for these common verb modifications are listed below (elements other than the verb are disregarded here):

LEXVB + PRTZ: watch + ING
LEXVB + PASV + PRTZ: be + ING watched
LEXVB + LMDR + PRTZ: ? ? ? be + ING watching
LEXVB + CRLV + PRTZ: hav + ING watched
LEXVB + PASV + LMDR + PRTZ: ? ? ? be + ING being watched
LEXVB + PASV + CRLV + PRTZ: hav + ING been watched
LEXVB + LMDR + CRLV + PRTZ: ? ? ? HAV + ING been watching
LEXVB + PASV + LMDR + CRLV + PRTZ: ? ? ? hav + ING BEEN being watched

As the question marks indicate, a number of these forms – those containing the modification LMDR – do not conform to the patterns of accepted English usage today. As a constraint applicable at the stage of verb modification, then, we must specify that the modification LMDR cannot apply when the infrastructure is to be participialized.

We conclude this section with a few examples of absolute adjectival participial clauses which give some idea of the various verb forms which may occur, as well as the range of position in the matrix clause which these participles may occupy. These clauses are italicized in the following sentences:

*turning suddenly*, the player kicked the ball into the net (IS: the player turn suddenly)
we have reading problems at school because the children, *being neglected at home*, fail to develop good reading habits (IS: SOMEONE neglect the children at home)

*having achieved a certain level of material prosperity,* we are now confronted with the problem of other values (IS: we achieve a certain level of material prosperity)

Willy, *having been caught in the act,* had no choice but to confess (IS: SOMEONE catch Willy in the act)

In the following example, we encounter two features alluded to in remarks earlier in this chapter: the possibility of retaining the subject as an expressed element in the surface structure, and the modification of the verb by passivization. When the subject of a participle is expressed, it must be regarded as having an adverbial function, as in this sentence:

the speaker, his requests having been denied by the chairman, marched from the rostrum

The infrastructures here are:

IS1: the speaker march from the rostrum
IS2: the chairman deny his requests

The dependent clause is generated as follows:

PASV: his requests be denied by the chairman
CRLV: his requests have been denied by the chairman
PRTZ: (his requests) having been denied by the chairman

Adverbial participial clauses like this one modify the verb. Hence, they are inserted into the matrix clause by means of clause-element-replacing embedding. The matrix clause must be regarded as containing a dummy adverb THUS which may stand at those points in the infrastructure where an adverb may normally stand, or to which it may be intra- or extraposed:

IS1: THUS the speaker THUS march THUS from the rostrum THUS

When the participle contains a possessive pronoun which refers to a specific noun, it should be placed as close as possible to the noun to which that pronoun refers. Thus, the participial clause in question could appear either at the beginning or the end of the matrix clause, i. e.:

E / 2: (his requests) having been denied by the chairman + the speaker march from the rostrum

E / 2: the speaker march from the rostrum + (his requests) having been denied by the chairman

We proceed, embedding the participle immediately after the noun to which it refers:

E / 2: the speaker + (his requests) having been denied by the chairman + march from the rostrum

Next, the matrix clause is modified:

FNTZ / 1 (= PAST, PSNM): the speaker + (his requests) having been denied by the chairman + marched from the rostrum

Since the subject of the participial clause, *his requests*, is not identical to the noun to which the clause refers, it remains in the surface structure:

SOP: "The speaker, his requests having been denied by the chairman, marched from the rostrum."

A participial clause may contain as many as two auxiliary verbs, e. g., *having been (denied)*. It is possible to delete these auxiliaries to signal certain shades of meaning which are analogous to the actional and statal meanings which arise in the passive modifications of German. In both languages, the larger conceptual categories of process and result are incorporated into morphological and syntactical structures at a number of points, including the present one. In effect, participialization by itself implies a process of the kind represented by the lexical verb (which may explain why the modification LMDR is redundant in participial constructions), while the modification CRLV plus participialization indicates the result of the process. By the inclusion of the passive voice in these transformations, yet a third meaning can be expressed: that of a stable condition reached as the result of the process. This meaning is conveyed, not by any further modification, but rather by the deletion of the auxiliaries. These three meanings can be seen in variant forms of the example used earlier:

the speaker etc.
1) his requests being denied by the chairman (PASV + PRTZ: in progress)
2) his requests having been denied by the chairman (PASV + CRLV + PRTZ: end of process)

342

3) his requests . . . . . . denied by the chairman (PASV + CRLV +
PRTZ + D / AUXX: resultant state)

The third of these examples would be generated as follows:

IS2: the chairman deny his requests
PASV: his requests be denied by the chairman
CRLV: his requests have been denied by the chairman
PRTZ: (his requests) having been denied by the chairman
D / AUXX: (his requests) . . . . . . denied by the chairman

Through the operation D / AUXX, these participial constructions
can be modified to convey yet a third shade of meaning, that of a
resultant state.

It is also possible to incorporate the participle much more closely
into the noun phrase by embedding it before the noun to which it
refers — that is, to make it a prenominal attributive participle. In
order to do this, certain changes are necessary: the lexical verb must
be commentized, and then the grammatical subject. There is a
further constraint: only verb complement adverbs (VCAdv) and
unpreceded noun objects may stand before the participle in this
construction. We will consider the latter case in a subsequent section
of this chapter. At this point, we will turn our attention to those
infrastructures which contain adverbs. One of these appears in the
sentence:

they discussed a persistently recurring problem

The constituent infrastructures are:

IS1: they discuss a problem
IS2: a problem recur persistently

First, the dependent infrastructure is participialized:

PRTZ / 2: (a problem) recurring persistently

Next follow the two transformations which are characteristic of
these prenominal participial constructions, as we will call them: the
commentization of the lexical verb, followed by that of the grammatical subject of the participialized infrastructure:

C /LEXVB: (a problem) persistently recurring
C / SJ: (a) persistently recurring (problem)

When the latter sequence is embedded, it is inserted into the matrix clause in such a way that the noun of the participial clause stands before the corresponding noun of the matrix clause, as follows:

IS1: they discuss a problem
E / 2: they discuss a + (a) persistently recurring (problem) + problem

After the matrix clause is modified:

FNTZ / 1 (= PAST, PSNM): they discussed a + (a) persistently recurring (problem) + problem

the duplicated elements of the participial clause are deleted as redundant:

D / EE: they discussed a + ( . . . ) persistently recurring ( . . . ) + problem
SOP: "They discussed a persistently recurring problem."

The same kind of construction may appear when the verb has been subjected to the modification PASV. The sentence:

we visited a village reconstructed systematically by archeologists

contains an attributive adjectival participial construction. From the analysis of these constructions earlier in this chapter, we know that this would be generated thus:

IS1: we visit a village
IS2: archeologists reconstruct a village systematically
PASV: a village be reconstructed systematically by archeologists
CRLV: a village have been reconstructed systematically by archeologists
PRTZ: (a village) having been reconstructed systematically by archeologists
D / AUXX: (a village) . . . . . . reconstructed systematically by archeologists

This is embedded by being placed after the noun corresponding to the subject noun in the participialized infrastructure:

E / 2: we visit a village + (a village) reconstructed systematically by archeologists
FNTZ / 1 (= PAST, PSNM): we visited a village + (a village) reconstructed systematically by archeologists

Ultimately, the redundant subject of the participial clause is deleted:

D / EE: we visited a village + (. . .) reconstructed systematically by archeologists

SOP: "We visited a village reconstructed systematically by archeologists."

It might be added here that the speaker could also intrapose the adverb *systematically* to a position immediately before the lexical verb to form the equally correct utterance:

we visited a village systematically reconstructed by archeologists

Native speakers of English know that the sentence above could be so reorganized that the participial phrase could precede the noun, i. e.:

we visited a systematically reconstructed village

As noted above — and in contrast to German — only verb complement adverbs may precede the participle. Thus, the sentence:

? ? ? we visited a by archeologists reconstructed village

is not acceptable English. This means that passivized infrastructures which are to be transformed into prenominal participles must contain a dummy subject which can be deleted. Thus, the sentence above:

we visited a systematically reconstructed village

would of necessity reflect the infrastructures:

IS1: we visit a village
IS2: SOMEONE reconstruct a village systematically

Initially, the derivation proceeds in the same way as that for absolute participial constructions:

PASV / 2: a village be reconstructed systematically by SOMEONE

CRLV: a village have been reconstructed systematically by SOMEONE

PRTZ: (a village) having been reconstructed systematically by SOMEONE

D / AUXX: (a village) . . . . . . reconstructed systematically by SOMEONE

At this point, the commentizations typical of attributive constructions are applied:

C / LEXVB: (a village) systematically by SOMEONE reconstructed

C / SJ: (a) systematically by SOMEONE reconstructed (village)

The agent prepositional phrase can be deleted as an empty element:

D / EE: (a) systematically . . . reconstructed (village)

Upon embedding, this is placed before the referent noun of the matrix clause:

E / 2: we visit a + (a) systematically reconstructed (village) + village

FNTZ /1 (= PAST, PSNM): we visited a + (a) systematically reconstructed (village) + village

The elements of the participial clause which duplicate those of the matrix clause are deleted as redundant:

D / EE: we visited a + ( . . . ) systematically reconstructed ( . . . ) + village

SOP: "We visited a systematically reconstructed village."

This is the origin of the use of the participle as adjective, as it is called in traditional grammar.

There are numerous variants of this type of construction which are widely used in everyday English. Some of the more common of these are exemplified in these sentences:

Smith is a well-known lawyer
William was only a mixed-up kid
Jones is a highly-thought-of physician

Each of these is generated in the same way as the prenominal participial constructions above, yet each contains a slightly different feature which requires a separate examination. The first sentence could be analyzed into the following infrastructures:

IS1: Smith be a lawyer
IS2: SOMEONE know a lawyer well

The first group of transformations generate an absolute participle:

PASV: a lawyer be known by SOMEONE well
CRLV: a lawyer have been known by SOMEONE well
PRTZ: (a lawyer) having been known by SOMEONE well
D / AUXX: (a lawyer) . . . . . . known by SOMEONE well

The next group changes the final sequence into an attributive participle:

C / LEXVB: (a lawyer) by SOMEONE well known
C / SJ: (a) by SOMEONE well known (lawyer)
D / EE: (a) ... well known (lawyer)

This is then embedded in the matrix clause, which is in turn modified:

E / 2: Smith be a + (a) well known (lawyer) + lawyer
FNTZ / 1: (= PSNM): Smith is a + (a) well known (lawyer) + lawyer
D / EE: Smith is a + ( ... ) well known ( ... ) + lawyer
SOP: "Smith is a well-known lawyer."

The next example illustrates the effect on participial constructions of the presence of a verb particle (VPART) in the infrastructure. Thus, the sentence:

William was only a mixed-up kid

comes from the infrastructures:

IS1: William be only a kid
IS2: SOMEONE mix a kid up

The word *up* in IS2 is a verb particle, and it remains closely associated with the verb throughout the derivation:

PASV: a kid be mixed up by SOMEONE
CRLV: a kid have been mixed up by SOMEONE
PRTZ: (a kid) having been mixed up by SOMEONE
D / AUXX: (a kid) ... ... ... mixed up by SOMEONE

When the lexical verb is commentized, the verb particle *up*, because it is closely linked to the verb, accompanies it to sequence-final position:

C / LEXVB: (a kid) by SOMEONE mixed up
C / SJ: (a) by SOMEONE mixed up (kid)
D / EE: (a) .. mixed up (kid)

This is embedded as in the previous example:

E / 2: William be only a + (a) mixed up (kid) + kid
FNTZ / 1 (= PAST, PSNM): William was only a + (a) mixed up (kid) + kid

347

D / EE: William was only a + ( . . . ) mixed up ( . . . ) + kid
SOP: "William was only a mixed-up kid."

The last of the three sentences illustrates one of the peculiarities of the English passive: there are some verbs where the object of a preposition, rather than the nominal or direct object of the verb, becomes the subject of the verb in the passive voice. The normal pattern is exemplified by this transformation:

the director approved *the project*$_{\text{NOMNL}}$ → PASV, etc: *the project*$_{\text{SJ}}$ was approved by the director

Depending on the valence of the verb, it is possible to have passive subjects which in their infrastructures are the objects of prepositions, as e. g.:

Jim made a fool of *Fred* → PASV, etc.: *Fred* was made a fool of . . . by Jim

the management did away with *the whole section* → PASV, etc.: *the whole section* was done away with . . . by the management

When verbs with this valence characteristic are used in participial constructions, the preposition is attached to the lexical verb. This is evident in the sentence:

Jones is a highly-thought-of physician

This is derived from the infrastructures:

IS1: Jones be a physician
IS2: SOMEONE think of a physician highly

When IS2 is passivized, the object of the preposition *of* becomes the subject of the passive verb:

PASV: a physician be thought of . . . highly by SOMEONE

After this stage, the derivation proceeds as before:

CRLV: a physician have been thought of highly by SOMEONE
PRTZ: (a physician) having been thought of highly by SOMEONE

D / AUXX: (a physician) .. .. .. thought of highly by SOMEONE

When the lexical verb is commentized, the preposition, because of its valence bond with the verb, accompanies it:

C / LEXVB: (a physician) highly by SOMEONE thought of
C / SJ: (a) highly by SOMEONE thought of (physician)
D / EE: (a) highly . . . thought of (physician)
E / 2: Jones be a + (a) highly thought of (physician) + physician
FNTZ / 1 (= PSNM): Jones is a + (a) highly thought of (physician) + physician
D / EE: Jones is a + ( . . . ) highly thought of ( . . . ) + physician
SOP: "Jones is a highly-thought-of physician."

All of the prenominal participial constructions examined so far have the common feature that the participle in the surface structure is accompanied by some kind of adverbial modifier. There is another class of attributive participial constructions in which the participle is preceded by a noun. These tend to be formulaic in character, and their use is subject to various lexical and semantic restrictions. Nevertheless, it is clear that each of them can be related to, and interpreted as, the surface pattern of an underlying infrastructure. The first of these subclasses is exemplified by the following expressions:

a heart-rending story
a hair-raising experience
a thirst-quenching beverage
interest-bearing securities
a blood-curdling cry
a back-breaking task

To show how these can be generated, let us analyze the following sentence:

she told us a heart-rending story

The infrastructures here are:

IS1: she tell us a story
IS2: a story rend SOMEONE'S heart

The second infrastructure is participialized thus:

PRTZ: (a story) rending SOMEONE'S heart

As in the case of all prenominal attributive participles, the lexical verb must be commentized:

C / LEXVB: (a story) SOMEONE'S heart rending

And then the subject is, too:

C / SJ: (a) SOMEONE'S heart rending (story)

What has happened is that the direct object has come to stand just before the lexical verb. There is a constraint on these constructions in English which specifies that only a single, simple element may stands before the participle — whether adverb or noun. Consequently, noun modifiers like *SOMEONE'S,* as well as prepositions, must be removed at this point:

D / PREP&MOD: (a) . . . heart rending (story)

The remainder of the derivation proceeds as before:

E / 2: she tell us a + (a) heart rending (story) + story
FNTZ / 1 (= PAST, PSNM): she told us a + (a) heart rending (story) + story
D / EE: she told us a + ( . . . ) heart rending ( . . . ) + story
SOP: "She told us a heart-rending story."

As a matter of orthographic convention in English, nonadverbial elements are usually linked to the participle with a hyphen.

The next group of participles differs from those above in that these contain the modification PASV plus related transformations:

a smoke-filled room
grief-stricken relatives
a drug-crazed maniac
airborne freight
a water-soaked garment
a stage-struck girl
a blood-stained shirt

The patterns of generation by which these expressions are produced can be seen in the sentence:

they met in a smoke-filled room

The constituent infrastructures are:

IS1: they meet in a room
IS2: smoke fill a room

The participial clause must first be passivized and subjected to the usual associated modifications:

PASV: a room be filled by smoke
CRLV: a room have been filled by smoke
PRTZ: (a room) having been filled by smoke
D / AUXX: (a room) ...... filled by smoke
C / LEXVB: (a room) by smoke filled
C / SJ: (a) by smoke filled (room)

Since only a single, simple element may stand before the participle, the preposition must be deleted:

D / PREP&MOD: (a) ... smoke filled (room)
E / 2: they meet in a + (a) smoke filled (room) + room
FNTZ / 1 (= PAST, PSNM): they met in a + (a) smoke filled (room) + room
D / EE: they met in a + ( ... ) smoke filled ( ... ) + room
SOP: "They met in a smoke-filled room."

As a transition to the next category, the expression *well-spoken* might be mentioned, as in:

John is a well-spoken man

This is typical for a small number of idiomatic phrases, e. g., *well-read, widely-traveled,* etc. The infrastructures behind the sentence above are:

IS1: John be a man
IS2: a man speak well

What distinguishes this and the following participial constructions from those analyzed above is the absence of the modification PASV: The derivation of IS2 thus begins with CRLV:

CRLV: a man have spoken well
PRTZ: (a man) having spoken well
D / AUXX: (a man) ... spoken well
C / LEXVB: (a man) well spoken
C /SJ: (a) well spoken (man)

This is then embedded:

E / 2: John be a + (a) well spoken (man) + man
FNTZ / 1 (= PSNM): John is a + (a) well spoken (man) + man
D / EE: John is a + ( ... ) well spoken ( ... ) + man
SOP: "John is a well-spoken man."

There is a rather large group of expressions in English, many having to do with the characteristics of human beings, which at first glance appear to have the form of participles, but on closer inspection may be seen to be nouns with a participial ending and preceded by an adjective, e. g., *stiff-necked, two-faced, long-lived, keen-sighted, cool-headed, light-hearted, narrow-minded, slack-jawed, slender-hipped, small-breasted, close-mouthed, thin-lipped, heavy-footed,* and the like. The same construction may also be found in phrases describing objects, as in *flat-bottomed, twin-engined, double-breasted,* etc. On our interpretation, the sentence:

Smith is a cool-headed diplomat

would reflect the infrastructures:

IS1: Smith be a diplomat
IS2: a diplomat have a cool head

What is distinctive about this construction is the deletion of the lexical component of the verb *have*, which occurs in due course in the generation of the participle. As in the foregoing construction, PASV does not occur; the derivation begins with CRLV:

CRLV: a diplomat have had a cool head
PRTZ: (a diplomat) having had a cool head
D / AUXX: (a diplomat) . . . had a cool head

The form *had* is a lexical verb here, and hence unaffected by D /AUXX. The derivation proceeds then as follows:

C / LEXVB: (a diplomat) a cool head had
C / SJ: (a) a cool head had (diplomat)

The form *had* contains the morphemes *HAVE + ED*. At this point, the lexical component *HAVE* is deleted, but not the participial morpheme *-ED*:

D / *have*: (a) a cool head . . . -ed (diplomat)

The remaining morpheme *-ED* will ultimately combine with the noun *head* to form what might be called a "pseudoparticiple." Since this element will acquire the form, indeed, the function, of a participle, the single element *cool* may be retained, though other elements must be deleted:

D / PREP&MOD: (a) . . . cool head -ed (diplomat)

From this point on, the derivation continues without change:

E / 2: Smith be a + (a) cool head -ed (diplomat) + diplomat
FNTZ / 1 (= PSNM): Smith is a + (a) cool head -ed (diplomat) +
   diplomat
D / EE: Smith is a + ( . . . ) cool head -ed ( . . . ) + diplomat
SOP: "Smith is a cool-headed diplomat."

Given the unusual nature of this kind of derivation, one further
example might not be unwarranted:

Tom bought a double-breasted suit

This is the product of the following transformations:

IS1: Tom buy a suit
IS2: a suit have a double breast
CRLV / 2: a suit have had a double reast
PRTZ: (a suit) having had a double breast
D / AUXX: (a suit) . . . had a double breast
C / LEXVB: (a suit) a double breast had
C / SJ: (a) a double breast had (suit)
D / have: (a) a double breast -ed (suit)
E / 2: Tom buy a + (a) double breast -ed (suit) + suit
FNTZ / 1 (= PAST, PSNM): Tom bought a + (a) double breast -ed
   (suit) + suit
D / EE: Tom bought a + ( . . . ) double breast -ed ( . . . ) + suit
SOP: "Tom bought a double-breasted suit."

The last category of prenominal participial constructions in English to be considered here comprises a series of phrases, most of
which involve metaphoric descriptions of the human body: *baby-
faced, bat-eared, bone-headed, bug-eyed, chicken-hearted, lily-
livered, rock-ribbed, rubber-jointed, hook-nosed, eagle-beaked,
pigeon-toed, lantern-jawed*, etc. On our interpretation, these represent the condensed participial forms of comparisons containing
the preposition *like*; thus, the expression *baby-faced* means that the
individual so described has a face like a baby, a *bat-eared* person has
ears like bat's wings, etc. By way of example, the sentence:

he was a chicken-hearted coward

would be generated thus:

IS1: he be a coward

IS2: a coward have a heart like a chicken
CRLV: a coward have had a heart like a chicken
PRTZ: (a coward) having had a heart like a chicken
D / AUXX: (a coward) . . . had a heart like a chicken

The distinctive transformation in the generation of this construction is the commentization of the object (here, *a heart*) before the lexical verb and subject are so treated:

C / OJ: (a coward) had like a chicken a heart
C / LEXVB: (a coward) like a chicken a heart had
C / SJ: (a) like a chicken a heart had (coward)
D / *have*: (a) like a chicken a heart . . . -ed (coward)

As in earlier cases, the preposition *like* and all modifiers are removed from the nominal elements:

D / PREP&MOD: (a) . . . . . . chicken . . . heart -ed (coward)
E / 2: he be a + (a) chicken heart -ed (coward) + coward
FNTZ / 1 (= PAST, PSNM): he was a + (a) chicken heart -ed (coward) + coward
D / EE: he was a + ( . . . ) chicken heart -ed ( . . . ) + coward
SOP: "He was a chicken-hearted coward."

Summarizing the descriptions of prenominal participial constructions, we note, first of all, that there are ten transformations which may be applied to change an infrastructure into a participle of some kind: PASV, CRLV, PRTZ, D / AUXX, C / OJ, C / LEXVB, C / SJ, D / EE, D / *have*, D / PREP&MOD, and ultimately E / . . ., when the participialized infrastructure is embedded in its matrix clause. Not every operation is used in generating each kind of construction. In the list of participial constructions which follows, we begin with the infrastructure, which must have the appropriate component elements; we then indicate the transformations which are to be applied to that infrastructure; and finally give the form of the participle as it appears, after embedding and the changes subsequent thereto, in the surface structure. The participles we have examined are:

1) IS: SOMEONE reconstruct a village systematically → PASV, CRLV, PRTZ, D / AUXX, C / LEXVB, C / SJ, D / EE, E / . . ., etc., SOP: " . . . a systematically reconstructed village . . .";
2) IS: SOMEONE know a lawyer well → PASV, CRLV, PRTZ, D / AUXX, C / LEXVB, C / SJ, D / EE, E / . . ., etc., SOP:

"... a well-known lawyer ... "; these procedures also generate phrases like *a mixed-up kid* and *a highly-thought-of physician;*

3) IS: a story rend SOMEONE'S heart → PRTZ, C / LEXVB, C / SJ, D / PREP&MOD, E / ..., etc., SOP: "... a heart-rending story ... ";

4) IS: smoke fill a room → PASV, CRLV, PRTZ, D / AUXX, C / LEXVB, C / SJ, D / PREP&MOD, E / ..., etc., SOP: "... a smoke-filled room ... ";

5) IS: a man speak well → CRLV, PRTZ, D / AUXX, C / LEXVB, C / SJ, E / ..., etc., SOP: "... a well-spoken man ... ";

6) IS: a diplomat have a cool head → CRLV, PRTZ, D / AUXX, C / LEXVB, C / SJ, D / *have*, D / PREP&MOD, E / ..., etc., SOP: "... a cool-headed diplomat ... ";

7) IS: a coward have a heart like a chicken → CRLV, PRTZ, D / AUXX, C / OJ, C / LEXVB, C / SJ, D / *have*, D / PREP&MOD, E / ..., etc., SOP: "... a chicken-hearted coward ... "

As this comparison shows, the transformations PRTZ, D / AUXX, C / LEXVB, and C / SJ are common to all prenominal attributive participles; the others are used to generate specific subtypes of this construction.

CHAPTER 18

THE PARTICIPIAL CONSTRUCTIONS OF GERMAN

As in English, the participle in German is an infrastructure which has assumed the function of an adjective or adverb. As in English, too, participles may be either attributive or absolute; in contrast to English, however, an attributive participle must precede an nominal element — there are no postnominal attributive participles. The two kinds of adjectival participles are exemplified by the following sentences:

die *auf Liegestühlen ruhenden* Gäste genossen die herrliche Sonne (attributive and adjectival)

die Gäste, *auf Liegestühlen ruhend,* genossen die herrliche Sonne (absolute and adjectival)

The adverbial participle, always absolute, is represented by the following sentence:

*von diesem Gesichtspunkt aus betrachtet,* kann die Partei nur Verluste erwarten (absolute and adverbial)

The morphosyntactic changes subsumed under the rubric of participialization (PRTZ) in German resemble those of English: the addition of a participle marker -*d* to the last verb form present, whether a lexical verb or an auxiliary; and the deletion of the subject, though this may in some cases be only temporary. Upon embedding, adjectival clauses are placed near or next to the noun in the matrix clause by means of clause-element-restricting embedding, while adverbial participles displace dummy adverbs in the matrix clause and are inserted into that structure by clause-element-replacing embedding.

Several examples of the various adjectival participles are contained in the following sentence:

" . . . Felix Genzmer und auf Genzmer bezugnehmend Hans Kuhn haben ausgehend von der Frage, wieviel Sagenkenntnis der Hörer zum vollen Verständnis des jeweiligen Edda-Liedes mitbringen müsse, gefolgert, daß eine ergänzende Begleitprosa unerläßlich sei" (Siegfried Beyschlag, "Das Nibelungenlied." in: *Zur germanisch-deutschen Heldensage,* ed. Karl Hauck, Wege der Forschung, Bd. 14 [Darmstadt: Wissenschaftliche Buchgesellschaft, 1965], p. 227).

This complex sentence contains no fewer than six infrastructures, three of them participles:

IS1: Felix Genzmer und Hans Kuhn DAS folgern
IS2: Hans Kuhn auf Genzmer Bezug nehmen
IS3: Felix Genzmer und Hans Kuhn von der Frage ausgehen
IS4: der Hörer viel Sagenkenntnis zum vollen Verständnis des jeweiligen Edda-Liedes mitbringen
IS5: eine Begleitprosa unerläßlich sein
IS6: eine Begleitprosa ETWAS ergänzen

The participial construction *auf Genzmer bezugnehmend* is typical of an absolute adjectival participle. The underlying infrastructure is first modified by participialization, and then embedded in its matrix clause:

IS2: Hans Kuhn auf Genzmer Bezug nehmen
PRTZ: (Hans Kuhn) auf Genzmer Bezug nehmend

Since the subject of the participialized infrastructure is identical in form to the noun to which it refers, it does not appear in the surface structure:

IS1: Felix Genzmer und Hans Kuhn DAS folgern
E / 2: Felix Genzmer und + (Hans Kuhn) auf Genzmer Bezug nehmend + Hans Kuhn DAS folgern

After a number of intervening steps:

SOP: "Felix Genzmer und auf Genzmer bezugnehmend Hans Kuhn . . ."

The second of these participles is also an absolute adjectival participle, but it is instructive because it exemplifies a possible subsidiary adjustment in the position of the lexical verb, and because it shows how participialization can operate in conjunction with other simple transformations to produce relatively complicated sentences. This participle:

. . . ausgehend von der Frage, wieviel Sagenkenntnis der Hörer zum vollen Verständnis des jeweiligen Edda-Liedes mitbringen müsse . . .

contains as a dependent clause an indirect information question which stands in apposition to the noun *Frage*. The participial structure in question would thus be generated as follows:

IS4: der Hörer viel Sagenkenntnis zum vollen Verständnis des jeweiligen Edda-Liedes mitbringen

FNTZ / 4 (= MODL, SJNC, PSNM): der Hörer viel Sagenkenntnis zum vollen Verständnis des jeweiligen Edda-Liedes mitbringen müsse

ITRGZ: der Hörer WIEVIEL Sagenkenntnis zum vollen Verständnis des jeweiligen Edda-Liedes mitbringen müsse

T / ITRG: WIEVIEL Sagenkenntnis der Hörer zum vollen Verständnis des jeweiligen Edda-Liedes mitbringen müsse

Clauses in apposition are embedded by clause-element-restricting embedding, i. e., by being attached to the noun which they are expansions of:

IS3: Felix Genzmer und Hans Kuhn von der Frage ausgehen

E / 4: Felix Genzmer und Hans Kuhn von der Frage + WIEVIEL Sagenkenntnis der Hörer zum vollen Verständnis des jeweiligen Edda-Liedes mitbringen müsse + ausgehen

The matrix clause is now modified by participialization:

PRTZ / 3: (Felix Genzmer und Hans Kuhn) von der Frage + WIE-VIEL etc. müsse + ausgehend

In these constructions, the topicalization of the lexical verb is optional:

T / LEXVB: ausgehend (Felix Genzmer und Hans Kuhn) von der Frage + WIEVIEL etc. müsse

Since the subjects of the participial clause are identical to the referent nouns in the matrix clause, those elements need not appear in the surface structure:

IS1: Felix Genzmer und Hans Kuhn DAS folgern

E / 3: Felix Genzmer und Hans Kuhn ++ ausgehend (Felix Genzmer und Hans Kuhn) von der Frage + WIEVIEL Sagenkenntnis der Hörer zum vollen Verständnis des jeweiligen Edda-Liedes mitbringen müsse ++ DAS folgern

After modifying the matrix clause and other changes, this becomes:

SOP: "Felix Genzmer und Hans Kuhn ... ausgehend von der Frage, wieviel Sagenkenntnis der Hörer zum vollen Verständnis des jeweiligen Edda-Liedes mitbringen müsse, ..."

The third participle in this sentence is an attributive participle, and hence functions as an integral part of the noun phrase in which it stands. The phrase in question is *eine ergänzende Begleitprosa*, which reflects the infrastructure:

IS6: eine Begleitprosa ETWAS ergänzen

Participialization takes place as before:

PRTZ: (eine Begleitprosa) ETWAS ergänzend

In the case of English, we observed that it was possible to transform these constructions into adjectival modifiers by commentizing, first, the lexical verb, and then the subject noun. Since the lexical verb is already in final position in German, it is unnecessary to commentize that. The subject noun, however, is moved to final position:

C / SJ: (eine) ETWAS ergänzend- (Begleitprosa)

The empty element *ETWAS* can be conveniently deleted at this point, and the appropriate adjective ending added:

D / EE: (eine) ... ergänzende (Begleitprosa)

This expression is then inserted into the matrix clause before the noun which corresponds to the noun with which the participial clause ends:

IS5: eine Begleitprosa unerläßlich sein
E / 6: eine + (eine) ergänzende (Begleitprosa) + Begleitprosa unerläßlich sein

After the finitization of the matrix clause, the marginal elements of the participial clause, which are identical to the contiguous elements of the matrix clause, are deleted:

FNTZ / 5 (= SJNC, PSNM): eine + (eine) ergänzende (Begleitprosa) + Begleitprosa unerläßlich sei
D / EE: eine + ( ... ) ergänzende ( ... ) + Begleitprosa unerläßlich sei
SOP: " ... eine ergänzende Begleitprosa unerläßlich sei."

When the subject of the participialized infrastructure is not identical to a specific noun in the matrix clause, that subject may be retained in the surface structure, as in the following quotation:

"Um zwölf Uhr kommen sie alle aus dem Portal, jeder dem nächsten die Tür haltend, alle in Mantel und Hut und immer zur gleichen Zeit, immer um zwölf Uhr" (Peter Bichsel, "Die Beamten," *Eigentlich möchte Frau Blum den Milchmann kennenlernen*, [Olten: Walter, 1964], p. 29).

The phrase which interests us here is the participial construction, *jeder dem nächsten die Tür haltend*, in which the word *jeder*, from its form, must be construed as being in the nominative case. This illustrates the principle that, when the subject phrase is not exactly the same as the referent noun in the matrix clause, the subject of the participial clause may appear in the surface structure. On this interpretation, the infrastructure underlying this participial clause would be:

IS: jeder dem nächsten die Tür halten

Participialization would then have the following effect:

PRTZ: (jeder) dem nächsten die Tür haltend

This phrase would then be embedded as such in the matrix clause without the ultimate deletion of *jeder*.

We have observed at several points that the auxiliary verbs are usually deleted in the last steps of the derivation. In recognizing these patterns of deletion, we are able to explain a number of phenomena by means of participialization which otherwise would appear to be unrelated to any larger structural features of the language. The following sentence contains one such case:

neben ihm saß der Pianist, den Kopf im Nacken (after Thomas Mann from Duden Grammatik 1969:§1044)

The phrase *den Kopf im Nacken* refers obviously to *der Pianist*, and yet the precise relationship of the expression to the matrix clause is by no means evident. Taking note of the fact that that the noun *den Kopf* is in the accusative case, we may postulate a lost form *habend* of which *den Kopf* may be construed as direct object. On the basis of these conjectures, then, we may analyze this sentence as containing the two infrastructures:

IS1: der Pianist neben ihm sitzen
IS2: der Pianist den Kopf im Nacken haben

Up to the point of deletion, the generation of this sentence is follows the same pattern as the other examples in this section:

PRTZ / 2: (der Pianist) den Kopf im Nacken habend
E / 2: der Pianist + (der Pianist) den Kopf im Nacken habend + neben ihm sitzen
FNTZ / 1 (= PAST, PSNM): der Pianist + (der Pianist) den Kopf im Nacken habend + neben ihm saß
T / FV: saß der Pianist + (der Pianist) den Kopf im Nacken habend + neben ihm
T / X: neben ihm saß der Pianist + (der Pianist) den Kopf im Nacken habend

At this point, the superfluous verb form *habend* and the redundant subject noun are deleted as empty elements:

D / EE: neben ihm saß der Pianist + ( . . . ) den Kopf im Nacken
. . .
SOP: "Neben ihm saß der Pianist, den Kopf im Nacken."

As speakers of German know, forms like *ruhend, haltend, habend,* etc. represent only one kind of participle, the socalled present participle. Past participles, forms like *geruht, gesehen, gekommen,* etc., are perhaps even more common in participial constructions than present participles. Our next task is to extend the application of the transformation PRTZ to include these forms as well. As it happens, we will be able to retain the rule which specifies that the essential verb modification involved in participialization is the addition of *-d* to the last verb form present. What must be added is that certain common verb modifications must occur before that rule can be applied. Let us approach this problem by considering the following example:

er brachte ihm die vom Kaufmann zur Kundenwerbung verwendeten Bilder ins Geschäft

On the basis of our previous conclusions, we can conjecture at this point that the two infrastructures which are present are:

IS1: er ihm die Bilder ins Geschäft bringen
IS2: der Kaufmann die Bilder zur Kundenwerbung verwenden

361

In order to transform IS2 into the phrase *die vom Kaufmann zur Kundenwerbung verwendeten Bilder,* two steps are necessary preliminary to the operation PRTZ: first, the common verb modification PASV must be applied; and second, the verb must also undergo the modification TRMV. Only then may the transformation PRTZ be applied. Performing these operations on our example produces the following sequences:

IS2: der Kaufmann die Bilder zur Kundenwerbung verwenden
PASV: die Bilder vom Kaufmann zur Kundenwerbung verwendet werden
TRMV: die Bilder vom Kaufmann zur Kundenwerbung verwendet worden sein
PRTZ: (die Bilder) vom Kaufmann zur Kundenwerbung verwendet worden seiend

(Our rule states that the last verb form present is modified to form the participle by the addition of *-d.* In the case of the verb *sein,* an *-e-* is inserted for the sake of euphony, producing *seiend* instead of ? ? ? *seind.*) At this point, the auxiliary verbs may be deleted and the subject commentized:

D / AUXX: (die Bilder) vom Kaufmann zur Kundenwerbung verwendet., . . . . .
C / SJ: (die) vom Kaufmann zur Kundenwerbung verwendet- (Bilder)

This sequence is now embedded in its matrix clause:

E / 2: er ihm die + (die) vom Kaufmann zur Kundenwerbung verwendet- (Bilder) + Bilder ins Geschäft bringen

Once this point has been reached, the remainder of the derivation proceeds by the familiar steps of finitization and topicalization:

FNTZ / 1 (= PAST, PSNM): er ihm die + (die) vom Kaufmann zur Kundenwerbung verwendet- (Bilder) + Bilder ins Geschäft brachte
T / FV: brachte er ihm die + (die) vom Kaufmann zur Kundenwerbung verwendet- (Bilder) + Bilder ins Geschäft
T / X: er brachte ihm die + (die) vom Kaufmann zur Kundenwerbung verwendet- (Bilder) + Bilder ins Geschäft
D / EE: er brachte ihm die + ( . . . ) vom Kaufmann zur Kundenwerbung verwendet- ( . . . ) + Bilder ins Geschäft

The appropriate adjective endings may be added to the participle at this point:

SOP: "Er brachte ihm die vom Kaufmann zur Kundenwerbung verwendeten Bilder ins Geschäft."

So as to throw into relief the differences between transitive and intransitive verbs in regard to this phenomenon of participialization, let us analyze the following sentence by the procedures which we have applied above:

die Polizei suchte das aus der Bank verschwundene Geld

The infrastructures here are:

IS1: die Polizei das Geld suchen
IS2: das Geld aus der Bank verschwinden

Because *verschwinden* is an intransitive verb, it cannot form a passive voice. It can and must undergo the modification TRMV, however:

TRMV: das Geld aus der Bank verschwunden sein

Participialization of this sequence yields:

PRTZ: (das Geld) aus der Bank verschwunden seiend
D / AUXX: (das Geld) aus der Bank verschwunden . . .
C / SJ: (das) aus der Bank verschwunden- (Geld)

Once this stage has been reached, the remainder of the derivation proceeds as in the previous example:

E / 2: die Polizei das + (das) aus der Bank verschwunden- (Geld) + Geld suchen
FNTZ / 1 (= PAST, PSNM): die Polizei das + (das) aus der Bank verschwunden- (Geld) + Geld suchte
T / FV: suchte die Polizei das + (das) aus der Bank verschwunden- (Geld) + Geld
T / X: die Polizei suchte das + (das) aus der Bank verschwunden- (Geld) + Geld
D / EE: die Polizei suchte das + ( . . . ) aus der Bank verschwunden- ( . . .) + Geld
SOP: "Die Polizei suchte das aus der Bank verschwundene Geld."

There are some limitations on the kind of intransitive verb which may form a participial construction with the modification TRMV: in general, only those which indicate, not the final stage of a process, but a state or condition which appears after the process is complete. Thus, one cannot say ? ? ? *ein geschlafenes Kind* or ? ? ? *ein gelaufenes Kind*, although it would be perfectly correct to apply this modification to a finite form, e. g., ! *das Kind hat geschlafen* or ! *das Kind ist gelaufen.* Only when these verbs are lexically modified to indicate a resultant state or condition can they form this kind of participial construction, e. g.:

! das eingeschlafene Kind
! das in den Wald gelaufene Kind

In our discussion of the modifications of the verb, we noted that the modal auxiliaries of German have a complete conjugation, including forms such as participles (e. g., *gewollt, gekonnt*), whereas the modals of English contain only a very few finite forms (e. g., *can, would, must,* etc.). Thus, constructions containing attributive participles are occasionally encountered, e. g.:

" ... eine das Christentum nicht verleugnen könnende, gebrochen heroische Entscheidung ... " (Gottfried Weber, *Das Nibelungenlied: Problem und Idee*, [Stuttgart: Metzler, 1963], p. 206).

The phrase which we are concerned with as an example of an attributive modal auxiliary is *eine das Christentum nicht verleugnen könnende ... Entscheidung*. This would be generated as follows:

IS1: ... eine Entscheidung ...
IS2: eine Entscheidung das Christentum nicht verleugnen

This is first modified by the addition of a modal, and then participialized:

MODL: eine Entscheidung das Christentum nicht verleugnen können
PRTZ: (eine Entscheidung) das Christentum nicht verleugnen könnend

The commentization of the subject typical of attributive participles follows:

C / SJ: (eine) das Christentum nicht verleugnen könnend- (Entscheidung)

This is then embedded in the noun phrase of IS1:

E / 2: ... eine + (eine) das Christentum nicht verleugnen kön-
nend- (Entscheidung) + Entscheidung ...
D / EE: ... eine + ( ... ) das Christentum nicht verleugnen
könnend- ( ... ) + Entscheidung ...
SOP: " ... eine das Christentum nicht verleugnen könnende Entscheidung ... "

The modification MODL may only be used in the absence of that
for the terminative aspect (TRMV); either of these may be applied
after that for the passive voice (PASV). Thus we have a constraint on
the combination of these verb modifications like that observed in
the case of the infinitive: oPASV + oTRMV or oMODL, i. e., either
TRMV or MODL may follow PASV, it being understood that all
three are optional.

Participles are sometimes regarded merely as adjectives which in
turn may assume the function of adverbs. While this interpretation is
not entirely incorrect, it is incomplete because it ignores the generative processes which are presupposed by our comprehension of the
utterance. In this sentence, for example:

verlassen blieb Hans zurück

we understand somehow that Hans is the one who has been *verlassen*
'abandoned'. By admitting the possibility of extensive deletion of
empty elements in these participial constructions, we can show that
adverbs such as this one are merely special cases of the general
patterns of participialization which have already been described. On
the pattern of our earlier derivations, we can reconstruct the infrastructures in this sentence as follows:

IS1: Hans zurückbleiben
IS2: JEMAND Hans verlassen

As we are dealing with a "past participle" here, one which reflects
the statal passive, we must subject IS2 to the common verb modifications for the passive voice (PASV) and the terminative aspect
(TRMV), followed by the deletion of *worden*:

PASV: Hans VON JEMANDEM verlassen werden
TRMV: Hans VON JEMANDEM verlassen worden sein
D / *worden*: Hans VON JEMANDEM verlassen ... sein

At this point, participialization may take place:

365

PRTZ: (Hans) VON JEMANDEM verlassen seiend
D / AUXX: (Hans) VON JEMANDEM verlassen . . .
E / 2: Hans + (Hans) VON JEMANDEM verlassen + zurückbleiben
FNTZ / 1 (= PAST, PSNM): Hans + (Hans) VON JEMANDEM
  verlassen + zurückblieb
T / FV: blieb Hans + (Hans) VON JEMANDEM verlassen + zurück
T / X: (Hans) VON JEMANDEM verlassen + blieb Hans zurück

Now the various empty elements may be deleted:

D / EE: ( . . . ) . . . verlassen + blieb Hans zurück
SOP: "Verlassen blieb Hans zurück."

Patterns of derivation such as this one show how participles functioning as "free adverbs" may be generated through participialization.

There is another construction in which a participle may stand alone in German when used as a noun. In light of the foregoing analyses, the sentence:

Franz wollte Reisender werden

must be regarded as reflecting the infrastructures:

IS1: Franz JEMAND werden
IS2: JEMAND reisen

As before, the second infrastructure is participialized:

PRTZ: (JEMAND) reisend

In order to transform this into an attributive participle, the subject noun must be commentized:

C / SJ: . . . reisend (JEMAND)

This is then embedded in the matrix clause immediately before the common element:

E / 2: Franz + reisend (JEMAND) + JEMAND werden

Now the matrix clause may be finitized:

FNTZ / 1 (= MODL, PAST, PSNM): Franz + reisend (JEMAND)
  + JEMAND werden wollte
T / FV: wollte Franz + reisend (JEMAND) + JEMAND werden
T / X: Franz wollte + reisend (JEMAND) + JEMAND werden

When the empty elements are deleted, the participle assumes the appropriate adjective endings:

D / EE: Franz wollte + reisend-er ( . . . ) + . . . werden
SOP: "Franz wollte Reisender werden."

The following case is essentially the same, yet it is complicated by additional steps involving the modification of the participialized verb:

er sprach mit einem Angestellten

Following the patterns established above, we may assume that this contains the following infrastructures:

IS1: er mit einem JEMAND sprechen
IS2: JEMAND1 JEMANDEN2 anstellen

To begin with, IS2 is subjected to the common verb modifications which generate the statal form of the passive voice:

PASV: JEMAND2 VON JEMANDEM1 angestellt werden
TRMV: JEMAND2 VON JEMANDEM1 angestellt worden sein
D / worden: JEMAND2 VON JEMANDEM1 angestellt . . . sein

This sequence is then participialized, and the auxiliary deleted:

PRTZ: JEMAND2 VON JEMANDEM1 angestellt seiend
D / AUXX: JEMAND2 VON JEMANDEM1 angestellt . . .

This subject is commentized to make it into an attributive participle, which is then embedded:

C / SJ: VON JEMANDEM1 angestellt (JEMAND2)
E / 2: er mit einem + VON JEMANDEM1 angestellt (JEMAND2) + JEMAND sprechen

The finite verb is then modified, and the usual topicalizations take place:

FNTZ / 1 (= PAST, PSNM): er mit einem + VON JEMANDEM1 angestellt (JEMAND2) + JEMAND sprach
T / FV: sprach er mit einem + VON JEMANDEM1 angestellt (JEMAND2) + JEMAND
T / X: er sprach mit einem + VON JEMANDEM1 angestellt (JE-MAND2) + JEMAND

Here, all of the dummy elements are deleted, and the participle equipped with the appropriate adjective ending:

D / EE: er sprach mit einem + . . . angestellt . . . -en ( . . . ) + . . .
SOP: "Er sprach mit einem Angestellten."

A variant of this construction occurs when words like *etwas* and *nichts* appear as subjects of the participial clause, the specific difference being the omission of the operation C / SJ, the commentization of the subject. A typical case would be the expression *etwas längst Vergessenes* in the sentence:

das erinnerte mich an etwas längst Vergessenes

This sentence manifests the infrastructures:

IS1: mich das an ETWAS erinnern
IS2: JEMAND ETWAS längst vergessen

The dependent clause would be modified thus:

PASV: ETWAS VON JEMANDEM längst vergessen werden
TRMV: ETWAS VON JEMANDEM längst vergessen worden sein
D / *worden*: ETWAS VON JEMANDEM längst vergessen . . . sein
PRTZ: (ETWAS) VON JEMANDEM längst vergessen seiend
D / AUXX: (ETWAS) VON JEMANDEM längst vergessen . . .

When generating attributive adjectival constructions, the subject would normally be commentized at this point. When the subject of the participial clause is an indefinite pronoun like *etwas, nichts, viel(es), alles,* etc., however, this step is omitted, and the clause in question is attached. to the common element in the matrix clause as if it were an absolute adjectival clause; because the clause is in fact attributive, it assumes the adjective endings required by the case of the referent in the matrix clause:

IS1: mich das an ETWAS erinnern
E / 2: mich das an ETWAS + (ETWAS) VON JEMANDEM längst vergessen + erinnern
FNTZ / 1 (= PAST, PSNM): mich das an ETWAS + (ETWAS) VON JEMANDEM längst vergessen + erinnerte
T / FV: erinnerte mich das an ETWAS + (ETWAS) VON JEMANDEM längst vergessen
T / X: das erinnerte mich an ETWAS + (ETWAS) VON JEMANDEM längst vergessen

By deletion, all empty elements are removed; the participle receives the appropriate adjective ending:

D / EE: das erinnerte mich an ETWAS + ( ... ) ... längst vergessen ... -es

SOP: "Das erinnerte mich an etwas längst Vergessenes."

The deletion of *seiend* helps us to understand those constructions where several words or phrases appear to depend upon an adjective, e. g., the expression *für das Land günstig-* in the sentence:

das war eine für das Land günstige Entwicklung (Erben 1973:§265)

This sentence can be derived from the two infrastructures:

IS1: das eine Entwicklung sein
IS2: eine Entwicklung für das Land günstig sein

The second of these is transformed into an attributive participle, and then embedded:

PRTZ / 2: (eine Entwicklung) für das Land günstig seiend

C / SJ: (eine) für das Land günstig seiend- (Entwicklung)

E / 2: das eine + (eine) für das Land günstig seiend- (Entwicklung) + Entwicklung sein

FNTZ / 1 (= PAST, PSNM): das eine + (eine) für das Land günstig seiend- (Entwicklung) + Entwicklung war

T / FV: war das eine + (eine) für das Land günstig seiend- (Entwicklung) + Entwicklung

T / X: das war eine + (eine) für das Land günstig seiend- (Entwicklung) + Entwicklung

As in other cases, the elements of the participial clause which duplicate those of the matrix clause are deleted, as is the redundant participle *seiend*:

D / EE: das war eine + ( ... ) für das Land günstig-e ( ... ) + Entwicklung

SOP: "Das war eine für das Land günstige Entwicklung."

This derivation helps to explain many constructions where various syntactic elements appear to depend upon a mere adjective. On our interpretation, such adjectives are really nucleus complements with *sein*, and the associated syntactic elements are in fact components of a participialized infrastructure.

Up to now, we have proceeded on the assumption that the five types of clauses in German were formed by five different sets of rules: finitization (FNTZ) produces finite clauses, infinitivization (INFZ) produces infinitives, participialization (PRTZ) generates participles, etc. Peculiar to German is a construction which combines the modifications INFZ and PRTZ; together, they produce what might be called a "participialized infinitive." This hybrid clause type is exemplified by the following sentence:

das war ein nicht zu billigender Schritt

From the patterns established in this and earlier chapters, we infer that this sentence can be interpreted as reflecting two infrastructures:

IS1: das ein Schritt sein
IS2: JEMAND einen Schritt nicht billigen

In order to generate the sentence above, we must first modify the dependent clause; the first step is to infinitivize it:

INFZ / 2: (JEMAND) einen Schritt nicht zu billigen

As in the case of some other infinitive constructions, the subject is completely suppressed, and the direct object is transformed by subjectivization into the pseudosubject:

SJCTZ: ( . . . ) ein Schritt nicht zu billigen

This sequence is then subjected to participialization:

PRTZ: (ein Schritt) nicht zu billigend

To become an attributive participle, the pseudosubject must be commentized:

C / SJ: (ein) nicht zu billigend- (Schritt)

In this form, it is embedded into the matrix clause:

E / 2: das ein + (ein) nicht zu billigend- (Schritt) + Schritt sein
FNTZ / 1 (= PAST, PSNM): das ein + (ein) nicht zu billigend-
(Schritt) + Schritt war
T / FV: war das ein + (ein) nicht zu billigend- (Schritt) + Schritt
T / X: das war ein + (ein) nicht zu billigend- (Schritt) + Schritt
D / EE: das war ein + ( . . . ) nicht zu billigend-er ( . . . ) + Schritt
SOP: "Das war ein nicht zu billigender Schritt."

Only infrastructures containing accusative objects can become participialized infinitives, because the object of the infinitive, e. g., *einen Schritt*, becomes the pseudosubject of the participle and eventually the noun modified by that participle.

# CHAPTER 19

## A COMPARISON OF THE PARTICIPIAL CONSTRUCTIONS
## OF ENGLISH AND GERMAN

In form and function, the participles of English and German, and the constructions in which they stand, are very similar. Most, though not all, of the differences between the two languages in regard to this construction derive from differences in their infrastructures, chiefly from the different position of the verb — medial in English, but final in German — as well as from the role and position of the subject in English. We will examine the major points of contrast below.

As to form, both languages restrict the number of verb modifications which can be applied to lexical verbs which are subsequently participialized. English excludes LMDR, permitting only PASV and CRLV; German also admits PASV, but excludes combinations of TRMV and MODL, while permitting either separately. Both languages have a special participial morpheme: -ING is added to the first verb form of English; -D is attached to the last verb form in the German verb complex. In addition, the modification PRTZ requires the deletion of the grammatical subject in both languages.

As to function, participles can be either adjectival or adverbial. Their relation to the matrix clause is also of two kinds, absolute and attributive. All adverbial participles are absolute; participles which are adjectival in function may be either absolute or attributive. The following sentences illustrate adverbial participles, which by definition must be absolute:

the members of the association paraded through the streets, *obstructing traffic*
die Vereinsmitglieder zogen durch die Straßen, *den Verkehr behindernd*

The question whether an absolute participle is adjectival or adverbial is sometimes not easy to answer, because every participle has a deleted subject which has some referent in the matrix clause. When the referent is the act of marching, as in the examples above, the participle is, so to speak, relatively adverbial. When the referent is clearly a noun, as in the examples which follow, we know we are dealing with an absolute adjectival participle:

> *smoking his pipe,* the old gentleman sat in his easy chair and read the newspaper
>
> *seine Pfeife rauchend,* saß der alte Herr im Lehnstuhl und las die Zeitung

In these sentences, the connection with *the old gentleman* and *der alte Herr* is unmistakable.

When we turn to attributive participles, we discover some significant differences between English and German. In both languages, the embedding of attributive participles is by clause-element-restricting embedding. The difference lies in where the participial clause is placed: in English it is placed immediately after the referent noun, in German, before it:

> the gentleman reading the newspaper is the proprietor
> der die Zeitung lesende Herr ist der Inhaber

These participles are embedded by placing the deleted subject of the participial clause immediately after the referent noun in English, immediately before it in German:

> the gentleman + (the gentleman) reading the newspaper
> der + (der) die Zeitung lesende (Herr) + Herr

By a subsequent series of transformations, it is possible to generate a participial clause in English which is quite similar to the prenominal adjectival participles of German. The constraints are two in number: first, the infrastructure must undergo PASV, when transitive, and CRLV in every case; and second, the postverbal domain may contain, after deletions, only a verb complement adverb (VCAdv). These conditions are largely responsible for the terror which the participial constructions of German strike into the hearts of English-speaking students. Thus, while one can easily speak of:

> ! die neulich vom Institutsleiter für die Universitätsbibliothek bestellten Bücher

in German, one cannot say in English:

> ? ? ? the recently by the department chairman for the university library ordered books

Only the verb complement adverb *recently* may precede the verb:

373

! the recently ordered books

This phrase would be generated thus:

IS1: . . . the books . . .
IS2: SOMEONE order the books recently
PASV: the books be ordered recently BY SOMEONE
CRLV: the books have been ordered recently BY SOMEONE
PRTZ: (the books) having been ordered recently BY SOMEONE
D / AUXX: (the books) . . . . . . ordered recently BY SOMEONE

Now follow the two transformations which are essential for the transformation of any such sequence into a prenominal attributive participle:

C / LEXVB: (the books) recently BY SOMEONE ordered
C / SJ: (the) recently BY SOMEONE ordered (books)
D / EE: (the) recently . . . ordered (books)

It is in this form that the participle is embedded:

E / 2: the + (the) recently ordered (books) + books
D / EE: the + ( . . . ) recently ordered ( . . . ) + books
FNTZ / 1, etc., SOP: " . . . the recently ordered books . . . "

All prenominal participles are subject to those two restrictions, and are generated in this fashion.

A final point of contrast between English and German is the participialized infinitive, e. g.:

eine durchaus anzuerkennende Leistung

This construction simply has no counterpart in English.

# CHAPTER 20

## THE ENGLISH GERUNDIVE

Like the infinitive, the gerundive arises from the partial transformation of an infrastructure into a noun. We must stipulate that the transformation is partial, because certain elements which appear in the infrastructure may continue to be associated with the verbal element, even though its syntactic role is that of a noun. Indeed, the distinction between the three kinds of gerundive in English depends to a great extent on the degree to which these associated elements are retained or altered in form. (The following is a reinterpretation of Thomas 1965:108-112.)

The first of the three patterns which gerundivization may produce in English — we will call it the "Gerundive 1" form — may be represented in symbols as follows:

GNDZ1 →
1) LEXVB; optionally PASV and / or CRLV
2) FVF + $ING_G$
3) Subj → POSS('S)
4) D / EE

The first of these steps has to do with the verb and its modifications; it states that any lexical verb may undergo this transformation, and that the verb modifications PASV (passivization) and CRLV (current relevance), either or both, may also be applied. The second step adds the suffix -$ING_G$ to the first verb form present after Step 1; for our purposes, this suffix is distinguished from the $ING_L$ introduced by the verb modification LMDR (limited duration) by the subscript "G". In the third step, the subject is changed into the corresponding possessive forms: nouns add 's, and pronouns assume the form appropriate to their person and number, e. g.:

| Subj | POSS('S) |
|------|----------|
| John | John's |
| the town | the town's |
| SOMEONE | SOMEONE'S |
| I | my |

| she | her |
| we | our, etc. |

In the fourth and final step of this transformation, "empty elements" (EE) are deleted. An empty element may be either an artificial element introduced to complete a syntactic pattern, e. g., *SOMEONE*, or an auxiliary verb form which loses its function in the phrase, or an element which has already been stated, so that a repetition of that element strikes the speaker or writer as labored and unnecessary.

Let us see how this transformation works by studying a few examples. In the following sentence, the Gerundive 1 form is italicized:

*reading the riot act to them* will not help

The infrastructure underlying this gerundive is:

IS: SOMEONE read PERSONS the riot act

Transforming the second nominal object (2NnOj), first to a pronoun object (PRNMZ / 2NnOj), then to a prepositional object (I / Prp), and then commentizing it (C / OjPhr), produces:

SOMEONE read the riot act to them

After this modification of the nominal − part of the formation of the infrastructure − the first verb form present is modified at Step 2 by the affixation of $ING_G$:

Step 2: SOMEONE read+$ING_G$ the riot act to them

At this point, the subject is changed into the possessive form:

Step 3: SOMEONE'S read+$ING_G$ the riot act to them

Next, the infrastructure, modified as above, is embedded into the matrix clause, which is then finitized:

E / GND: SOMEONE'S read+$ING_G$ the riot act to them + will not help

Finally, empty elements are deleted:

D / EE: . . . read+$ING_G$ the riot act to them + will not help
SOP: "Reading the riot act to them will not help."

The following derivation exemplifies the passive voice as it appears in the Gerundive 1 construction, as well as another pattern of deletion:

the proposal is now in the process of *being reviewed by the committee*

The infrastructure of the gerundive, italicized above, is:

IS: the committee review the proposal

Before gerundivization proper, the passive voice transformation PASV is applied:

PASV: the proposal be reviewed by the committee

We combine Steps 2 and 3:

GNDZ1: the proposal's being reviewed by the committee

After embedding, we have:

E / GND: the proposal is now in the process of + the proposal's being reviewed by the committee

In this context, the phrase *the proposal's* is clearly redundant, and hence may be deleted:

D / EE: the proposal is now in the process of + . . . being reviewed by the committee

SOP: "The proposal is now in the process of being reviewed by the committee."

A final example of the Gerundive 1 shows a more complex pattern of verb modification:

*the envelope's having already been opened* casts suspicion on the butler

The infrastructure underlying the gerundive is:

IS: SOMEONE already open the envelope

Note that the adverb *already* is an intraverbal adverb, and as such will stand after the first auxiliary. The verb modifications are two in number:

PASV: the envelope be already opened by SOMEONE

CRLV: the envelope have already been opened by SOMEONE

At this point, the process of gerundivization may take place:

GNDZ1: the envelope's having already been opened by SOMEONE

After embedding, we have:

E / GND: the envelope's having already been opened by SOMEONE + casts suspicion on the butler

Now we delete the empty elements:

D / EE: the envelope's having already been opened ... + casts suspicion on the butler
SOP: "The envelope's having already been opened casts suspicion on the butler."

Not surprisingly, the Gerundive 2 is similar in some ways to the form we have just described, and yet there are some differences which are reflected in the following operations:

GNDZ2 →
1) LEXVB only
2) FVF + $ING_G$
3) Subj → POSS('S); 1NnOj → POSS(OF); 2NnOj → PrpOj
4) VcAdv → (Subj) + Adj
5) POSS('S) + . . . + VERB → VERB + POSS(OF); optional; may apply only when 1NnOj is not present
6) D / EE; when Subj is deleted, then I / THE.

The first step indicates that, whereas the Gerundive 1 forms were found to undergo optionally both passivization (PASV) and current relevance (CRLV), the Gerundive 2 forms may undergo neither. Step 2, on the other hand, is the same, i. e., the suffixing of $ING_G$ to the first verb form, which in light of Step 1 must be the lexical verb. In Step 3, the subject is transformed into the appropriate possessive form with 's the first noun object into the possessive form with *of*; these forms are exemplified in the following table:

| *Nominal* | *POSS('S)* | *POSS(OF)* |
|---|---|---|
| Tom | Tom's | of Tom |
| the table | the table's | of the table |
| SOMEONE | SOMEONE'S | OF SOMEONE |
| I | my | of me |
| he | his | of him, etc. |

Any second noun object present must be transformed into a prepositional object. In Step 4, any verb complement adverb (VcAdv), a one-word adverb which is distinguished from a verb complement phrase (VcPhr), must be transformed into the corresponding adjective and placed after the subject, which at this point is in the possessive case. Step 5 introduces a number of complications, for which reason it will be discussed later. Step 6 is contingent on Step 4: as we have seen, "empty elements" may almost always be deleted; when the subject is such an empty element and it is deleted, then the element *THE* must be inserted in its place.

Again let us consider some examples involving the Gerundive 2 form, in order to make these transformations somewhat less abstract. In the following sentence, the Gerundive 2 is italicized:

*Tom's eloquent reading of the story to the children* impressed us

The infrastructure behind the gerundive is:

IS: Tom read the children the story eloquently

The phrases *the story* and *the children* are the first and second noun objects, respectively, and *eloquently* is a verb complement adverb. Step 2 changes the verb:

Step 2: Tom reading the children the story eloquently

The next step applies to the nouns of the phrase:

Step 3: Tom's reading of the story to the children eloquently

Then the verb complement adverb *eloquently* is transformed into an adjective and placed after the subject:

Step 4: Tom's eloquent reading of the story to the children

At this point, we may embed this gerundive into its matrix:

E / GND: Tom's eloquent reading of the story to the children + impressed everyone

As there is no element susceptible of deletion, this stage is the final one:

SOP: "Tom's eloquent reading of the story to the children impressed everyone."

The formulas, as they were spelled out above, admit of two variations which must now be described. As to the first, when the subject is a pronoun, it naturally assumes the form appropriate to its person and number, e. g.:

IS: we read the story
GNDZ2: our reading of the story

The second variation arises when there is no expressed subject, as in this example:

*the eloquent reading of the story* impressed everyone

This Gerundive 2 clause must be generated as follows:

SOMEONE read the story eloquently
GNDZ2:
Step 2: SOMEONE reading the story eloquently
Step 3: SOMEONE'S reading of the story eloquently
Step 4: SOMEONE'S eloquent reading of the story

As the subject here is an empty element, it may be deleted. Step 6, however, stipulates that, if the subject is an empty element, and if it has been deleted, then the element *THE* must be inserted in its place:

Step 6a: . . . eloquent reading of the story
Step 6b: THE eloquent reading of the story
SOP: "The eloquent reading of the story impressed everyone."

There is yet another transformation which can apply to these Gerundive 2 forms. While the following phrases are identical in surface structure, most native speakers of English would agree that they reflect a different deep structure:

1) the magnificent singing of the Ave Maria
2) the magnificent singing of the choir

It requires only a moment's reflection to realize that the nouns in the *of*-phrase stand in a different relation to the word *singing* in each case: in the first, the Ave Maria is what is being sung; in the second, it is the choir which is singing. If these two phrases in fact have different deep structures, we must then show the steps by which they, too, arise from the infrastructures which, on our theory, lie at the root of all completed clauses.

Let us posit these two infrastructures, relying on our understanding of the phrases:

IS1: SOMEONE sing the Ave Maria magnificently
IS2: the choir sing magnificently

It is apparent that we can account for the first phrase by the rules we have already set up:

IS1: SOMEONE sing the Ave Maria magnificently
      GNDZ2:
Step 2: SOMEONE singing the Ave Maria magnificently
Step 3: SOMEONE'S singing of the Ave Maria magnificently
Step 4: SOMEONE'S magnificent singing of the Ave Maria
Step 6: THE magnificent singing of the Ave Maria

Applying the same rules to the second case leads to a different result:

IS2: the choir sing magnificently
      GNDZ2:
Step 2: the choir singing magnificently
Step 3: the choir's singing magnificently
Step 4: the choir's magnificent singing

Since nothing is to be deleted, Step 6 does not apply.

Our inquiry now shifts to the question of how the following two patterns are related:

the choir's magnificent singing (generated above)
the magnificent singing of the choir (to be explained)

To begin with, we note that the two possessive forms of English can, under certain circumstances, be regarded as interchangeable, e. g.:

my best friend's name is Tom
the name of my best friend is Tom

In light of this feature of the language, it seems likely that the second of the two gerundives just referred to may be derived from the first. It is this step which we can now include in our set of generative rules for the Gerundive 2 form as Step 5:

5) POSS('S) + ... + VERB → VERB + POSS(OF); optional; may apply only when 1NnOj ist not present

This formula states that, when there is no first noun object present in the infrastructure which could be transformed by Step 3 into a possessive phrase with *of*, then the subject of the gerundive – now in the possessive form as POSS('S) — may be shifted to the postverbal position, taking the form of POSS(OF). Step 6 will then apply, and the missing subject will be replaced by the element *THE*. Let us see how this applies to the examples above.

We have already developed the infrastructure:

IS: the choir sing magnificently

as far as Step 4:

Step 4: the choir's magnificent singing

If we now apply Step 5, we change *the choir's* to *of the choir* and move it to a position immediately following the verb:

Step 5: ... magnificent singing of the choir

Since the subject has vacated its position by this move, Step 6 applies, and *THE* is inserted:

Step 6: THE magnificent singing of the choir

In consequence of this derivation, we can explain the difference between the two phrases:

1) the magnificent singing of the Ave Maria
2) the magnificent singing of the choir

as being due to different infrastructures, and as arising out of the operation of Step 5 in the second example.

By way of checking our results, let us apply Step 5 to the following gerundive:

the choir's magnificent singing of the Ave Maria

The infrastructure would be:

IS: the choir sing the Ave Maria magnificently
  GNDZ2:
Step 2: the choir singing the Ave Maria magnificently
Step 3: the choir's singing of the Ave Maria magnificently
Step 4: the choir's magnificent singing of the Ave Maria
Step 5: ... magnificent singing of the choir of the Ave Maria
Step 6: THE magnificent singing of the choir of the Ave Maria
SOP: ? ? "The magnificent singing of the choir of the Ave Maria ..."

The presence of two *of*-clauses raises questions as to their relation to one another, and the gerundive phrase as a whole seems unclear. The presence of a first noun object *of the Ave Maria* compels us to omit Steps 5 and 6.

The third and final pattern, Gerundive 3, is the simplest of all. The first two steps are the same as for the Gerundive 2 form, the third quite different:

GNDZ3 →
1) LEXVB only
2) FVF + $ING_G$
3) D / everything except the verb form

The third step of the procedure calls for the deletion of every element of the infrastructure except the verb and its affix. The Gerundive 3 appears in sentences like:

the team took another *beating* last week
the dentist put in two *fillings* today

On the basis of the context, we may restore the infrastructure of the former sentence as follows:

IS: SOMEONE beat the team

Steps 1 and 2 produce:

Steps 1 and 2: SOMEONE beating the team

The next, however, involves deletion:

Step 3: . . . beating . . .

This, then, is embedded into the matrix clause:

E / GND: the team took another + beating + last week
SOP: "The team took another beating last week."

In the area of the gerundive in general, and in the case of the Gerundive 3 form in particular, we are very close to the border line between morphology and syntax. Only the presence of the morpheme -$ING_G$ betrays the existence of an underlying infrastructure which has been transformed into a nominal consisting of a single word.

CHAPTER 21

THE GERMAN GERUNDIVE

As in English, the infrastructure of German may be transformed into certain kinds of structures which function in their matrix clauses as nouns, i. e., infinitives and gerundives. The former were described in an earlier chapter; the gerundive of German is analyzed below. The patterns of formation of this structure in German are somewhat less complex than those of English, though the procedures comprising the transformation of gerundivization (GNDZ) are roughly the same in both languages. The transformation itself may be broken down into the following steps:

1) the verb may optionally undergo the common verb modifications for the passive voice (PASV), for the terminative aspect (TRMV), and for the modal auxiliary (MODL) — in certain combinations; the last verb form present (LVF) remains in the neutral form, i. e., no further ending is added;

2) both the subject and the accusative object, when present, are changed into the appropriate possessive forms: either into the genitive case, into objects of the preposition *von*, or into a possessive pronoun;

3) one-word adverbs from the adverbo-nominal (AVNOM) tagmeme are transformed into adjectives; adverbs functioning as nucleus complements (NCOMP) normally retain their position;

4) adverbial phrases from the AVNOM tagmeme, as well as possessive expressions generated at Step 2 which are shifted to that tagmeme, are commentized;

5) empty elements, including certain auxiliary verbs, are normally deleted;

6) when the subject has been commentized by the operation of Steps 2 and 4, or when it has been deleted as an empty element at Step 5, its place may be taken by a pointer word, usually *ein* or *das* (I / PW).

These changes may be summarized as formulas in the following way:

GNDZ →

1) LEXVB; oPASV + oTRMV + oMODL
2) Subj, AccObj → POSS:
   (PW + NOUN) → (PW + NOUN)$_{gen}$
   ($\emptyset$ + NOUN) → *von* + ($\emptyset$ + NOUN)$_{dat}$
   Pronoun → Pronoun$_{poss}$
3) Adverbs$_{AVNOM}$ → Adjectives
4) C / AvPhr$_{AVNOM}$, NnPhr$_{AVNOM}$
5) D / EE
6) I / PW when Subj = $\emptyset$

Let us illustrate the application of these rules by analyzing a number of examples which have been taken from the work of an author who uses this grammatical structure quite frequently. Page references in the following presentation refer to Marie Luise Kaschnitz, *Engelsbrücke: Römische Betrachtungen* (Fischer Bücherei 820 [Frankfurt: Fischer Bücherei, 1967] ).

The first examples have to do with elements in the clause nucleus. In the case of a simple intransitive verb, only the subject and the verb are present. The gerundive in the phrase:

wegen seines Fortgehens (p. 162)

reflects the infrastructure and derivation:

IS: er fortgehen
GNDZ (Step 2): sein fortgehen
SOP: " . . . sein(es) Fortgehen(s) . . ."

(Here, as in the sequel, the entire phrase containing the gerundive will be cited. However, we will pass over the otherwise normal step of embedding in, and generation of, the matrix clause, so as to focus more closely on the various features of this verb modification. It suffices to recall that the gerundive functions syntactically as a noun, and that it replaces the dummy element *DAS* in its matrix clause.)

Not infrequently, the subject is an empty element, as in this example:

. . . kamen wir dann ins Schwatzen (p. 11)

This must be derived from the infrastructure thus:

IS: JEMAND schwatzen
GNDZ:

Step 2: JEMANDS schwatzen
Step 5: ... schwatzen

When the gerundive at this point is not preceded by any pointer word, the word *das* or *ein* may be inserted:

Step 6: DAS schwatzen
SOP: " ... (in da)s Schwatzen ... "

Not only subjects, but also objects, may be empty elements, e. g., as in the phrase:

beim Aufschreiben (p. 7)

This gerundive would be derived as follows:

IS: JEMAND ETWAS aufschreiben
GNDZ:
Step 2: JEMANDS VON ETWAS aufschreiben

The commentization of the prepositional phrase *VON ETWAS* here is, strictly speaking, unnecessary, since it will be deleted in the next step; however, it is included here for the sake of completeness and consistency:

Step 4: JEMANDS ... aufschreiben VON ETWAS
Step 5: ... aufschreiben ...
Step 6: DAS aufschreiben
SOP: " ... (bei)m Aufschreiben ... "

The following examples show now nucleus complements may be retained in the gerundive; in the first case, the complement is an adjective with *sein*:

das Alleinsein (p. 87)
IS: JEMAND allein sein
GNDZ:
Step 2: JEMANDS allein sein
Step 5: ... allein sein
Step 6: DAS allein sein
SOP: " ... das Alleinsein ... "

Prepositional phrases frequently appear as nucleus complements, as in this case:

das Um-Atem-Ringen (p. 104)

This is generated as follows:

IS: JEMAND um Atem ringen
GNDZ:
Step 2: JEMANDS um Atem ringen
Step 5: ... um Atem ringen
Step 6: DAS um Atem ringen
SOP: "... das Um-Atem-Ringen ..."

Clause nucleus adverbs (CLNAV), especially *nicht*, may be included in the gerundive, as well as the reflexive pronoun, e. g.:

das Sichnichtzurechtfinden (p. 152)
IS: sich JEMAND nicht zurecht finden
GNDZ:
Step 2: sich JEMANDS nicht zurecht finden
Step 5: sich ... nicht zurecht finden
Step 6: DAS sich nicht zurecht finden
SOP: "... das Sichnichtzurechtfinden ..."

Most of the complexities attending the generation of these gerundives have to do with the way in which subjects, objects, and adverbs in the infrastructure are transformed. Both subject and object are transformed into possessives; when preceded by an article, the possessive takes the form, in most instances, of the genitive case of the noun phrase in question. As in the two examples which follow, it is not possible to tell from the form of the gerundive alone whether the genitive which accompanies it has been transformed from a subject or an object in the infrastructure − only the sense of the expression can provide the basis for that determination, as in this phrase:

das Heraufdrängen der Piraten und das Aufrollen des Taus (p. 32)

As the derivations below will show, the noun in the first gerundive is the subject, but in the second, it is the object in its respective infrastructure:

das Heraufdrängen der Piraten
IS: die Piraten heraufdrängen
GNDZ:
Step 2: der Piraten heraufdrängen

Since the adverbo-nominal noun phrase *der Piraten* is not a pronoun, it is commentized:

Step 4: ... heraufdrängen der Piraten

No pointer word now precedes the gerundive; hence, *DAS* may be inserted:

Step 6: DAS heraufdrängen der Piraten
SOP: " ... das Heraufdrängen der Piraten ... "

In the second gerundive, the noun phrase is derived from the object in the infrastructure:

das Aufrollen des Taus
IS: JEMAND das Tau aufrollen
GNDZ:
Step 2: JEMANDS des Taus aufrollen

Indeclinable elements are commentized:

Step 4: JEMANDS ... aufrollen des Taus

Empty elements are now deleted, and *DAS* inserted:

Step 5: ... aufrollen des Taus
Step 6: DAS aufrollen des Taus
SOP: " ... das Aufrollen des Taus ... "

When the subject or object are not preceded by articles, the possessive form which the noun assumes is that of a prepositional phrase with *von*, as in this derivation:

mit dem Vorzeigen von Photographien (p. 53)
IS: JEMAND Photographien vorzeigen
GNDZ:
Step 2: JEMANDS von Photographien vorzeigen
Step 4: JEMANDS ... vorzeigen von Photographien
Step 5: ... vorzeigen von Photgraphien
Step 6: DAS vorzeigen von Photographien
SOP " ... (mit) dem Vorzeigen von Photographien ... "

Adverbial prepositional phrases in the AVNOM tagmeme are commentized in the same way; cf. the following example:

bei seinem Auftauchen an diesem Abend allerdings kam er aus dem Gefängnis (p. 182)

The word *allerdings* is an intersentence adverb, and can be disgarded. The fact that the prepositional phrase *an diesem Abend* follows the gerundivized verb *Auftauchen,* and yet precedes the finite verb *kam* of the matrix clause shows conclusively that *an diesem Abend* belongs to the gerundive, and is not merely an adverbial expression modifying *kam.* Its function as an adverb in the AVNOM tagmeme can also be demonstrated by means of the contradiction test, applied to a finitized form of the same infrastructure:

er ist an diesem Abend aufgetaucht
er ist an diesem Abend NICHT aufgetaucht

This difference in function is reflected in the treatment of the phrase *an diesem Abend* in the process of gerundivization:

IS: er an diesem Abend auftauchen
GNDZ:
Step 2: sein an diesem Abend auftauchen
Step 4: sein . . . auftauchen an diesem Abend
SOP: " . . . sein Auftauchen an diesem Abend . . . "

One-word adverbs from the adverbo-nominal field may be transformed into declined adjectives, as in the following:

das krampfhafte Zurückwerfen des Kopfes (p. 104)

This is derived from the following infrastructure:

IS: JEMAND den Kopf krampfhaft zurückwerfen
GNDZ:
Step 2: JEMANDS des Kopfes krampfhaft zurückwerfen
Step 3: JEMANDS des Kopfes krampfhaft- zurückwerfen
Step 4: JEMANDS krampfhaft- zurückwerfen des Kopfes
Step 5: . . . krampfhaft- zurückwerfen des Kopfes
Step 6: DAS krampfhaft- zurückwerfen des Kopfes
SOP: " . . . das krampfhafte Zurückwerfen des Kopfes . . . "

It might be added that the insertion of a pointer word after deletion of the subject is optional, not obligatory. This is illustrated in the following derivation:

nichts von sanftem Die-Augen-Schließen (p. 142)

This is derived from the infrastructure below as follows:

IS: JEMAND sanft die Augen schließen
GNDZ:
Step 2: JEMANDS sanft die Augen schließen

Step 3: JEMANDS sanft- die Augen schließen
Step 5: . . . sanft- die Augen schließen

At this point, it would be possible to introduce a pointer word such as *DAS*. However, the author has chosen not to exercise this option, and hence the next step is:

SOP: " . . . (nichts von) sanftem Die-Augen-Schließen . . . "

Earlier in this description of the gerundive, reference was made to the range of applicability of the various common verb modifications. We find in general three patterns: (1) a modification by the addition of a modal auxiliary (MODL); (2) by the passive voice transformation (PASV); or (3) by PASV plus the modification for the terminative aspect (TRMV), usually followed by the deletion of *worden*, so that the gerundive in effect displays the form of the statal passive. The next three examples show how these patterns are produced. First, the modification MODL:

das Auf-die-Gasse-laufen-Müssen (p. 155)
IS: JEMAND auf die Gasse laufen
GNDZ:
Step 1 (MODL): JEMAND auf die Gasse laufen müssen
Step 2: JEMANDS auf die Gasse laufen müssen
Step 5: . . . auf die Gasse laufen müssen
Step 6: DAS auf die Gasse laufen müssen
SOP: " . . . das Auf-die-Gasse-laufen-Müssen . . . "

In like fashion, the modification PASV can be applied, with the interchange of active subject with instrumental prepositional object, and active object with passive subject, which always accompanies this transformation of the verb:

das Angesprochenwerden von Menschen (p. 87)
IS: Menschen JEMANDEN ansprechen
GNDZ:
Step 1 (PASV): JEMAND von Menschen angesprochen werden
Step 2: JEMANDS von Menschen angesprochen werden
Step 4: JEMANDS . . . angesprochen werden von Menschen
Step 5: . . . angesprochen werden von Menschen
Step 6: DAS angesprochen werden von Menschen
SOP: " . . . das Angesprochenwerden von Menschen . . . "

Not infrequently, these infrastructures have empty elements as both subject and object:

das leichte Hingetragen werden (p. 61)
IS: ETWAS JEMANDEN leicht hintragen
GNDZ:
Step 1 (PASV): JEMAND VON ETWAS leicht hingetragen werden
Step 2: JEMANDS VON ETWAS leicht hingetragen werden
Step 3: JEMANDS VON ETWAS leicht- hingetragen werden
Step 4: JEMANDS leicht- hingetragen werden VON ETWAS
Step 5: ... leicht- hingetragen werden ...
Step 6: DAS leicht- hingetragen werden
SOP: " ... das leichte Hingetragenwerden ... "

When the infrastructure undergoes both modifications, PASV and TRMV, the resulting form *worden* is often deleted, so that the gerundive form reflects the statal passive, e. g.:

das selbstverständliche Aufgehobensein (p. 123)
IS: ETWAS JEMANDEN selbstverständlich aufheben
GNDZ:
Step 1 (PASV): JEMAND VON ETWAS selbstverständlich aufgehoben werden
Step 1 (TRMV): JEMAND VON ETWAS selbstverständlich aufgehoben worden sein
Step 1 (D / *worden*): JEMAND VON ETWAS selbstverständlich augehoben ... sein
Step 2: JEMANDS VON ETWAS selbstverständlich aufgehoben sein
Step 3: JEMANDS VON ETWAS selbstverständlich- aufgehoben sein
Step 4: JEMANDS selbstverständlich- aufgehoben sein VON ETWAS
Step 5: ... selbstverständlich- aufgehoben sein ...
Step 6: DAS selbstverständlich- aufgehoben sein
SOP: " ... das selbstverständliche Aufgehobensein ... "

At the beginning of this section, it was observed that, in gerundivization, the subject and the object, if present, are transformed into the corresponding possessive forms, i. e., either into nouns in the genitive case, or into objects of the preposition *von*. There are some exceptions to this rule, to which we now turn our attention.

For example, there are cases in which the object is not transformed into a possessive and then commentized. The object nouns in this instances are almost all nucleus complements; distinguished by their generality, they tend to have no clear or specific reference, but have an almost adverbial function. Thus, in the example:

beim Prosaschreiben (p. 130)

no specific prose work is being referred to; rather, it is the act of writing in a certain style to which this phrase makes reference. This phrase is derived as follows:

IS: JEMAND Prosa schreiben
GNDZ:
Step 2: JEMANDS Prosa schreiben

In this kind of construction, Step 2 applies only to the subject of the verb. Step 4 is omitted here.

Step 5: ... ... Prosa schreiben
Step 6: DAS Prosa schreiben
SOP: " ... (bei)m Prosaschreiben ... "

On the other hand, the same infrastructure with Step 4 included in the derivation would also generate an acceptable gerundive:

IS: JEMAND Prosa schreiben
GNDZ:
Step 2: JEMANDS von Prosa schreiben
Step 4: JEMANDS schreiben von Prosa
Step 5: ... schreiben von Prosa
Step 6: DAS schreiben von Prosa
SOP: " ... das Schreiben von Prosa ... "

Both alternatives, with and without Step 4, are available to the speaker of German.

Plural nouns not preceded by an article may also have a quasi-adverbial character, as in this example:

[das] Watschengeben (p. 101; *die Watsche* 'box on the ears')

This, too, may be derived without Step 4:

IS: JEMAND JEMANDEM Watschen geben
GNDZ:
Step 2: JEMANDS JEMANDEM Watschen (*not:* von Watschen) geben

Step 5: ....... Watschen geben
Step 6: DAS Watschen geben
SOP: " ... das Watschengeben ... "

Certain pronouns, too, share the quality of generality which is a condition for the exception to the rule which we have expressed as the omission of Step 4; cf. the following:

das Alleswissen (p. 52)
IS: JEMAND alles wissen
   GNDZ:
Step 2: JEMANDS alles (*not*: von allem) wissen
Step 5: ... alles wissen
Step 6: DAS alles wissen
SOP: " ... das Alleswissen ... "

In these three cases, the object of the verb is in effect a nucleus complement (NCOMP), and hence serves more to amplify and complete the action represented by the verb than to indicate any specific object or entity.

There are other cases where the apparent subject of the gerundivized verb retains its form and position, that is, where it does not take the form of a possessive, and where it is not commentized. In these instances, too, we may detect a kind of adverbial function not altogether different from that observed in connection with the object nouns just described. The use of the word "apparent" suggests that these are not the real subjects of their verbs; our analysis indicates that they are nouns used in a kind of comparison, a function which will be represented in the infrastructure by placing them in a second infrastructure with the elements *SO + WIE* 'just as'. This means that the infrastructure behind the gerundive:

das Alte-Dame-Leben (p. 85)

is not:

IS: (eine) alte Dame$_{SUBJ}$ leben

but rather the conflated infrastructures:

ISS: JEMAND SO + WIE eine alte Dame leben + leben

On this hypothesis, gerundivization would proceed as follows:

Step 2: JEMANDS SO + WIE eine alte Dame leben + leben

When empty elements are deleted, the second verb, since it repeats an existing element, is eliminated:

Step 5: ... + ... eine alte Dame leben + ...

In the case of the uncommentized objects described above, we noted that they were characterized by the absence of pointer words before them. There is a general prohibition against two articles, *das* and *ein*, following one another. Therefore, when DAS is to be inserted, we delete the pointer word *eine* at Step 5, too:

Step 5: ... + ... ... alte Dame leben + ...
Step 6: DAS alte Dame leben
SOP:" ... das Alte-Dame-Leben ... "

This pattern of derivation, with its conflated infrastructures, helps to explain the following gerundive:

ein lustiges Schaubudenflimmern (p. 75)

As before, this may be interpreted by assuming the presence of a second infrastructure introduced by the element *WIE*:

ISS: ETWAS lustig + WIE Schaubuden flimmern + flimmern
    GNDZ:
Step 2: VON ETWAS lustig + WIE Schaubuden flimmern + flimmern
Step 3: VON ETWAS lustig- + WIE Schaubuden flimmern + flimmern
Step 5: ... lustig- + ... Schaubuden flimmern + ...
Step 6: EIN lustig- Schaubuden flimmern
SOP: " ... ein lustiges Schaubudenflimmern ... "

The following gerundive may be interpreted in like fashion:

ob ihres Greisenstolperns (p. 76)
ISS: sie SO + WIE Greise stolpern + stolpern
    GNDZ:
Step 2: ihr SO + WIE Greise stolpern + stolpern
Step 5: ihr ... + ... Greise stolpern + ...

Before fusing the elements *Greise* and *stolpern*, the author adds an -*n* to the noun. In so doing, she is assimilating this structure to another pattern in the language, i. e., that characteristic of nominal compounds whereby an -*n*- is frequently introduced between the constituent elements — hence the final form:

SOP: " . . . Ihr(es) Greisenstolpern(s) . . . "

In all of these cases, the nouns in question have an almost adverbial character because of the comparison implied.

In the foregoing discussion of the gerundive, the attempt was made to identify and describe the characteristic patterns by which an infrastructure can be transformed into a kind of noun. Yet there are other gerundive constructions which cannot be completely explained by application of the rules and procedures which were presented above. These fall into two categories, which might be called "undergerundivized" and "overgerundivized" constructions.

The first of these is exemplified by a gerundive which appears in the context of a discussion of the literary properties of the *Hörspiel* or radio play:

"Mit dieser Art der Struktur [i. e., eine gleichsam schwebende Reihung], wie überhaupt mit allem Positiven des dichterischen Hörspiels, seinem erregenden Ahnenlassen und *seinem Geheimnisvoll-vor-dem-inneren-Auge-Vorüberziehen*, kann die Bühne nichts anfangen, und es ist zu bezweifeln, ob die Fernsehleinwand da der richtige Hintergrund ist" (p. 119; italics added).

According to the patterns set forth earlier, one would expect, in place of the italicized expression, the gerundive:

seinem geheimnisvollen Vor-dem-inneren-Auge-Vorüberziehen

on the grounds that a one-word adverb in the infrastructure should, at Step 3, take the form of an adjective. We must ask whether this constitutes a clumsy application of the structures of the language on the part of this author, or whether some other factor is at work which would motivate this exception to the structures as we have defined them. Let us approach the problem by reconstructing an infrastructure which could underlie both the original phrase, as well as the expected form above:

IS: es geheimnisvoll vor dem inneren Auge vorüberziehen

The key question is, to what does *es* refer? If it refers to *das Hörspiel*, then we can construct the finite clause:

das Hörspiel zieht geheimnisvoll vor dem inneren Auge vorüber

This by itself does not make much sense, and seems to contradict the implication of the context, namely, that this mysterious movement before the inner eye is an effect of the performance of the radio play, and not the radio play itself. Building on this observation, we may postulate a lost gerundive into which the phrase itself was once embedded. By placing this phrase within another gerundive, and then deleting certain dummy elements, we can bring meaning and structure into harmony with one another. The infrastructures, on this hypothesis, would be:

IS1: es + GND2 + HABEN
IS2: ETWAS geheimnisvoll vor dem inneren Auge vorüberziehen

Here, the *es* in IS1 refers to *das Hörspiel*, and the *ETWAS* in IS2 to the content of a radio play. In this derivation, we notice that the gerundive from IS2 is "undergerundivized," in that Step 3 has been omitted. Let us reconstruct the derivation of the phrase, and then look for some reason for this unexpected step. The infrastructures above evolve further as follows:

GNDZ / 2:
Step 2: VON ETWAS geheimnisvoll vor dem inneren Auge vorüberziehen
Step 3: (omitted!)
Step 5: . . . geheimnisvoll vor dem inneren Auge vorüberziehen

The resulting gerundive, as a noun, is embedded in its matrix clause:

E / 2: es + geheimnisvoll vor dem inneren Auge vorüberziehen + HABEN

The matrix clause, too, is gerundivized:

GNDZ / 1:
Step 2: sein + geheimnisvoll vor dem inneren Auge vorüberziehen + HABEN
Step 5: sein + geheimnisvoll vor dem inneren Auge vorüberziehen + . . .
SOP: " . . . sein Geheimnisvoll-vor-dem-inneren-Auge-Vorüberziehen . . . "

The question is, what has the author accomplished by the omission of Step 3 in the generation of IS2? Put another way, what is the communicative difference between:

1) sein geheimnisvolles Vor-dem-inneren-Auge-Vorüberziehen
2) sein Geheimnisvoll-vor-dem-inneren-Auge-Vorüberziehen

supposed to be? The answer lies in the relation of the word *geheimnisvoll* to the phrase as a whole, and in the difference in meaning implied by the different functions which it has in those two phrases. The former means 'its mysterious (property of) passing before the inner eye', whereas the latter means 'its (property of) mysteriously passing before the inner eye'. The difference between these two expressions can be made somewhat more clear by using parentheses to indicate the lines of dependency in each of the two expressions:

(1) $(_4$ seinem $(_3$ geheimnisvollen $(_2$ vor-dem-inneren-Auge $(_1$ Vor-überziehen$)_1)_2)_3)_4$

(2) $(_5 (_4$ seinem$)_4$ $(_3$ geheimnisvoll $(_2$ vor-dem-inneren-Auge $(_1$ Vor-überziehen$)_1)_2)_3)_5$

It seems altogether clear that the author chose to "undergerundivize" IS2 in order to insure that the reference of the adverb *geheimnisvoll* would be unambiguous. But how could it be ambiguous? There is a potential source of ambiguity in the fact that the first of the two expressions above could be derived from either of two pairs of infrastructures, either from:

IS1: es geheimnisvoll + GND2 + HABEN
IS2: ETWAS vor dem inneren Auge vorüberziehen

or from:

IS1: es + GND2 + HABEN
IS2: ETWAS geheimnisvoll vor dem inneren Auge vorüberziehen

By omitting Step 3 in the derivation of IS2 in the second of these two pairs, the author indicated unmistakably that *geheimnisvoll* was to be part of IS2 rather than IS1, and that the latter of the two possibilities was intended. We conclude that "undergerundivization" here is not a failure to control the structures of the language, but rather a means of preventing ambiguity.

If we have managed to offer some explanation for one case where the infrastructure in question seemed to have only partially or incompletely undergone the transformation of gerundivization, we must now turn to the opposite case, those which have been "overgerundivized," i. e., those which have been so completely transformed that their connection with any infrastructure is in doubt. This situation is exemplified by the following:

sein sonderbares Verhalten (p. 11)

Though this looks at first glance like a gerundive, we find, when we try to reconstruct its infrastructure, that an element is missing:

IS: er (sich? ) sonderbar verhalten

In modern German, the verb *verhalten* cannot be used without an object of some kind, either a noun or a pronoun; often it is used reflexively. This requirement constitutes a barrier between the infrastructure postulated above and the phrase in question. For this reason, the phrase cannot be considered a gerundive, even though it looks like one; it must be regarded as a common noun. In order to be treated as a gerundive, a phrase must be capable of being transformed from a gerundive into an infrastructure by the stages and steps which have been described above. Where the language has so changed that this essential feature of convertibility has been lost, we have crossed the boundary which separates syntax and morphology. The form of words like *Verhalten* then becomes the object of historical linguistics, and not of a generative syntax of the current language.

Another example of this phenomenon is the expression:

mein Erstaunen (p. 11)

Again the noun here has a form which suggests that it is a verb used as a noun; indeed, the dictionary tells us that a verb *erstaunen* exists and is common use. Nevertheless, this is not a gerundive because it cannot be converted into an infrastructure in which the elements are combined according to the patterns of the language. The phrase presupposes the infrastructure:

IS: ich erstaunen

from which we would expect to derive the finite clause:

? ? ? ich erstaune

As the question marks indicate, however, this sequence is unacceptable in German: one can say either ! *ich staune* or ! *das erstaunt mich*, but not ??? *ich erstaune*. Again, because the phrases cannot be converted into an infrastructure which could in turn be converted into a finite clause or infinitive, we must conclude that *Erstaunen* here is a noun, and not a gerundive.

Nevertheless, we must not lose sight of the fact that the gerundive is a functional variant of an infrastructure, and not a form-class. The practical thrust of this observation is that there are cases where the same verb may function in one instance as a gerundive, and also have a related form which is a noun. The distinguishing characteristic is always that of convertibility. We find these two conditions exemplified in the following expressions:

ihr bloßes Da-Sein (p. 22) 'their merely being present'
unseres irdischen Daseins (p. 28) 'our earthly existence'

The question here is: are we dealing with a verb form which has become fixated as a noun, or with an infrastructure transformed into a gerundive? If these expressions can be converted to infrastructures, and thence to finite clauses which make sense, then we know we have a gerundive before us. If this procedure results in an unacceptable or dubious utterance, then the verb form must be regarded as a noun. Let us apply this test to these two expressions.

The former evidently reflects the infrastructure:

IS: sie bloß da sein

If we now finitize this infrastructure, we can generate the sentence:

sie sind bloß da 'they are merely there'

Since this makes sense, we may assume that the original expression is indeed a gerundive. Now let us apply the same test to the other expression. Its infrastructure may be reconstructed as:

IS: wir irdisch da sein

which in turn can be transformed into the finite clause:

? ? wir sind irdisch da ? ? 'we are here in an earthly manner'

While one would be reluctant to characterize this as nonsense, it is not at all apparent when it means. Hence, it is likely that the original phrase represents an adjective plus a noun. It is noteworthy that the author sensed the difference between these two constructions, and tried to represent it orthographically, writing *Da-Sein* for the gerundive, but *Dasein* for the noun. It is the potential for convertibility, however, which enables us to distinguish between nouns as a morphological category, and gerundives as end-products of a generative process described in detail in the pages above.

# CHAPTER 22

## A COMPARISON OF THE ENGLISH AND GERMAN
## GERUNDIVES

The mode of generation of these forms has been set forth in the two preceding chapters; our purpose here is to identify the important features of the construction in English and German, and to compare those of the two languages in this regard. To begin with, the gerundives of both languages are noun phrases, and impose in similar fashion a hierarchical ordering on the elements of their infrastructures in that the verb becomes the noun proper and the center of the phrase, whereas the nominal and adverbial elements become satellites to that verb.

As far as the morphology of the gerundive is concerned, only English has a special element to mark this function of the infrastructure: the suffix -$ING_G$. To be sure, as the subscript suggests, this affix appears also as the sign of the verb modification LMDR (limited duration), as well as the mark of the transformation PRTZ (participialization). German has no characteristic marker for its gerundives, though at times the confusing and inaccurate term "infinitive" is applied to the neutral form when it appears in the function of a gerundive.

The English gerundives may be divided into three subclasses labeled the Gerundive 1, the Gerundive 2, and the Gerundive 3 forms. As was noted in Chapter 20, the Gerundive 1 of English is characterized by the fact that the noun which functions as the first noun object of the verb in the infrastructure retains that relationship even after gerundivization, whereas in Gerundive 2 forms it becomes a possessive noun. Similarly, one-word adverbs retain that function in Gerundive 1, but become attributive adjectives in Gerundive 2. This distinction is exemplified in the following phrases:

    IS: John sell the farm suddenly
    Gerundive 1: John's selling the farm suddenly
      or: John's suddenly selling the farm
    Gerundive 2: John's sudden selling of the farm

If we regard such transformations of the noun objects as the hallmark of the gerundive, we can say that Gerundive 1 constructions in English are "undergerundivized" in this regard, whereas the Gerundive 2 pattern constitutes the norm. Conversely, Gerundive 3 forms, which are generated by the total deletion of all nonverbal elements, are "overgerundivized," e. g.:

Gerundive 3: . . . selling . . .

In the examination of the German gerundive, it was found convenient to apply the terms "over-" and "undergerundivization" to comparable (though not identical) features of that construction. Undergerundivization was detected in gerundives derived from certain conflated infrastructures, e. g.:

sein Geheimnisvoll-vor-dem-inneren-Auge-Vorüberziehen

in which one step in the derivation was omitted. Whereas this is typical of a whole class of gerundives in English (the Gerundive 1), it is as *ad hoc* phenomenon in German.

Overgerundivization in German was applied to cases in which nouns like *Verhalten* and *Erstaunen* have lost the feature of convertibility which is essential to a gerundive. These are comparable to the English Gerundive 3, which consists of a gerundivized verb, and nothing more, e. g.:

two *fillings*
a *beating*, etc.

While differing in a number of details, the gerundives of English and German betray an underlying resemblance to one another.

# CHAPTER 23

## SOME FINAL OBSERVATIONS

In the foregoing twenty-two chapters, a system of rules has been presented, through the application of which sentences may be constructed in both English and German. A summary of these may be found in Chapter 2. At this point, the author wishes to offer a number of general observations on the nature of language and of syntax which are implicit in, or presupposed by the generative-tagmemic approach taken in this book.

The first point is the departure from the method followed by many in the last two decades, since the appearance of Noam Chomsky's *Syntactic Structures* (1957). After much experimentation, the fundamental formula for the analysis of syntactic structure, i. e., S → NP + VP, was rejected as inadequate to an interpretation of the syntax of either language. Its deficiencies are three in number. First, it omits any mention of the clause, which is the cornerstone of syntax, because it is in the clause that the nonverbal elements of the sentence enter into their primary relationship with the verb. A sentence may be defined as a single clause, or as two or more clauses in an ordered relationship.

Second, the formula NP + VP as the basic structure of the clause evidently reflects one facet of the structure of English, i. e., the position of the subject before the lexical verb, perhaps also the notions of psychological subject and psychological predicate (again, cf. Brockhaus 1969). Moreover, while the formula can be interpreted as a kind of primitive infrastructure, it is too simple to do justice to the complexities either of German or of English. As was shown, a more differentiated conception of the infrastructures of these languages is essential to an adequate description of the sentences produced by native speakers.

Third and finally, the arrow which represents the process of syntactic generation needs redefinition. As used in most cases in American linguistics, it represents an interchange of categories such that one symbol is replaced by one or more others, as in the formula "S → NP + VP," where the element "S" is to be replaced by "NP + VP." One cannot generate all of the correct sentences and only the correct sentences of a language by this method, if one assumes that "correct" also means "idiomatic," because the criteria of idiomaticity lie in part outside of the language itself in the context in which the sentence is uttered. It is for this reason that the systems of rules set forth in this book admit of so many variations. For, in the last analysis, the rules of syntax do not tell us how to make up sentences — they tell us how *not* to make up sentences. The determination as to which of several possible "correct" combinations of syntactic elements is selected in a given case will depend upon the circumstances in which the sentence is formed — specifically on the communicative hierarchy of elements which has been referred to in this book as the "topic" and the "comment" of the utterance. The assumption that a system of rules can specify the form in which an utterance will appear ignores the creative element in the use of language. The generative-tagmemic approach adopted as the basis of the present work attempts to specify, not the form of the finished sentence, but rather the limits at every stage within which the speaker must operate if he is to use these languages in a fashion acceptable to the speech community of which he is a member. In this sense, the author has tried to realize in a practical way the conception of language described by Wilhelm von Humboldt:

"Die Sprache . . . ist nämlich die sich ewig wiederholende Arbeit des Geistes, den artikulierten Laut zum Ausdruck des Gedanken fähig zu machen. Unmittelbar und streng genommen, ist dies die Definition des jedesmaligen Sprechens; aber im wahren und wesentlichen Sinne kann man auch nur gleichsam die Totalität dieses Sprechens als die Sprache ansehen. Denn in dem zerstreuten Chaos von Wörtern und Regeln, welches wir wohl eine Sprache zu nennen pflegen, ist nur das durch jenes Sprechen hervorgebrachte einzelne vorhanden und dies niemals vollständig, auch erst einer neuen Arbeit bedürftig, um daraus die Art des lebendigen Sprechens zu erkennen und ein wahres Bild der lebendigen Sprache zu geben." (von Humboldt 1973:36)

In this book we have concentrated on the problems of word order, to the neglect of other aspects of English and German. Within the limits set by this restriction, we may regard the sum total of the rules for the construction of English and German sentences as "ein wahres Bild der lebendigen Sprache[n]", and the application of those rules "die Art des lebendigen Sprechens".

# WORKS CITED

Agricola, E. at al., edd. 1969-1970. Die deutsche Sprache: Kleine Enzyklopädie in zwei Bänden. 2. vols., continuously paginated. Leipzig: Bibliographisches Institut.

Allen, Harold B., ed. 1964. Readings in Applied English Linguistics. 2nd ed. New York: Appleton-Century-Crofts.

Bach, Emmon. 1962. "The Order of Elements in a Transformational Grammar of German." Language 38:263-269.

Bloomfield, Leonard. 1935. Language. London: Allen & Unwin.

Bolinger, Dwight. 1952. "Linear Modification." Publications of the Modern Language Association 67:1117-1144. Rpt. in Bolinger 1965:279-307.

—. 1965. Forms of English: Accent, Morpheme, Order. Edd. Isamu Abe & Tesuya Kanekiyo. Cambridge, Mass.: Harvard Univ. Press.

Brinkmann, Hennig. 1971. Die deutsche Sprache: Gestalt und Leistung. 2nd ed. Düsseldorf: Schwann.

Brockhaus, Klaus. 1969. "Subjekt und Prädikat in Grammatik und Logik." Linguistische Berichte 1:19-26.

Chomsky, Noam. 1957. Syntactic Structures. Janua Linguarum, IV. The Hague: Mouton.

—. 1959. Review of B. F. Skinner, Verbal Behavior (New York, 1957). Language 35:26-58. Rpt. in Fodor & Katz 1964:547-578.

—. 1964. "Current Issues in Linguistic Theory." Fodor & Katz 1964:50-118.

—. 1965. Aspects of the Theory of Syntax. Cambridge, Mass.: MIT Press.

Cook, Walter A., SJ. 1967. On Tagmemes and Transforms. Washington, D.C.: Georgetown Univ. Press.

—. 1969. Introduction to Tagmemic Analysis. Transatlantic Series in Linguistics. New York: Holt, Rinehart & Winston.

Coppieters, Rudy. 1969. "A Survey of Sentence Patterns with 'to + infinitive.' " Revue des Langues Vivantes 35:294-312.

Curme, George O. 1952. A Grammar of the German Language. 2nd ed. New York: Ungar.

Dal, Ingerid. 1962. Kurze deutsche Syntax auf historischer Grundlage. 2nd ed. Sammlung kurzer Grammatiken germanischer Dialekte, B, 7. Tübingen: Max Niemeyer.

Daniels, Karlheinz. 1963. Substantivierungstendenzen in der deutschen Gegenwartssprache. Sprache und Gemeinschaft: Studien, Bd. 3. Düsseldorf: Schwann.

Di Pietro, Robert J. 1971. Language Structures in Contrast. Rowley, Mass.: Newbury House.

Diver, William. 1963. "The Chronological System of the English Verb." Word 19:141–181.

—. 1964. "The Modal System of the English Verb." Word 20:322-352.

Duden: Die Grammatik der deutschen Gegenwartssprache. 1959. Edd. Paul Grebe et al. Der große Duden, Bd. 4. Mannheim: Bibliographisches Institut.

—. 1973. 3rd ed. Edd. Paul Grebe et al. Der große Duden, Bd. 4. Mannheim: Bibliographisches Institut.

Duden: Hauptschwierigkeiten der deutschen Sprache. 1965. Edd. Günther Drosdowski et al. Der große Duden, Bd. 9. Mannheim: Bibliographisches Institut.

Erben, Johannes. 1972. Deutsche Grammatik: Ein Abriß. 11th ed. München: Hueber.

Fichtner, Edward G. 1970. "Clause Formation and Sentence Building: A Generative Model of German Syntax." Die Unterrichtspraxis 3:7-28.

Fillmore, Charles J. 1965. Indirect Object Constructions in English and the Ordering of Transformations. Monographs on Linguistic Analysis, No. 1. The Hague: Mouton.

Firbas, Jan. 1964. "On Defining the Theme in Functional Sentence Analysis." Travaux Linguistiques de Prague 1:267-280.

Fodor, Jerry A. & Katz, Jerrold J. 1964. The Structure of Language: Readings in the Philosophy of Language. Englewood Cliffs, New Jersey: Prentice-Hall.

Fries, Charles C. 1952. The Structure of English. New York: Harcourt, Brace & World.

Gunter, Richard. 1966. "On the Placement of Accent in Dialogue: A Feature of Context Grammar." Journal of Linguistics 2:159-179.

Hathaway, Baxter. 1967. A Transformational Syntax: The Grammar of Modern American English. New York: Ronald Press.

Helbig, Gerhard. 1969. "Valenz, Tiefenstruktur und Semantik." Glottodidaktika 3-4:11-46.

—. 1970. Referat von Arbeitsgruppe 23: Probleme der Valenztheorie. Deutsch als Fremdsprache 7,3:212.

—, ed. 1971a. Beiträge zur Valenztheorie. Janua Linguarum, Series Minor, 115. The Hague: Mouton.

—. 1971b. Theoretische und praktische Aspekte eines Valenzmodells." In: Helbig 1971a:31-50.

— & Buscha, Joachim. 1974. Deutsche Grammatik: Ein Handbuch für den Ausländerunterricht. Leipzig: VEB Verlag Enzyklopädie.

Humboldt, Wilhelm von. 1973. "Einleitung zum Kawi-Werk." Rpt. in: Wilhelm von Humboldt. Schriften zur Sprache. Ed. Michael Böhler. Universal-Bibliothek, Nr. 6922-24. Stuttgart: Reclam.

Jacobs, Roderick A. & Rosenbaum, Peter A. 1968. English Transformational Grammar. Waltham, Mass.: Blaisdell.

Kaufmann, Gerhard. 1971. "Hat der deutsche Konjunktiv 'ein voll ausgebautes Tempussystem'?" Zielsprache Deutsch 51-62.

Killinger, Robert & Doppler, Alfred. 1950. Deutsch: richtig gesprochen — richtig geschrieben. Salzburg: Andreas-Verlag.

König, G. & Nickel, G. 1970. "Transformationelle Restriktionen in dem Verbalsyntax des Englischen und Deutschen." In: Probleme der kontrastiven Grammatik. Sprache der Gegenwart: Schriften des Instituts für deutsche Sprache in Mannheim, Bd. VIII: Jahrbuch 1969. Düsseldorf: Schwann. Pp. 70-81.

Krohn, Robert et al. 1971. English Sentence Structure. Ann Arbor: Univ. of Michigan Press.

Kufner, Herbert L. 1962. The Grammatical Structures of English and German: A Contrastive Sketch. Contrastive Structure Series. Chicago: Univ. of Chicago Press.

Langendoen, D. Terence. 1969. The Study of Syntax: The Generative-Transformational Approach to the Structure of American English. Transatlantic Series in Linguistics. New York: Holt, Rinehart & Winston.

Lederer, Herbert. 1969. Reference Grammar of the German Language. New York: Scribners.

Lees, Robert B. 1960a. "A Multiply Ambiguous Adjectival Construction." Language 36:207-221.

—. 1960b. The Grammar of English Nominalizations. International Journal of Applied Linguistics, 26,3,2. Bloomington, Indiana: University Press.

Lindgren, Kaj B. 1964. "Syntaktische Probleme beim deutschen Infinitiv I." Neuphilologische Mitteilungen 65:317-332.

—. 1966. "Methodische Probleme der Syntax der Infinitive." Wirkendes Wort 16:156-165.

—. 1967. "Syntaktische Probleme beim deutschen Infinitiv II." Neuphilologische Mitteilungen 68:69-86.

Live, Anna H. 1967. "Subject-Verb Inversion (in English)." General Linguistics 7,1:31-49.

Lohnes, Walter F. W. & Strothmann, Friedrich W. 1968. German: A Structural Approach. New York: Norton.

Long, Ralph B. 1961. The Sentence and its Parts: A Grammar of Contemporary English. Chicago: Univ. of Chicago Press.

Moser, Hugo, ed. 1965. Das Ringen um eine neue deutsche Grammatik. Wege der Forschung, Bd. 25. Darmstadt: Wissenschaftliche Buchgesellschaft.

Moulton, William G. 1962. The Sounds of English and German. Contrastive Structure Series. Chicago: Univ. of Chicago Press.

Nilsen, Don L. F. 1968. "English Infinitives." Canadian Journal of Linguistics 13:83-93.

Noblitt, James S. 1972. "Pedagogical Grammar: Towards a Theory of Foreign Language Materials Preparation." International Review of Applied Linguistics 10:313-331.

Ries, John. 1927. Was ist Syntax? Ein kritischer Versuch. 2nd ed. Rpt. Darmstadt: Wissenschaftliche Buchgesellschaft, 1967.

Sandmann, Manfred. 1940. "Substantiv, Adjektiv, Adverb und Verb als sprachliche Formen: Bemerkungen zur Theorie der Wortarten." Indogermanische Forschungen 57:81-112. Rpt. in Moser 1965:186-216.

Schipporeit, Luise. 1971. Tenses and Time Phrases in Modern German. München: Hueber.

Schubiger, Maria. 1965. "English Intonation and German Modal Particles - A Comparative Study." Phonetica 12:65-84.

Schwarze, Christoph. 1972. "Grammatiktheorie und Sprachvergleich." Linguistische Berichte 21:15-29.

Stickel, Gerhard. 1970. Untersuchungen zur Negation im heutigen Deutsch. Schriften zur Linguistik. 1. Braunschweig: Vieweg.

Sundby, Bertil. 1970. Front-Shifted "-ing" and "-ed" Groups in Present-Day English. Scripta Minora: Studier utg. av Kungl. Humanistiska Vetenskapsfundet i Lund, 1970-1971:1. Lund: CWK Gleerup.

Taha, Abdul Karim. 1960. "The Structure of Two-Word Verbs in English." Language Learning 10:115-122. Rtp. in Allen 1964:130-136.

Tesnière, Lucien. 1965. Eléments de syntaxe structurale. 2nd ed. Paris: Klincksieck.

Thomas, Owen. 1965. Transformational Grammar and the Teacher of English. New York: Holt, Rinehart & Winston.

Wagner, K. Heinz. 1968. "Verb Phrase Complementation: A Criticism." Journal of Linguistics 4:89-91.

Waterman, John T. 1957. "The Possessive Case in German." German Quarterly 30:95-97.

Whitehall, Harold. 1956. Structural Essentials of English. New York: Harcourt, Brace & World.

# INDEX

In addition to page citations, this index includes all of the technical terms, phrases, and definitions used in this work, as well as the abbreviations and symbols which express them. The letters *E, G,* and *EG* stand for 'English', 'German', and 'English as well as German', respectively, and groups of entries headed by those symbols appear in that order. The abbreviations *sp.* and *incl.* stand for the words 'specifically' and 'including', respectively, and introduce a series of sub-entries which are separated from one another by virgules (" / "); *v.* and *q.v.* mean *vide* 'see' and *quod vide* 'which see'. The ampersand ("&") follows the last letter of the alphabet, and is in turn followed by the Arabic numerals.

ambiguity, syntactic, E 42—43.
apposition: v. embedding (E), apposition in; infinitive (INF), G, adjective /noun, with, *sp.* NOUN + INF.
aspect, G 123—126; continuative (CNTV) 125 126 134; terminative (TRMV) 16 117 124 126 134. *See also* mood, subjunctive (SJNC), G; participle (PRT), G, terminative aspect in; process and result; verb, modifications of, G, tense and aspect in.
asyntactic elements: v. elements, asyntactic.
attributive participles: v. participle (PRT), EG, form of.
*auch*, as clause nucleus adverb (CLNAV), G 87—88.
auxiliary, modal (MODL), E 16 111—112 115 139—141; —, G 16 117 139—141; concurrent and prospicient conjugations of 130—133 140; generation of 118 119 134—135; *werden* as 131 133. *See also* participle (PRT), G, auxiliary, modal, forms of.
auxiliary verb: v. auxiliary, modal; verb, auxiliary.
AUXX 'auxiliary verbs': v. participle (PRT), EG, auxiliary verbs, deletion of (D / AUXX).
AUX1 'first auxiliary': v. verb, auxiliary, first (AUX1).
AUX 2 / 3 / 4 'second / third / fourth auxiliary': v. verb, auxiliary, first (AUX1).
AVBLZ 'adverbialization': q.v.
AVNOM 'adverbo-nominal': q.v.
AV&AUX1 'adverb resulting from the adverbialization of forms following the first auxiliary': v. sentence, correlative, comparative / confirmative.

Basic transformations, E: v. transformations, basic, E.
*BE* 'the verb *to be*', E: contrasted with E lexical verb (LEXVB) 62—63; topicalization of one-word forms of 145—146 147 159 161 162 206.
BE1 'first form of *BE* present': v. transformations, topic-comment redistribution (TCR), E.
Bloomfield, Leonard 11.

C 'commentization': q.v.
CF 'clause formation': v. clause, formation of.
Chomsky, Noam 11—12; criticism of theories of 402—403.
CJNLZ 'conjunctionalization': q.v.
clause, contrary-to-fact, E: v. clause, finite, E, contrary-to-fact.
clause, finite, E 143—189; contrary-to-fact, generation of 146—147; dependent (DFCL), commentization of 237 258—259 264—265 329; —, G 190—202; —, EG: differences between 203—204. *See also* topicalization (T), G, in finite clauses; transformations, E, *sp.* basic / THERE- / topic-comment redistribution (TCR); verb, finite (FV), G, *sp.* position of / topicalization of.
clause, formation of (CF) 14 16. *See also* finitization (FNTZ); gerundivization (GNDZ); infinitivization (INFZ); participialization (PRTZ).
clause, matrix: v. embedding (E), matrix clause.

clause, noun (NNCL) 218. *See also* embedding (E), noun clauses, of.

clause, relative (RLCL) 17 218; –, E 154–156; deletion of relative adverb / pronoun in 154–156; –, G, indefinite 231–232. *See also* embedding (E), relative clause (RLCL), of; topicalization (T), G, in finite clauses.

clause, subordinate (SBCL) 17. *See also* embedding (E), subordinate clauses (SBCL), of.

clause, types of 14 16–17 217–219.

clause-element-replacing / restricting embedding: v. embedding (E).

clause nucleus adverb (CLNAV): v. adverb, nucleus, clause (CLNAV), G.

clause-restricting embedding: v. embedding (E).

C / LEXVB 'commentization of lexical verb': v. participle (PRT), E, lexical verb, commentization of (C/LEXVB).

CLNAV 'clause nucleus adverb': v. adverb, nucleus, clause (CLNAV), G.

CN 'clause nucleus': v. nucleus, clause (CN).

CNTV 'continuative aspect': v. aspect, continuative (CNTV), G; verb, modifications of, G, tense and aspect in.

C / OjPhr 'commentization of object phrase': v. phrase, object, commentization of (C / OjPhr).

comment 28 57. *See also* topic and comment.

commentization (C) 18 29.

commentization of first noun object (C / 1NnOj): v. ob-

ject, noun, first, commentization of (C / 1NnOj).

commentization of grammatical subject (C / SJ): v. participle (PRT), EG, subject, grammatical, commentization of (C / SJ).

commentization of lexical verb (C / LEXVB): v. participle (PRT), E, lexical verb, commentization of (C / LEXVB).

commentization of object phrase (C / OjPhr): v. phrase, object, commentization of (C / OjPhr).

complement, nucleus (NCOMP), G 15 74–86 106; adjective / adverb as 85; noun as 80–85 103–105; prepositional phrase as 74–80; with *sein* 85–86.

complement, verb (VCOMP), E 15 50–54 106; constituents of 50; intraposition (INPOS) of 182–183 185–187. *See also* adverb, complement, verb (VCAdv); phrase, complement, verb (VCPhr).

complement adverb, verb (VCAdv): v. adverb, complement, verb (VCAdv), E.

complement phrase, verb (VCPhr): v. phrase, complement, verb (VCPhr), E.

concurrent modal conjugation: v. auxiliary, modal (MODL), G, concurrent and prospicient conjugations of.

conjunctionalization (CJNLZ) 17 226.

context, influence of 25 29.

continuative aspect (CNTV): v. aspect, continuative (CNTV), G.

contradiction: v. nucleus, clause (CN), G, role of negation in defining.

co-valent elements: v. valence.

CRLV 'current relevance': v. relevance, current (CRLV), E.

C / SJ 'commentization of grammatical subject': v. participle (PRT), EG, subject, grammatical, commentization of (C / SJ).

C / 1NnOj 'commentization of first noun object': v. object, noun, first, commentization of (C / 1NnOj).

D 'deletion': q.v.

D / AUXX 'deletion of auxiliary verbs': v. participle (PRT), EG, auxiliary verbs, deletion of (D / AUXX).

deletion (D) 18 29–32 33.

deletion of auxiliary verbs (D / AUXX): v. participle (PRT), EG, auxiliary verbs, deletion of (D / AUXX).

deletion of preposition followed by all modifiers (D / PREP&MOD): v. participle (PRT), E, preposition followed by all modifiers, deletion of (D / PREP &MOD).

dependent finite clause (DFCL): v. clause, finite, E, dependent (DFCL).

DFCL 'dependent finite clause': v. clause, finite, E, dependent (DFCL).

direct object: v. nominal (NOMNL), E.

DO, as auxiliary, E: v. verb, auxiliary, first (AUX1).

"double infinitive construction": v. verb, finite (FV), G, position of, in "double infinitive construction."

D / PREP&MOD 'deletion of preposition followed by all modifiers': v. participle (PRT), E, preposition fol-

lowed by all modifiers, deletion of (D / PREP&MOD).

dummy topic, ES as: v. topic, dummy, ES as.

duration, limited (LMDR), E 16 108–109 138 340.

E 'embedding': q.v.

EDICT-rules: v. rules, EDICT.

EE 'empty element': v. element, empty (EE).

element, asyntactic, intersentence adverb as 34.

element, empty (EE) 123.

ellipsis: basis for, in language 29; patterns of 29–34.

embedding (E) 18 217–219; apposition in 219; clause-element-replacing 219 338; clause-element-restricting 218–219 338 358; clause-restricting 232; finite clauses, of 217–232; matrix clause 15; noun clauses (NNCL), of 225–228; relative clauses (RLCL), of 219–221 221–225, indefinite, G 231–232; subordinate clauses (SBCL), of 228–231. See also gerundive (GND) / infinitive (INF) / participle (PRT), EG, embedding of.

empty element (EE): v. element, empty (EE).

ES, insertion of (I / ES), G, in infinitive constructions 286–287 290 299–301 302–304 306 319, instances of 289–308 passim.

ES as dummy topic: v. topic, dummy, ES as.

EXPOS 'extraposition': v. infrastructure (IS), E, adjustments to.

extraposition (EXPOS): v. infrastructure (IS), E, adjustments to.

lexical verb (LEXVB): v. verb, lexical (LEXVB).

LMDR 'limited duration': v. duration, limited (LMDR), E.

LVF 'last verb form': v. verb form, last (LVF).

Manifestation, verb of, E 178.

matrix clause: v. embedding (E), matrix clause.

MDLAV 'modal adverb': v. adverb, modal (MDLAV), G.

meaning: v. semantics; valence.

*Mitspieler*: v. valence.

MOD 'modifiers': v. participle (PRT), E, preposition followed by all modifiers, deletion of (D / PREP&MOD).

modal adverb (MDLAV): v. adverb, modal (MDLAV), G.

modifications of verb: v. verb, modifications of.

MODL 'modal auxiliary': v. auxiliary, modal (MODL), EG.

mood, indicative (INDC), E 112–115;
–, G 126–127.

mood, subjunctive (SJNC), E 16 113–115;
–, G 16 120–122 126–127 135–136.

morphosyntactic rules: v. rules, morphosyntactic.

MS 'morphosyntactic rules': v. rules, morphosyntactic.

NCOMP 'nucleus complement': v. complement, nucleus (NCOMP), G.

NNCL 'noun clause': v. clause, noun (NNCL).

NEG 'negative (element)': v. negation, G.

negation, G 78–80.

*NEITHER*, E: v. sentence, correlative, comparative.

*nicht*, G: as clause nucleus adverb (CLNAV) 87; as modal adverb (MDLAV) 93. *See also* negation, G.

NOM 'nominal element': q.v.

nominal (NOMNL), E 15 38–44; "direct objects" in 38; extraposition (EXPOS) of 182–183 185 186 187; formula for generation of 41; "indirect objects" in 38 43; in juxtaposition to verb particle (VPART) 45–46.

nominal element (NOM), infinitive in matrix clause with 235 236 253. *See also* gerundive (GND), E, nominal element (NOM), possessive forms of.

NOMNL 'nominal': q.v.

nonrestrictive intraverbal adverb: v. adverb, intraverbal (ITVAV), E.

nonspecific noun: v. noun, specific/nonspecific.

"normal" word order, G: v. verb, finite (FV), G, position of.

noun, G: v. complement, nucleus (NCOMP), G, noun as; adverbo-nominal (AVNOM), G, noun as.

noun, object, in E participle: v. participle (PRT), E, infrastructures (IS) containing, with.

noun, specific / nonspecific, G 82–84; adverbo-nominal (AVNOM), as 88; compared to E 101–102; nucleus complement (NCOMP), as 82.

noun object, first (1NnOj); v. object, noun, first (1NnOj).

nucleus, clause (CN), G 15; defined 73; role of negation in determining 78–80.

nucleus adverb, clause: v. adverb, nucleus, clause (CLNAV), G.

participle (PRT), G (cont.):
(MODL) in 364, forms of 119; auxiliary verbs, deletion of (D / AUXX) 362 363; embedding (E) of 356 358–370 *passim* 373; form of 356, absolute 357 358 365–366, attributive, *sp.* postnominal 356 / prenominal 359–360; function of 356, adjectival 356–360 366–369, adverbial 365–366; infinitive, participialized 370–371 374; infrastructures (IS) containing, with *haben* 360–361 / *sein* 369; lexical verb as, form of 116–117; noun, as 366–368; passive voice (PASV) in 361–363 365; subject, grammatical, commentization of (C / SJ) 359 362 363 364 366 367 369 370; terminative aspect (TRMV) in 361–363 363–364; topicalization of lexical verb (T / LEXVB) in 357–358;
–, EG 372–374. *See also* subject, grammatical (SJ), G, deletion of.

particle, verb (VPART), E 15 44–49 106; accent on 49 51–52; distinguishing between preposition and 48–49 51; in juxtaposition to nominal (NOMNL) 45–46. *See also* participle (PRT), E, infrastructure (IS) containing, with.

PAST 'past tense': v. tense, EG, past (PAST).

PASV 'passive voice': v. voice, passive (PASV), EG.

person and number (PSNM), E 16 113–115 140–141;
–, G 16 120–122 135–136 140–141.

personal pronoun, unaccented:
v. pronoun, personal, unaccented (UPPRN), G.

phrase, complement, verb (VCPhr), E: defined 50; topicalization of 144.

phrase, object (OjPhr), E 42; commentization of (C / OjPhr), *sp.* application of, to nominal (NOMNL) 39 40 / when obligatory 48; distinguishing between prepositional phrase and 42–43.

phrase, prepositional, E: agent (AgPhr) 107–108 234 350–351; distinguishing between adnominal and adverbial 52–53; distinguishing between object phrase (OjPhr) and 42–43; distinguishing between verb particle (VPART) and 48–49;
–, G: agent (AgPhr) 116–117. *See also* adverbonominal (AVNOM), G, prepositional phrase as; complement, nucleus (NCOMP), G, prepositional phrase as.

PNTR 'past anterior': v. tense, G, past anterior (PNTR).

pointer word 82 83.

possessive form with 'S / OF (POSS['S] / POSS[OF]): v. gerundive (GND), E, nominal element (NOM), possessive forms of.

POSS(OF / 'S) 'possessive form with OF / 'S: v. gerundive (GND), E, nominal element (NOM), possessive forms of.

post-FV topicalization of adverb (T / AV): v. topicalization (T), G, in finite clauses.

postnominal participles, E: v. participle (PRT), E, form of.

postverbal adjective (PVAJ): v. transformations, topic-comment redistribution (TCR).

SJ2 'subject of embedded infinitive': v. infinitive (INF), EG, embedded, topicalization of subject of.

*SO*, E: v. sentence, correlative, comparative / confirmative.

SOP 'standard orthography and punctuation': q.v.

specific noun: v. noun, specific / nonspecific.

standard orthography and punctuation (SOP) 15.

statal passive: v. voice, passive (PASV), G.

structure, syntactic: v. syntax.

SUBJ 'subject': q.v.

subject (SUBJ) = tagmeme of E 15    58–60    103–105 107–108 165 180 182 233.

subject, grammatical (SJ) 18 58–59;
   –, G: deletion of, in infinitivization (INFZ) 283 285 327, in participialization (PRTZ) 356 358;
   –, EG: commentization of, v. participle (PRT), EG, subject, grammatical, commentization of (C / SJ); function of 101 103.

subjectivization    (SJCTZ)    17 239–240 242 243–244 250 291 295 296.

subject-raising, EG: v. infinitive (INF), EG, embedded, topicalization of subject of.

subordinate clause: v. clause, subordinate (SBCL).

syntactic ambiguity: v. ambiguity, syntactic.

syntax: definition of, as word order    9–10    12–13    18 402–403; nature of rules of 403; theories of 11–13.

T 'topicalization': q.v.

tagmeme: defined 15; elements occupying 15. *See also* infrastructure (IS), EG.

T / AV 'post-FV topicalization of adverb': v. topicalization (T), G, in finite clauses.

TCR 'topic-comment redistribution (transformations)': v. transformations, topic-comment redistribution (TCR).

tense, E: past (PAST) 16 112–113;
   –, G: future 131; past (PAST) 16 120–122 124 135; past anterior (PNTR) 19 125 135. *See also* verb, modifications of, G, tense and aspect in.

terminal adverb (TRMAV), E: v. adverb, terminal (TRMAV), E.

terminative aspect (TRMV), G: v. aspect, terminative (TRMV), G.

THE, insertion of (I / THE): v. gerundive (GND), E, THE, insertion of (I / THE).

THERE,    insertion    of (I / THERE): v. transformations, THERE-, E.

THERE-transformations:    v. transformations, THERE-, E.

T /OJ2 'topicalization of object of embedded infinitive': v. infinitive (INF), EG, embedded, topicalization of object of.

topic,    dummy,    ES    as, G 294–295.

topic and comment: basis for, in language 27–28 29;
   –, E 41–42 46 160–161 164 167;
   –, G 28–29.

topic-comment    redistribution (TCR)    transformation:    v. transformation, topic-comment redistribution (TCR).

topicalization (T) 18 29;
   –, E: style as reason for 188–189;
   –, G: in finite clauses, of, *sp.*

verb, modifications of (cont.): aspect, terminative (TRMV); auxiliary, modal (MODL); mood, subjunctive (SJNC); person and number (PSNM); tense, past (PAST); voice, passive (PASV).

verb complement: v. complement, verb (VCOMP), E.

verb complement adverb (VCAdv): v. adverb, complement, verb (VCAdv).

verb complement phrase (VCPhr): v. phrase, complement, verb (VCPhr).

verb-first / last / second word order: v. verb, finite (FV), G, position of.

verb form, first (FVF), E 108−110 112.

verb form, last (LVF), G 18 116 122.

verb forms (VFF) 112. *See also* transformations, THERE-, E.

verb forms up to and including the first form of *BE* (VFF+BE1): v. transformations, THERE-, E.

verb particle (VPART), E: v. particle, verb (VPART), E.

VFF 'verb forms': q.v.

*verbum dicendi*, E: v. infinitive (INF), E, *verbum dicendi* in constructions with.

VFF+BE1 'verb forms up to and including the first form of *BE*': v. transformations, THERE-, E.

VM 'verb modifications': v. verb, modifications of, EG.

voice, passive (PASV), E 16 107−108;

−, G 16 116−117 134; actional and statal forms of 127−129;

−, EG 138. *See also* participle (PRT), EG, passive voice (PASV) in.

VPART 'verb particle': v. particle, verb (VPART), E.

W *'werden'* (G auxiliary verb): q.v.

*werden* (G auxiliary verb): v. auxiliary, modal (MODL), G; voice, passive (PASV), G.

works cited 404−407;

Zero-object, E 257−258.

zero-complement, G: in the construction $INF_{SJ} + \emptyset + sein$ 294.

zero-predicate, E: in the construction $INF + BE + \emptyset$ 244. *See also* transformations, THERE-, E, with *BE*.

'Z-rules': v. rules, morphosyntactic (MS).

*zu*, deletion of: v. infinitive (INF), G, *zu*, deletion of.

& 'before, up to, following'.

1NnOj 'first noun object': v. object, noun, first (1NnOj).

2NnOj 'second noun object': v. object, noun, second (2NnOj).